Unless the Threat of Death Is Behind Them

Unless the Threat of Death Is Behind Them

Hard-Boiled Fiction and Film Noir

John T. Irwin

The Johns Hopkins University Press
Baltimore

©2006 The Johns Hopkins University Press
All rights reserved. Published 2006
Printed in the United States of America on acid-free paper
9 8 7 6 5 4 3 2 1

The Johns Hopkins University Press
2715 North Charles Street
Baltimore, Maryland 21218-4363
www.press.jhu.edu

Library of Congress Cataloging-in-Publication Data

Irwin, John T.
Unless the threat of death is behind them : hard-boiled fiction and film
noir / John T. Irwin.
p.   cm.
Includes bibliographical references and index.
ISBN 0-8018-8435-7 (acid-free paper)
1. Detective and mystery stories, American—History and criticism.
2. Noir fiction, American—History and criticism. 3. Detective and mystery
films—United States—History and criticism. 4. Film noir—United States—
History and criticism. 5. Private investigators in literature. 6. Detectives in
literature. 7. Masculinity in literature. 8. Masculinity in motion pictures.
9. Men in literature. 10. Men in motion pictures. I. Title.
PS374.D4178 2006
813'.087209—dc22   2006008094

A catalog record for this book is available from the British Library.

For my brother Billy

Contents

Preface

In the preface to my previous book of literary criticism, *The Mystery to a Solution: Poe, Borges, and the Analytic Detective Story*, I explained that it was the first of a three-book project whose other two planned volumes would be titled *"Apollinaire Lived in Paris. I Live in Cleveland, Ohio": Approaches to the Poetry of Hart Crane* and *An Almost Theatrical Distance: Figuration and Desire in the Fiction of F. Scott Fitzgerald*. That project still continues, but accounting for the present book's appearance before the project's completion requires a brief explanation. After finishing *The Mystery to a Solution*, I started back to work on the Hart Crane book, but it occurred to me that since I had just written on the analytic detective story tradition that links Poe and Borges, I might as well go on to deal with the main offshoot of this tradition, hard-boiled detective fiction, and then with hard-boiled fiction's relation to film noir. And since one of the ongoing themes of *The Mystery to a Solution* is the undecidability between the numbers three and four, it seemed to me that the irruption of a fourth book within that three-book project was not unexpected. That three-book project is now back on track; indeed, even as you read this preface I am at work on Hart Crane's poetry, but I want to acknowledge here all those whose generous help and advice have contributed to the present book.

First, my thanks to Donald Yates and Mike Nevins, who both read the entire manuscript, caught errors, and made countless useful comments; next, Millard Kaufman and John Astin, who read the film noir chapters and gave me the benefit of their years of working in Hollywood; next, Dr. Melvin McInnis and Dr. Francis Mondimore, who both read chapter 5 and saw to it that my remarks on Woolrich's psychological make-up accurately reflected the way in which a psychoanalytic approach contemporaneous with the period during which Woolrich was writing would have understood Woolrich's sexuality and its effect on his fiction. Finally, I am grateful to the editors and journals that first published chapters of the book and who have given me permission to reprint them here: Sarah Spence at *Literary Imagination* (chap. 1, on Hammett),

Dave Smith at the *Southern Review* (chap. 2, on Chandler), and Gordon Hutner at *American Literary History* (chap. 3, on Cain). Needless to say, whatever strengths this book exhibits are in large part due to the generous advice and help I received during its composition from the above-mentioned individuals; any faults the book has are all my own.

Introduction

The first thing that a reader starting this book should be aware of is that, in spite of its subtitle, it is not a general overview of an entire fiction genre and its authors nor of an entire film genre and its auteurs. Rather, this book is a selective study of works by five seminal writers of the 1930s and '40s who established the themes and narrative structures of hard-boiled fiction and initiated the genre's popularity with the American reading public, and of certain key films of the 1940s that translated hard-boiled novels to the screen and in turn established many of the themes and cinematic techniques of film noir. The novels I've chosen to discuss by Hammett, Chandler, Cain, Burnett, and Woolrich are linked thematically: each evokes the struggle of the twentieth-century working American to become or stay his own boss, a struggle that plays out as a conflict between the professional and personal lives of these novels' protagonists. The hard-boiled detectives of Hammett and Chandler always resolve this conflict in favor of the professional, placing their work with its code and its demands above their personal relationships. Cain's two best novels, on the other hand, are cautionary tales, showing the disastrous results for their protagonists of allowing personal relationships to overwhelm their commitment to their work. In the novels by Burnett and Woolrich the struggle of the twentieth-century working American to become or stay his own boss takes on a larger, existential dimension as their protagonists try to maintain control of their own lives against obstacles that are posed less by persons they love or lust for than by the effects of time in Burnett's fiction and by fate in Woolrich's.

The reader will notice that throughout the book, in addition to the five authors from the thirties and forties that I discuss, the names of two other American writers keep coming up—Edgar Allan Poe and F. Scott Fitzgerald. Poe, as the inventor of the detective story, is of necessity a continuing presence in any discussion of hard-boiled detective fiction considered as the major twentieth-century offshoot of the genre he founded—that is, in any discussion of the degree to which Poe's influence and example, positive or negative, either as something to be emulated or avoided, contributed to the creation of the new genre. Fitzgerald, on the other hand, is an ongoing presence in the book because he is, I argue, the contemporary high-art novelist whose work most closely resembles thematically that of the five popular novelists I discuss, thus suggesting the artistic ambitions animating the best of these hard-boiled writers.

After examining in the first five chapters the principal works of each of the hard-boiled novelists mentioned, I briefly summarize in the sixth chapter the tradition of the detective story from its founding by Poe in the middle of the nineteenth century up to that point in the 1920s when Hammett initiated the hard-boiled genre, a summary that provides a basis for my reading of the conditions and causes from which this new type of the detective story emerged and that offers an estimate of the genre's literary and cultural significance. In the book's last two chapters, I discuss the way in which hard-boiled fiction of the thirties and forties prepared the audience and provided the material for those seminal Hollywood movies that initiated the American film noir genre, whose black-and-white cycle lasted for twenty years and produced some three hundred films.

Unless the Threat of Death Is Behind Them

CHAPTER ONE

"Where Their Best Interest Lies"

Hammett's *The Maltese Falcon*

1

Over the last ten or fifteen years I have reread Dashiell Hammett's *The Maltese Falcon* at least once, sometimes twice, a year and accompanied each rereading with a viewing of John Huston's film version. Some readers may dismiss this annual rereading of the same book as either boring or silly, or merely obsessive-compulsive. I hope to find on examination that it's neither boring nor silly, and though I may accept "obsessive-compulsive," I reject the "merely."

I can account in part for my returning again and again to *The Maltese Falcon* on the practical grounds that I was using the book to work on a long narrative poem, begun in 1981 and finished in 1997, called *Just Let Me Say This About That.* It was written in blank verse, and given its subject matter, I wanted its diction to be as colloquial and American, as hard-nosed, energetic, and unsentimental, as I could make it. So I reread *The Maltese Falcon* periodically to remind myself of the kind of idiomatic, knowing, skeptical sound I wanted the poem to have, and I found that whenever I'd been working on the blank verse for a long time and the cadences and diction of Wordsworth's *Prelude* or Marlowe's dramas had begun to creep in, reading Hammett's prose washed them away quick. So there is part of the reason for my going back continually to the book, but only the smaller part. The bigger one's not so quickly nor so easily described.

Let me start that description by saying that for me *The Maltese Falcon* is the emotional and intellectual equivalent of comfort food, that particular dish each one of us has that's familiar, always appetizing, and that serves to console or reassure us when we're low or sick or suffer some reversal. It's a work so intelligent, with dialogue so witty and a view of life so worldly-wise, presented with such formal economy and flawless pacing and yet such fun to read, that it continually renews my belief in the principle that art and brains can transform just about anything, no matter how lowly or unpromising that thing might seem, into something intelligent, moving, and worthy—indeed, that art and brains could translate a pulp genre into the big leagues with one book. It has always seemed to me somehow appropriate that in the same de-cade in which Hammett demonstrated the high-art possibilities of the hard-boiled detective genre with the publication of *The Maltese Falcon* (1930), his friend William Faulkner demonstrated, with the publication of *Absalom, Absalom!* (1936)—the story of two amateur detectives puzzling over the facts of a very old murder, trying to solve the mystery of why a man killed his best friend and half-brother—that the gothic detective genre, founded by Poe in the Dupin stories, was capable of being translated into the very highest realms of literary art. In what follows I hope to show why it does not seem to me at all inappropriate to mention Hammett's achievement in the same breath with Faulkner's.

II

Most critics of *The Maltese Falcon* and most readers who have read it more than once have sensed the importance for the novel's overall meaning of the Flitcraft story, which Sam Spade tells Brigid O'Shaughnessy at the start of chapter 7, ostensibly as a way of killing time, while they wait in Spade's apart-ment for Joel Cairo to show up. The story of Flitcraft, a little over a thousand words in length, is usually treated by critics as a parable, as Spade's way of obliquely telling Brigid, with whom he is becoming romantically involved, his view of life and the world, of telling her the sort of person he is.

According to Spade, Flitcraft, a successful businessman in Tacoma, left his office one day to have lunch and never came back; he vanished "like a fist when you open your hand."[1] Flitcraft was happily married, had two young children, a thriving real estate business, owned his own home, had a new Packard, "and the rest of the appurtenances of successful American living" (64). (One can imagine Hammett relishing that last phrase as if it had been copied from an ad for some new appliance that aimed to become the next criterion of successful American living. Hammett had, of course, worked for a while in the 1920s as the advertising manager for a jewelry store.) At the time of his disappearance, Flitcraft was worth about two hundred thousand dollars, and while his affairs were in order, there were still enough loose ends to suggest that he hadn't planned to disappear. Indeed, he had called a friend that morning and made a date to play golf that afternoon.

Spade became involved in the Flitcraft case about five years later. He was working for a large detective agency in Seattle, when Mrs. Flitcraft hired the agency to send someone to investigate a man she'd seen in Spokane who looked a lot like her husband. Spade was sent, found Flitcraft, who had changed his name to Charles Pierce, and found that Flitcraft now owned his own automobile business, had a wife and baby son, owned a home in a Spokane suburb, "and usually got away to play golf after four in the afternoon during the season." Spade interviewed Flitcraft and learned that he had "no feeling of guilt," since he had "left his first family well provided for." But Flitcraft was concerned that he wouldn't be able to make the "reasonableness" of what he'd done "clear to Spade" (65).

It seems that on the day he disappeared Flitcraft had been going to lunch when he walked past a building site, and a steel beam fell and hit the sidewalk so close that a chip from the sidewalk flew up and scratched his cheek. More shocked than frightened, Flitcraft said "he felt like somebody had taken the lid off life and let him look at the works": "Flitcraft had been a good citizen and a good husband and father, not by any outer compulsion, but simply because he was a man who was most comfortable in step with his surroundings. . . . The life he knew was a clean orderly sane responsible affair. Now a falling beam had shown him that life was fundamentally none of these things. . . . He knew then that men died at haphazard like that, and lived only while blind chance spared them. . . . What disturbed him was the discovery that in sensibly ordering his affairs he had got out of step, and not into step, with life" (66).

Flitcraft immediately decided that he had to adjust himself "to this new glimpse of life" and that if life "could be ended for him at random by a falling beam," then "he would change his life at random by simply going away" (66).

He left that afternoon for Seattle, took a boat to San Francisco, then wandered around for a couple of years before drifting back to the Pacific Northwest. He settled in Spokane and got married again: "His second wife didn't look like the first, but they were more alike than they were different. You know, the kind of women that play fair games of golf and bridge and like new salad-recipes." Spade's final comment on the story is "I don't think he even knew he had settled back naturally into the same groove he had jumped out of in Tacoma. But that's the part of it I always liked. He adjusted himself to beams falling, and then no more of them fell, and he adjusted himself to them not falling" (67).

And thus, as abruptly as the story began, it ends, with Spade's listener, Brigid, remarking, "How perfectly fascinating" (67). (One can imagine her saying these words in a tone whose brittle enthusiasm suggests her true reaction to the tale: "It may mean the world to you, but it's chopped liver to me.") In fact, Hammett suggests that Brigid's inability to grasp the meaning of Flitcraft's story is somehow gender-related. Flitcraft had originally agreed to talk to Spade in order to explain his actions and make their "reasonableness explicit." Spade says of that explanation: "I got it all right, . . . but Mrs. Flitcraft never did. She thought it was silly. Maybe it was" (66). At any rate, the first Mrs. Flitcraft wanted a divorce "after the trick he had played on her—the way she looked at it" (65). So it's not just Brigid that doesn't get Flitcraft's story, it's the first Mrs. Flitcraft as well.

Clearly, one of the structural purposes of Flitcraft's story in the novel, this tale that Spade tells Brigid while they are alone together in his apartment waiting for Joel Cairo to arrive, is that it foreshadows the novel's final scene between Spade and Brigid (again alone together in his apartment, this time waiting for the police to arrive), when Spade explains to her in great detail why he's going to turn her in for Miles Archer's murder. Needless to say, Brigid doesn't grasp that explanation either. At one point in the scene, Spade tells her that if she gets a break, she'll only serve twenty years and he'll wait for her, but if she doesn't, they'll hang her and he'll always remember her, and Brigid says, "Don't, Sam, don't say that even in fun. Oh, you frightened me for a moment! I really thought you—You know you do such wild and unpredictable things that–." To which Spade replies, "Don't be silly. You're taking the fall" (223).

Brigid's comment that Spade does "such wild and unpredictable things" is meant to remind us of a similar exchange between the two in that earlier scene at Spade's apartment. After Spade finishes the story of Flitcraft, Joel Cairo arrives and gets into an argument with Brigid that turns violent just as the police show up at Spade's door. Leaving Brigid in the living room holding a gun on Cairo, Spade stalls the police, telling them they can't come in without a search warrant. But when the sounds of a scuffle in the living room and Cairo's cries for help create probable cause, the police go in, and Spade, in order to keep the cops from "pulling the whole lot of them in" (79), manufactures an incredible story that the scuffle and the call for help were part of an elaborate gag to razz the cops. By sheer bravado and the craziness of the story, Spade makes the cops uncertain enough about whether they're being kidded that finally they leave, taking Cairo with them. At this point, Brigid tells Spade, "You're absolutely the wildest person I've ever known," adding a bit later, "You're altogether unpredictable" (85–87). The phrase "wild and unpredictable" to describe Spade's conduct appears three more times during this scene, culminating in his remark that if Brigid won't tell him what she knows about the case, then his "way of learning is to heave a wild and unpredictable monkey-wrench into the machinery. It's all right with me, if you're sure none of the flying pieces will hurt you" (90).

So it's clear that when Brigid, in that final scene, thinks Spade's joking about turning her over to the cops and says, "You know you do such wild and unpredictable things," the phrase comes bearing a load of freight that leads directly back to the story of Flitcraft. For the story that Spade tells Brigid at the start of that earlier scene is essentially a tale about a man who has learned from a close brush with accidental death that life is not "a clean orderly sane responsible affair," since men live "only while blind chance" spares them. And Flitcraft's response to "this new glimpse of life" is to match his behavior to it, like to like: the random unpredictability of an individual's behavior responding to the haphazardness of events as a way, in Flitcraft's words, of getting "into step with life." The parable of Flitcraft presents, in effect, a rationale for doing "wild and unpredictable things," and just so that the reader won't miss the connection between Flitcraft's behavior and Spade's, Hammett links the two with an image. Just as Flitcraft says that the falling beam which almost killed him sent "a piece of the sidewalk" flying up to cut his cheek, so Spade tells Brigid that if he has to heave "a wild and unpredictable monkey-wrench into the machinery" in order to learn what's going on, she may be hurt by "the flying pieces."

From a flying "piece of the sidewalk" to "flying pieces" of machinery seems like a short step, though the images are separated by twenty-five pages of text, but before we assume we know what this linking of Flitcraft's revelation about life to Spade's unpredictable actions means, we should look more closely at what Flitcraft's encounter with the falling beam actually teaches him. The accident demonstrates that there is no necessary connection between the way a man leads his life and the time and manner of his death. As a successful businessman, Flitcraft sees that being "a good citizen-husband-father," leading an "orderly sane responsible" life, has bought him nothing, no assurance either about longevity or about an appropriately dignified, honored, and loving end. Had he been hit by the beam, he would have died a very young man with a wife and two small children, died senselessly and horribly on a city street surrounded by strangers. What he learns is the difference between life-as-being and life-as-having, between what one is and what one owns, between life as the simple persistence of individual consciousness in time and life as the accumulation of people, property, habits, whatnot, by an individual during the course of his existence. And Flitcraft's response to this traumatic event reminds us of the kind of response Sigmund Freud described as occurring in children's play when youngsters attempt to master a trauma by reenacting it as a game.

According to Freud, in *Beyond the Pleasure Principle* (1920), the child is originally in "a *passive* situation" as regards the trauma; he experiences it as something beyond his control, something he must helplessly endure, and thus he is "overpowered by the experience." But, "by repeating it, unpleasurable though it was, as a game," he takes "an *active* part"; in voluntarily initiating the repetition he achieves a kind of mastery of the trauma by switching from a passive to an active role in relation to it.[2] And this is precisely what Flitcraft does. In response to the falling beam, the trauma of almost losing his life-as-being, Flitcraft voluntarily reenacts the event by losing, by actively giving up, his life-as-having. He leaves behind all those people, things, and habits that had previously constituted his life. He symbolically replays his own death and thus seems to regain active control of his own fate.

III

I emphasize the circumscribed character of the lesson Flitcraft learned from the falling beam (i.e., that there is no necessary relationship between the way a man lives his life and the time and manner of his death) at some length precisely because this rigorously delimited sense of the event's significance serves both to explain the ease with which Flitcraft, once beams no longer fell, settled back into a life so much like the one he had left, and also to combat an influential reading of the Flitcraft episode that in effect sees it as an *ur-existentialist* fable—an interpretation that to my mind overstates the falling beam's lesson. The origin of this interpretation seems to be Steven Marcus's 1974 essay "Dashiell Hammett and the Continental Op," in which, as part of a discussion of Hammett's Continental Op stories, Marcus gives a reading of the Flitcraft tale, a story he calls "the most important or central moment" in *The Maltese Falcon* and "one of the central moments in all of Hammett's writing."[3] After briefly summarizing the Flitcraft episode, Marcus concludes that the tale is "about among other things . . . the ethical irrationality of existence, the ethical unintelligibility of the world," and that what Flitcraft learns from the incident of the falling beam is "that life is inscrutable, opaque, irresponsible, and arbitrary—that human existence does not correspond in its actuality to the way we live it." One gets the sense from Marcus that this must have been a load-bearing beam indeed. He says that Flitcraft, in responding to this new insight by leaving his wife and children, "acts irrationally and at random, in accordance with the nature of existence." Yet to act at random, to act in an unpredictable manner, is not necessarily to act irrationally. Indeed, the whole point of Flitcraft's telling Spade his story is that he wants to make clear to him the "reasonableness" of his actions. But Marcus goes on to comment on Flitcraft's falling back into his old way of life a few years later that "here we come upon the unfathomable and most mysteriously irrational part of it all—how despite everything we have learned and everything we know, men will persist in behaving and trying to behave sanely, rationally, sensibly, and responsibly. And we will continue to persist even when we know that there is no logical or metaphysical, no discoverable or demonstrable reason for doing so. It is this sense of sustained contradiction that is close to the center—or to one of the centers—of Hammett's work. The contradiction is not ethical alone; it is metaphysical as well. And it is not merely sustained; it is sustained with pleasure" (196).

So it's not just Flitcraft's sudden leaving of his previous life that's irrational but also his returning to a similar life two years later. In trying to account for Marcus's reading of the Flitcraft episode, one is left with the sense that his interpretation resulted from a back-pressure of the film on the novel. Marcus begins his essay by telling us that he was first introduced to *The Maltese Falcon* at the age of twelve when he saw the John Huston film and that it was only years later, after he'd read and reread the book and reseen the movie, that he "could begin to understand why the impact of the film had been so memorable": "The director, John Huston, had had the wit to recognize the power, sharpness, integrity, and bite of Hammett's prose—particularly the dialogue—and the film script consists almost entirely of speech taken directly and without modification from the written novel. . . . Huston had to make certain omissions. Paradoxically, however, one of the things that he chose to omit was the most important or central moment in the entire novel. It is also one of the central moments in all of Hammett's writing. I think we can make use of this oddly 'lost' passage as a means of entry into Hammett's vision or imagination of the world" (194). The omitted passage is, of course, the story of Flitcraft, and the reasoning implicit in Marcus's argument is that since the Flitcraft episode is central to the novel and, indeed, to all Hammett's writing, because it expresses parabolically his "vision or imagination of the world," the episode's worldview pervades the entire book, coloring the dialogue to which Huston's film is so faithful. The omitted Flitcraft episode is, then, the hidden center around which the visible memorableness of the movie orbits, and though Marcus ostensibly sets out to explain the striking quality of the film in terms of the novel's worldview, he in fact ends up interpreting Flitcraft's story in terms of a preexisting sense of what constitutes the film's memorableness, its place in cultural and film history.

As we know, Huston's *The Maltese Falcon* was one of the first great examples of American film noir, a genre originally described and named by French film critics at the end of World War II. As the well-known story goes, the French hadn't been able to get new American movies during the years of the war and the German occupation, and then suddenly, with the peace, there was an influx into French theaters of American films made between 1940 and 1945, among which was a type of film whose scripts were based on the hard-boiled fiction of writers like Hammett, Chandler, and Cain and whose visual style and subject matter, as distinct from the prewar American films the French were used to, had substantially darkened. Indeed, one of these critics, Jean Pierre Chartier, titled his 1946 article in *Revue du Cinema* "The Americans Are Making Dark Films Too"[4]—the *too* clearly evoking the author's sense that this dark subject matter had already been a staple of such prewar French films as Marcel Carné's *Quai des Brumes, Hôtel du Nord,* and *Le Jour se lève,* Julien Duvivier's *Pépé le Moko,* and Sacha Guitry's *Le Roman d'un tricheur.* What these critics clearly responded to in this new genre of American films was a worldview that could be assimilated to the most influential contemporary French thought, the existentialist philosophy and literature of Sartre and Camus. For hadn't Camus once said that the book that was "both the inspiration and the model" for *The Stranger* was James M. Cain's *The Postman Always Rings Twice*? (At least that's what it says in the blurb on the back of my paperback edition of Cain's novel. Of course, whether or not Camus actually said this is of no interest to me because that's not the point. Rather, the point is this characteristic strategy, illustrated by the paperback blurb, of trying to give hard-boiled detective fiction an intellectual and aesthetic cachet by associating it with existentialism and Camus, which is to say, this strategy of trying to establish the seriousness of some aspect of American popular culture by showing that the French take it seriously, the same ploy that would have us believe that Jerry Lewis is a comic genius because the French made him a member of the Legion of Honor or that Mickey Rourke is a great actor because he's all the rage in Paris.)

At the start, then, in the very critiques that identified and named the genre, film noir had been associated with existentialism, and as this association became a commonplace of subsequent discussions of the genre, it exercised a retrospective influence on critical readings of the hard-boiled detective novels from which many of the films were adapted. In a 1976 article in *Sight and Sound* entitled "No Way Out: Existential Motifs in the Film Noir," Robert Porfirio, discussing Huston's *The Maltese Falcon*, says that "the film's one unfortunate omission is the Flitcraft parable Spade tells Brigid O'Shaughnessy, for this is our only chance to peep into Spade's interior life. And what it reveals is that Spade is by nature an existentialist, with a strong conception of the randomness of existence."[5] In that same year Charles Gregory, writing in the *Journal of Popular Film*, characterized the worldview of film noir by citing the Flitcraft story, which he paraphrased at some length, commenting that "French critics have admired Spade's anecdote for its 'existential' nature, proving Hammett's philosophic grasp of a world ruled by chance rather than Divine Order. . . . Steven Marcus has noted in his introduction to some Continental Op stories that this passage means that 'life is inscrutable, opaque, irresponsible, and arbitrary.'"[6]

However, it seems to me an enormous, and ultimately unjustifiable, leap to go from a tale illustrating that there's no necessary connection between the way one leads one's life and the time and manner of one's death to a reading that finds life to be inscrutable, opaque, irresponsible, and arbitrary, particularly since the conclusion of Flitcraft's story is his ending up voluntarily leading the same kind of life he had previously abandoned. Indeed, I've evoked at some length this back-pressure of film noir criticism on the interpretation of hard-boiled detective fiction because I want to free the Flitcraft episode, and thus Hammett's novel as a whole, from this retrospective existentialist overlay, a frame of reference that reduces the real complexity of the Flitcraft story and diminishes the richness of the novel whose worldview it informs.

IV

Part of the appeal of Flitcraft's adventure for me is that it belongs to a much older and more interesting tradition than that provided by existentialism. To begin with, it has always reminded me of one of Hawthorne's best short works, the 1835 tale "Wakefield," about a man who, "under the pretence of going a journey, took lodgings in the next street to his own house, and there, unheard of by his wife or friends, and without the shadow of a reason for such self-banishment, dwelt upwards of twenty years. During that period, he beheld his home every day, and frequently the forlorn Mrs. Wakefield. And after so great a gap in his matrimonial felicity—when his death was reckoned certain, his estate settled, his name dismissed from memory, and his wife long, long ago, resigned to her autumnal widowhood—he entered the door one evening, quietly, as from a day's absence, and became a loving spouse till death."[7]

One sees immediately the structural resemblance between Wakefield and Flitcraft, two men who leave a former life suddenly, for no reason apparent to those left behind, and then, after an absence of two or twenty years, return, either to that former life or to its equivalent. And what for me gives these stories their peculiar power is that they both seem to be modern reworkings of the story of Job—which is to say that Job, Wakefield, and Flitcraft are all men who lose their "lives" without losing their life, men who are either deprived of or voluntarily give up their life-as-having while retaining their life-as-being and who in one way or another ultimately recover the former, with some recognition of the difference between the two accruing to the readers of their stories if not to the men themselves. Examining the similarities and differences among the three stories will make clear what gives the Flitcraft episode its special quality and how the significance of that episode pervades the whole novel.

Like the Flitcraft episode, the story of Job is concerned with the sudden, apparently undeserved reversal of fortune that can be suffered by a good man, but whereas such a reversal is only threatened in Flitcraft's case (a close brush with a falling beam) and its cause explained by the random nature of accidents, it is actually endured by Job, who loses his possessions, sons and daughters, health, and peace of mind, and its cause explained as the will of God. God has permitted Satan to test his servant Job, who "was perfect and upright" and who "feared God, and eschewed evil" (Job 1:1), because Satan said that Job's rectitude was merely a function of how greatly he had been blessed with the good things of life. So God allows Satan to remove all Job's possessions (offspring, wealth, health, tranquillity, but with the stipulation that he not kill him) to prove that Job, no matter how much he suffers, will remain faithful, that he will not, as Satan predicted, curse God to his face.

Clearly, in Flitcraft's case, it makes sense to explain a single close encounter with a falling beam (which can instantly wipe out all Flitcraft is and has) by invoking the random, haphazard component of existence, but in the case of Job, such an explanation is ruled out by the sheer number and frequency of the disasters befalling the same man; indeed, so many that they can not be random and coincidental, they must be intentional and meaningful. But such a scenario necessarily raises the further question of what kind of intention or will, what kind of meaning, can lie behind bad things happening to good people. The Job story is, then, front-loaded by the repetitive nature of its hero's sufferings for an explanation involving intention rather than chance. This is not to say that God willed this good man's sufferings but rather that His will permitted Satan to test His servant, presumably knowing that Job would remain faithful through his trials and gain even greater favor in the eyes of the Lord. Thus, at the conclusion of the narrative, God speaks out of a whirlwind, rebukes the false comforters, and makes "the latter end of Job's life" more blessed than the beginning, giving him seven sons and three daughters to replace those that were lost and returning his herds of sheep, camels, oxen, and she-asses but doubling their numbers. Job is further blessed with a long life, living to see "his sons, and his sons' sons, even four generations" (Job 42:16).

Granted, the Book of Job as we have it seems to be the work of more than one author, with various parts written at different periods. The book's prologue (chaps. 1 and 2: the dialogue of God and Satan, and the disasters that Satan inflicts on Job) and epilogue (chap. 42: the restoration of God's blessings and prolongation of Job's life in which to enjoy those blessings) are both written from an omniscient viewpoint, with the writer knowing what goes on both in heaven and in the mind of God. In contrast, the large middle portion of the narrative (chaps. 3–41: the dialogue of Job and his comforters, and the concluding statement by God from the whirlwind) is written from a limited viewpoint associated with Job. Given the book's various authors, compilers, or revisers, it is not surprising that the work, in terms of its overall meaning, often seems at cross-purposes with itself. The long middle section is a text illustrating patience in adversity as personified by Job, and evoking, in the dialogue of Job and his three false comforters and in God's closing statement, that it is pointless—indeed, presumptuous—for man to inquire into the ways of God, to try to puzzle out, for example, why bad things happen to good people.

Yet this moral is clearly undercut by the prologue, which provides just such an explanation in the story of God's allowing Satan to test his servant's rectitude. Even more puzzling is the epilogue, in which Job gets back all he'd lost and then some, for if the point of the dialogue between God and Satan at the start of the book had been, on the one hand, Satan's assertion that Job worshiped God only because God had showered him with blessings and built a "hedge about him, and about his house" (Job 1:10) and, on the other hand, God's rejoinder that Job would remain faithful even if he lost all he had, then certainly this ending seems to undermine that point. For Satan could argue that Job only remains faithful to God because he knows he will ultimately have all his blessings restored, that is, that the necessary connection between conduct and rewards, between worshipful service and God's blessings, is still intact, even though it may be delayed for a while by Job's trials, and that Job thus continues to worship God only because he has expectations of some return. Satan might then propose that the only true test of Job's motives would be for God to break absolutely the connection between conduct and rewards by letting Satan deprive Job not only of his life-as-having but also of his life-as-being. But that is, as we noted, the one thing God specifically forbids Satan from doing, for the overall point of the book as it now exists is to reaffirm the long-term link between one's behavior and one's deserts.

The Old Testament has, of course, no clearly defined notion of a blessed afterlife. God and the angels are in heaven, and on occasion, room is made there for exceptional persons such as Elijah and Enoch. But because the Old Testament isn't so much interested in the survival of individuals in the next world as in the survival of a people in this one, its notion of every person's fate at death is that they descend to a place of darkness called Sheol, similar to the classical underworld of shades. Lacking the sense of a commonly available blessed afterlife, the Book of Job must make the link between conduct and compensation visible *within* its hero's lifetime, unlike the New Testament, in which the notion of personal immortality would allow Job's two-part trajectory (first, patience and faithfulness in adversity; second, ultimate compensation) to be distributed on either side of death and thereby to define the difference between this life and the next. The Book of Job gives a further indication of its lack of interest in the fate of individuals in the detail of the sudden death of Job's ten children and their subsequent compensatory replacement by ten new children. The impersonality of this ten-for-ten reimbursement speaks volumes. Interestingly enough, the Flitcraft story exhibits in its modern way as little interest in the notion of compensation in the next world for behavior in this one as does the Book of Job in its Old Testament way. Flitcraft never considers any form of metaphysical response to the perceived injustice of a good life ending in a random, premature death. Indeed, one can imagine him agreeing with Brigid O'Shaughnessy's remark, "I'm not heroic. I don't think there's anything worse than death" (39).

Considering the relationship of the stories of Job and Flitcraft, we can see that in the case of Job the *repetitive* nature of the disasters that beset him mark them as intentional and meaningful (that "half-credence in the supernatural" caused "by *coincidences* of so seemingly marvelous a character that, as *mere* coincidences, the intellect has been unable to receive them," as Poe says)[8] and that the *singular*, the one-shot, nature of the event that happens to Flitcraft (the falling beam) marks it as random and meaningless. We should note in this regard that Job, Flitcraft, and Wakefield are all married men and that Job and Flitcraft both have families and have enjoyed success in their work (in Wakefield's case, no mention is made of children or of any kind of employment)—which is simply to say that all three have a settled domestic existence and that two of them have successful lives beyond the family. They are men who have settled into a routine in their lives: Wakefield is described as "a man of habits"; indeed, his life had been so unremarkable, says the narrator, that no one who knew him "could have anticipated" (76) this "very singular step" (77). And Spade says that Flitcraft's "habits for months" before his disappearance "could be accounted for too thoroughly to justify any suspicion of secret vices, or even of another woman in his life" (64), adding that Flitcraft had reestablished this same habitual lifestyle in his new incarnation, even down to the detail of his usually getting away "to play golf after four in the afternoon during the season" (65).

What I would draw attention to here is the difference between the repetitive, habitual, or routine character of Flitcraft's life and the singular character of the event that threatens him (the falling beam) in order to point out that this event is not, strictly speaking, "singular," not something that could happen only once to Flitcraft and never again; as long as the falling beam didn't kill Flitcraft, beams could theoretically fall on the sidewalk near him every day as he goes to lunch. What the *exceptional* occurrence of the falling beam stands for in Flitcraft's story is the most important, absolutely singular event that can occur in his or anyone's life after their birth, the only life-encompassing event that cannot be repeated: one's own death. This is clearly why Flitcraft's response to this random event, his decision to get himself "into step with life" by matching the random component in existence with a random component in his own behavior by suddenly leaving his life of settled habits, doesn't work. For the very singularity of one's death doesn't permit its being incorporated into a rule of living, into something that presumes the possibility of repetition. One might think of it by analogy with the way that mathematicians use the word *singularity* to refer to the center of that theoretical phenomenon known as a black hole, that is, an object whose mass is so great that it captures its own radiation and at whose center the mathematics of quantum mechanics—the known laws of physics that describe the rest of the universe—break down, and where time and space as we know them cease to exist. We each have our own personal black hole coming at some point in our lives, and there's no actual way of matching any sort of human behavior, short of suicide, to the reality of that one-and-only, once-and-for-all occurrence.

One can respond to an associative evocation (such as the falling beam) of that real singularity by a symbolic action (Flitcraft's abrupt leaving of his life-as-having), but whether one interprets Flitcraft's sudden departure as a psychological move that aims to master a traumatic event passively suffered by transforming it into something actively replayed in symbolic form, thus metaphorically reasserting one's control over one's own fate, or as a philosophical move that existentially enacts the primacy of life-as-being over life-as-having, no symbolic (i.e., repetitive) action can ever put one's life "into step," as Flitcraft says, with something that has no second step. So Flitcraft's solution of suddenly leaving his old life and wandering around for two years (a wandering that doubtless represents a series of sudden, random leave-takings attempting to replicate the first one) falls of its own weight, for if one's own death is an unrepeatable event, then sudden violent evocations of the possibility of one's own death are only a slightly-less-frequent occurrence and, given the singularity of the former and the rarity of the latter, neither is worth trying to make the basis of a design for living.

If Flitcraft's subsequent adjustment of his life to the fact of no more beams falling involves his settling "back naturally into the same groove he had jumped out of in Tacoma," then this same recapturing of the central character by repetition, after an initial instance of extraordinary behavior, is acted out in "Wakefield." Hawthorne refers to Wakefield's sudden disappearance as "this very singular step" (77) and speaks of "the singularity of his situation" in dissevering "himself from the world" by giving "up his place and privileges with living men, without being admitted among the dead," characterizing Wakefield's as the "unprecedented fate to retain his original share of human sympathies, and to be still involved in human interests, while he had lost his reciprocal influence on them" (79). Certainly this language of "singularity" and of the "unprecedented" evokes Wakefield's sudden leaving of his life-as-having as an exceptional figure of the singularity of his own death, but what distinguishes Wakefield's fate from Flitcraft's is that after his disappearance Wakefield continues to haunt his old surroundings. He constructs his new existence around the very absence his departure created in his home and marriage. Having abruptly left a domestic routine, he establishes another routine in watching over the empty place that had once been his: "We must leave him, for ten years or so, to haunt around his house, without once crossing the threshold, and to be faithful to his wife, with all the affection of which his heart is capable, while he is slowly fading out of hers. Long since, he had lost the perception of singularity in his conduct" (78); what had started as a "very singular step," in terms of both its oddness and its random, unpremeditated quality, soon became, through its prolongation, something unremarkable, just another habit for this "man of habits" (77).

If, when a man dies, he "shall return no more to his house, neither shall his place know him any more" (Job 7:10), then when Wakefield, on the spur of the moment, decides one evening to return to *his* home after a twenty-year absence, Hawthorne seems to echo Job when he thunders, "Stay, Wakefield! Would you go to the sole home that is left you? Then step into your grave!" (80). And I would argue that there is yet another Jobean reference that has been present all along in the name of the tale's central character, for Wakefield's name has always seemed to me to be an allusion to Goldsmith's *The Vicar of Wakefield*, a novel that, in its story of Mr. Primrose's many trials patiently endured and the ultimate restoration of his lost blessings (including a daughter he had thought was dead), has long been acknowledged as based on the Book of Job.

Where Hammett gives us a reason for Flitcraft's disappearance, Hawthorne leaves the motive for Wakefield's departure and twenty-year absence a matter of conjecture to the end. He focuses instead on the effect that stepping out of one's accustomed place can have: "Amid the seeming confusion of our mysterious world, individuals are so nicely adjusted to a system, and systems to one another and to a whole, that, by stepping aside for a moment, a man exposes himself to a fearful risk of losing his place forever. Like Wakefield, he may become, as it were, the Outcast of the Universe" (80). And yet it may be precisely that sense of "a fearful risk" that is the key to understanding Wakefield's actions. Hawthorne tells us that Wakefield's character is compounded of "a quiet selfishness," a "peculiar sort of vanity," a "disposition to craft," and "a little strangeness" (76). One can easily imagine that such an individual, who has been immersed for some years in a habitual domestic existence, might well feel the perverse attraction of this "fearful risk," feel his vanity, craftiness, and peculiarity drawn suddenly and irresistibly toward an action precisely because it is the one thing *he should not do,* the one thing that, since it is clearly opposed to his own best interests, represents a supreme test of the self's freedom and perhaps of its cleverness as well. Such a risky manipulation of the conditions of one's existence might well appeal to Wakefield as a means of demonstrating that he is a creature of habit not out of necessity but out of free choice, of demonstrating this by suddenly choosing to step out of his domestic routine with the vain self-assurance that only he would be crafty enough to do so and still be able to resume his former life at will.

My reading of Wakefield's possible motives for his sudden departure and prolonged absence has obviously been influenced by Poe's explication, in his 1845 tale "The Imp of the Perverse," of that basic, primitive psychological component he calls *perverseness.* And yet, in failing to provide a definite interpretation of Wakefield's motives while encouraging the reader to speculate, Hawthorne in effect authorizes each reader to make an interpretation of his own. And this sense, combined with Hawthorne's frequent rhetorical warnings to Wakefield during the tale that his sudden departure from home and continued absence are actions directly opposed to his own self-interest, and his further suggestion that these actions are without any discernible purpose, points us toward that psychological principle concerning which Poe says the self's only object is to vex itself.

V

All of which brings us to a final question: If, as I have suggested, "Wakefield" and the Book of Job are the allusive backgrounds for Flitcraft's story, then how does placing his story in this context alter or enrich our reading of Hammett's novel? Let me start with the book's central eponymous object and note that the Maltese falcon has a dual significance in the book, in part because there seem to be two falcons. On the one hand, there is the fantastic golden, jewel-encrusted statue, which Gutman says was sent by the Order of the Hospital of St. John of Jerusalem to the Emperor Charles V in 1531 as tribute to show that, even though Charles had given the island to the Order, "Malta was still under Spain" (128); a statue that is hijacked on the way to Charles V by "a famous admiral of buccaneers" (129) and thus launched on an obscure four-hundred-year trajectory through the hands of various possessors, some of whom do, and some of whom do not, know what the object is. But what we must keep in mind is that no one in the novel has ever actually seen this object (not even Gutman). Its existence has simply been deduced by Gutman from examining historical documents. On the other hand, there is the actual foot-high statue of a falcon made of lead and coated with black enamel, a fake that Cairo and Gutman conclude was produced by the Russian general Kemidov when Gutman's attempt to buy the statue from him in Istanbul alerted the Russian to its true value. And while the former statue is the one Gutman and Spade are seeking, it is the latter they end up with.

What becomes clear as Gutman discusses the original Maltese falcon with Spade is that its value is a function not just of its material (gold and precious jewels) and workmanship (crafted by Turkish slaves in the castle of St. Angelo) but of its uniqueness (dare I say its singularity?) and its historical provenance, as an art dealer would say. When Gutman asks Spade if he has "any conception of how much money can be made out of that black bird" (111), Spade says no, but adds that if Gutman tells him what it is, he'll figure out the profits. To which Gutman replies, "'You couldn't do it, sir. Nobody could do it who hadn't a world of experience with things of that sort, and'—he paused impressively—'there aren't any other things of that sort. '"So at the start Hammett codes the golden bird as singular, and in the very next exchange he associates it with death. Gutman asks Spade if he really doesn't know what the black bird is, and Spade says, "I know what it's supposed to look like. I know the value in life you people put on it" (112). And of course, before the novel is done, four people will have been murdered, and two more will be facing a possible death penalty for murder. Indeed, it is precisely the ambiguity of the statue's signification, in part a function of there being two falcons, that Hammett intends to make use of, for while the golden bird is coded as unique and associated with death, thus capable of serving as a figure for the singularity of one's own death, it is also coded as long-lived, as an object whose historical longevity, whose ability to survive its creators and all its subsequent possessors, makes it capable, like other objects of this sort, such as the pyramids, of serving as a figure of immortality.

It would not, of course, be the first time in English literature that a bird simultaneously evoked death and immortality, as any reader of Keats's "Ode to a Nightingale" knows. When Keats contemplates the impersonal species-longevity of the bird and its song compared to the uniqueness of his own song and his personal mortality, he exclaims, "Thou wast not born for death, immortal Bird!" And it certainly wouldn't be the first time in American literature that a black bird, as the falcon is frequently referred to in the novel, was associated with death (consider the most famous poem by the detective genre's inventor).

So we have a novel whose characters are pursuing the golden statue of a bird, a statue whose existence may be nothing more than the interpretive dream of the obsessive Gutman, a putative object that serves as a figure at once of the singularity of one's own death and of the traditional golden dream of the great good thing associated with that singularity in the Christian West, the dream of personal immortality after death, of being given back one's life after losing one's life. But what these characters actually find is a leaden statue of a bird with a string of violent deaths in its wake. Of course, a falcon is a bird of prey and thus already associated with death. And does one really need to invoke Shakespearean imagery to establish "lead" and "the leaden" as common evocations of death? or, on the other hand, cite the fact that since gold has no oxide and thus doesn't corrupt when buried, it has traditionally functioned as a figure of immortality? No, I think it is sufficient to note that *The Maltese Falcon* plays itself out as a quest for possession of a golden possibility than ends with possession of a leaden singularity, a pursuit that is an ironic enough, not to say a cynical enough, inversion of the quest-romance structure underlying hard-boiled detective fiction to satisfy even the most hard-boiled reader.

But there is more. Looking again at the scene in Spade's apartment in which he tells Brigid the story of Flitcraft, we realize that this tale of an explained disappearance, whose central figure was found to be still alive, corresponds to a tale Brigid had told Spade earlier in her own apartment about an unexplained disappearance, in which the missing person was presumed to be dead. Responding to Spade's question about Floyd Thursby, her protector and the supposed killer of Miles Archer, Brigid says that she had met him in the Orient: "There was a story in Hongkong that he had come out there, to the Orient, as bodyguard to a gambler who had had to leave the States, and that the gambler had since disappeared. They said Floyd knew about his disappearing. I don't know. I do know that he always went heavily armed." When Spade asks her if she's in physical danger, she says yes and adds, "I'm not heroic. I don't think there's anything worse than death" (39). It's a line that resonates through the entire novel, evoking not only Brigid's worldview but that of most of the other characters as well. For if nothing is worse than death, if death is a total loss of everything one has or is (as it seems to be for Flitcraft, for example), then human conduct, no longer restrained by the hope or fear of an afterlife, is governed only by the kinds of rewards and punishments that can be assessed in this world and by the kind of limited human means that exist for judging that conduct.

There is something else in Brigid's remark as well, for certainly Hammett intends for the reader to hear this comment, made by an American woman in the 1920s, as both an echo and a repudiation of a moral dictum from an earlier era, the dictum that for a woman forcible sexual violation was "a fate worse than death," a fate to be resisted at the cost of one's life, if necessary. And certainly Hammett further intends that on a second reading of the novel we should grasp the deeper point of this echo, understand that, although a certain type of conventionally moral woman might consider forced sexual intercourse to be a fate worse than death, for Brigid, who thinks there's no fate worse than death, sexual intercourse, in fact or in prospect, becomes a means of deflecting or delivering death to someone else (as when she sexually entices Miles Archer up a dark alley to put a bullet through his heart) or of manipulating men to do her bidding (as when she tells Spade that she doesn't have enough money if she has to bid for his loyalty, then asks provocatively, "Can I buy you with my body?" [59]). The answer, of course, is yes—temporarily. But her echoic invocation of an older morality regarding women's virtue also functions as an ironic underlining of the "helpless female" role she plays with Spade, a role Spade characterizes as her "schoolgirl manner, stammering and blushing and all that" (57). After Spade tells Brigid the Flitcraft story in his apartment, before Cairo arrives, Brigid tries again to convince Spade that he should trust her completely because she trusts him completely, as evidenced by her coming to his apartment: "I don't have to tell you how utterly at a disadvantage you'll have me, with him here, if you choose. . . . And you know I'd never have placed myself in this position if I hadn't trusted you completely." To which Spade succinctly replies, "That again!" and then goes on to explain, "You don't have to trust me, anyhow, as long as you can persuade me to trust you" (67).

But perhaps the fullest resonance of Brigid's remark that there is nothing worse than death only comes in that concluding scene at Spade's apartment, in which Gutman, Cairo, and Wilmer Cook take Spade prisoner at gunpoint after Brigid has led him into a trap, comes as that distinction between life-as-being and life-as-having (which is part of the point of the Flitcraft story) resurfaces in one of the most intriguing moments of the novel.

Though held at gunpoint, Spade begins bargaining with Gutman about the black bird, demanding not only the money Gutman had promised him but also a fall guy for the police to pin the murders on. When Spade suggests they give the police Wilmer, Gutman at first rejects the notion, saying, "I feel towards Wilmer just exactly as if he were my own son" (187). Spade then suggests they give the police Cairo, and Cairo, who at the beginning of the bargaining had warned Spade that "though you may have the falcon yet we certainly have you" (183), flies into a rage and says, "You seem to forget that you are not in a position to insist on anything" (192). To which Spade replies, "If you kill me, how are you going to get the bird? And if I know you can't afford to kill me till you have it, how are you going to scare me into giving it to you?" When Gutman points out that "there are other means of persuasion besides killing and threatening to kill," Spade says, "Sure, . . . but they're not much good unless the threat of death is behind them to hold the victim down. See what I mean? If you try anything I don't like I won't stand for it. I'll make it a matter of your having to call it off or kill me, knowing you can't afford to kill me." Gutman affably warns Spade that such situations require delicate judgment on both sides, since men may forget "in the heat of action where their best interest lies and let their emotions carry them away." To which Spade just as affably replies, "That's the trick, from my side, . . . to make my play strong enough that it ties you up, but yet not make you mad enough to bump me off against your better judgment" (193).

It is one of the shrewdest exchanges in a novel noted for the quality of its dialogue, and certainly from the reader's viewpoint part of the exchange's force derives from its structural resemblance to the Flitcraft story. Consider the similarity of the two situations: Flitcraft confronts the real possibility of his own violent death in the incident of the falling beam, while Spade confronts the same possibility in being captured by three armed men who he knows have killed before. Flitcraft responds to this possibility with a typical psychological move: he splits the endangered object (his life) in two and then, separating his life-as-being from his life-as-having, he voluntarily sacrifices the latter either as a philosophical gesture to reassert control of his own destiny or as a psychological defense mechanism to master a trauma, a reply that, as Flitcraft eventually learns, doesn't work as a rule of life.

Spade, on the other hand, responds to the possibility of his own death not by any symbolic action but by trying to manipulate that death's real singularity through another being/having distinction. Cairo says that though Spade *has* the falcon, they most certainly *have* him, but Spade demonstrates that their *having* him (and thus the falcon) depends entirely on their willingness and ability to exercise an ultimate sanction over his *being*, a sanction that, if exercised, will make his being and their having vanish together. It is precisely the real possibility of his own death (and the loss with it of the secret of the falcon's whereabouts) that Spade wields like a weapon when he tells Gutman that he will certainly make it a matter of their having to kill him if they try to extract the information through torture. Convinced by their conversation of Spade's willingness to take this risk, Gutman agrees to make Wilmer the fall guy, telling Wilmer, in a kind of Jobean postscript to this dialogue of having and being, "Well, Wilmer, I'm sorry indeed to lose you, and I want you to know that I couldn't be any fonder of you if you were my own son; but—well, by God!—if you lose a son it's possible to get another—and there's only one Maltese falcon" (204).

Though at first glance the obvious difference between Flitcraft's and Spade's cases seems to be the type of death each confronts (for Flitcraft random and accidental, for Spade intentional), yet in describing the death Spade risks, Hammett makes clear that to some extent it too would be accidental, that while Gutman and his associates simply intend to learn the whereabouts of the falcon, they might accidentally kill Spade in the heat of action. Thus the deaths Flitcraft and Spade face differ as an accident at random (any number of variables could have altered the time and position of Flitcraft and the falling beam in relation to each other) differs from a work-related accident; also, there is enough human agency involved in the death Spade is threatened with that Spade's reasoning with his captors allows him to avoid this death, allows him the kind of negotiation denied to Flitcraft and the falling beam.

There is in the novel, of course, one death whose randomness resembles to some degree the one that almost befell Flitcraft—Miles Archer's. Brigid kills Archer with a gun she had borrowed from Floyd Thursby, her former protector, in order to get rid of Thursby by pinning Archer's murder on him. But as Spade makes clear in his climactic conversation with Brigid, since all she'd needed was a murder victim that could be plausibly linked to Thursby, any number of people could have been the possible victim, including Spade if he, instead of Archer, had volunteered to shadow Brigid and Thursby that evening. The element of haphazardness in Miles Archer's death accounts, then, for the ultimate appropriateness of Spade's telling the story of Flitcraft's brush with random death to Archer's killer; for as Spade also makes clear in that final conversation with Brigid, he suspected her of being Archer's killer from the moment the police told him the physical circumstances of the murder. He tells Brigid that Archer had had "too many years' experience as a detective to be caught like that by a man he was shadowing. Up a blind alley with his gun tucked away on his hip and his overcoat buttoned . . . but he'd've gone up there with you, angel, . . . and then you could've stood close to him in the dark and put a hole in him" (220).

This brings us to the core of that climactic conversation between Spade and Brigid and to the central moral dilemma facing Spade in the novel: he has allowed himself to become sexually involved, even perhaps to fall in love, with a woman he believes is a murderer. This involvement with Brigid is the last instance I want to examine of the way that the story of Flitcraft, with its allusive background in "Wakefield" and the Book of Job, informs the entire novel.

There is this curious asymmetry about the stories of Job, Wakefield, and Flitcraft: all three men have wives, but where Wakefield and Flitcraft leave their wives (Wakefield for twenty years, Flitcraft for good) as part of giving up their life-as-having, Job does not lose *his* wife when he's deprived of his blessings. Job's wife survives to comfort him with the words, "Dost thou still retain thine integrity? curse God, and die" (Job 2:9). Indeed, it has always seemed to me part of the Jewish humor of Job that it is not the death of his wife but her survival that its author means for us to number among Job's trials. Similarly, there seems to be no great bond of affection between Wakefield and his wife or between Flitcraft and his first wife. Wakefield leaves his spouse without hinting what he intends to do and returns twenty years later without a word of explanation, while Flitcraft, says Spade, "had no feeling of guilt" (65) for what he'd done: "He loved his family, he said, as much as he supposed was usual, but knew he was leaving them adequately provided for, and his love for them was not of the sort to make absence painful" (66).

I would say that the ease, not to say the apparent callousness, with which Flitcraft leaves his wife and family is related, on the one hand, to Wakefield's cavalier treatment of his wife and, on the other, to Spade's behavior with Brigid. For if Spade had suspected from the very beginning that Brigid killed Miles Archer, then his becoming sexually, if not romantically, involved with her suggests he knew their liaison had a brief life span built into it, for precisely those reasons he gives Brigid in their final conversation. Depending on how you count, there are seven or eight of these prompting his decision to "send her over," and at least two are crucial. He says that "no matter what I wanted to do now it would be absolutely impossible for me to let you go without having myself dragged to the gallows with the others" and, further, that if he did let her go, then she'd have something on him and he'd have something on her, and "I couldn't be sure you wouldn't decide to shoot a hole in *me* some day" (226–27).

Spade understands that what could easily result, one way or the other, from his continuing their affair is his own death. But when Spade first told Brigid that he was turning her in for reasons he must have known all along, she says, "You've been playing with me? Only pretending you cared—to trap me? You didn't care at all? You didn't—don't—l-love me?" To which he replies, "I think I do. What of it?" (223–24). And then, after rehearsing the reasons for turning her in, he says, "Now on the other side we've got what? All we've got is the fact that maybe you love me and maybe I love you," and when she objects that he must know whether he loves her or not, he says, "I don't. It's easy enough to be nuts about you. . . . But I don't know what that amounts to. Does anybody ever? But suppose I do? What of it? Maybe next month I won't. I've been through it before—when it lasted that long. Then what? Then I'll think I played the sap. And if I did it and got sent over then I'd be sure I was the sap. Well, if I send you over I'll be sorry as hell—I'll have some rotten nights—but that'll pass" (227).

If Spade's point is that this too shall pass away, then we see here the dark side of repetition, the side expressed not by Job but by Ecclesiastes: the sense that if repetition in the case of Flitcraft, Wakefield, and Job equates with a kind of domestic routine whose attributes are comfort and safety and the familiar (Flitcraft is said to be "a man who was most comfortable in step with his surroundings. He had been raised that way. The people he knew were like that" [66]), then the other side of such a settled, predictable life may well be a feeling of senseless repetition, of a universal existential boredom (what Wallace Stevens called "the celestial ennui of apartments"), the sense that if there is no once-and-for-all in life (short of one's own death), then there's nothing that's supremely valuable, nothing whose worth isn't continually eroded by endless repetition or instantiation, what one might call the Jake-it's-Chinatown syndrome or the dark side of Kant's mathematical sublime. And thus one might see in an exceptional event (such as the pursuit of a fabulous statue that may or may not exist, or a short-term love affair with an attractive and dangerous woman that might or might not result in one's own death) a figurative evocation of that ultimate singularity, similar to the one provided by the falling beam in Flitcraft's case, see that such an exceptional event (a once-in-a-lifetime adventure or an affair that's too hot not to cool down) has meaning and value in a life only through a constitutive opposition to all that is routine, repetitive, familiar, and humdrum. When Gutman tells Spade the history of the Maltese falcon, he begins by saying, "This is going to be the most astounding thing you've ever heard of, sir, and I say that knowing that a man of your caliber in your profession must have known some astounding things in his time" (127). This may be true enough, though to judge the detective business from what we know of Spade's work both with Spade and Archer and with the big detective agency in Seattle that sent him looking for Flitcraft, that business amounts essentially to tail jobs, tracking down missing persons, and divorce work—fairly routine. Indeed, the only thing Spade, during the course of the exceptional case of the Maltese falcon, recounts from his own working life that struck him as extraordinary is the story of Flitcraft.

And here perhaps is the full meaning of the novel's structural link between Flitcraft's random-action response to his new view of life-as-random-event and Spade's method of "wild and unpredictable" behavior as a "way of learning" (90) what's going on. For while Flitcraft's response may be a temporary psychological or philosophical reply to "a new glimpse of life," it cannot be prolonged. And since Spade knows this, because he knows Flitcraft's whole story and has apparently understood it better than Flitcraft himself (that is, understood the meaning of his ultimate return to a domestic environment and a workaday world), he employs this random-action response, this "wild and unpredictable" behavior, simply as a professional ploy, a psychological tool to disrupt his opponents' settled plans and keep his enemies off balance—

a method that must be only occasionally and unpredictably applied, since random action loses its psychological effect if it becomes expected and routine.

If, then, the case of the Maltese falcon is the great adventure of Spade's career as a detective (as it is most certainly the best detective novel of Hammett's career as an author), and if his affair with the beautiful, sensuous murderess Brigid is the most exciting and memorable liaison in his life, then his decision both to complete the case and end the affair by "sending over" Brigid for Archer's murder is essentially the decision to choose repetition over singularity (as figured by the exceptional), to choose life over death (the death he knows could easily occur if the affair continued) or, more exactly, to choose *his* life, and thus allow himself to be recaptured by repetition.

Because the ending of the film version of *The Maltese Falcon* is so memorable (the closing of the elevator's grated door, so like the door of a prison cell, in front of Brigid's face in close-up as she stands next to a policeman, then the closing of the grated, translucent glass door as the elevator descends into darkness, like the fall through the trapdoor of a scaffold, as Tom Polhaus and Spade, carrying the falcon, descend the stairs of the scaffold) people often forget that that is not the way the book ends. The novel's final scene takes place the next morning, when Spade comes into his office and finds his secretary Effie Perrine sitting in his chair reading the newspaper account of the case. She asks him, "Is that—what the papers have—right?" When he says yes, and adds, "So much for your woman's intuition," referring to her earlier belief in Brigid, Effie asks, "You did that, Sam, to her?"

> He nodded. "Your Sam's a detective." He looked sharply at her. He put his arm around her waist, his hand on her hip. "She did kill Miles, angel," he said gently, "offhand, like that." He snapped his fingers.
>
> She escaped from his arm as if it had hurt her. "Don't, please, don't touch me," she said brokenly. "I know—I know you're right. You're right. But don't touch me now—not now." Spade's face became pale as his collar. The corridor-door's knob rattled. Effie Perrine turned quickly and went into the outer office, shutting the door behind her. When she came in again she shut it behind her. She said in a small flat voice: "Iva is here."
>
> Spade, looking at his desk, nodded almost imperceptibly. "Yes," he said, and shivered. "Well, send her in." (229)

Iva, of course, is Miles Archer's widow, with whom Spade had been having an adulterous affair before the novel's start and of whom he had grown tired and begun to avoid by the time Archer was killed. During the earlier part of the novel, Iva had repeatedly sought out Spade, expecting that with her husband's death their liaison would lead to a more permanent union, indeed, even asking Spade at one point if *he* had killed Miles so that they could be together. And now, with the extraordinary case of the Maltese falcon and the affair with Brigid over, repetition recaptures Spade in both the professional and the personal spheres: he returns to work at his office the next morning, and his former lover walks back into his life—Spade's shiver of revulsion suggesting that, faute de mieux, he will resume their liaison.

Job's wife, who had told him to curse God and die, is still there waiting around when Job's blessings are restored; Wakefield returns to his wife after twenty years; Flitcraft takes a second wife "who didn't look like the first, but they were more alike than they were different" (67); and Spade ends up with Iva, the woman with whom he'd been involved at the beginning. Are these mere coincidences, or are they somehow related to that recurring situation in *The Maltese Falcon* of Spade telling parabolic stories or giving elaborate explanations that both reveal his inner life and account for his actions only to have those stories and explanations not be understood by the women who hear them? Flitcraft had originally been concerned about whether he could make the reasonableness of what he had done clear to Spade, and Spade says, "I got it all right, . . . but Mrs. Flitcraft never did" (65). And neither does Brigid when Spade tells her Flitcraft's story, any more than she understands Spade's explanation of why he must send her over for Miles Archer's murder:

> "Listen. This isn't a damned bit of good. You'll never understand me, but I'll try once more and then we'll give it up. Listen. When a man's partner is killed he's supposed to do something about it. It doesn't make any difference what you thought of him. He was your partner and you're supposed to do something about it. Then it happens we were in the detective business. Well, when one of your organization gets killed it's bad business to let the killer get away with it. . . . I'm a detective and expecting me to run criminals down and then let them go is like asking a dog to catch a rabbit and let it go. It can be done, all right, and sometimes it is done, but it's not the natural thing. The only way I could have let you go was by letting Gutman and Cairo and the kid go. That's—"
>
> "You're not serious," she said. "You don't expect me to think that these things you're saying are sufficient reason for sending me to the—"
>
> "Wait till I'm through and then you can talk." (226)

Spade interposes here a new third term into the opposition between life-as-being and life-as-having, which is to say, life-as-doing. He in effect tells Brigid that for him what he is what he does, not what he has. He says, "I'm a detective," just as, on the morning after turning Brigid over to the police, when Effie asks, "You did that, Sam, to her?" he says, "Your Sam's a detective." And though Effie knows he's right, she, like Brigid, doesn't seem to understand—either doesn't understand or doesn't want to face what she does understand: that for Spade no merely personal relationship can ever be as important as his work, as what he does and thus what he is. Indeed, Spade even claims that what a man does can become so much a part of his nature that it's almost an instinctive reflex, like a dog catching rabbits, and that, though one can on occasion act against that reflex, "it's not the natural thing."

In Spade's view a man may *have* a wife and family, like Flitcraft, may be "a good citizen and a good husband and father," but *being* a husband and father is not what he *is*. His wife and family are part of his life-as-having, but his work is the practical embodiment of his life-as-being. When Flitcraft decides to stop wandering around, decides that random action can't be a rule of life, he returns, in effect, to steady work. And Spade makes clear the priorities involved in that return: "He had been living in Spokane for a couple of years as Charles—that was his first name—Pierce. He had an automobile business that was netting him twenty or twenty-five thousand a year, a wife, a baby son, owned his own home in a Spokane suburb, and usually got away to play golf after four in the afternoon during the season" (65). It is, in effect, simply the successful businessman's return to success, this time selling cars in Spokane rather than real estate in Tacoma, a work success that permits his reestablishment of a second wife and family, home and lifestyle, that, in its impersonal substitution for the first wife and family and "the rest of the appurtenances of successful American living," makes the Book of Job's ruthless substitution of ten new children for the ten Job lost seem like child's play—no pun intended.

Though Hawthorne tells us nothing about what Wakefield does for a living (whether he has a profession or a business) and nothing about how he supports himself during the twenty years he surreptitiously keeps watch over his home and wife, he does tell us something about Wakefield's character (he had "a peculiar sort of vanity" coupled with "a disposition to craft") that resonates with something in Spade's character as evoked by Effie's remark to Spade, "You always think you know what you're doing, but you're too slick for your own good, and some day you're going to find it out" (29), and evoked again later in a conversation between Lieutenant Dundy and Spade when the former says, "'It'd pay you to play along with us a little, Spade. You've got away with this and you've got away with that, but you can't keep it up forever.' 'Stop me when you can,' Spade replied arrogantly" (73). As we noted earlier, there is about Wakefield's twenty-year escapade the sense that part of its attraction for him was his feeling that only he would be clever enough, adept enough to manipulate his life this way and pull it off. And something of that same quality is at the core of Spade's character as well: the pro's sense that what he is, is what he knows how to do, and that his success in wielding his knowledge and ability makes him to some degree a law unto himself.

In that same vein, any event that could have befallen Flitcraft and left him still in possession of his faculties (his self-consciousness and unique personality), whatever possessions it might have deprived him of, could never have affected what he was, his ability to work and succeed and thus his ability to reconstitute his life as having. And this sense that no merely personal relationship can ever be as important to a man as his work or profession is presented in that final conversation between Spade and Brigid as the opposition between a professional commitment and a personal one, between what one owes to one's business partner as opposed to one's bed partner, to Miles Archer but not to Brigid O'Shaughnessy. Indeed, you don't even have to like or respect your business partner, you only have to have made a professional commitment to him; then, to let a merely personal connection override that professional one, is, as Spade says, "bad business. . . . It's bad all around—bad for that one organization, bad for every detective everywhere" (226).

I don't claim that this sense—that what a man *does* (and thus, *is*) takes precedence over any mere personal relationship he may *have*—is something peculiarly American, but I do claim that it is typically American and that the delineation of this sense has created some of the central moments in some of the most characteristic works of twentieth-century American literature: from Gatsby's famous remark (after the failure of his quest to recover Daisy and thus confirm that through his own brains and work, he has bested Tom's inherited wealth, a remark made after he realizes Daisy might in fact have loved Tom at some point in their marriage) that this momentary betrayal on Daisy's part was "In any case . . . just personal";[9] to Spade's story of Flitcraft and his subsequent explanation of why one owes more to a partner than to a lover; and on to *Death of a Salesman*, in which Willy Loman's wife and sons are left in the wake of what it takes for a salesman not just to be liked but to be well liked.

This deep American secret (that most men know, many women suspect, and few women can accept, which is to say, don't understand, don't see why something that is of primary importance to them might be of secondary importance to their partners) animates the novel on one level. Hence the incomprehension exhibited in turn by the first Mrs. Flitcraft, by Brigid, and finally by Effie in the novel's last scene, when Sam puts his arm around her waist and she escapes "as if it had hurt her," saying "Don't, please, don't touch me. . . . You're right. But don't touch me now—not now" (229). Effie has seen how little personal relationships mean to Sam, and she is disturbed because she wonders what she herself means to him. But she shouldn't have worried, because as far as Spade is concerned she doesn't have a personal relationship with him, no matter what she may think is her due after her years of faithful service as his secretary. She has only a professional relationship, she is one of his organization and thus covered by that same sense of responsibility that Spade says he owed his dead partner Miles Archer. Or, as Spade says to Effie earlier in the novel, when he leaves her alone in his office with the body of Captain Jacobi to wait for the police and tell them an edited version of the truth, "You're a damned good man, sister" (167).

VI

These seem to me to be some of the things going on in The Maltese Falcon, some of the matters at issue in the book's evocation of the interplay among the repetitive (ordinary daily routine), the exceptional (an event like Flitcraft's falling beam or Spade's extraordinary case of the Maltese falcon or his love affair with Brigid), and the singular (one's own death) in any life, an evocation that speaks not only to questions the novel shares with works like the Book of Job and "Wakefield" but also to its own exceptional place and the place of its genre in the routine lives of twentieth-century Americans. For in the lives of many readers, hard-boiled detective fiction has served for decades now as precisely that vicarious experience of the exceptional (in its character as a figure of the singular) that releases readers temporarily from the humdrum and routine of their own lives and then returns them to their lives with a renewed appreciation of the pleasures of the humdrum and the routine. And The Mal-

tese Falcon, in making, as it were, a self-reflexive gesture toward its genre by thematizing the interplay among the repetitive, the exceptional, and the singular, makes us see that the ceaseless repetition that constitutes the very stuff of our lives only has meaning in a constitutive opposition with the possibility of the exceptional, on the one hand, and the certainty of the singular, on the other—makes us sees that what keeps the ceaseless repetition of life from becoming empty and meaningless, from boring us to death, is the possibility of the exceptional, and that what gives life its weight, its seriousness, is that sense of the once-and-for-all that flows from the certainty of the singular. It is not so much that "death is the mother of beauty," as Stevens says, as that death is the mother of meaning and value, that, to alter Spade's statement slightly, when it comes to meaning and value, "they're not much good unless the threat of death is behind them."

CHAPTER TWO

Being Boss

Chandler's *The Big Sleep*

I

Like Dashiell Hammett, Raymond Chandler turned to the writing of detective fiction to support himself when his previous line of work as a salaried employee of a business ran out. Hammett had joined the Pinkerton Detective Agency as an operative in 1915 at the age of twenty, worked for them until the summer of 1918, when he was inducted into the army, and then rejoined Pinkerton's in 1920, only to have his career as a professional detective ended a year later, when a recurrence of the tuberculosis he'd contracted in the army made strenuous surveillance work impossible. He left Pinkerton's in December 1921 and began writing for a living, publishing the first Continental Op story in *Black Mask* magazine in October 1923. Though Hammett returned briefly to a salaried position in 1926, working as advertising manager for Samuels Jewelry Company in San Francisco, his health again forced him to give up a steady job, and he went back to writing.

Similarly, when Chandler returned to the United States from serving in the Canadian Army during World War I, he settled in Los Angeles and in 1922 took a job in the accounting department of the Dabney Oil Syndicate, which had been "formed to develop the Ventura Avenue oil fields," as biographer Frank MacShane notes.[1] Company president Joseph Dabney later founded another firm, South Basin Oil, and Chandler worked first as its auditor and then as vice president, becoming "in effect the person in charge of the Los Angeles office" and "Dabney's right-hand man" (MacShane, 35). Chandler continued with Dabney for ten years until in 1932 he was fired for alcoholism and for having affairs with female employees. At the age of forty-four, at the height of the Depression, Chandler suddenly had to find another way of making a living, and detective fiction seemed like something he could do.

In calling attention to Hammett's and Chandler's employment histories immediately prior to the start of their writing careers, I mean to focus my initial discussion of *The Big Sleep* both on the similarity between Hammett's Spade and Chandler's Marlowe as regards their professional careers and on the difference between these two characters and Hammett's earlier detective, the anonymous little fat man known as the Continental Op, the central figure in many of Hammett's short stories and in his first two novels, *Red Harvest* (1929) and *The Dain Curse* (1929).

Spade, Marlowe, and the Op are, of course, all private investigators, but where Spade and Marlowe are self-employed, the Op is a salaried operative of a large agency, his boss the taciturn, imperturbable Old Man. Significantly, Sam Spade does not begin *The Maltese Falcon* as his own boss; he has a partner in the firm of Spade and Archer—at least until the evening of the day on which the novel's action starts. One of the first things Hammett has Spade do the morning after Archer's murder is tell his secretary Effie Perrine to "have the *Spade & Archer* taken off the door and *Samuel Spade* put on."[2] John Huston, in his film version of *The Maltese Falcon,* emphasizes this moment of unsentimental erasure by expanding the scene's dialogue, having Spade tell Effie, "Oh, have Miles's desk moved out of the office and have SPADE & ARCHER taken off all the doors and windows and, er, have SAMUEL SPADE put on," a move that makes clear Spade's intention not only to be his own employer but also to be the sole principal in the new agency.

Spade's eagerness, not to say brutal abruptness, in establishing himself as an independent operator in the wake of Archer's death suggests that the decisive shift in Hammett's fiction from the Continental Op in the first two novels to Sam Spade in the third is the main character's freedom from being the paid employee of a large business, a firm that dictates the cases he works on, the hours he keeps, the fees he charges, and his code of conduct. As the

Op explains to a prospective client in the 1924 story "The Girl with the Silver Eyes": "I'd like to handle this thing for you, but I'm not sure that I can. The Continental is rather strict, and, while I believe this thing is on the level, still I am only a hired man and have to go by the rules. Now if you could give us the endorsement of some firm or person of standing . . . "[3] Clearly, the Op initially doubts the prospective client's story, and his agency's rules require him, if he has this sort of suspicion, to get the name of someone of known probity to vouch for the client. Compare this with the initial encounter between Spade and Brigid O'Shaughnessy in his office, when she tells him her name is Wonderly, then gives him a story about trying to get her underage sister Corinne away from a man named Thursby, who'd brought her from New York to San Francisco. Spade, of course, takes the case, accepting a two-hundred-dollar retainer, and when, on the day after Archer is killed (presumably while shadowing Thursby), Brigid admits to Spade that "that story I told you yesterday was all—a story," Spade says, "Oh, that, . . . We didn't exactly believe your story. . . . We believed your two hundred dollars. . . . I mean that you paid us more than if you'd been telling the truth . . . and enough more to make it all right" (33).

Where the Op is governed by the operating procedures of his agency ("The Continental's got rules against taking bonuses or rewards,"[4] he tells his client in *Red Harvest*), Spade's code of conduct is, in the words of Lewis Carroll's White Knight, something of his own invention. Spade suspects that Brigid is lying, but he accepts her case because she's willing to pay more than the going rate and because she's a real looker, a consideration evoked in that moment when Archer enters the office while Brigid and Spade are talking, sizes Brigid up, and then, when Brigid isn't looking, glances at Spade and makes "a silent whistling mouth of appreciation" (8).

Of course, the trade-off between working for yourself and working for a large agency is that what you gain in independence or self-satisfaction by being your own boss, you give up in steady income, personnel support, and establishment credentials. The regularly salaried Op has any number of agency employees like Dick Foley or Mickey Linehan he can call on in an investigation, branch offices to be contacted for information or to follow up a lead, and the added financial muscle of a large company retained by big businesses (banks, insurance companies, law firms), a company that maintains a cordial working relationship with police departments everywhere. None of the things that, as the genre develops, a solo private eye has. Spade takes Brigid's case, then, despite his suspicions, because this is precisely the type of questionable client or ambiguous assignment that a lone investigator or a small partnership must have in order to survive. After all, the people likely to hire a single private detective rather than a large agency are either those who can't afford the fees charged by the latter, with its high overhead, or those whose motives, background, or business won't bear close scrutiny, people who want a man who needs the work, plays it close to the line, and sometimes steps over the line for his client's benefit. As private detective Alec Rush explains in Hammett's "The Assistant Murderer" (1926) when his client refuses to give Rush his name or explain his relationship to the woman he wants shadowed,

> What you did, on a guess, was go to one of the big agencies and tell 'em your story. They wouldn't touch it unless you cleared up the fishy points. Then you ran across my name, remembered I was chucked out of the department a couple of years ago. "There's my man," you said to yourself, "a baby who won't be so choicy!" . . . No matter. I ain't sensitive about it. I can talk about politics, and being made the goat, and all that, but the records show the Board of Police Commissioners gave me the air for a list of crimes that would stretch from here to Canton Hollow. All right, sir! I'll take your job. It sounds phony, but maybe it ain't. It'll cost you fifteen a day and expenses."[5]

Similarly, in *The Dain Curse* (1929), the Continental Op novel that immediately precedes *The Maltese Falcon,* we're told that the first murder victim, Louis Upton, had once been a private detective with an "agency of his own—till '23, when him and a guy named Harry Ruppert were sent over for trying to fix a jury."[6]

Spade actively cultivates a reputation for stepping over the line: When Brigid asks him near the novel's end if he would still have turned her over to the police if the falcon had been real, he says, "Don't be too sure I'm as crooked as I'm supposed to be. That kind of reputation might be good business—bringing in high-priced jobs and making it easier to deal with the enemy" (227). And earlier, when Joel Cairo tries to hire Spade to recover the falcon for a fee of five thousand dollars, then pulls a gun and attempts to search his office, Spade, after knocking Cairo unconscious and ransacking his pockets, coolly continues negotiating the terms of his contract with this new and slightly groggy client, knowing the type of person Cairo is and the type Cairo thinks Spade is:

> "Right. And it's a legitimate proposition." Spade's face was solemn except for wrinkles at the corners of his eyes. "You're not hiring me to do any murders or

burglaries for you, but simply to get it back if possible in an honest and lawful way."

"If possible," Cairo agreed. His face also was solemn except for the eyes. "And in any event with discretion." (52–53)

In accepting a two-hundred-dollar retainer from Cairo, Spade not only takes on the kind of client the Op, in following the agency's rules, would have had to refuse, but he also violates a basic conflict-of-interest principle governing any person who acts as another's paid agent, for his conversation with Cairo has made it clear that Cairo's interests are almost certainly at odds with those of his other client, Brigid.

In making Spade his own boss and, in effect, the creator and arbiter of his own professional code of conduct, Hammett introduces into *The Maltese Falcon* both a moral ambiguity and a resultant range of dramatic possibilities denied the Continental Op. One need only compare the lengthy scene at the novel's end, in which Spade tells Brigid that even though they may love each other, he's still going to turn her in for Miles Archer's murder, with the scene at the end of the 1925 story "The Gutting of Couffignal," in which the Princess Zhukovski, who has just been captured by the Op and accused of robbery and murder, suddenly throws herself at him, offering him the proceeds from the looting of the island and her body as well. His response sounds like a trial run for Spade's reply to Brigid: The Op says he won't do what she asks "because I like being a detective, like the work. And liking work makes you want to do it as well as you can. Otherwise there'd be no sense to it. That's the fix I am in. I don't know anything else, don't enjoy anything else, don't want to know or enjoy anything else. You can't weigh that against any sum of money . . . in the past eighteen years I've been getting my fun out of chasing crooks and tackling puzzles, my satisfaction out of catching crooks and solving riddles. It's the only kind of sport I know anything about, and I can't imagine a pleasanter future than twenty-some years more of it. I'm not going to blow that up!"[7]

When the Princess reminds him that it's not just money she's offering but her favors as well, he thinks, "That was out. I don't know where these women get their ideas," and says, "You think I'm a man and you're a woman. That's wrong. I'm a manhunter and you're something that has been running in front of me. There's nothing human about it. You might just as well expect a hound to play tiddly-winks with the fox he's caught" (34). When the Princess tells him that she's simply going to leave the room and get away because the Op, who's hobbled by a badly sprained ankle, won't shoot her, given his high ideals, he warns her not to try, and as she's about to pass through the door, he pots her in the leg, adding, "I had never shot a woman before. I felt queer about it" (38).

The Op's remark about letting the Princess go being like expecting "a hound to play tiddly-winks with the fox he's caught" anticipates the hunting image Spade uses with Brigid: "I'm a detective and expecting me to run criminals down and then let them go free is like asking a dog to catch a rabbit and let it go. It can be done, . . . and sometimes it is done, but it's not the natural thing" (226). But where Spade says it isn't "natural" for a detective to let a criminal go, the Op distinguishes the man/woman relationship from that between man-hunter and prey by saying of the latter, "There's nothing human about it," a distinction Spade explains to Brigid as the difference between a personal and a professional relationship, the professional presumably involving no purely human considerations.

The major difference in the two scenes is that the Op's refusal to be bribed with money or sex seems almost perfunctory, there having been no previous evidence of his character's moral ambiguity or of any corner-cutting in his professional conduct (indeed, the little fat man's response to the leggy princess ["I don't know where these women get their ideas"] seeming almost Victorian), there is, on the other hand, ample indication that Spade has stepped over the line in small matters before and thus might well be tempted to do so in a large one. We also know that, whether or not he loves Brigid, he has certainly made love to her and that, as he says, "it's easy enough to be nuts about" her (227). Consequently, what is only a kind of a pro forma temptation scene in the Op story, its main interest being the detail of the Op's shooting the princess in the leg, becomes in the novel the emotional climax, a scene in which Hammett, by having Spade pile up reason after reason for turning Brigid in, makes clear just how tempted Spade is to let her go, since any *one* of these reasons would have sufficed for a disinterested person to reach the same conclusion.

Spade's refusal to give up being a detective, to give up what he does and thus what he is, for whatever relationship he might have with Brigid, gives this scene, and with it the novel as a whole, a recognizably modern-American emotional feel. For if the desire for personal freedom has been a defining trait of our national character since the pioneers set out to own and work their own land, and if the twentieth-century urban survival of that desire for a free-dom grounded on economic independence has often been the attempt to con-trol one's own destiny, be one's own boss, by owning one's own business, then

Spade's unwillingness to let Brigid go and thus become her partner in crime is not just a refusal to let personal considerations outweigh professional ones; it's a refusal to let a novel, which began with the violent dissolution of one partnership, end with the establishment of another partnership whose ties are tighter and demands greater (because of the sanctions entailed by mutual culpability) than those associated with any mere contractual engagement, either marital or professional.

This shift in Hammett's protagonists, from a salaried operative at a large agency, either public or private, to a self-employed lone wolf (from the Continental Op to Spade), is embodied in the career transitions of both Alec Rush, who, after having been dismissed from the police department runs a one-man private detective operation in "The Assistant Murderer," and Spade himself, who once worked, as he tells us, for "one of the big detective agencies in Seattle" (64–65). But what is equally interesting is that this trajectory within the fiction paralleled one in Hammett's own life, from being a salaried Pinkerton operative to becoming a freelance writer. Indeed, in *The Dain Curse*, Hammett draws a comparison between detective work and fiction-writing, evoking the difference between the two as essentially that between working for someone else and working for yourself. The Op accuses the writer Owen Fitzstephan of "snooping around" when he becomes too inquisitive about the Op's case, and Fitzstephan replies,

"Are you—who make your living snooping—sneering at my curiosity about people and my attempts to satisfy it?"

"We're different," I said. "I do mine with the object of putting people in jail, and I get paid for it, though not as much as I should."

"That's not different," he said. "I do mine with the object of putting people in books, and I get paid for it, though not as much as I should." (22)

The difference, of course, is the way each gets paid for his work—salary versus royalty, employment versus ownership. It's also interesting that while Hammett was finishing up, during the spring of 1929, the novel that would complete, with the creation of Sam Spade, the fictional transition from salaried operative to self-employed detective, Hammett was himself in the process of leaving his wife and family for good, moving in October of that year from San Francisco to New York. His wife, Jose, to whom *The Maltese Falcon* was dedicated when it appeared on Valentine's Day, 1930, eventually got a Mexican divorce in 1937, and though Hammett sent his wife and two daughters money over the years, he never contributed regularly to their support. Nor did he ever marry again, though he had several liaisons, the longest of these, lasting off and on for almost thirty years, with Lillian Hellman, whom he met in late 1930. Indeed, Hammett's subsequent involvements with women after leaving his wife were largely shaped by his desire that each party maintain maximum independence, and certainly the length of his involvement with Hellman was in part the result of her being someone with her own work to pursue.

What these parallel trajectories in Hammett's fiction and biography (from salaried to self-employed, from emotional or economic entanglement to personal freedom) suggest is that the first great practitioner of hard-boiled detective fiction, in creating the main outlines of this new genre, not only turned away, as critics have noted, from the type of plot-driven analytic detective story invented by Edgar Allan Poe in the Dupin tales to write character-driven stories that focused on the brutal reality of crime and the mundane reality of professional detection, but that he also installed at this new genre's emotional center the problem of masculinity in modern, capitalist America.

In the old American South (and certainly Hammett's roots in rural Maryland were more southern than northern) it was said that a man wasn't a man till his father said he was, but in urban twentieth-century America, North and South, many have felt that a man wasn't a man until he was his own boss; until, in a country one of whose founding ideals was the personal freedom that comes with economic independence, he had achieved some form of self-employment. Significantly, Hammett's great-grandfather had owned his own general store in St. Mary's County, Maryland, a business prosperous enough for him to buy a farm called "Hopewell and Aim" in 1827, though the store remained his and his family's principal source of income for another generation. Hammett's grandfather inherited the store, prospering for a time but ultimately losing the business in 1889. He subsequently moved his extended family, including his son, Richard, and his daughter-in-law, to "Hopewell and Aim," where in 1894 Dashiell was born. In 1900, Richard Hammett, looking for work, moved his family first to Philadelphia and then to Baltimore. He held a series of salaried jobs ranging from traveling salesman to streetcar conductor to clerk, and in 1908 he tried to start his own business, with Dashiell quitting high school in September to help out when his father became ill. The business failed the next year, and Dashiell took a series of odd jobs with various companies before landing at Pinkerton's in 1915.

It must have seemed to Hammett that his family, up to the point at which he became a writer, had acted out the American dream in reverse, going from his great-grandfather, who'd owned his own business and bought land, to his father and himself, who moved from place to place as hourly wage earners or salaried employees. Yet this apparent retrogression in Hammett's family may simply have reflected the movement from rural to urban, from nineteenth- to twentieth-century America. Obviously, most American men still aren't their own bosses. Yet if the economic independence that goes with self-employment remains a traditional male ideal, a constant value in the collective consciousness, then the sense of being a wage-slave at another's beck and call may contribute to a sense of impaired masculinity, a sense of impairment often aggravated by the financial demands of a wife and family, by responsibilities that keep a man from striking out on his own and setting up in business for himself. It is this emotional vein in the American male psyche that the parallel work-trajectories in Hammett's fiction and life reflect, a vein that also explains Spade's and Hammett's refusal or repudiation of entangling personal relationships that would compromise that freedom. And it is hard-boiled detective fiction's mining of this vein after Hammett that accounts in large part for the genre's continuing appeal.

II

It may seem that we've followed a circuitous path to talk about Raymond Chandler's *The Big Sleep*, but the point that the trajectory in Hammett's detective fiction reaches with the creation of Sam Spade is the point at which Chandler begins *his* novelistic career, with the decision to make his ongoing protagonist the self-employed, lone-wolf private eye Philip Marlowe—a natural enough choice given that Chandler always acknowledged Hammett as the creator of the hard-boiled detective genre and said that he'd taught himself to write fiction by exhaustively analyzing and imitating Hammett's work. Moreover, as we noted, Chandler too became a freelance writer of detective fiction after his career as a salaried employee abruptly ended. Recalling, almost thirty years after his firing, his time at the South Basin Oil Company, Chandler said, "I was an executive in the oil business once, a director of eight companies and a president of three, although actually I was simply a high-priced employee" (MacShane, 35). In interviews Chandler never gave the real reason for his firing, preferring to say, "My services cost them too much. . . . Always a good reason for letting a man go" (40).

Given all the parallels we've traced, it's not surprising that one of the first things we learn about Marlowe in *The Big Sleep* is that before going out on his own, he'd been a salaried operative who was fired. Marlowe tells his client General Sternwood:

> "I worked for Mr. Wilde, the District Attorney, as an investigator once. His chief investigator, a man named Bernie Ohls, called me and told me you wanted to see me. I'm unmarried because I don't like policemen's wives."
>
> "And a little bit of a cynic," the old man smiled. "You didn't like working for Wilde?"
>
> "I was fired. For insubordination. I test very high on insubordination, General."
>
> "I always did myself, sir. I'm glad to hear it."[8]

So Marlowe had been fired not for something sleazy like being a drunk or having affairs with the secretaries but for something honorable and manly, for not obeying orders, for acting like his own boss—an explanation that sits well with his client.

But who exactly is this client to whom Marlowe offers his explanation? Critics have noted that General Sternwood bears a structural resemblance to Joseph Dabney, the owner of the South Basin Oil Company. Sternwood and Dabney had both become rich from the southern California oilfields. As Marlowe leaves the Sternwood mansion after his first meeting with the General, he looks out over the terraced lawn and sees, some miles below, "the old wooden derricks of the oilfield from which the Sternwoods had made their money. Most of the field was public park now, cleaned up and donated to the city by General Sternwood. But a little of it was still producing in groups of wells pumping five or six barrels a day. The Sternwoods, having moved up the hill, could no longer smell the stale sump water or the oil, but they could still look out of their front windows and see what had made them rich. If they wanted to. I didn't suppose they wanted to" (18).

The passage is significant for several reasons. First, it presents Sternwood, financially independent and thus very much his own boss, as someone whose fortune comes from a business physically dirty, as suggested by the smell of "the stale sump water" and the oil, and perhaps morally dirty as well, as suggested by the image's recurrence at the novel's end, when Marlowe discovers that the sump has become the final resting place of the General's murdered son-in-law and friend Rusty Regan. Second, it indicates the characteristic process by which the Sternwoods, like many affluent American families, rose away from the origins of their wealth—in this case quite literally by moving up the hill from their oilfield—and by which they laundered their money, represented in this case again quite literally by the General's cleaning up part of the field and donating it to the city for a public park, a philanthropic gesture typical of the way the founders of great American dynasties had made the public forget, or no longer care about, the ruthless, often corrupt, ways their fortunes had been amassed. Third, the detail of the Sternwoods being able to look out their front windows and see what had made them rich, but Marlowe's doubting that they wanted to, suggests that no matter how much General Sternwood has physically sanitized the place, there is something that the filth of oil and sump water symbolizes that he hasn't been able to clean up; something, either in his character, which allowed him to make that much money, or else in the prolonged possession of that wealth, which has been passed on to and has corrupted his two daughters—these two being the Sternwoods who don't want to look too closely into the place and process from which their money and position came.

Given that the professional connection between Marlowe and Sternwood turns out to be the single most important relationship in *The Big Sleep*, energizing the entire novel as it drives Marlowe to discover the fate of the General's friend Rusty Regan (despite the other characters wanting him to drop the investigation), and given that this relationship bears a resemblance to that of Chandler and Joseph Dabney, we must consider how the real-life friendship influenced, or was incorporated into, Chandler's imagining of the fictive one. We know that Chandler respected and liked the older man and that the respect and liking seem to have survived Chandler's dismissal. In fact, if he blamed anyone for his firing other than himself, it was John Abrams, an independent oil operator who had married into the Dabney family and who subsequently worked for South Basin Oil (MacShane, 36). Abrams and Chandler didn't get along (Chandler was, by all accounts, not an easy person to get along with, especially when he'd been drinking). Indeed, one can also imagine that there was a certain tension between the man who'd previously been Dabney's most trusted employee and a new family member who perhaps thought that the position of Dabney's chief assistant should be held by someone who was related to him, if only by marriage. Whatever the root of the ill feeling, by 1931–32, when Chandler's drinking and philandering had begun to interfere with his work, it was Abrams who spearheaded the effort to force him out. He brought Chandler's conduct to Dabney's attention and urged Dabney to fire him. When Chandler later learned of Abrams' actions, he threatened to sue Abrams for slander (40), but nothing ever came of the threat, and in 1932 Chandler was dismissed.

The memory of this situation probably served as a resource for Chandler when, after having spent some six years writing short stories and learning the craft of detective fiction but not making enough money to support himself and his wife, he began his first novel (and with it a writing career that would ultimately make him financially independent), a resource for imagining the emotions involved in the story of an oil millionaire who enlists the aid of a detective to get and keep his irresponsible younger daughter out of trouble, a detective who, though only a hireling, is more loyal to and better serves his interests than any member of his own family. If there is something of Dabney (and of Chandler's feelings for him) in General Sternwood, then, judging by the novel, those feelings must have been ambivalent by the time Chandler came to create the character, involving both a residual respect and affection that had animated ten years of loyal service and a resentment that those ten years hadn't counted at least as much as the familial tie between in-laws. So Chandler begins his first novel, on the one hand, with a scene in which Marlowe accounts to General Sternwood for his having been fired as an investigator for the DA's office with an explanation clearly more honorable and more manly than any Chandler could have offered Dabney about his conduct at South Basin Oil and, on the other hand, a scene in which the General comes across as someone who, though he has the financial wherewithal to control his own destiny, has lost, either in the process of acquiring his wealth or through the ongoing possession of it, moral or spiritual authority over his family, lost the ability to influence or control his spoiled daughters by any but economic means.

The novel juxtaposes two characters who are each associated with a certain kind of personal freedom, each evoked as men unwilling to take orders from others. One has achieved a form of economic independence by working as a self-employed detective, able to accept or refuse clients or jobs on the basis of his own judgment; the other is economically independent because he is a millionaire. The former has maintained his personal independence of thought and action by adjusting his style of living to whatever level of remuneration his work is capable of producing consistent with its allowing him to stay his own man. He can make this sacrifice because he is financially responsible for no one but himself. Chandler emphasizes this link between a man's limiting his personal responsibilities and his being free to conduct his business as he sees fit by having Marlowe, just before he tells Sternwood that he was fired for insubordination, inject into his spoken résumé what seems at first an extraneous bit of information ("I'm unmarried because I don't like policemen's wives") but whose point soon becomes apparent. For while Marlowe never married, General Sternwood, a widower, has, and he now finds himself saddled with the sole responsibility for two daughters, as well as with the responsibility he feels for the way they've turned out, both because of the character traits inherited from him and because of his indifferent interest in their upbringing. His estimate of his daughters is unvarnished: "Vivian is spoiled, exacting, smart and quite ruthless. Carmen is a child who likes to pull wings off flies. Neither of them has any more moral sense than a cat. Neither have I. No Sternwood ever had. . . . Vivian went to good schools of the snob type and to college. Carmen went to half a dozen schools of greater and greater liberality, and ended up where she started. I presume they both had, and still have, all the usual vices. If I sound a little sinister as a parent, Mr. Marlowe, it is because my hold on life is too slight to include any Victorian hypocrisy. . . . I need not add that a man who indulges in parenthood for the first time at the age of fifty-four deserves all he gets" (10–11).

If indulging in parenthood late in life brings its own punishment, then the General, who has enough money to defy or ignore anyone else's will, is being punished by having his independence coerced through a member of his family: He's being blackmailed by Arthur Gwynn Geiger, a rare book dealer who, as Marlowe later discovers, traffics in upscale pornography. Geiger has sent Sternwood a batch of IOUs totaling three thousand dollars and signed by his younger daughter, Carmen, with a note saying, "In spite of the legal uncollectability of the enclosed, which frankly represent gambling debts, I assume you might wish them honored" (9–10). Sternwood says that he had been blackmailed some months before by a man named Joe Brody, once again through Carmen, and that he'd paid Brody, who he thinks was "some kind of gambler" (12), five thousand dollars to leave her alone. Marlowe asks the General if he's questioned Carmen about the IOUs from Geiger, and Sternwood says in effect that he hasn't because he didn't want to be lied to: "She would suck her thumb and look coy" (10). Marlowe then advises him to pay Geiger, saying that "it's a question of a little money against a lot of annoyance," that "there has to be something behind it" (which Marlowe suspects, and which Sternwood must know, as evidenced by his having paid off the earlier blackmailer), and that it would take a "lot of chiselers an awful lot of time to rob you of enough so that you'd even notice it." To which the General replies coldly, "I have my pride, sir" (11).

It is precisely that pride, both personal and familial, and the acute sense of honor associated with a military officer (implied by Sternwood's title) that, Marlowe says, Geiger is counting on for his scheme to work. The blackmail note's cleverness is the distinction it makes between a legally enforceable debt and a debt of honor, the latter being the one which, Geiger suggests, one gentleman to another, Sternwood will recognize and make good, because the General would never allow his daughter to disgrace the family name by welching on a debt or a bet. But of course Geiger's note is also a fishing expedition, since it takes the form not of a demand for payment but rather of a gentlemanly notification to a father about his daughter's actions: Geiger wants to see just how sensitive the General's sense of family honor is, the lengths he'll go to keep the Sternwood name free of scandal, and also to judge the extent to which Sternwood's possible knowledge of any other of Carmen's scandalous escapades (knowledge that might be suggested by a willingness to pay hush money in this instance) would make him ripe for an even bigger squeeze, either by delving deeper into Carmen's past or by luring her into trouble.

When Sternwood tells Marlowe that he doesn't want to pay Geiger or go to the police with the matter, Marlowe agrees to take the case. But Marlowe senses that the General has another, unspoken reason for wanting a private investigator rather than the cops to handle the case. Earlier in their conversation Sternwood had asked Marlowe how much he knew about the family, and Marlowe had replied, "I'm told you are a widower and have two young daughters, both pretty and both wild. One of them has been married three times, the last time to an ex-bootlegger who went in the trade by the name of Rusty Regan" (8). Sternwood admits, "I'm very fond of Rusty. A big curly-headed Irishman from Clonmel. . . . He was the breath of life to me—while he lasted. He spent hours with me . . . telling me stories of the Irish revolution. . . . It was a ridiculous marriage, of course, and it probably didn't last a month, as a marriage. . . . He went away a month ago. Abruptly, without a word to anyone. Without saying good-by to me. That hurt a little. . . . I'll hear from him again one of these days. Meantime I'm being blackmailed again" (8–9). By the end of their interview Marlowe feels sure that Sternwood has brought him in rather than the police because the old man fears his son-in-law might be mixed up in the blackmail attempt, feels certain that what Sternwood really wants is not just for Marlowe to take Geiger off his back but also to find Rusty Regan, make sure he's all right, and establish that he's not linked to either Geiger or Joe Brody.

Much of the ensuing drama turns on Marlowe's efforts to maintain his independence of thought and action by not succumbing to the financial or sexual allures of Sternwood's daughters. As soon as Marlowe's interview with the General ends, this struggle begins. The butler says that the older daughter, Vivian Regan, would like to see him before he leaves. He finds her in her room, reclining on a chaise-longue, with her slippers off, showing lots of leg and nibbling on a drink—that is to say, finds her exhibiting a casualness, not to say carelessness, of manner that bespeaks her sense of dealing with someone very much her inferior. Her opening remarks make this explicit: "So you're a private detective. . . . I didn't know they really existed, except in books. Or else they were greasy little men snooping around hotels" (15). Vivian wants to find out, without coming out and asking, whether her father has hired him to look for Rusty Regan, and she sets out to get the upper hand by putting Marlowe on the defensive, throwing up to him the stereotype of the lone private detective as someone who makes his living doing sleazy divorce work, someone whose moral ambiguity, social unsavoriness, and financial need make him more likely to blackmail a client than to prevent a client from being blackmailed. Chandler himself had no illusions about the type of person drawn to detective work, remarking once that "the real-life private eye is a sleazy little drudge from the Burns Agency, a strong-arm guy with no more personality than a blackjack" and with "about as much moral stature as a stop and go sign." The character of Marlowe is, of course, a creation against type, a sort of battered knight-errant in a profession peopled by unethical journeymen, a man, as Chandler says, whose "moral and intellectual force is that he gets nothing but his fee," that he tries to "protect the innocent, guard the helpless and destroy the wicked . . . and that he must do this while earning a meagre living in a corrupt world" (MacShane, 70).

Given that Marlowe's moral stature is in some sense a function of the meagerness of the living he earns, Vivian is playing to Marlowe's strength by throwing up to him the social and economic gap between them. Marlowe lets her high-hat him for a while as she tries to get information without placing herself under the obligation of asking for it, and then, when she says that she doesn't like his manners, he lets her have it: "I'm not crazy about yours. . . . I didn't ask to see you. You sent for me. I don't mind your ritzing me or drinking your lunch out of a Scotch bottle. I don't mind your showing me your legs.

. . . I don't mind if you don't like my manners. They're pretty bad. I grieve over them during the long winter evenings. But don't waste your time trying to cross-examine me" (16). When she says that people don't talk to her like that, Marlowe delivers the final blow, asking her, "Just what is it you're afraid of, Mrs. Regan?" (17)

As the reader eventually learns, Vivian fears that if her father has hired Marlowe to look for Rusty Reagan, he'll discover that Regan was shot by Carmen during an epileptic seizure triggered by her rage at Regan's having rejected her advances. And more, that when Carmen told her sister what she'd done, Vivian, to avoid a scandal, called her gambler friend Eddie Mars, who had Regan's body disposed of and then created a diversion to make it look as if Regan had run off with Mars' wife. But at the time of his first conversation with Vivian, Marlowe knows none of this, and he ends their interview, after needling her just long enough to satisfy his pride, by telling her that her father didn't hire him to look for Regan.

Marlowe's sense of honor in his professional dealings is very much a matter of pride with him, and as Chandler says in "The Simple Art of Murder," his hero will take "no man's insolence without a due and dispassionate revenge" because "his pride is that you will treat him as a proud man or be very sorry you ever saw him."[9] As General Sternwood and Marlowe both share a taste for insubordination, so they both have a proud streak: It's why Sternwood balks at paying off Geiger and why Marlowe refuses to let Vivian treat him insolently—to ritz him, as he says—without putting her in her place and then making her squirm by asking what she's afraid of. The similarities between Sternwood and Marlowe—both proud, both insubordinate, one financially independent because he has all the money he'll ever need, the other because he's willing to adjust his lifestyle to his income—serve to underscore the big difference between them: that one is entangled in family responsibilities that threaten his independence and have put him in the position of needing the professional help of the other, whose suitability for this job is an independence of thought and action grounded on his being, and staying, free of such personal entanglements.

In engaging Marlowe, Sternwood in effect acknowledges the similarity between them, hiring him to act as a kind of surrogate father for Carmen—a role that gives Marlowe's attraction to and involvement with the General's other daughter an incestuous overtone, an overtone that foreshadows the ultimate solution to Rusty Regan's disappearance, that is, that he was killed by his sister-in-law because he rejected her advances, a fate that almost befalls Marlowe and for the same reason. And whether the sexual liaison Carmen had sought was with a brother-in-law or a father-surrogate, both bespeak that familial corruption Marlowe had sensed on his first visit to the mansion and of which he has to steer clear if he's to do his job.

Though there is, when they first meet, an obvious physical spark between Marlowe and Vivian, when they next meet she again brings up his profession's lack of class and cash. Looking around his seedy office, she says, "You don't put up much of a front":

> "Neither do the Pinkertons. . . . You can't make much money at this trade, if you're honest. If you have a front, you're making money—or expect to."
> "Oh—are you honest?" . . .
> "Painfully."
> "How did you get into this slimy kind of business then?"
> "How did you come to marry a bootlegger?"
> "My God, let's not start quarreling again."(51–52).

Though Vivian's approach involves the same high-class-deigning-to-talk-to low-class act she'd used earlier, she now tries to manipulate Marlowe with an implied compliment: he's too intelligent, has too much class, to be in this low line of work. But just as Marlowe wouldn't put up with her insolence earlier, he won't put up with her patronizing now. Vivian's "ritzing" act recalls Brigid O'Shaughnessy's "schoolgirl manner" (57) with Spade, and in each case the woman's performance is motivated by a need to manipulate the detective verbally in order to keep him from discovering what each has to hide: in one case the concealing of a murder, in the other the commission of a murder. And just as Brigid turns to a more straightforward sexual approach when her schoolgirl act fails, asking Spade, "Can I buy you with my body?" (59), so Vivian takes a similar tack when condescension gets her nowhere.

Vivian has come to his office because an envelope containing a nude picture of Carmen was delivered to the Sternwood mansion, a photo Marlowe recognizes as one taken of the drugged Carmen by Geiger at his home just before he was shot by the Sternwood's chauffeur, Owen Taylor, who was in love with Carmen. The photo's delivery was accompanied by a phone call demanding five thousand dollars, and Vivian has come to Marlowe for help in handling the matter discreetly, without her father having to learn of it. Marlowe asks if she can get five thousand in cash right away, and she says she might be able to borrow it from her friend Eddie Mars. When Marlowe agrees to help her, they become friendlier. But as they share a drink from his office bottle, she again tries to learn what her father has hired him to do, and when Marlowe says he can't tell her without clearing it with the General, Vivian, who's been holding the nude photo of Carmen, glances at it and remarks, "She has a beautiful little body, hasn't she?" When Marlowe agrees, she leans toward him and says:

> "You ought to see mine." . . .
>   "Can it be arranged?"
> She laughed suddenly and sharply and went halfway through the door, then turned her head to say coolly: "You're as cold-blooded a beast as I ever met, Marlowe. Or can I call you Phil?"
>   "Sure."
>   "You can call me Vivian."
>   "Thanks, Mrs. Regan."
>   "Oh, go to hell, Marlowe." She went on out and didn't look back. (55–56)

In this trenchant little exchange, Marlowe simultaneously gives Vivian a lesson in manners and in the limits of their relationship. In their first meeting she'd simply taken for granted that her higher status gave her the right to treat him with a certain familiarity, even with contemptuous casualness. But now she's changed her tone, asking permission to address him by his given name. He grants her request, but when she tries to reciprocate by having him call her Vivian, he demurs, using instead the reserved "Mrs. Regan" to make clear that theirs is a formal relationship, governed wholly by the professional contract he has with her father. In effect, he reminds her of the difference in status and position, of that professional boundary between them she'd tried to overstep from her side in their first encounter but that he refuses to overstep from his side in this one. He also addresses her as "Mrs. Regan" to remind her that, though she might make sexual innuendoes and though he might be attracted to her, she is still a married woman, and any dalliance would be adulterous. The irony, of course, is that Vivian knows she's no longer a married woman, but she can't say that without admitting that she knows Regan is dead.

Marlowe's willingness to remain, as Chandler describes the private detective in "The Simple Art of Murder," "a relatively poor man" (20) as the price for remaining his own boss is a recurring motif not just in his interactions with Vivian Regan but in those with Eddie Mars as well. When Marlowe first meets Mars inside Geiger's empty house, Mars says,

"Convenient. . . . The door being open. When you didn't have a key."

"Yes. How come *you* had a key?"

"Is that any of your business, soldier?"

"I could make it my business?"

. . . "And I could make your business my business."

"You wouldn't like it. The pay's too small." (65)

This your-business-my-business dialogue is meant to emphasize that Marlowe has kept his moral independence by being a one-man operation, while his opposite, the mobster Eddie Mars, is a big-businessman, whose actions, even though he is his own boss, are often determined by the need to maintain a large organization or put up the kind of front that, as Marlowe had told Vivian, an honest detective couldn't afford. And like any big business, Mars' casino, the Cypress Club at Las Olindas, has operating expenses: Its owner needs to have, as Marlowe says, the local law in his pocket "and a well-greased line into L.A. In other words, protection" (66). Later in the novel, when Marlowe asks Captain Gregory of the Missing Persons Bureau about the police efforts to locate Rusty Regan, Gregory discounts the theory that Regan's disappearance had anything to do with the near-simultaneous disappearance of Mrs. Eddie Mars, that is, that the two tried to run away together and that Mars had found and killed them both: "Jealousy is a bad motive for his type. Top-flight racketeers have business brains. They learn to do things that are good policy and let their personal feelings take care of themselves" (116).

Thinking it over later, Marlowe agrees that Mars would never be involved "in a double murder just because another man had gone to town with" his wife: "It might have annoyed him, but business is business, and you have to hold your teeth clamped around Hollywood to keep from chewing on stray blondes. If there had been a lot of money involved, that would be different. But fifteen grand wouldn't be a lot of money to Eddie Mars" (119–20). The fifteen grand referred to is the amount Rusty Regan was reputed to carry in cash, but Eddie Mars is after much more than that. He wants the Sternwood millions, and he's got enough on the two daughters (murder and accessory to murder after the fact) to collect once they inherit, or perhaps sooner. As Marlowe figures it out at the end, that was the whole point of Geiger's initial attempt at blackmail. He tells Vivian: "Eddie Mars was behind Geiger, protecting him and using him for a cat's-paw. Your father sent for me instead of paying up, which showed he wasn't scared about anything. Eddie Mars wanted to know that. He had something on you and he wanted to know if he had it on the General too. If he had, he could collect a lot of money in a hurry. If not, he would have to wait until you got your share of the family fortune, and in the meantime be satisfied with whatever spare cash he could take away from you across the roulette table" (209).

It was a good plan, and it would have worked if Marlowe hadn't gotten involved in the original blackmail case and then started looking for Rusty Regan because he'd sensed that was what the General really wanted. Since neither Mars nor Vivian want Marlowe nosing around the Regan disappearance, the first thing they have to do is find out exactly why the General hired him. But once Marlowe learns that Mars has a link to Geiger (he was Geiger's landlord) and that Vivian knows Mars, they have to convince Marlowe that theirs is simply the relationship of a casino owner to a good customer, convince him that the money flows in both directions across Mars' roulette tables, not just from Vivian to the man who's blackmailing her. To this end they stage an elaborate charade on the evening Marlowe goes to see Mars at the Cypress Club.

Before that charade begins, Mars offers Marlowe a fee for handling the Joe Brody murder case and keeping Mars' name out of it, saying "I'm used to paying for nice treatment." Since his client was General Sternwood, Marlowe had handled the Brody murder so as to keep Carmen's name out of it, but he'd sensed that the network of connections between Mars and Sternwood's daughters was such that it might be impossible to protect Carmen if he didn't shield Mars as well. Yet Marlowe also knows that Mars' offer is really an attempt to co-opt his services in any future investigation of Rusty Regan's disappearance, so he (unlike Spade, who accepted a retainer from both Brigid O'Shaughnessy and Joel Cairo) refuses to take on a client whom he senses may pose a conflict of interest with an existing client, and in so doing, he invokes his independence as a small businessman: "I get paid for what I do. Not much by your standards, but I make out. One customer at a time is a good rule" (123).

When Mars mentions in passing that Vivian Regan is at the club that evening and winning heavily at roulette, Marlowe stops by the wheel on his way out, and the performance begins. Vivian wants to stake all her winnings on one spin, but the table can't cover her bet, so the croupier sends for Mars, who personally covers it on the condition that the next spin be only for her. Vivian wins thirty-two thousand dollars and then asks Marlowe to drive her home. As Marlowe goes to get his car, he sees a man waiting in the fog and watches as Mars' gunsel Lanny sticks up Vivian when she comes out of the club. Marlowe turns the tables on Lanny, recovers Vivian's purse, and then drives off with her. Realizing that their act is falling apart, Vivian again throws herself at Marlowe, offering to spend the night at his apartment. But when Marlowe replies, "What has Eddie Mars got on you?" she freezes and says,

> "So that's the way it is" . . .
> "That's the way it is. Kissing is nice, but your father didn't hire me to sleep with you. . . . The first time we met I told you I was a detective. Get it through your lovely head. I work at it, lady. I don't play at it." (141)

When Vivian asks why he thinks Mars has something on her, he says, "He lets you win a lot of money and sends a gunpoke around to take it back for him. You're not more than mildly surprised. . . . I think the whole thing was just some kind of an act. If I wanted to flatter myself, I'd say it was at least partly for my benefit" (141–42). In "an icy drawl" Vivian tells him to take her home, and Marlowe can't resist the chance to give her the needle one more time, "You won't be a sister to me?" (143).

Little does Marlowe realize that on this particular evening he's playing a double header against the Sternwood girls. When he gets home after dropping Vivian off, he finds that Carmen, having conned the manager into letting her into his apartment, is in his bed naked. Once more that evening he has to explain to one of Sternwood's daughters the difference between a personal and a professional relationship, saying that even though he's "the guy that keeps finding" her "without any clothes on" (145), that's not due to any sexual interest but because he's been hired by her father to keep her out of mischief: "It's a question of professional pride. You know—professional pride. I'm working for your father. He's a sick man, very frail, very helpless. He sort of trusts me not to pull any stunts" (146). When he asks her to get dressed and leave, she calls him "a filthy name," and Marlowe thinks, "I didn't mind what she called me, what anybody called me. But this was the room I had to live in. It was all I had in the way of a home. In it was everything that was mine, that had any association for me, any past, anything that took the place of a family. Not much; a few books, pictures, radio, chessmen, old letters, stuff like that. Nothing. Such as they were they had all my memories. I couldn't stand her in that room any longer"(147).

In a passage that's as explicit as he ever gets, Chandler makes clear just how rigorously and how self-consciously Marlowe has circumscribed his life-as-having in order to achieve the maximum independence of his life-as-being:

His rented room and meager possessions (like his office, which had evoked Vivian's comment about not putting up much of a front) bespeak the near-complete subordination of economic concerns, of his personal standard of living, to his need to be his own man, to be insubordinate in speech and action if he chooses, and when he adds that these possessions, paltry as they may be, are what take "the place of a family" in his life, one gains the full sense of a personal life sacrificed to a professional one. Yet still there are limits to how far Marlowe will let business relationships intrude into his private space, for when Carmen calls him a filthy name in his own room, client's daughter or not he gives her three minutes to get dressed and get out or he'll throw her into the hall naked and toss her clothes out after her. After she leaves, Marlowe looks at his bed: "The imprint of her head was still in the pillow, of her small corrupt body still on the sheets. I put my empty glass down and tore the bed to pieces savagely" (148). This gesture of tearing his bed apart after a woman had lain in it recurs in Chandler's next-to-last and most ambitious novel, *The Long Goodbye* (1953), but for a different reason and with an entirely different emotional resonance. But more of that later.

The morning after Marlowe's back-to-back encounters with Vivian and Carmen he says he feels like he has "a hangover . . . from women" (149), but he still has another scene to play with each Sternwood daughter. The first is with Carmen, when he returns the pistol he had taken away from her earlier at Joe Brody's apartment and she asks him to teach her to shoot, down at one of the family's old oil wells. Marlowe agrees, drives her there, and after setting up a target, suddenly becomes the target himself as Carmen empties the gun at him, a gun Marlowe had loaded with blanks because he suspected Carmen had killed her brother-in-law, Rusty Regan, under the same circumstances and for the same reason. Carmen has an epileptic seizure, and Marlowe drives her home and sees Vivian one last time, telling her what has just happened and what he suspects about her husband's disappearance. What Chandler creates out of this final encounter is both an explanatory scene in which Marlowe seeks confirmation of his suspicions (his theory of Regan's murder and the events that grew out of the attempt to cover it up) from Vivian and a final test of Marlowe's professional ethics and small-businessman independence. As he tells her what he knows and what he suspects, Vivian immediately reverts to her initial sense of private detectives as "greasy little men snooping around hotels," assuming that Marlowe's remarks are a prelude to blackmail. She offers him fifteen thousand dollars, and he says, "That would be the established fee," the same amount that Regan had on him when Carmen shot him and that Eddie Mars' man Canino would have taken from Regan's corpse as the fee for disposing of it after Vivian asked Mars for help. Marlowe, of course, refuses the money, and in his climactic set-speech tries once again to make her understand the kind of man he is, detailing all the things he has done and endured in handling the case: "I do all this for twenty-five bucks a day—and maybe . . . to protect what little pride a broken and sick old man has left in his blood, in the thought that his blood is not poison" (213)—which is to say that he is still working for his original client, the General, and not for Vivian and that, as he'd told Mars, "one customer at a time is a good rule."

Though he doesn't want Vivian's fifteen grand, he does want something else as the price of his silence: a promise that she'll take Carmen away to an asylum for treatment. When Vivian agrees, Marlowe leaves the Sternwood mansion for the last time, a leave-taking that recalls his meditation on the Sternwoods and their wealth the first time he left the house. But this time as he drives down the hill, he muses (in what is arguably the most poetic ending in hard-boiled detective fiction):

> What did it matter where you lay once you were dead? In a dirty sump or in a marble tower on top of a high hill? You were dead, you were sleeping the big sleep, you were not bothered by things like that. Oil and water were the same as wind and air to you. You just slept the big sleep, not caring about the nastiness of how you died or where you fell. Me, I was part of the nastiness now. Far more a part of it than Rusty Regan was. But the old man didn't have to be. (215–16)

Though Regan's body in the sump is now "a horrible decayed thing," as Vivian says, Marlowe feels that the moral nastiness surrounding the concealment of Regan's murder and the disposal of his body is a corruption far more repellent than the physical decay of a corpse in oily water, feels that in agreeing to continue the cover-up in order to protect his aged, ailing client he too has become part of this moral nastiness, shielding the General's violent and mentally unstable younger daughter and her spoiled and irresponsible sister from the legal consequences of their actions. But Marlowe knows that he is not simply a detective, not someone whose job it is to solve mysteries, apprehend killers or blackmailers, and bring them to justice. That was his task as an investigator for the district attorney, the job from which he was fired for insubordination. Now he is a *private* detective, hired by individuals, not by the public, to investigate what are often confidential matters and to keep the results of those inquiries private, a paid agent who must, in deciding on a course of action, weigh the often conflicting demands of loyalty to a client against the moral and legal responsibilities of citizenship.

In following the pattern set by Hammett in *The Maltese Falcon,* Chandler makes the central conflict in *The Big Sleep* dual: on the one hand, the struggle between the detective and the criminal, and on the other, the struggle between the detective and himself. It is the former that makes *The Big Sleep* a detective story, but it is the latter that Chandler counted on to make it a work of art. And he certainly never concealed his literary ambitions for the hard-boiled detective genre. In "The Simple Art of Murder," published in the *Atlantic Monthly* in 1944, he said that Hammett "demonstrated that the detective story can be important writing. *The Maltese Falcon* may or may not be a work of genius, but an art which is capable of it is not 'by hypothesis' incapable of anything" (17). Clearly, developing the genre's capabilities was Chandler's goal.

To generate the psychological complexity and dramatic moral tension associated with a literary novel, Chandler, like Hammett, chose to divide the detective's struggle with himself in two: the conflict between what the detective's professional ethics and personal pride would allow him to do for his client and what they would allow him to do for himself. The pattern that Chandler adopts in *The Big Sleep,* and maintains in the rest of the Marlowe novels, involves in the first case (where it's a question of what he will do for the client) a recurring scenario in which Marlowe enacts, whenever he steps over the line of legality in the client's behalf (like letting Sternwood's daughters get away with murder), a sort of economic punishment on himself to demonstrate that personal gain had nothing to do with his decision. Thus, when Marlowe visits the General for the last time, he offers to return his fee because he feels he's done an "unsatisfactory job" (197) in that, when Sternwood first hired him to handle the Geiger blackmail, Marlowe had assumed that Sternwood also wanted to know whether his son-in-law was mixed up in it, where Regan was, and why he had left suddenly without saying good-bye. Though his investigation has convinced him that Regan had no part in the blackmail, Marlowe hasn't been able to find Regan and has decided to quit looking for him, having been warned off by both the police and the DA and having learned that the Missing Persons Bureau has been working discreetly on the Regan disappearance all along, presumably at the request of Sternwood and the DA. He offers to return the fee, saying "it isn't a completed job by my standards" (200). But Sternwood won't let him quit and offers him a thousand dollars specifically to find Regan. Of course, Marlowe's decision to stop looking had been motivated largely by his suspicion that the daughter whom he'd been hired to keep out of trouble had murdered Regan, and when he verifies this suspicion in his final conversation with Vivian, he not only refuses her hush money but tells her that he won't be collecting the thousand-dollar fee from her father, either. Over the course of succeeding novels, Marlowe not only doesn't make much money, he doesn't keep much either, demonstrating time and again the independence and disinterestedness of his actions. And if that's how Marlowe behaves on his client's behalf, he is even more austere on his own, maintaining, as we have seen, the independence and professional ethics of a self-employed small-businessman in the face of periodic temptations involving money or sex, or both.

In creating the character of Marlowe, Chandler took this drive to be one's own boss (which he'd seen was the point of Hammett's move from the Continental Op to Sam Spade) and went one step further, making Marlowe not just self-employed but his own *sole* employee as well—the culmination of the quest to be one's own boss being the freeing of the boss from responsibility for anyone but himself. Even after Miles Archer had been killed and Spade had the agency all to himself, he still had Effie Perrine, his secretary and occasional quasi-operative, working for him, her performance eliciting the ultimate compliment: "You're a damned good man, sister" (167). But Marlowe doesn't even have a secretary, let alone an operative, and this lack of at least some ongoing work relationship only serves to emphasize Marlowe's isolation, the self-imposed loneliness entailed by his maintaining an absolute independence that can neither be compromised by temptations of love or money nor intimidated by threats or physical violence. The only thing that can make a dent in it is the passage of time.

III

In *The Big Sleep* Marlowe is thirty-three years old, and in the sixth Marlowe novel, *The Long Goodbye*, he is forty-two, but when *The Big Sleep* was published in 1939 Chandler was fifty-one and when *The Long Goodbye* was published in 1953 he was sixty-five. A nine-year span in Marlowe's fictional life equates with a fourteen-year stretch in Chandler's real one, and the increasing cynicism, weariness, and disillusion, not to say bitterness, critics have noted in Marlowe as the novels progress seem more characteristic of a man's transition from his early fifties to mid-sixties than from his early thirties to early forties. While *The Big Sleep, Farewell, My Lovely,* and *The Lady in the Lake* are to my mind the three best novels (in order of descending excellence) in the Chandler canon, the novel he seems to have tried hardest to make a work of art first and a detective story second, in which he tried to realize his full potential as a serious novelist without any hard-boiled generic qualification, was *The Long Goodbye,* his longest and most psychologically ambitious novel. *The Long Goodbye* is in crucial ways simply a rewriting of the materials of *The Big Sleep* with a deeper awareness, an older man's awareness, of the difficulty, the ultimate cost, of trying to maintain the kind of independence that characterized Marlowe in the earlier books. As Marlowe says to the heiress Linda Loring in *The Long Goodbye* after he has just made love to her in his bedroom (the first instance, by the way, of Marlowe's engaging in undoubted sexual intercourse in the first six novels), "I'm forty-two years old. I'm spoiled by independence. You're spoiled a little—not too much—by money."[10] And certainly both times Chandler uses the word *spoiled* in this passage he means both "excessively self-indulgent" and "psychologically damaged."

In reworking the materials of *The Big Sleep* in *The Long Goodbye,* Chandler repeats virtually every major element in the earlier story, some changed slightly, some substantially. In place of the millionaire General Sternwood and his two spoiled daughters, there is now the millionaire Harlan Potter and his two spoiled daughters, Linda Potter Loring and Sylvia Potter Lennox. Where Sternwood's son-in-law, Rusty Regan, initiates the first novel's action through his disappearance (i.e., through his death at the hands of his sister-in-law, Carmen), Potter's son-in-law, Terry Lennox, initiates the later novel's action when he gets Marlowe to help him disappear across the Mexican border after, as Marlowe later learns, allegedly killing his wife, Sylvia. Both Sternwood and Potter have been extremely fond of their sons-in-law: Sternwood said that Regan "was the breath of life to me" (8), and Potter had "liked Terry" Lennox because he "was a gentleman twenty-four hours a day instead of for the fifteen minutes" between the arrival of the guests and the first cocktail (134). Soon Lennox is the victim of an apparent suicide in a small Mexican town, a suicide faked, we ultimately discover, by an L.A. mobster named Mendy Menendez, whose life Lennox had saved during the war. When Marlowe refuses to believe that Lennox killed his wife and starts to look into his suicide, Menendez warns him off, engaging him, as Eddie Mars had, in big-businessman-versus-small-businessman repartee. Telling Marlowe that he's so "small time . . . it takes a magnifying glass to see" him (60), Menendez calls him in the course of a four-page exchange a piker, a cheapie, a peanut grifter, and a nickel's worth of nothing, before pronouncing his final judgment: "No dough, no family, no prospects, no nothing" (63). Menendez says that he, on the other hand, is "a big, bad man": "I make lots of dough. I got to make lots of dough to juice the guys I got to juice in order to make lots of dough to juice the guys I got to juice" (60). Like Eddie Mars, Menendez has the operating expenses (police protection) of a big business, and he also has a big front to keep up (he gives Marlowe a partial list of his possessions and obligations: two mansions, a yacht, four cars, a blonde wife, and two kids in private schools back east). Marlowe finally has enough and punches him hard in the stomach.

As in *The Big Sleep*, in *The Long Goodbye* Marlowe is physically attracted to his client's older daughter. This attraction wasn't consummated in the first novel (for reasons explored earlier), but in the later novel it is, and at the book's close the intimacy seems to be turning into something more serious, something that carries over into Chandler's next and last book, *Playback*, and seems likely to mitigate Marlowe's isolation as it threatens his independence.

In *The Big Sleep* Chandler had made Sternwood's younger daughter both morally bankrupt and mentally unstable, but in *The Long Goodbye* he divides these traits between two female characters, giving the moral decadence to Potter's younger daughter, the six-times married Sylvia Lennox, who's slept with everyone in her set, and the mental instability to Eileen Wade, the long-suffering wife of the alcoholic novelist Roger Wade. Eileen had been in love with Terry Lennox during the war, when he went under the name Paul Marston, and they'd been married in England before Lennox went on a commando raid to Norway and was apparently killed. Years later, at a party in Los Angeles, Eileen, now married to Wade, runs into Lennox, who had survived being badly wounded in Norway and captured by the Germans. Lennox is now married to Sylvia Potter, who is having an affair with Eileen's husband, Roger.

Though we never fully understand Eileen Wade's psychology or motivations, it seems that she'd kept herself going for years through a bad marriage to the alcoholic, womanizing Wade by clinging to the memory of her lost love Paul and to the image of herself that had gone into that romantically idealized wartime love affair. And then suddenly she ran into her beloved Paul and found him "the empty shell of the man" she'd known; he'd come back "a friend of gamblers, the husband of a rich whore, a spoiled and ruined man, and probably some kind of crook in his past life" (270–71), and something inside her snapped. She made the "rich whore" whom Lennox had married and who was having an affair with her present husband the representative of all the things that had gone wrong in her life, of all the dreams that had failed, so she killed Sylvia Lennox in revenge, not caring that Terry would be the prime suspect in his wife's murder, and then she killed her husband, Roger, because he had begun to suspect what she'd done.

When Marlowe pieces all this together, he confronts Eileen, knowing his suspicions would be difficult to prove but also knowing that *she* doesn't understand this and that in her mental state she might well do the state's work for it. That evening she kills herself and leaves a note acknowledging her responsibility for the deaths of Sylvia Lennox and Roger Wade and saying that Terry Lennox "should have died young in the snow of Norway, my lover that I gave to death. . . . Time makes everything mean and shabby and wrinkled. The tragedy of life . . . is not that the beautiful things die young, but that they grow old and mean. It will not happen to me" (270–71).

This sense that "time makes everything mean and shabby and wrinkled" weighs heavily on *The Long Goodbye,* and not just because Chandler wrote the book in his early sixties, when his health had begun to fail, but because he wrote it during what, as became increasingly clear, was to be his wife's final illness. Chandler's senior by eighteen years, Cissy had lied about her real age when they'd married, but she had been both his faithful companion through the infidelities and alcoholism that got him fired at South Basin Oil and the unfailing supporter of his decision to pursue writing as a new career. Moreover, she had provided the stable domestic environment that allowed Chandler to bring his drinking under control during his years as a writer, and now, during the writing of *The Long Goodbye,* he was faced with the loss of all that and with the knowledge that he himself might well have only one more chance to reach the level of literary achievement that he'd predicted, in "The Simple Art of Murder," the detective novel was capable of. And so, in *The Long Goodbye,* he reused structural elements from his first novel in order to emphasize, through the sameness of this material, just what was different about the later work, how it set out to examine the long-term consequences of Marlowe's drive always to be his own man, his own boss, to be self-contained and self-sufficient. As anyone who has lived past a certain age in the United States knows, philosophies of self-sufficiency are one thing at high noon in bright sunshine when you are twenty-five or thirty but a far different thing at three A.M. when one is about to be jettisoned into the penultimate void of retirement.

Chandler chose three main areas in which to differentiate *The Long Good-bye* from his earlier work and in particular from *The Big Sleep*. First, in a kind of modernist, self-reflexive gesture, he introduced the character of Roger Wade, an alcoholic best-selling novelist on the verge of a nervous breakdown as he struggles to finish his latest book. Marlowe is hired by Wade's wife and his publisher, Howard Spencer, to locate Wade (who had vanished), bring him home, and keep him sober long enough to complete his manuscript. (As Marlowe learns later, Eileen Wade had originally recommended him to Spencer as a private investigator because she knew he was a friend of Lennox and because Marlowe had the same initials, PM, as Paul Marston, the name under which Terry Lennox had married Eileen during the war.) As Spencer says in explaining to Marlowe why they're hiring him, "We want to save a very able writer who is capable of much better things than he has ever done" (75).

We know that writing *The Long Goodbye* was a long (three-and-a-half years) and difficult process for Chandler, who during this time was on the verge of physical and nervous collapse on several occasions from the strain of caring for his wife. Both Chandler and Cissy realized early on that she wouldn't recover from this illness, and Chandler's devoted, not to say obsessive, care of her was, in effect, a long good-bye—part atonement, perhaps, for his earlier marital lapses, part a desperate attempt to stave off for as long as possible an event that would leave him old and alone. After Cissy died in December 1954, he wrote to a friend, "In a sense I had said goodbye to her long ago. In fact, many times during the past two years in the middle of the night I had realized that it was only a question of time until I lost her. But . . . saying goodbye to your loved one in your mind is not the same thing as closing her eyes and knowing they will never open again" (MacShane, 223). After Cissy's death, Chandler fell off the wagon definitively and two months later attempted suicide, ending up in the psychiatric ward of the county hospital.

We have, then, in Chandler's writing of *The Long Goodbye* the case of a real novelist (with a history of alcoholism and in danger of a nervous breakdown) trying to finish a manuscript he hopes will raise his writing and its genre to a new level of achievement, a manuscript in which the main character is hired to look out for an alcoholic novelist on the verge of a nervous breakdown, a novelist who's having trouble finishing a book and whose publisher thinks he's "capable of much better things than he has ever done." And where the real novelist Chandler was driven to the point of emotional collapse and attempted suicide by his wife's death, the fictive novelist Wade is driven to the point of mental collapse by the suspicion that his wife has killed the woman he was having an affair with. Then Wade is himself killed by his wife, and the death made to look like suicide. The final infolding of this reflexive structure is that, while Marlowe is unable to look out for the unstable Wade well enough for him to finish his manuscript, Chandler successfully completes his own manuscript narrating Marlowe's failure, and the work of finishing *The Long Goodbye* was undoubtedly one of the things, if not the main thing, that sustained him during the long, despairing period of his wife's illness. Chandler had wanted her to see his most ambitious work in print and to share with him what he hoped would be the popular and critical acclaim it garnered. But just in case the novel's reception turned out to be less than he'd hoped for, Chandler also included in an exchange between Marlowe and Wade a line doubtless designed to anticipate critics' objections. Wade tells Marlowe that "a writer can tell when he's washed up . . . when he starts reading his old stuff for inspiration" (198), a line meant both to call attention to the reworking of material from *The Big Sleep* in *The Long Goodbye* and to counter in advance any reviewer's cavil that he had exhausted his resources and was repeating himself—by pointing out that this was a self-conscious reuse of material in the service of a different kind of novel.

Of course, Marlowe was always to some extent a function of Chandler's own personality, not perhaps an alter ego or an idealized self, as some critics have claimed, but certainly someone who shared traits and opinions with his creator, such as their mutual distaste for Southern California. But when Chandler created in *The Long Goodbye* another character resembling himself (Roger Wade) whom Marlowe was hired to look out for, this other figure's interaction with Marlowe indicated, and to some degree facilitated, a further superimposition of the sixty-two-year-old Chandler's concerns onto the figure of the forty-two-year-old detective. For what one notices almost immediately about the Marlowe of *The Long Goodbye* is that his sense of the abrasive, corrosive action of time and of one's inescapable mortality is more typical of someone entering old age than early middle age.

This brings us to the second area in which Chandler differentiates this novel from his earlier work, for in *The Long Goodbye* the tone substantially darkens, as if Marlowe's world-weariness had been suffused by Chandler's physical weariness. The Marlovian wisecracks, the ironic similes—which had in the earlier novels been his way of imaginatively mastering the venal, threatening, or tawdry aspects of his Southern California world, the verbal wit that had seemed, as in Wallace Stevens's definition of poetry, "a violence from within that protects us from a violence without, . . . the imagination pressing back against the pressure of reality"[11]—are either absent or reduced to being defenses not against external violence or vulgarity but against internal despair. They are replaced all too often by "serious" passages like this:

> No feelings at all was exactly right. I was as hollow and empty as the spaces between the stars. . . . Out there in the night of a thousand crimes people were dying, being maimed, cut by flying glass, crushed against steering wheels or under heavy tires. People were being beaten, robbed, strangled, raped, and murdered. People were hungry, sick; bored, desperate with loneliness or remorse or fear, angry, cruel, feverish, shaken by sobs. A city no worse than others, a city rich and vigorous and full of pride, a city lost and beaten and full of emptiness.
>
> It all depends on where you sit and what your own private score is. I didn't have one. I didn't care.(224)

The initial image here of hollowness, emptiness of feeling, recurs again and again in the novel, applied not just to the city (as at the passage's end) but also to most of the book's main characters. Roger Wade, for example, says his wife is as "empty" as a drinking glass turned upside down, "nothing there at all" (151), and Eileen, in her suicide note, says that when she met Paul Marston again as Terry Lennox, "he was the empty shell of the man I loved and married" (270). At the novel's end, when Marlowe meets Terry Lennox again, after plastic surgery and new papers have transformed him into Senor Cisco Maioranos, Marlowe in effect repeats Eileen's judgment, implying that it was easy for Lennox to change his identity by altering his appearance because there's nothing substantial inside, because he's "a moral defeatist" with "no relation to any kind of ethics or scruples" (310). And just so the reader doesn't miss the Eliotic provenance of the "hollow-man" imagery, Chandler inserts the following tongue-in-cheek exchange near the book's end. Inquiring if he may ask Marlowe a question, Linda Loring's black chauffeur, Amos, says,

> "'I grow old . . . I grow old . . . I shall wear the bottoms of my trousers rolled.' What does that mean, Mr. Marlowe?"
>
> "Not a bloody thing. It just sounds good."
>
> " . . . Nonetheless I admire T. S. Eliot very much."(293)

So Chandler gets the high-art allusion and gets to throw it away at the same time, hard-boiled fashion.

But of course Amos's quote from "The Love Song of J. Alfred Prufrock" has a double edge, for this image of someone growing older who contemplates adopting a more youthful style of dress to combat the sense of aging, if not aging itself, evokes Marlowe's own sense of growing older and lonelier, more isolated and depressed, a sense that leads him to become romantically involved with Linda Loring, the attractive heiress whom Amos has just dropped off at Marlowe's house for an assignation when he asks about the meaning of the Eliot quote.

But look again at the lengthy passage, quoted earlier, that begins with the image of Marlowe feeling hollow and empty and ends with the image of the city "full of pride . . . full of emptiness" and compare it to a typical moment from his earlier work. For example, the scene from *The Big Sleep* in which Marlowe, waiting in his car outside the pornographer Geiger's house in an upper-middle-class neighborhood, hears a shot and tries to enter the house by giving "the front door the heavy shoulder": "This was foolish. About the only part of a California house you can't put your foot through is the front door. All it did was hurt my shoulder and make me mad. I climbed over the railing again and kicked the French window in" (30). This image of the front door being the only part of a California house you can't put your foot through, coupled with the fact that behind that door a sleaze merchant has just photographed a naked, drugged young woman, is more effective as an evocation of hollowness, of an inner insubstantiality masked by an outer veneer of respectability, than anything Marlowe tells us in the passage from *The Long Goodbye*. It's not that one passage is more serious than the other; it's that the later excerpt is more solemn and slightly arty while the earlier is more artful and ironic, that the later tells us while the earlier shows us.

One could multiply such comparisons almost indefinitely. But of course if Chandler is aiming in *The Long Goodbye* to show us the human cost to Marlowe of his years spent cleaning up other people's garbage, then the novel has to enact some of his weariness, which is to say, some of his wordiness in facing, in summing up his sense, that he's been in this line of work too long—an awareness that typically comes to him at the end of the day when he returns to his empty house, in passages that begin "I got home late and tired and depressed" (261). It is Marlowe's depression and loneliness, his sense of growing older in isolation, that leads to the third main area of difference in *The Long Goodbye* from the earlier novels—his romance with Linda Loring.

When, at the novel's end, Marlowe invites Linda over for a drink and she shows up with an overnight case, something major has changed in his life. There has been an attraction between them since their first meeting, just as there was between Marlowe and Vivian in *The Big Sleep*. By paralleling moments and dialogue in the two novels, Chandler again goes to some lengths to call the reader's attention to that earlier flirtation (which led to nothing) as a contrasting background for this encounter (which leads to sex): When Vivian visits Marlowe's office the first time she says, "You don't put up much of a front" (51), while Linda on her first visit says, "Your establishment isn't exactly palatial. . . . . Don't you even have a secretary?" (181). Further, in the scene in which Marlowe makes clear that his attraction is to the good sister in each pair rather than the bad one, he tells Vivian, who has said that the Sternwood blood was always wild, "but it wasn't always rotten blood," that *her* blood isn't rotten (as distinct from Carmen's), that she's "just playing the part" (138), and he tells Linda Loring, just before he makes love to her, that "by all the rules you ought to be the same sort of shallow spoiled promiscuous brat your sister was. By some miracle you're not. You've got all the honesty and a large part of the guts in your family" (296). Finally, when Linda, after their lovemaking, leaves to catch a plane for Paris, Marlowe goes back into the bedroom and pulls "the bed to pieces" and remakes it, finding "a long dark hair on one of the pillows" and feeling "a lump of lead at the pit" of his stomach (300).

The scene is meant, of course, to recall the one in *The Big Sleep* in which Marlowe "tore the bed to pieces savagely" after he'd found not Vivian but Carmen in it naked; but where he'd ripped off the bedding in the earlier case to obliterate the imprint of Carmen's head on the pillow and her small corrupt body on the sheets, he does so here to wipe out any reminder, like that long dark hair on the pillow, of what he had and what he's lost. For Linda had asked him to come to Paris and marry her, and Marlowe, giving various halfhearted reasons, refused. Linda, sensing immediately that her money has put Marlowe off, says, "It's no disgrace to have money and no disgrace to marry it" (298), and asks what he's got to lose except "the loneliness of a pretty empty kind of life": "An empty house to come home to, with not even a dog or cat, a small stuffy office to sit in and wait. Even if I divorced you I'd never let you go back to that" (299). But Marlowe still refuses the proposal, refuses to become a kept man like Terry Lennox, and Linda tells him he's a "self-sufficient, self-satisfied, self-confident, untouchable bastard" (298). Though Marlowe and Linda part after one night, she has touched him more deeply than he realizes, and her memory haunts him in Chandler's last novel *Playback* (1958), the weakest Marlowe book.

In *Playback*, whose plot revolves around a kind of elaborate tail job better suited to a short story, Marlowe has two one-night stands, and on each occasion he tells the woman about Linda before they have sex. Thus, for example, in explaining to his client's secretary why he would rather make love at her place than his, he says, "I had a dream here once, a year and a half ago. There's still a shred of it left. I'd like it to stay in charge. . . . There was a woman. She was rich. She thought she wanted to marry me. It wouldn't have worked. I'll probably never see her again. But I remember."[12] Then, in the novel's last chapter, after the case is closed, Marlowe returns home, mixes himself a drink, and finds himself staring at the wall: "Wherever I went, whatever I did, this was what I would come back to. A blank wall in a meaningless room in a meaningless house" (166). But then the phone rings, and it's Linda Loring calling from Paris, saying that she hasn't been able to forget him, asking him to marry her, and offering to send him a plane ticket to Paris. Marlowe says he'll send her a plane ticket to L.A. instead, adding, "Take it, or don't come" (167). She says yes, and when Marlowe hangs up, he looks "around the empty room—which was no longer empty. There was a voice in it, and a tall slim lovely woman. There was a dark hair on the pillow in the bedroom. . . . The air was full of music" (168). So time and loneliness have finally worn him down, turning the hardboiled Marlowe, so it seems, into the hero of a Harlequin romance.

Part of this change in Marlowe was a function of the change in Chandler's own life during the years between his wife's death in 1954 and the appearance of *Playback* in 1958. Chandler's last five years bear an uncanny resemblance to those of the detective genre's inventor following Virginia Poe's death. Trying desperately to reestablish the stable domestic setting he had lost, Poe engaged in a series of quixotic courtings of, proposals to, and refusals by various women friends, interspersed with alcoholic episodes—a pattern repeated by Chandler. Following the precedent he'd set in *The Long Goodbye* with Roger Wade, Chandler again introduced into *Playback* a character, besides Marlowe, who was modeled on himself and then had this character, Henry Clarendon IV, engage the detective in a lengthy philosophical discussion. Clarendon, whom Marlowe happens to meet in the lobby of a resort hotel while investigating a suspect, describes himself as an elderly idler, a member of "what used to be called the upper classes," who has "spent many years in lobbies, lounges and bars . . .

in hotels all over the world" and has "outlived everyone" in his family (111). In describing Clarendon, Chandler includes two distinctive physical markers that make it clear he's "a cameo self-portrait":[13] Clarendon wears suede gloves with the cuffs turned back, and he never shakes hands because, he says, "My hands are ugly and painful. I wear gloves for that reason" (117). When he wrote *Playback,* Chandler was suffering from a painful skin disease that necessitated his wearing gloves (usually suede) and avoiding shaking hands.

Clarendon, lonely, bored, and idle, who has outlived everyone in his family and who foresees the day "when the stretcher carries me off to . . . a hospital" and they "put the oxygen tent over me and draw the screens around the little white bed" (111), suddenly asks Marlowe if he believes in God. When Marlowe answers, "If you mean an omniscient and omnipotent God who intended everything exactly the way it is, no," Clarendon replies, "But you should, Mr. Marlowe. It is a great comfort. We all come to it in the end because we have to die and become dust. Perhaps for the individual that is all, perhaps not" (114). Clarendon then rehearses the major objections to the notion of an afterlife, the main one from his point of view being that heaven would lack the exclusivity of a four-star hotel, and informs Marlowe that he's answering his questions about the person Marlowe's investigating—a gigolo who lives in the hotel and blackmails women—because the gigolo has had an affair with a wealthy divorcée whom Clarendon would like to marry. This sudden marital turn in a conversation that had largely been about last things, taken in conjunction with Linda Loring's reappearance in the final chapter, makes it seem as if the hard-boiled Marlowe of the earlier novels is a goner for sure, slated to pass between the Scylla and Charybdis of getting God or getting married. And indeed, in the unfinished story "Poodle Springs," begun during the last year of Chandler's life, he'd decided to marry Marlowe off to Linda, but, as he told his friend the English writer Ian Fleming, he also "planned to have his hero drink himself to death because he could not work any more" (Hiney, 269). But he abandoned the story because, he told another friend, the idea of Marlowe getting married, "even to a very nice girl, is quite out of character. I see him always in a lonely street, in lonely rooms, puzzled but never quite defeated" (270), the implication being that for Marlowe marriage would be tantamount to defeat.

Though it was a close call, Chandler remained true to the original conception of Marlowe at the end. Yet the notion that, if Marlowe married, he'd drink himself to death because he couldn't work any more was not some spur-of-the-moment conception but a possible outcome Chandler had envisioned ever since Marlowe had become involved with Linda in *The Long Goodbye.* Linda had said to him when she proposed the first time, "I'm a rich woman, darling, and I shall be infinitely richer. I could buy you the world if it were worth buying" (298). In refusing her proposal, Marlowe made it clear that they could never marry because she wouldn't give up her fortune and he wouldn't give up his work. At the end of *Playback,* the colloquy about who pays for the plane ticket and whether Marlowe goes to her or she comes to him raises this issue again, and Linda's acquiescence seems to suggest a compromise in which, if they marry, he will keep his job and his independence. But Chandler knew that such a compromise was an illusion, that in time the disparity between Linda's millions and Marlowe's hard-earned fees would take its toll and that either they would split up or Marlowe would give in to being kept and drink himself to death, having found—like Dick Diver in Fitzgerald's *Tender Is the Night,* who had tried to maintain his economic and professional independence by continuing his medical practice and research after marrying an heiress—that finally he couldn't beat his wife's money.

In contemplating as a possible fate for Marlowe his death from drink as a result of marrying money and quitting work, Chandler may have been influenced by another novel that, like *Tender Is the Night,* was published in 1934, Hammett's *The Thin Man*—which is to say, Chandler may have contemplated having Marlowe follow the Hammett trajectory, which ran from the salaried Continental Op through the self-employed Sam Spade to the retired private eye Nick Charles. When someone tries to hire Nick Charles as a detective at the novel's start, he explains that he hasn't worked in that line "since 1927" because "a year after I got married, my wife's father died and left her a lumber mill and a narrow-gauged railroad and some other things and I quit the Agency to look after them"[14]—though one has no sense from the novel what that "looking after" amounts to or that it's ever allowed to cut into his drinking time. Though Nick ends up taking the case of the missing inventor Clyde Wynant (the thin man of the title), a sea change has occurred in Hammett's detective fiction since the appearance of *The Maltese Falcon* four years earlier, for *The Thin Man*'s mystery story exists mainly as a frame on which to display the modern marriage of Nick and his rich wife, Nora, a relationship based on that of Hammett and Lillian Hellman and characterized by mutual independence, social and moral broad-mindedness, witty repartee, and the liberal application of alcohol. As Nick says when the case is wrapped up, "This excitement has put us behind in our drinking" (180).

Perhaps in imagining a possible end for Marlowe in "Poodle Springs," Chandler simply amalgamated the figure of Nick Charles with the fate of his creator, for *The Thin Man,* in which the professional detective marries money, retires, and drinks, was Hammett's last novel. He never again did any serious writing, and over the remaining seventeen years of his life he drank himself to death by degrees. Chandler must have realized that if Marlowe ever gave up his work, then his detective might as well be dead. But so too might his creator, and drinking himself to death was, as it turned out, a more likely end for the author than for the character.

In abandoning "Poodle Springs" and remaining true to his original vision of Marlowe, Chandler may have begun to realize that the attempt to deepen the character by aging him, by giving him a personal life and a possible mate, the attempt to raise hard-boiled detective fiction into the realm of high art by rendering his central character more psychologically complex, more vulnerable to the quotidian pressures of life, may have produced, in *The Long Good-bye,* a change in his work but not an improvement. For as a writer Chandler's depth had always been his surfaces. It's the reason why Marlowe is virtually inseparable, almost impossible to imagine apart, from the background of Los Angeles. Marlowe exists against, and in counterpoint to, the city's composite of hard surfaces and even harder superficiality, of mean streets and mansions, of Central Avenue and Beverly Hills, exists as someone who, as he tells Clarendon, doesn't believe in God (in any Absolute Consciousness or otherworldly sanction underpinning a cosmic moral order) and so must determine for himself "what we have instead of God,"[15] as Brett Ashley says in *The Sun Also Rises* when she decides "not to be a bitch" by ruining the young bullfighter Pedro Romero.

Certainly, many modern novels are about trying to discover, and then test the efficacy of, what it is we have instead of God, but Marlowe's answer to that problem was to some degree predetermined by the very nature of the hard-boiled genre he had inherited from Hammett. What Marlowe has instead of God is his work, the detective's special know-how and professional code of ethics, which allow him to navigate the materialistic, insubstantial L.A. world in which the front door is the only part of a house you can't put your foot through and in which a man must remain relatively poor to stay his own man. As a substitute for God, it may not be much, but it's not nothing, either. In the earlier novels it had been enough to hold him, to keep him from lapsing into sentimental illusions or succumbing to what Wallace Stevens called the nostalgias. In Fitzgerald's *Tender Is the Night,* Dick Diver said (and his wife throws the words up to him later, as his self-esteem begins to crumble under the pressure of trying to compete with her wealth) that "a man knows things and when he stops knowing things he's like anybody else," that "it's a confession of weakness for a scientist not to write."[16] In effect, Diver says that a man's special knowledge, the skill that is his work, is crucially what makes him a man. Consequently, what undermines Diver's sense of himself is his violation, by marrying a patient, of his own professional code and psychiatric expertise, his allowing himself to be co-opted by his wife's rarefied social world, a world that gives importance only to economic valuations of work (or anything else)—a world in which his wife's ever-increasing income for doing nothing dwarfs what he earns from his medical work and thus makes that work, and him along with it, seem paltry. No wonder that Marlowe's dedication to his work, the doing that is his being, by its very essence entails his placing no importance on monetary success and fosters a special wariness of being seduced from that resolve, under the pressure of age and loneliness, by an attractive heiress who wants him to marry into her world and values rather than the reverse.

The hard-boiled fiction of Hammett and Chandler did not just transform the amateur sleuth of the analytic genre into a salaried or self-employed private eye, it also annexed to the imagining of professional detective work questions about the place of work in the American psyche, in gender relations, in notions of personal success or failure, of personal freedom or its lack; and annexed such questions precisely during a period (the 1930s and '40s) when, because of the widespread unemployment of the Depression and the wholesale entry of women into the workforce during the war, issues of work and the economic, social, political, and psychological structures that work underpins seemed most pressing and problematic. To have done that while writing a novel as witty, intelligent, and appealing as *The Big Sleep* should have been enough to have satisfied even Chandler's literary ambitions.

CHAPTER THREE

Beating the Boss

Cain's *Double Indemnity*

I

The two writers most frequently associated with James M. Cain in any discussion of hard-boiled fiction are, of course, Dashiell Hammett and Raymond Chandler, and indeed the three men's lives and careers have much in common. Like Hammett, Cain was born and raised in Maryland, served in the U.S. Army during World War I, and contracted pulmonary tuberculosis as a result of that service. Like Chandler, who served in the Canadian Army, Cain actually saw combat. Cain and Hammett each received a disability pension from the government, and each spent time in various TB hospitals during the 1920s. (One wonders how much their both being "lungers," sharing perhaps a sense of life's brevity and fatality, contributed to the subject and tone of their novels.) All three turned to fiction writing after leaving other lines of work (Cain had previously been a newspaperman and managing editor of the *New Yorker*), and after the war each lived in California at some point and made it the setting for his best work. Indeed, the three so closely identified their main characters with the state and its state of mind that Hammett's Continental Op and Sam Spade seem impossible to imagine apart from the foggy streets of

San Francisco, while Chandler's Philip Marlowe and Cain's Frank Chambers and Walter Huff are equally inseparable from the harsh, sunlit world of Los Angeles and its environs.

Of course, Hammett, Chandler, and Cain all worked as Hollywood screenwriters, though only Chandler had any appreciable success in films, gaining his first screen credit for the script of Cain's *Double Indemnity* (1944), which he coauthored with the picture's director Billy Wilder. Chandler went on to write the original script for *The Blue Dahlia* (1946) and to adapt the Patricia Highsmith novel for Hitchcock's *Strangers on a Train* (1951). Cain, on the other hand, noted that, while several of his stories had "made legendary successes when adapted for films," he himself had "not been particularly successful" in the picture business: "Moving pictures simply do not excite me intellectually, or aesthetically. . . . I know their technique as exhaustively as anybody knows it . . . but I don't feel it."[1] The three writers also shared the same publisher, Knopf, for most of their careers, as well as a close working relationship with Alfred and Blanche Knopf.

The three were used to being grouped together by critics, an association Chandler and Cain both resented. Chandler wrote Alfred Knopf in February 1943, "I hope the day will come when I don't have to ride around on Hammett and James Cain, like an organ grinder's monkey. Hammett is all right. I give him everything. There were a lot of things he could not do, but what he did he did superbly. But James Cain—faugh! Everything he touches smells like a billygoat. He is every kind of writer I detest, a faux naif, a Proust in greasy overalls, a dirty little boy with a piece of chalk and a board fence and nobody looking. Such people are the offal of literature, not because they write about dirty things but because they do it in a dirty way."[2] As for the practice of labeling groups of writers, Cain commented, "Although I have read less than twenty pages of Mr. Dashiell Hammett in my whole life, Mr. Clifton Fadiman can refer to my hammett-and-tongs style and make things easy for himself" (Pref., 352). The twenty pages of Hammett Cain had read were from *The Glass Key* (1931), and Cain's reaction to the novel was "forget this goddamn book."[3] Later in his life, Cain would say that while he liked mystery writer Rex Stout, "he would not read Dashiell Hammett or Raymond Chandler" (Hoopes, 470). In contrast, Hammett left no written record of his opinion of Cain or Chandler, perhaps because Hammett's last novel, *The Thin Man*, appeared in the same year (1934) as Cain's first novel, *The Postman Always Rings Twice*, and five years before Chandler's first novel. While there is no record of Cain and

Hammett ever meeting, Chandler did meet Hammett once (and only once), at a dinner in January 1936 in Los Angeles for *Black Mask* magazine authors, and Cain in 1943, at a story conference with Billy Wilder in preparing the script for *Double Indemnity.*

There are, then, more than enough similarities in these three writers' lives and careers to account for the critical association of their works, but the obvious difference between Hammett and Chandler, on the one hand, and Cain, on the other, is that Hammett and Chandler wrote detective fiction exclusively, while Cain never wrote a straight detective story. Still, I would argue that it is precisely in relation to Hammett and Chandler that we can best understand the type of fiction Cain *did* write in *Double Indemnity* (1936) and *The Postman Always Rings Twice* (1934), his two most compelling books.

II

Double Indemnity began its life in print as an eight-part serial in *Liberty* magazine in 1936, its first appearance in book form being Cain's *Three of a Kind* (1943), where it was grouped with two other of his short works. It's the story of insurance salesman Walter Huff, who, in paying a call on a client one day, meets instead the client's wife, Phyllis Nirdlinger, finds himself immediately attracted to her, and guesses, when she asks if she could take out an accident policy for her husband without his having to know, that something fishy is going on: "I couldn't be mistaken about what she meant, not after fifteen years in the insurance business. I mashed out my cigarette, so I could get up and go. I was going to get out of there, and drop those renewals and everything else about her like a red-hot poker. But I didn't do it. . . . What I did do was put my arm around her, pull her face up against mine, and kiss her on the mouth, hard. I was trembling like a leaf."[4]

When Huff leaves, he realizes that he's been "standing right on the deep end, looking over the edge" and that all the time he was "trying to pull away from it, there was something in" him "that kept edging a little closer, trying to get a better look" (18). Phyllis shows up one evening at Huff's apartment, and Huff, once again feeling she's trying to tell him something without saying what she means, describes his state of mind with the same image: "I ought to quit, while the quitting was good, I knew that. But that thing was in me, pushing me still closer to the edge." So Huff steps over the edge and tells Phyllis what she's been trying to tell him with her exaggerated concern for her husband's safety, tells her she's been planning for something "accidentally-on-purpose . . . to fall on" her husband so that "he'll be dead" (20). Feigning outrage, Phyllis walks out, but when she returns the next night, Huff makes his decision: "Phyllis, you seem to think that because I can call it on you, you're not going to do it. You *are* going to do it, and I'm going to help you" (22).

Huff's two obvious motives are sex and money: he wants Phyllis and the insurance. But there are two other, less-than-obvious motives, and in associating the first of these with an irresistible impulse that has him standing at the edge of a drop, drawing closer and closer to get a better look, Cain echoes two Poe tales that are the origin of this particular motive in American crime fiction. In Poe's 1845 "The Imp of the Perverse," the narrator points out that there is one "innate and primitive principle of human action" which the phrenologists and all earlier moralists have overlooked, a principle he names "*perverseness.*"[5] He explains, "Through its promptings we act without comprehensible object, . . . act, for the reason that we should *not.*" He continues, "I am not more certain that I breathe, than that the assurance of the wrong or error of any action is often the one unconquerable *force* that impels us, and alone impels us to its prosecution" (1220–21).

The narrator then gives several examples of the impulse, with the last of these especially relevant to Huff: "We stand upon the brink of a precipice. We peer into the abyss. . . . Our first impulse is to shrink from the danger. Unaccountably we remain" (1222). The narrator says that precisely "because our reason violently deters us from the brink, *therefore,* do we the more impetuously approach it. . . . To indulge for a moment, in any attempt at *thought,* is to be inevitably lost; for reflection but urges us to forbear, and *therefore* it is, I say, that we *cannot*" (1223).

Besides sharing the same drawn-to-the-edge image for figuring perverseness, *Double Indemnity* and "The Imp of the Perverse" also share the same narrative situation—the confession of a murderer awaiting punishment. In "The Imp of the Perverse" the tale's narration takes place on the night before the narrator's execution, while in *Double Indemnity*'s last chapter we learn that Huff's narrative is supposedly the text of a notarized statement he's given Keyes, the head of his company's claims department, as part of an agreement to let Huff have a head start in getting away from the police, an arrangement Keyes hopes will avoid a trial and the resulting embarrassment to the company. Keyes gives Huff this option because he has already set in motion the machinery of his punishment; he has apparently made the same deal with Phyllis

Nirdlinger and booked passage for them both, unknown to one another, on the same steamship heading for Mexico, feeling certain that either Phyllis will kill Walter (as she has already tried unsuccessfully to do) or that Walter, who knows that the police will be waiting when the boat docks, will kill himself rather than submit to trial and execution. As it turns out, they both commit suicide, jumping overboard on their last night at sea. Interestingly enough, Huff's initial drawn-to-the-edge-of-a-drop image for the perverse impulse that leads to murder resonates in two subsequent leaps Huff takes in committing the crime and in enacting the punishment: one from the rear of a train when he's impersonating Nirdlinger and the other from the stern of a ship.

Cain and Poe had each previously used this device of a murderer's first-person narrative on the eve of punishment—Cain in his first novel *The Postman Always Rings Twice* and Poe in two earlier stories, "The Tell-Tale Heart" (1842) and "The Black Cat" (1843). We learn in the last chapter of *Postman* that the narrative is a statement written by Frank Chambers on death row, a statement intended for the prison chaplain Father McConnell: "If I get a stay, he's to hold on to it and wait for what happens. If I get a commutation, then, he's to burn it, and they'll never know whether there really was any murder or not, from anything I tell them. But if they get me, he's to take it and see if he can find somebody to print it." [6] In Poe's "The Black Cat" not only does the narrator recount his crimes from a "felon's cell," but he attributes the first of these to "the spirit of PERVERSENESS . . . , this unfathomable longing of the soul *to vex itself*—to offer violence to its own nature—to do wrong for the wrong's sake only." [7] Clearly, this brief discussion of perverseness in "The Black Cat" in 1843 was a trial run for the much longer, more detailed one in "The Imp of the Perverse" in 1845. But the main difference between "The Imp of the Perverse" and *Double Indemnity* is that the latter's narrator is motivated by a seemingly irresistible impulse to commit a crime (as in "The Black Cat"), while the former's narrator is driven by an irresistible impulse to confess one.

Besides sex, money, and perverseness, Huff has a further motive that gets mixed up with (and goes a way toward explaining) the perverse principle in his case. The speed with which Huff agrees to help Phyllis kill her husband for the insurance, and with which he then generates the plan for the perfect crime, makes clear he'd been thinking about this possibility long before they'd met. After working for fifteen years as an insurance agent, Huff has developed in dealing with prospective clients a sixth sense about the sorts of behavior or inquiries that indicate trouble. When Huff returns to his office after his first visit to Nirdlinger's house, he finds Keyes fuming about a client who'd "burned his truck up and tried to collect" on a policy Huff had written, and Huff says in his own defense, "I distinctly remember that I clipped a memo to that application when I sent it through that I thought that fellow ought to be thoroughly investigated before we accepted the risk. I didn't like his looks" (12). His alertness to questionable motives had already been established in the opening scene with Phyllis when, during a conversation about renewing her husband's automobile insurance, she'd suddenly asked, "Do you handle accident insurance?" and he'd thought: "Maybe that don't mean to you what it meant to me. . . . when there's dirty work going on, accident is the first thing they think of. . . . it's the one kind of insurance that can be taken out without the insured knowing a thing about it" (11).

From the outset Cain presents Huff as an experienced professional with a store of inside information, someone who's seen most of the tricks people can play to defraud insurance companies and who's tried to imagine new ones in order to guard against them. So we're not wholly surprised when he says that if the reader thinks he's nuts to suddenly throw in with Phyllis, then maybe he is, "but you spend fifteen years in the business I'm in, maybe you'll go nuts yourself. . . . You think it's a business . . . ? It's not" (29). It's more like a game of roulette, says Huff, and as an insurance agent he's "a croupier in that game": "I know all their tricks, I lie awake nights thinking up tricks, so I'll be ready for them when they come at me. And then one night I think up a trick, and get to thinking I could crook the wheel myself if I could only put a plant out there to put down my bet. That's all. When I met Phyllis I met my plant" (29–30). Although perverseness drives Huff to risk everything in this scheme, it's a perverseness fueled both by boredom with his work and by the moral indifference that work engenders: "I had seen so many houses burned down, so many cars wrecked, so many corpses with blue holes in their temples, so many awful things that people had pulled to crook the wheel, that that stuff didn't seem real to me any more. If you don't understand that, go to Monte Carlo . . . and watch the face of the man that spins the little ivory ball. . . . he wouldn't care. Not that baby" (30).

An additional element rounds out this last motive, a key element that comes through repeatedly in Huff's narration: a sort of intellectual pride, a professional's sense of superiority. In the novel's most engrossing passages—those in which Huff describes in detail first his plan to make the murder look like an accident and then the plan's execution—what's evident is Huff's pleasure both in exhibiting his own cleverness to the reader and in outwitting the people he works for. This theme—of an employee who is smarter and more experienced in his line of work than his employer and who consequently feels frustrated and resentful because, in terms of brains and ability, his boss should be working for him—is introduced in the very first scene between Huff and Keyes. Complaining to Huff about the performance of another unit of the company, Keyes says: "'I'm sending a memo to Norton about it. I think the whole thing is something the president of this company might well look into. Though if you ask me, if the president of this company had more . . .' He stopped and I didn't jog him. Keyes was one of the holdovers from the time of Old Man Norton, the founder of the company, and he didn't think much of young Norton, that took over the job when his father died. The way he told it, young Norton never did anything right, and the whole place was always worried for fear he'd pull them in on the feud" (13).

What Huff does to his company by murdering Nirdlinger and trying to collect the insurance is a more extreme, though doubtless similarly motivated, version of what Huff has seen Keyes doing in his tirades about young Norton: asserting and demonstrating (if only to himself) an employee's superiority to his boss. There is never any doubt in the novel that Huff admires and respects Keyes for his intelligence and professionalism, nor much doubt that he agrees with Keyes's opinion of their employer. What Huff questions is the wisdom of asserting an employee's superiority in a public venue in front of other employees, of seeking a confrontation. The particular way Huff chooses to show he's smarter than the boss can only demonstrate that fact, of course, if the boss is never allowed to realize that superiority. And if one of the reasons Huff explains his plan to Phyllis in such detail is his desire to have at least one other person at this point know of his cleverness, then one of the reasons he includes those detailed discussions in his confession to Keyes is that he wants the plan's ingenuity appreciated by a professional.

But obviously the reason *Cain* goes in for these detailed explanations of Huff's plan is that they make for the most engrossing writing in the book. One can see plainly Cain's awareness of where the narrative's real energy lies, for when the planning and execution of the first murder is finished, there is a palpable letdown in the book's excitement as Huff and Phyllis lie low and wait for the insurance company's first move, a relaxation in narrative tension that Cain quickly addresses with the step-by-step planning of a second (unsuccessful) murder, as Huff tries to rid himself of his partner in crime and pin her death on somebody else.

When Huff first tells Phyllis he'll help kill her husband, he asks what she's been planning to see if she's already "gummed it up" for his scheme "with some bad move of her own" (24). She says she'd been considering an accidental drowning in the swimming pool, "as though he hit his head diving or something," but Huff tells her that's an amateur's plan and a one-way ticket to the death-house: "In the first place, some fool in the insurance business, five or six years ago, put out a newspaper story that most accidents happen in people's own bathtubs, and since then bathtubs, swimming pools, and fish ponds are the first thing they think of. When they're trying to pull something, I mean. There's two cases like that out here in California right now. Neither one of them are on the up-and-up, and if there'd been an insurance angle those people would wind up on the gallows" (24–25).

Huff then explains how a professional would approach the job: "There's three essential elements to a successful murder. . . . The first is, help. One person can't get away with it. . . . The second is, the time, the place, the way, all known in advance—to us, but not to him. The third is, audacity. That's the one that all amateur murderers forget. They know the first two, sometimes. But that third, only a professional knows. . . . Be bold. It's the only chance to get away with it" (25–27). For Huff, Phyllis's "swimming pool idea" isn't audacious enough, and besides, "there's no money in it" because "all the big money on an accident policy comes from railroad accidents." Huff explains that insurance companies know from statistics that "the spots that people think are danger spots, aren't danger spots at all," that "the figures show not many people get killed, or even hurt, on railroad trains," and that as a sales gimmick insurance companies write accident policies with "double indemnity for railroad accidents." He tells her that when they pull off his scheme they're going to "cash a $50,000 bet" because his plan "is a beauty, if I do say so myself. I didn't spend all this time in this business for nothing" (27).

However, the doubling of the insurance payment is not the only, or perhaps even the main, attraction of the railroad accident scheme. Rather, it's that he's spent a long time working out the details of a plan that draws on fifteen years of professional experience and that this scheme will require all his cleverness, dexterity, and nerve to execute. Indeed, the plan's complexity of execution is what Huff counts on to make it undetectable, for he intends to use his company's own actuarial information and investigative procedures against it. As an insurance man, Huff knows that the statistical probability of committing premeditated murder by pushing someone off the rear observation platform of a slow-moving train leaving a station is virtually nonexistent; and that since there's no likelihood of this method actually resulting in the intended victim's death, there are no recorded instances of its having been tried. He also knows that his company's standard operating procedure in such matters is to consider the statistical probability of this sort of death being murder and, if that probability is zero, then to conclude, absent any other evidence to arouse their suspicions, that the death was a freak accident. Huff knows it's precisely the audacity of appearing to commit a murder in a situation where it seems no premeditation could be sure of causing the victim's death that is his plan's best chance of success. Also, the high level of planning, nerve, and execution that pulling off such a plan requires make it the ultimate demonstration of his superiority to his job, or at least to his boss, young Norton. Thus, when Phyllis tells Huff that her husband is planning to drive to his college reunion in Palo Alto and that she hasn't been able to persuade him to take the train, Huff says his deal to help her with the murder is off: "Listen, it's the train or we don't do it. . . . Just pulling off some piker job, that don't interest me. But this, hitting it for the limit, that's what I go for" (43). When Nirdlinger accidentally falls and fractures his leg, necessitating a train trip to his reunion, Huff and Phyllis get their chance.

Clearly, the challenge of "hitting it for the limit" is an important part of Huff's motivation, for in committing a crime so intricate and audacious that only a man of his caliber could bring it off, Huff seems to redeem (or at least rebel against and thus gain a measure of freedom from) those fifteen years of servitude selling insurance, years that had made him go nuts enough to throw in with Phyllis. And this final motive of beating the boss links Cain's tough-guy fiction to the hard-boiled detective fiction of Hammett and Chandler.

III

In the two previous chapters I argue that a major thematic trajectory in the works of Hammett and Chandler is the detective's movement from being a salaried employee of a large private agency (the Continental Op and Spade) or of the DA's office (Marlowe) to being a self-employed, independent operator and that, paralleling this trajectory, is another in which the detective avoids compromising his hard-won and precariously maintained economic and personal freedom through an entangling relationship with a woman. As the resentment of having a boss—of not being one's own man and thus not being fully a man—is addressed by the first trajectory in Hammett's and Chandler's fiction, so it is addressed in a different way by the beating-the-boss scenario in Cain's *Double Indemnity*. Whereas the former trajectory is based on the assumption that being boss means being the better man, or at least more of a man than the employee, the latter scenario aims to show that becoming boss is less often a matter of ability, hard work, and dedication than of wealth, class, and connections, as suggested by the inept and inexperienced young Norton succeeding his father as company president rather than a more qualified insurance man like Keyes. Certainly another reason why Huff confesses his plan to Keyes in such detail is that he expects Keyes, given his opinion of young Norton, immediately to understand this display of ingenuity at the boss's expense.

When Huff opts for beating rather than being the boss, it's clearly not because he doesn't have another choice. Huff tells us at one point that, because of the competition he'd been getting for automobile insurance from companies that also lent "money on a member's car": "I organized a little finance company of my own, had myself made a director, and spent about one day a week there. It didn't have anything to do with the insurance company, but it was the one way I could meet that question that I ran into all the time: 'Do you lend money on a car?'" (35). That Huff has the business sense and entrepreneurial energy to start and run his own company is what Cain wants the reader to register before Huff takes that perverse gamble of "hitting it for the limit."

If Huff's opting for immediate gratification in both the professional and personal spheres marks him as someone who, unlike Spade and Marlowe, chooses to let his life-as-having suddenly preempt his life-as-being, then that clearly accords with what Cain said was the ongoing theme of all his work: "I . . . write of the wish that comes true, for some reason a terrifying concept, at least to my imagination. . . . My stories have some quality of the opening of a forbidden box . . . and the reader is carried along . . . by his own realization that the characters cannot have this particular wish and survive" ("Pref.," 353). The image of opening a forbidden box, of a dangerous wish suddenly gratified, leads Cain in the next sentence to mention "Pandora, the first woman," and certainly in his best books the main female character, as the object of that forbidden wish, is usually the one who sets things in motion. The central irony in *Double Indemnity*, of course, is that while Huff clearly prides himself on being an experienced professional in dealing with insurance fraud, an insider who takes pleasure in showing Phyllis why her swimming-pool-accident idea is an amateur's plan compared to his railroad-accident scheme, it is in fact Phyllis who turns out to be the really experienced one when it comes to killing people. As Huff learns from Keyes at the end, Phyllis is suspected of four other murders and is linked to five more suspicious deaths.

In the wake of her father's accident, Lola Nirdlinger tells Huff she suspects that her stepmother killed her real mother, who had suffered from lung problems. Phyllis, a nurse who "specialized in pulmonary diseases" (83), was caring for her in a cabin at Lake Arrowhead in the dead of winter when Lola's mother succumbed to pneumonia under questionable circumstances. A year later Phyllis married Lola's father. But the plot thickens when Huff learns from Keyes that three children had died of pneumonia in a sanatorium "in the Verdugo Hills about a quarter of a mile from this place where she [Phyllis] was head nurse," that she "was over there too much, and she seemed to take too much interest in the children up there," and finally that "*one* of those children was related to . . . [the first] Mrs. Nirdlinger," who "became executrix for quite a lot of property the child was due to inherit" (115–16). The property eventually passed to Mrs. Nirdlinger and, on her death, to her husband. With Nirdlinger's death it would pass to Lola, with Phyllis as her legal guardian, and the final part of the plan seemed clear: "Lola was next" (117).

Although Phyllis's murders share a certain pulmonary monotony, Huff prides himself on the brilliant uniqueness of his plan to kill Phyllis's husband and make it look like an accident. Hiding in the back of the Nirdlingers' sedan when Phyllis drives her husband to the train station, Huff, at a prearranged signal on a dark, deserted street, grabs Nirdlinger from behind and, using one of Nirdlinger's own crutches, breaks his neck. Huff then switches places with Nirdlinger and boards the train, a switch facilitated by the fact that the two men are the same general height and build, wearing the same color suit, and that Huff's foot has been bandaged in the same way as Nirdlinger's broken one. After saying good-bye to her "husband" at the station so that the porter and conductor notice, Phyllis drives the car containing Nirdlinger's body to an agreed-on spot by the railroad tracks where the slow-moving train with Huff on board must pass on its way out of Los Angeles. Meanwhile Huff, with his hat pulled low and looking down at his feet as if concentrating on the crutches, has made his way back to the train's rear observation platform. When the train reaches the spot, Huff jumps off, then he and Phyllis leave Nirdlinger's body by the tracks and drive back to their respective homes.

Smart and audaciously executed, Huff's plan is, as Huff realizes when he learns of Phyllis's past from Keyes, only tactically clever compared to the overall strategic sweep of Phyllis's plan to end up, through a series of murders (including Huff's, after he helped her eliminate Nirdlinger), with the property that had originally belonged to the child she'd killed at the sanatorium, a murder whose motive she'd tried to disguise by killing two other children at the same time. This is what Huff understands as he lies in the hospital recovering from Phyllis's attempt to kill him and listens to Keyes. For clearly, it was one thing for Phyllis, as a nurse who specialized in pulmonary diseases, to bring about the deaths from pneumonia of three children in a sanatorium and of a woman with lung problems in a deserted cabin in the dead of winter, but it was another thing entirely to kill a healthy, vigorous man in his mid-forties and not have it look suspicious. For that Phyllis needed the help of an expert.

Keyes tells Huff they've also learned of "five cases, all before the three little children, where patients died under" Phyllis's care, "two of them where she got property out of it" (118–19). Three of the five died of pneumonia, and "the older two were operative cases" in which "she found out some way to do it with the serum, combining with another drug" (119). Huff had told Phyllis the most important element needed in order to get away with murder was audacity, the element "all amateur murderers forget" and "only a professional knows" (25). What Huff meant by audacity was a reasoned policy of playing the wild card, of taking a bold risk in the execution of a plan (as when Huff takes Nirdlinger's place and boards the train in plain view of the conductor, porter, and all the passengers), but for sheer audaciousness, Phyllis easily trumps that with nine murders (seven of which have the same cause of death and six of patients under her care), though the audacity in her case comes not from reasoned policy but from pathology. Keyes tells Huff, "She's a pathological case . . . an out-and-out lunatic" (115, 118), which shouldn't have surprised Huff, since Phyllis's instability had been hinted at early on. At their third meeting, after Huff has volunteered to help kill her husband, Phyllis says,

> "Maybe I'm crazy. But there's something in me that loves Death. I think of myself as Death, sometimes. In a scarlet shroud, floating through the night. . . .
>
> It seems as though I'm doing something—that's really best for him [Nirdlinger], if he only knew it. Do you understand me, Walter?"

"No."

"Nobody could." (23–24)

It's hard to imagine that Huff, given the forethought involved in his plan, wouldn't have been alerted by this conversation and inquired into his prospective partner-in-crime's background, precisely because one of the two conditions on which the success of his scheme depends (besides the zero actuarial probability of murdering someone under those circumstances) is the absence of any other evidence to arouse suspicion, a condition that would be demolished by Phyllis's past coming to light.

Cain suggests that this lapse in Huff's judgment is the result of shrewdness being temporarily overruled by lust: Huff describes what he originally felt for Phyllis as "some kind of unhealthy excitement that came over me just at the sight of her" (95). But Huff's sense of his own superiority may also have contributed—his sense that he's a pro while Phyllis is just another unhappy, frustrated housewife fantasizing about doing away with her husband, that he's the actual initiator and thus in complete control of the situation (a feeling encouraged by Phyllis's pretense that he sexually seduced her rather than the reverse). So Huff's only inquiry is to ask Phyllis "what she'd been figuring on" for Nirdlinger's accidental death. Still, we should note in Huff's defense that if he *had* made the kind of inquiry needed to uncover Phyllis's past, such an investigation, even if it uncovered nothing damaging, would nevertheless have prevented his plan from going forward, because no matter how discreet, any inquiry thorough enough to be useful would surely have left a trace, something that would come to light in an insurance investigation of Nirdlinger's death. And Huff knows that part of his company's standard operating procedure in large claims cases is to investigate both the beneficiary of the policy and the agent who wrote it.

Letting himself into Keyes's office one night to check on the progress of the Nirdlinger investigation, Huff listens to a Keyes Dictaphone memo regarding young Norton's "proposal to put Agent Huff under surveillance for his connection with the Nirdlinger case" (85). Keyes disagrees, saying that, although the agent "is automatically under suspicion" in such a case, he has checked the facts and the records as well as Huff's "whereabouts the night of the crime, and find[s] he was at home all night. This in my opinion lets him out" (85–86). Yet if there had been any inkling that Huff had carried out his own investigation of Phyllis, Keyes would have instantly known that Huff was his man.

However complex Huff's motivation may have been in falling for Phyllis and helping kill her husband, his revulsion for her after they commit the murder is simple and straightforward. Lying awake in bed on the night of the killing, he says, "I knew then what I had done. . . . I had killed a man to get a woman. I had put myself in her power, so there was one person in the world that could point a finger at me, and I would have to die. I had done all that for her, and I never wanted to see her again as long as I lived. That's all it takes, one drop of fear, to curdle love into hate" (62).

Once Huff warns Phyllis she's under surveillance, the two are able to see little of each other. The separation and Huff's corrosive fear of Phyllis's cracking up or slipping up, plus his knowledge, gleaned from listening to another Keyes Dictaphone memo, that Beniamino Sachetti, Lola's former boyfriend, has visited Phyllis every night for a week, gradually make clear to Huff that to save himself he must take drastic action: "I don't know when I decided to kill Phyllis. It seemed to me that ever since that night, somewhere in the back of my head I had known I would have to kill her, for what she knew about me, and because the world isn't big enough for two people once they've got something like that on each other." Huff's decision comes when he realizes that he won't be able to keep Lola (whom he'd been romancing during the hiatus from seeing Phyllis) from revealing her suspicions about her stepmother in open court, not just the theory that Phyllis had killed Lola's real mother but the fact that Lola had seen Phyllis trying on black dresses in a store the week before her father's death. Huff says, "The idea that Lola would put on an act like that in the courtroom, and that then Phyllis would lash out and tell her the truth, that was too horrible for me to think about" (95). Even if Phyllis kept her head in court and said nothing, Lola's accusations would still compromise Huff because it would come out that Lola had told him her suspicions immediately after Nirdlinger's death and that Huff hadn't reported them to Keyes—indeed, that he'd discouraged Lola from pursuing an inquiry.

IV

The method Huff selects to kill Phyllis recalls Frank and Cora's method of disposing of her husband in *The Postman Always Rings Twice*—a car accidentally going over a cliff. But whereas in Phyllis's case the drop is supposed to kill her, in the case of Cora's husband a blow to the back of Nick's head does the trick before the car is pushed over the edge. There are of course numerous similarities between Cain's first novel and *Double Indemnity*, sharing as they do the story of a husband murdered by his wife and her lover and the subsequent fate of the two killers. Apparently Cain got the original idea for *The Postman Always Rings Twice* after a conversation with his friend, the playwright Vincent Lawrence. The two had been discussing the 1927 Ruth Snyder–Judd Gray murder trial, a sensational case now best remembered for the front-page photo in the *New York Daily News* of Ruth Snyder in the electric chair at the moment of her execution, a photo snapped by a reporter with a concealed camera strapped to his ankle. As Cain's biographer Roy Hoopes tells it, "Albert Snyder was a mild little Long Islander and art editor of *Motor Boating* magazine. His wife Ruth and her lover, Judd Gray, a corset salesman, conspired to murder Snyder, then turned on each other after the murder" (Hoopes, 232–33). What Lawrence told Cain was that "when Ruth Snyder packed Gray off to Syracuse where he was to stay the night she murdered her husband, she gave him a bottle of wine, which he desperately wanted on the train. But he had no corkscrew with him and dared not ask the porter for one, for fear it would be the one thing they'd remember him by. When the police lab analyzed it, they found enough arsenic to kill a regiment of men." Cain's response was: "That jells the idea I've had for just such a story; a couple of jerks who discover that a murder, though dreadful enough morally, can be a love story too, but then wake up to discover that once they've pulled the thing off, no two people can share this terrible secret and live on the same earth. They turn against each other, as Judd and Ruth did" (233).

In *Postman*, Frank turns on Cora because the district attorney intimidates him, immediately after he regains consciousness from the auto accident, into swearing out an attempted-murder complaint against her to prove his own non-complicity. And Cora, who feels she's being left alone to take the rap, dictates, in revenge for Frank's betrayal, a full confession to her lawyer Katz's assistant (under the impression he's a cop) detailing Frank's part in the murder. But when Katz succeeds in getting Cora off with a six-month suspended sentence for manslaughter, she and Frank find they're still in love with each other and that they're going to have a child. At this point fate intervenes: there's another automobile accident (a real one this time, with Frank driving), in which Cora is killed and for which Frank is wrongly convicted of murder and sentenced to death, justice being served the second time around, as the book's title suggests. The novel ends with Frank awaiting execution, saying to the reader: "Father McConnell says prayers help. If you've got this far, send up one for me, and

Cora, and make it that we're together, wherever it is" (120). Though in *Postman* the murderous couple's love for each other ultimately prevails over their mutual fear and revulsion in the·wake of the killing ("Yellow is a color you figure on in murder," says Katz [78]), the opposite result was, as Cain knew, much likelier, and the several resemblances between *Postman* and *Double Indemnity* may well be Cain's way of inviting the reader to compare the two and appreciate the grimmer realism of Huff and Phyllis both planning to eliminate the other.

Besides the similar love triangles in each novel, there is a resemblance in the involvement of insurance companies and, as we noted, in the methods of the crimes (both actual and prospective), the latter extending to the similarity between Phyllis's original plan to drown Nirdlinger in the swimming pool and Frank and Cora's first, unsuccessful attempt to kill Nick. Cora is to go into the bathroom while Nick is bathing, blackjack him, then hold his head under till he drowns, lock the bathroom door from the inside, climb out the window onto the porch roof, and down a ladder Frank has placed there. Frank says, "I got the idea from a piece in the paper where a guy had said that most accidents happen right in people's own bathtubs" (17), clearly the same newspaper story Huffs refers to in nixing Phyllis's plan, saying that "since then bathtubs, swimming pools, and fish ponds are the first thing they think of" (24–25).

But luckily Frank and Cora's first attempt doesn't work, because just after Cora blackjacks Nick, a fuse blows, all the lights in the building go out, and Cora can't see to hold Nick under— "luckily" because, while Cora is sapping Nick in the tub, a motorcycle policeman has stopped by the diner downstairs and seen Frank standing by the ladder against the porch roof. When the policeman leaves and the lights suddenly go out, Frank yells for Cora to stop what she's doing, and they pull the unconscious Nick out of the tub and call an ambulance. Frank says later that it was a dumb plan: "Even if we had gone through with it they would have guessed it. . . . Because look how quick that cop knew something was wrong. . . . Soon as he saw me standing there he knew it" (24). Similarly, Huff tells Phyllis regarding her own "swimming pool job," which she thinks is "so slick nobody would ever guess it": "They'd guess it in two seconds, flat. In three seconds, flat, they'd prove it, and in four seconds, flat, you'd confess it" (25–26).

The insurance company's investigation of Nirdlinger's death was, of course, planned on by Huff when he decided to "hit it for the limit," but in the case of Nick Papadakis, the insurance angle comes as a surprise to the killers. As Katz explains it to Frank, five days before his death Nick took out a ten-thousand-dollar insurance policy on himself with Cora as the beneficiary, but without her knowledge. Consequently, when Cora is arraigned for Nick's murder and Frank's attempted murder (because she was supposedly driving the car that was in fact pushed over the cliff), a representative of Nick's insurance company testifies to the policy's terms. When Katz asks him if he is "an interested party to this proceeding," seeking "to escape payment of this indemnity, on the ground that a crime has been committed," and the insurance man says yes, Katz asks him a carefully worded final question: "You really believe . . . that this woman killed her husband to obtain this indemnity, and either tried to kill this man, or else deliberately placed him in jeopardy that might cause his death, all as part of a plan to obtain this indemnity?" (70–71). When the man again says yes, Katz, in a surprise move, immediately pleads Cora guilty on both charges.

What Katz had learned when Nick's safe deposit box was opened was that Nick had several insurance policies with different companies and that the insurance agent who had written them was also the one who had sold him the ten-thousand-dollar policy just before his death. The insurance agent had stopped by Nick's place one day because Papadakis's auto insurance had almost expired. Nick renewed the auto insurance, and the agent ended up selling him a personal accident policy as well. But Katz discovered that two of Nick's old policies "*still had a week to run*" at the time of his death, each for ten thousand dollars and each a public liability bond. By forcing Frank to sign a complaint for attempted murder against Cora, the district attorney had fixed it so that if he convicted Cora of both charges, then Frank could "bring suit against her for injuries sustained as a result of that murder," and the two bonding companies would be "liable for every cent of their policies to satisfy that judgment" (80). Katz then arranges a meeting with representatives of all three insurance companies, explains the situation, and brokers a deal in which the two bonding companies each put up five thousand dollars to cover the ten-thousand-dollar personal accident claim of the third company. The third company agrees to pay the claim and have its representative, at Cora's sentencing hearing, retract his earlier statement and say instead that he was now sure Nick's death was an accident, his certainty evidenced by his company's willingness to honor the policy. When the insurance representative contradicts his previous testimony, Katz, knowing that "if an insurance company didn't believe she was guilty, a jury would never believe it" (82), asks to "withdraw the pleas of guilty and allow the cases to proceed" (83), and the DA, realizing he's been outsmarted, agrees to a plea of manslaughter with a six-month suspended sentence.

Just as a large part of the most interesting "business" in *Double Indemnity* involves Huff's letting the reader in on an insurance company's professional secrets, so a substantial portion of the reader's interest in *Postman* lies in the intricate maneuvering of Katz in playing off one insurance company against another to get the verdict he wants. In making insurance companies protagonists in his two best books, Cain was drawing on his personal experience as an insurance salesman in 1914 and on conversations with his father, who had been a vice president of the insurer U.S. Fidelity and Guaranty since 1918. Cain had also verified "the insurance details in *Postman*" with the "AAA men in Los Angeles" when he was working on the manuscript, and one executive had told him: "This stuff of yours . . . is right from beginning to end. . . . No insurance man will laugh at you for it, and it's so right that you ought to write more stuff along this line. . . . All the big crime mysteries in this country are locked up in insurance company files, and the writer that gets wise to that one of these days is going to make himself rich" (quoted in Hoopes, 258). No doubt the remark encouraged Cain to revisit this material in *Double Indemnity*, for clearly insurance companies offered Cain the kind of alternative investigative agency to the police that private detective firms offered Hammett and Chandler—agencies with divided loyalties vis-à-vis their clients, their employees, their business, and the law: organizations constantly faced with morally and legally ambiguous situations, which is to say, with the stuff of hard-boiled fiction.

Since Frank and Cora kill her husband to be together and in possession of his business, Nick's policy simply serves as the excuse for Katz's machinations at the trial and for creating (as part of a standard hard-boiled aura) the sense of a system, collusive and manipulable, perhaps even wholly corrupt, comprising the police, the DA, lawyers, and insurance firms. But in *Double Indemnity* the insurance industry is the very stuff of the novel. By setting the book's action in this specific business, Cain can treat human existence and some of its more alarming but predictable vicissitudes within a context of statistical probability and corporate decision making, a context that gives these events a dual focus: personal, humane, moral, on the one hand, and professional, commercial, expedient, on the other. Expanding on his remark that fifteen years in the insurance business had made him go nuts, Huff says:

> You think it's a business, don't you, just like your business, and maybe a little better than that, because it's the friend of the widow, the orphan, and the needy in time of trouble? It's not. It's the biggest gambling wheel in the world. . . . You

bet your house will burn down, they bet it won't, that's all. What fools you is that you didn't *want* your house to burn down when you made the bet, and so you forget it's a bet. That don't fool them.... a hedge bet don't look any different than any other bet. But there comes a time, maybe, when you *do* want your house to burn down, when the money is worth more than the house. And right there is where the trouble starts. (29)

In Huff's view the insurance business is not only a kind of legalized gambling that makes money by playing on people's fear of disasters but also a commercial mechanism, one of whose inevitable side effects is to attach a bounty to certain disastrous acts, as when Huff observes that since accident coverage can be taken out without the insured even knowing about it, "there's many a man walking around today that's worth more to his loved ones dead than alive, only he don't know it yet." Huff aims to justify his decision to defraud his company on the grounds that insurance companies are morally suspect, allowing practices such as writing accident coverage without the insured's knowledge. (As Huff says, "No physical examination for accident. On that, all they want is the money" [11]). But one also senses that Cain intends for us to recognize Huff's planning, with its stress on foreseeing every eventuality and addressing it in advance, as something that grows naturally out of the very idea of insurance. For the essence of the business is nothing if not forethought and precaution, and thus Huff's fifteen years in the insurance business have not only made him a little nuts, they've also made him what he is—calculating, cold-blooded, opportunistic. Indeed, his company understands the potentially corrupting effect of Huff's line of work, for as Keyes says in his Dictaphone memo, the agent is automatically under suspicion in large-claim cases. It's in the context of this insurance ethos that Huff makes his play, one that almost succeeds because of the unwitting help of another employee who also thinks he's smarter than the boss—something Huff probably counted on.

Huff knows from the start that his scheme's success depends on surviving the scrutiny of his friend Keyes, whose first appearance in the novel establishes him as "a wolf on a phony claim" (12): Foiling the man who tried to collect after setting fire to his own truck, Keyes complains that the way the company's now being run under young Norton "they'd have paid that claim" if he hadn't intervened (13). Keyes, "the best claim man on the Coast, . . . was the one I was afraid of," says Huff. On the day after Nirdlinger's death Huff, as the agent who wrote the policy, has an interview with Keyes and young Norton, who's "so busy trying to act like his father he doesn't seem to have time for much else" (63). The tension between Keyes and Norton immediately dictates the course of the discussion. First, Norton claims that the company's not liable because Nirdlinger's death is a "clear case of suicide," pointing out that Nirdlinger took out his accident policy "in absolute secrecy," then when "he fractured his leg, . . . didn't put a claim in" because he knew he was going to kill himself and if he'd put in a claim "*the family would find out about this policy and block him off*" (65). Unable to keep quiet any longer, Keyes begins throwing books of actuarial tables on suicide in front of Norton, saying "*there's not one case here out of all these millions of cases of a leap from the rear end of a moving train*" because no one could jump off a train going "a maximum of fifteen miles an hour . . . with any real expectation of killing himself" (67–68). Keyes adds that Norton should study these books, and he "might find out something about the insurance business":

> "I was raised in the insurance business, Keyes."
> "You were raised in private schools, Groton, and Harvard. While you were learning how to pull bow oars there, I was studying these tables." (67)

Clearly, the tension between Keyes and Norton is a matter not only of generational difference but of class jealousy as well.

Since Keyes's patronizing explanation of why it can't be suicide is delivered with another employee present, Norton feels he's been shown up and thus, as a way of reasserting his authority, he has to be just as skeptical when Keyes proposes that Nirdlinger's death is murder. When Norton asks him what he's got to go on, Keyes says, "Whoever did this did a perfect job. There's nothing to go on. Just the same, it's murder" (68), and the beneficiary of the policy, says Keyes, is the prime suspect. Prompted by "hunch, instinct, and experience," Keyes recommends they go against practice in this case because "there's a couple of things about this that make me think that practice is" what "they're going to count on, and take advantage of." He suggests they immediately file "an information of suspected murder" against Phyllis, have her arrested and held "the full forty-eight hours incommunicado that the law allows" (69), thus separating her from her unknown accomplice while the police sweat her with everything they've got. But Norton refuses, saying that if the interrogation produced nothing, "she could murder us in a civil suit." Then Norton, implying that he, unlike Keyes (who is simply a department head), must, as president, keep the big picture in mind, points out that they have an advertising budget of a hundred thousand dollars a year publicizing the company "as the friend of the widow and orphan": "We spend all that for goodwill, and then . . . we lay ourselves open to the charge that we'd accuse a woman of *murder* even, rather than pay a just claim" (70).

Norton rejects Keyes's recommendation, and at the coroner's inquest the jury returns a verdict that Nirdlinger died "by a broken neck" in a fall from a train "in a manner unknown to this jury." The verdict surprises Norton, but not Huff, who'd foreseen the company's suicide defense and told Phyllis to bring a minister with her to the inquest on the pretext of having him confer with the undertaker about funeral arrangements. Huff knows that once the jury thinks "it's a question of burial in consecrated ground" (72), they'd never bring in a verdict of suicide.

Though Norton admits the company's suicide defense is sunk after the inquest, he's still not convinced by Keyes's murder theory because, after speaking with the police, who had also suspected murder, he finds they've since "given up that idea," adding tartly, "They've got their books too, Keyes" (73). Nevertheless, Norton says he's not going to pay the Nirdlinger claim, that he's going to force Phyllis to sue, hoping in the meantime some new evidence will turn up. As Keyes and Huff are leaving Norton's office, Keyes, still fuming about what he considers Norton's incompetence, suddenly realizes what the true solution to Nirdlinger's death must be, that Nirdlinger must have been killed somewhere else and his body left by the tracks. And just as suddenly he realizes that Nirdlinger never boarded the train and that the result of the inquest has been doubly disastrous for the company because now they'd have to contend with all "those sworn identifications" of Nirdlinger's corpse by various passengers saying that he was the man they'd seen on the train, contend with them if they went back into court and tried to prove it was someone else. Huff had of course planned on those identifications: "That was why I took such care that nobody on that train got a good look at me. I figured the crutches, the foot, the glasses, the cigar, and imagination would be enough" (75), plus the fact that the first person at the inquest to identify Nirdlinger's corpse would be Phyllis, to get the ball rolling. Noting that old man Norton would have taken his recommendation on how to handle the case, Keyes laments, "If that guy keeps on trying to run this company, the company's sunk. You can't take many body blows like this and last. . . . Just sheer, willful stupidity!" (76). The invocation of what young Norton's father would have done recalls the ending of that earlier scene when the son, in refusing to charge Phyllis with murder, said that he, like his father, would "do the conservative, safe thing, I don't get mixed up with the other kind."

> "Old Man Norton could take a chance."
> "Well I'm not my father!"
> "It's your responsibility." (71)

On that word *responsibility* hinges the difference between Keyes and Huff regarding the boss they both feel superior to, and between Frank Chambers and Huff regarding the alternatives of being boss and beating the boss. Cain surely intends the reader to notice the paralleling of real and symbolic father-son relationships between old man Norton and young Norton and between Keyes and Huff. Keyes thinks young Norton has betrayed his dead father's business legacy by ignoring his example in running the company, an example embodied by Keyes and ignored by young Norton when he fails to take Keyes's advice. Huff, on the other hand, admires and respects Keyes's professional acumen (indeed, fears it), and he also seems to have a real affection for the older man. In many ways he looks on Keyes as a professional father figure. Yet just as Keyes believes young Norton has betrayed his real father in the way he runs the company, so Huff betrays Keyes with his scheme to defraud the company. To the extent that Keyes's repeatedly expressed scorn for young Norton's abilities has contributed to Huff's decision to try to beat the boss, Huff has missed the point of Keyes's objections. Keyes doesn't object to the *role* of the boss, to the concept or necessity of there being someone with ultimate authority and responsibility at work; rather, he objects to the specific occupant of that role, to the role's being gained by inheritance rather than experience and hard work. Keyes is willing to help young Norton learn how to do his job by giving him advice or even do the job in his stead. In contrast, Huff's plan isn't part of a scheme to be boss in Norton's place. Huff's betrayal of his employer, as an attempt to subvert the notion of the boss as better man, strikes a blow at the very role itself.

The Oedipal resonance of Huff's crime—the killing of a husband and father by a younger man in love with the older man's wife—seems only appropriate to the novel's background of betrayed fathers and father figures. Cain had, of course, addressed some of these issues previously in *Postman,* but the added wrinkle there was that the older man whom Frank killed in order to get his wife had also been Frank's boss, a man who had given him a job and generally treated the drifter, if not like a son, then like a younger brother. Although

Frank and Cora plan on her inheriting Nick's diner, Frank doesn't intend to run it. Rather, once Cora's suspended sentence is up, he wants them to sell the diner, take the insurance money, and hit the road together. But Cora, who'd won a high school beauty contest in her native Iowa and a trip to Hollywood, ruefully recalls her arrival in L.A. and her abrupt descent into the food-service business: "I got off the Chief with fifteen guys taking my picture, and two weeks later I was in the hash house" (12). Though she loves Frank, she thinks his idea of the road, with its freedom to go "anywhere we choose" (13), is just another name for the hash house, and adds, "I want to work and be something, that's all" (14). Frank says he wants them to go drifting together because "I've got to get out of here, or I go nuts" (92), but Cora tells him, "You've been trying to make a bum out of me ever since you've known me, but you're not going to do it. . . . We stay here. . . . We amount to something" (93). She plans to use Nick's insurance to fix up the diner, get a liquor license, and have Frank run the place. Though Frank makes various stabs at recovering that total freedom from responsibility he calls "the road," including running off to Mexico with another woman for a week while Cora is away on a trip, Cora ultimately prevails, telling him, first, that she's pregnant and, second, that she's figured out a way for him to be completely free of her if that's what he wants. They'll go to the beach and both swim out as far as they can and if Frank chooses, he can swim back in and leave her there to drown. Of course, he chooses to save her, and driving back, he seems ready to become the proprietor of Nick's business when the auto accident intervenes.

Frank's reluctance to give up his freedom for the responsibilities of being boss and Huff's decision to try to beat rather than become the boss point up a crucial difference between independence and freedom that distinguishes Cain's two best books from Hammett's *The Maltese Falcon* and Chandler's *The Big Sleep*. In becoming their own bosses, Spade and Marlowe each seek economic independence in order to ground independence of thought and action, while their avoidance of entangling personal relationships, their seeking freedom from the responsibilities of a wife and family, are part of a larger discipline, one that subjects the personal to the professional, that places their responsibilities to business partners, employees, or clients and to their own professional code of ethics above their individual lusts for women or wealth. This choice, though self-centered, is not so much selfish as self-defensive, a more or less conscious drawing in of the self's boundaries to those responsibilities each man can be sure of fulfilling.

In contrast, Frank Chambers and Walter Huff seek a more or less capricious freedom from the responsibilities and demands work entails (Chambers from work in general and Huff from a specific job he finds boring and from an employer to whom he feels superior)—an irresponsibility regarding work that's of a piece with their impulsive, spur-of-the-moment adulterous affairs and the murders these lead to, murders of men to whom each of the killers had a prior business obligation, one a boss (Nick), the other a client (Nirdlinger). If the ongoing subject of Cain's fiction, "the wish that comes true," is, as he says, "a terrifying concept," then its terror resides mainly in the usually infantile or adolescent irresponsibility of these wishes.

V

In earlier chapters I suggested that the choice confronting Hammett's and Chandler's protagonists between a man's work and his personal life (one always decided in favor of work in their books) is a conflict that figures significantly for their contemporary F. Scott Fitzgerald. Adumbrated in *The Great Gatsby* (1925), this conflict between a man's career and what Gatsby memorably calls the "just personal" takes center stage in *Tender Is the Night* (1934). As we noted previously, the brilliant, ambitious psychiatrist Dick Diver commits a cardinal sin against his professional code when he marries a patient. Since, in the largely Freudian terms in which the practice of psychiatry is imagined in the novel, the doctor is a father figure for the patient, this marriage symbolically repeats the trauma that had originally precipitated Nicole Warren's mental illness (her father's having committed incest with her when she was a teenager), a repetitive psychological structure whose consequences Dick must face when the young movie star Rosemary Hoyt enters his life. Rosemary is the daughter of a doctor, and though Dick tries at first to damp her attraction to him and control his attraction to her by assuming a fatherly stance, he ultimately repeats with Rosemary the same "father-daughter" coupling he had previously enacted with Nicole.

Dick's emotional bond to Nicole as his wife clouds his objective judgment of her as his patient, and he finds himself organizing his professional life as a psychiatrist more and more around providing Nicole with a supportive environment. He finally gives up his practice and part ownership of the Swiss sanitorium (which Nicole's money had secured for him) as well as his research and writing, realizing that whatever professional life he has left has been reduced to being simply his wife's doctor. As his working life collapses, so too does Dick's self-esteem, while at the same time he increasingly resents Nicole's psychological and emotional neediness and her ever-increasing inherited wealth, which makes him feel like a kept man.

At one point in the novel (bk. 2, chap. 14), when Dick is still trying to make a go of the Swiss sanitorium, Fitzgerald follows him through a typical workday to give the reader a sense of how talented and dedicated a psychiatrist he is and how much his personal dilemma has begun to undermine his work. And Fitzgerald uses this same day-in-the-life ploy in his next (and last) novel, the unfinished *The Last Tycoon* (1941), where the narrator, Cecilia Brady, spends the whole of chapter 3 trying to give the reader "a glimpse of him [Monroe Stahr] functioning" as chief of production at a movie studio,[8] Stahr's character being modeled on Irving Thalberg, M-G-M's head of production and husband of movie star Norma Shearer. With the death of *his* movie-star wife Minna Davis, Stahr's personal life had virtually ended, and he threw himself totally into his work. Fitzgerald's description of Stahr's workday and of the behind-the-scenes activity of filmmaking are some of the best parts of the book, as well as some of the best writing in all of Fitzgerald. The book's main action, centering on Stahr's working life—his attempt to retain control of the studio (i.e., to stay boss) by simultaneously fending off the efforts of Communists to infiltrate the writers' union and of his partner Pat Brady to force him out—is counterpointed by the sudden reawakening of his personal life when he meets and suddenly falls in love with a woman who uncannily resembles his dead wife. It seems clear from Fitzgerald's notes for the novel's unfinished portion that the ensuing conflict between Stahr's work and his personal life would have been the meat of the completed book.

When Edmund Wilson published the unfinished manuscript of *The Last Tycoon* in 1941, he included as an appendix to the text many of Fitzgerald's notes for the unfinished portion, among which was the now-famous line "There are no second acts in American lives."[9] If what Fitzgerald meant by this comment, as I have always assumed, is that Americans, especially American men, have trouble developing emotionally or intellectually, trouble maturing, that they often grow old without ever growing up, then Fitzgerald himself had to face, in the years after publishing *The Great Gatsby,* the difficulty both in his professional life of continuing to grow his talent after the early triumph of that novel and in his personal life of becoming a mature, responsible adult, a husband and father who had to support and care for an emotionally erratic, and at last, mentally ill, wife, and raise a young daughter, and who had to do all this while making a living and battling alcoholism. Clearly, the strategy he adopted in trying to mature his talent in *Tender Is the Night* and *The Last Tycoon* was to make these novels' central subject the problem of an American man's becoming fully adult, of his having a second act in both his professional and personal lives as these two impinged on each other.

Fitzgerald understood that the very stuff of his personal life (his love affair with Zelda, their marriage, and what came after) had always been the basic material of his life as a fiction writer. His professional and personal lives were inextricably entangled precisely because he'd made the latter the subject of the former. Where Dr. Diver had merged these two spheres by marrying his patient, Fitzgerald had merged them by marrying the principal female character in his fiction, a situation he characterizes in Dick's case (and perhaps his own as well) with a reference to Svengali and Trilby. Whereas Nicole's mental illness had played havoc both with Dick's career and their home life, her money bringing about his final emasculation, Zelda's instability had created constant turmoil in Fitzgerald's life as a writer and as a husband and father, and her increasing jealousy of his work (both because of the time it took away from his being with her and because of her own artistic ambitions) had almost, Fitzgerald felt by the time he finished *Tender,* unmanned him.

The crisis came during the period when Zelda was in therapy at the Phipps Clinic in Baltimore and started writing a novel about insanity, which Scott felt poached on the same material he was using for *Tender Is the Night.* At a joint interview with Zelda and her psychiatrist in May 1933, Fitzgerald said he wanted Zelda to stop writing about this subject, considering her use of this material a measure of her hostility toward him and her jealousy of his work and adding that she thought she had the right "to destroy me completely in order to satisfy herself."[10] In *A Moveable Feast* (1964) Hemingway claimed to have discerned this jealousy early on and warned Scott. In the scene in which Fitzgerald consults Hemingway about Zelda's accusations of Scott's penile inadequacy, Hemingway tells him that Zelda is saying this "to put you out of business. That's the oldest way in the world to put people out of business. . . . Zelda just wants to destroy you."[11]

After the agonizing struggle of finishing *Tender Is the Night* and its relative lack of financial success, Fitzgerald spent the rest of the 1930s caring for Zelda, raising his daughter, struggling with drink and depression, and trying to work his way out of debt by writing for the movies. When he began his last novel at the end of the decade, a novel that, judging by the finished chapters, would have been his third masterpiece along with *Gatsby* and *Tender,* he chose as his main character a man who had been a great success as a combination businessman/artist but who found himself threatened on all sides by people who wanted to put him out of business, threatened at just the moment when his long-dormant personal life was reawakening through the love of a young woman. Stahr's struggle to stay in the picture business and the way the sharpness of his professional judgment becomes clouded by events in his personal life was a subject related to, and drawing its inspiration and energy from, Fitzgerald's own effort to stay in business both as a serious fiction writer, by writing this novel, and as a human being, through his love affair with Sheilah Graham—an affair over which the memory of Scott's life with Zelda must have hovered like a ghost image much as the image of Stahr's dead wife hung over his new love Kathleen.

The similarity between Hammett's and Chandler's fiction, on the one hand, and Fitzgerald's, on the other, regarding this conflict between professional and personal throws into stronger relief the difference between Cain's work and that of the two detective writers. For while that insider's view of an insurance salesman's workday Cain provides in *Double Indemnity* might seem to have much in common with what Fitzgerald does in *Tender Is the Night* and *The Last Tycoon* in showing us, respectively, the workday of a clinical psychiatrist and the production chief of a Hollywood studio, these demonstrations are made to entirely different ends. Where Dick Diver and Monroe Stahr would certainly have agreed with Hammett's Continental Op that "liking work makes you want to do it as well as you can,"[12] Walter Huff would say instead, "Doing work as well as you can doesn't necessarily mean (or make) you like it." And precisely because no ringing endorsements of his profession characterize Huff—rather, just the opposite—the conflict between personal and professional in Cain's fiction more closely resembles that in Fitzgerald's: it is a real conflict that could go either way, not a setup.

Unlike Hammett and Chandler, who were committed to writing a genre linked to a specific profession, a genre in which the main character's line of work or the main character himself (as with the Continental Op or Marlowe) carries over from book to book, Cain was not so committed, and consequently there is no front-loaded bias to the professional winning out over the personal. When Huff allows himself to be seduced by Phyllis into using his professional knowledge of insurance fraud to help murder her husband, he does what Sam

Spade won't do at the end of *The Maltese Falcon* when he refuses to betray his code and put his professional expertise at Brigid's service just because he happens to be "nuts about her." In effect, Spade refuses to let his life-as-having (the possession of Brigid) overwhelm his life-as-doing (the specialized knowledge that makes him what he is). The very possibility of this conflict between professional and personal tilting in the latter's favor, as it does when Dick Diver's brilliant career as a psychiatrist is destroyed by his marriage, or as it might well have done in the unfinished *Last Tycoon* if Stahr had lost control of the studio because of his love affair with Kathleen, is the essential difference between the hard-boiled quality of Cain's novels and those of Hammett and Chandler.

Who's the Boss?

W. R. Burnett's *High Sierra*

I

If Hammett's and Chandler's best detective fiction has as its underlying theme the main character's becoming or staying his own boss and Cain's best has as its the main character's trying to beat or outwit his employer, then W. R. Burnett's *High Sierra* (1940) situates itself in relation to these works by addressing the question of who's actually the boss and whether bosses are necessary.

During his long working life, William Riley Burnett (1899–1982) enjoyed equally successful careers as novelist and screenwriter. A native of Ohio and descendant of a family long active in state politics, Burnett, after being turned down for army service in World War I and briefly studying journalism at Ohio State, worked in vaudeville, insurance sales, and in factories before he got, through his family's political connections, a job with the Ohio Bureau of Labor Statistics in the early 1920s. Finding the work boring, he set out to learn the craft of fiction in his spare time. Realizing his son's unhappiness as a state employee, Burnett's father gave him a job in 1927 as desk clerk at the Northmere Hotel in Chicago, one of the repossessed hotels the elder Burnett managed, and young Burnett found in the city a subject to match his growing ability as a storyteller. Burnett's work at the hotel brought him in contact with small-time underworld figures, and through an acquaintance he began learning as much as he could about the Chicago mobs, research that resulted in his first novel, *Little Caesar* (1929), the story of the rise and fall of Rico Bandello. The novel received glowing reviews, was a main selection of the Literary Guild, and in 1930 Warner Bros. turned it into a movie that made Edward G. Robinson a star in the role of Rico. That same year Warners offered Burnett a screenwriting contract, and his dual career began.

Over his working life Burnett would publish more than thirty-five books and have as many more screenplays (on which he did both credited and uncredited work) produced as films, among these Howard Hawks's *Scarface* (1932); John Ford's *The Whole Town's Talking* (1935); Raoul Walsh's *High Sierra* (1941), on which he collaborated with John Huston; Frank Tuttle's *This Gun for Hire* (1942); John Farrow's *Wake Island* (1942), for which he received an Academy Award nomination; John Huston's *The Asphalt Jungle* (1950); and John Sturges's *The Great Escape* (1963), for which he received another Academy Award nomination. Of Burnett's novels, the three best are *High Sierra, The Asphalt Jungle* (1949), and *Little Caesar,* in that order. In this chapter I focus on the first, invoking the other two for comparison.

II

High Sierra is the story of Roy Earle, "the Indiana bank robber and last of the old Dillinger mob,"[1] pardoned from a life sentence in prison through the corrupt intervention of Big Mac M'Gann. M'Gann wants Earle to lead a gang of inexperienced young crooks in robbing a luxury hotel in Tropico Springs, California (a setting modeled on Palm Springs). As the novel opens, Roy is driving cross-country from the Midwest and remembering during the long trip through the Nevada-California desert his boyhood on an Indiana farm. Earle's memories of his bucolic younger years (comprising the book's entire first chapter) "were of that far-off time, a generation ago" and "seemed to a worried man heading downhill like the morning of the world, a true Golden Age." In these memories "it was always summer" (1), memories of the swimming-hole, the Saturday afternoon baseball game, his Aunt Minnie and her "home-made ice cream in the summer-house," and "those long hot evenings" when "Roma Stover, the yellow-haired girl from across the road, came sidling over shyly" and the two would swing on "the big farm gate" and laugh at noth-

ing (3–4). Suggesting the nostalgic iconography of a Norman Rockwell painting (indeed, at one point Roy even cites a poem by the nineteenth-century Indiana bard James Whitcomb Riley to describe Aunt Minnie), these memories
are meant not only to evoke the complexity of Earle's interior life, distinguish-
ing the aging outlaw from a more superficially drawn gangster-type like *Little
Caesar*'s young Rico Bandello, a character driven solely by his desire to be the
toughest in the gang and end up as boss, but also to provide an insight into
Roy's motives as the novel progresses, motives very much at odds with what
one would expect from an experienced bank robber and ex-con. Further, Roy's
memories set up at the start an opposition between nineteenth-century-rural
and twentieth-century-urban America (the world he was raised in versus the
world he now lives in) that gives his character dramatic tension and his story
a sociological/historical dimension. This opposition in Roy's psyche between
the summer fields of a family farm and the city streets of fast cars, machine
guns, and police shootouts makes him seem, says one character, like "a cross
between a farmer and a refined gorilla" (5).

Earle is headed for a fishing camp in the mountains near Tropico Springs
to meet the other members of the gang Big Mac's put together for the job, two
small-timers named Red Hattery and Babe Kozak. Earle's role as a professional
is, says Big Mac, to "kind of hold these jitterbugs down. Ain't one of 'em over
twenty-five. Punks" (8). The other member of the gang, Louis Mendoza, the
night desk clerk at the Tropico Hotel, is the inside man for the robbery. When
Earle arrives at the fishing camp, he finds that Kozak has brought along Marie
Garson, a former L.A. dance-hall girl, and he tells Red, the leader of the group
up to that point, "give her some dough and send her back to L.A." (26). When
Red informs Kozak and Marie, Kozak says, "He's not the boss no more than we
are" (28). In spite of Earle's reputation for toughness as a member of the Dillinger gang, Kozak is unimpressed: "You can have your Roy Earle. . . . He may
be a powerhouse to some people, but he's a blowed-out fuse to me." Even Red
admits to being surprised by Earle's appearance: "Can you feature him being
Roy Earle! Why, his hair's getting gray around the edges and he looks sort of
old and he's kind of fat around the middle. Only he ain't exactly fat, just kind
of soft." But Marie disagrees, "I say he's got a hard eye on him. . . . He's tough,
don't you worry" (27).

At the novel's start, Earle is only thirty-seven, but his six years in prison
have prematurely aged him. At Earle's first meeting with Big Mac after his
pardon, Mac is "so upset . . . by the change in Roy's appearance" that he doesn't

"even shake hands or speak," while Earle, with "an allgone sensation in the pit of his stomach," has to put "his hands into his coat pockets so Mac wouldn't see how they shook" (7). Prison has wrecked Earle's nerves, and on his solitary drive out west he suffers repeatedly from night sweats, loneliness, and bouts of depression. Earle has become "prison-conditioned," feeling he doesn't "belong with the people outside." He doesn't "know how to act with them" (18), and as he drives through the Nevada-California desert "his chronic sense of loneliness" is "increased by this bleak and deserted country" (21) and by his sense of the "indifference of nature" (20). The youthful memories that preoccupy him during the day invade his dreams at night, troubling his sleep. Earle's stretch in the pen has not only aged him, it has made him confront the limitations of his own mortality, the flood of boyhood memories being part of the introspection and the predictable stocktaking of one's life that a sense of growing older brings. But Earle's time in prison has also left him with doubts about how well he'll function as boss of this young gang of small-time crooks. When Mac tells him about bossing the Tropico Springs job, Earle thinks that what he really needs is "a long rest" instead, but since he owes Mac his freedom, he's got to accept his role.

If Earle has doubts about himself, he senses on meeting the "jitterbugs" that they have doubts about him as well: "these three kids, none of them over twenty-five; all of them members of a generation which was not his own, all thinking probably that he was an old phutz and a has-been" (25). But Roy soon convinces Red and Babe he's in charge. Something in his eyes and in his manner makes clear he's the last person in the world you want to cross. Meanwhile, Marie, told that Earle wants her to leave, goes to Roy to plead her case. She says she knows about the Tropico job but that she didn't learn it from Red or Babe but from Louis Mendoza: "Louis thinks he's a bearcat with women and made a strong play for me behind Babe's back. I just kidded him along and he bragged what a big shot he was and said we'd all be wearing diamonds. . . . So Louis's your headache, not us." Earle decides she can stay, thinking, "That dame's got something on the ball. She may be of more use to me than the punks" (30).

As their acquaintance develops, Roy and Marie discover they have much in common. At one point, Marie asks him how he kept from going nuts in prison, and he says a lot of guys did.

> "But not me. I got the jitters bad, I'll admit. I still got 'em. But all I thought about was a crash out. . . ."

"I get it. You always hope you can get out. That keeps you going. . . . I know. I been trying to crash out all my life." (36–37)

Marie says that first she crashed out of her family and her abusive father in San Francisco and came to L.A. to work in a dime-a-dance joint but got "sick of being pawed by Mexicans and Filipinos and a lot of stinking old men. So Babe come along and I crashed out." When Roy asks her if she's "thinking up another crash," Marie says "Maybe" (37).

Though hooking up with Roy is what she has in mind, at this point Roy's not interested in Marie because on his drive across the desert he'd met a young girl name Velma traveling with her grandparents, Pa and Ma Goodhue, from Ohio to L.A., and he can't get her off his mind. Not only do the grandparents remind Earle of his own folks, but blonde-haired Velma reminds him of his dead boyhood sweetheart Roma Stover. Roy's interest in the girl is further engaged because she has a clubfoot and walks with a limp—not that Roy is a foot fetishist, but where he couldn't do anything about Roma's dying, he can, in unconsciously projecting her image on Velma, do something about Velma's being crippled, thus curing (and so symbolically restoring) a person who represents the dead world of his past and who will hopefully give him renewed access to that innocent, rural world and its values.

As embodiments of Roy's own midwestern background, the Goodhues and Velma become unwitting psychological counters: Roy arranges and pays for an operation to correct Velma's clubfoot with the idea of ultimately proposing marriage to her, seeing such a union and the extended family it would bring as a way of becoming again the man he'd been twenty years before. With this in mind, Roy begins to think of the Tropico Springs job as his last big caper, its take large enough to let him go straight with Velma and her family. But the Goodhues have an additional significance for Roy and his past. Not only had they been small, midwestern farmers like Roy's folks, but they'd also lost their farm to a bank during the Depression and, as such, evoke a class and region favorably disposed to the Dillinger gang's bank-robbing. As Big Mac and Roy remember:

"When Johnny was running wild, a lot of people were with him. Back in Indiana, Ohio, and Illinois half the farmers were getting their farms took away from them. The bankers foreclosed till there was nothing left to foreclose. And when Johnny'd knock over one of them banks for a big wad, the farmers would yell: 'Attaboy, Johnny. You're doing fine'". . . .

"That's no lie. Why, half the country people in the Midwest were pals of ours. They'd never turn us up. Johnny used to go home and have dinner with his old man every once in a while, and he'd sit out on the front porch . . . right in broad daylight." (67)

Clearly, Roy feels the Goodhues are people who'll understand if their prospective in-law ever has to reveal his past.

Pa and Ma Goodhue's situation functions in the narrative as a counterpoint to that of Roy and Marie. Just as Roy says that the hope and constant planning for "crashing out" kept him from going nuts in prison (this last big caper to bankroll his going straight being simply another instance of this dream), and just as Marie had crashed out of her family and then the L.A. dance hall and now plans to crash out of her abusive relationship with Babe Kozak, so the Goodhues have followed the reverse trajectory—from the independence of owning their own farm, to losing it to a bank, to moving out to California and living in the cramped house of their married daughter. When Roy brings his friend Doc Parker to the daughter's house to examine Velma's foot, he's surprised by the change in the Goodhues: "Pa and Ma were not like themselves. They seemed shrunken and very old. It was this room maybe. Or maybe they were beginning to feel their dependence. Folks used to a free existence didn't take to living off of people or being handed charity. It did something to them" (94).

This sense of financial dependence as the loss of "free existence" intersects the novel's questioning both of the real boss's identity and of whether bosses are necessary. When Marie asks Roy how he "got mixed up in bank robbery and stuff," Roy says,

> I just never seemed to fit in no place. I tried helping Elmer [Roy's brother] on the farm. But that wasn't no life for me, except a man was his own boss. Even in school the teacher used to gripe me. And I got a bellyful of bosses before I was through. . . . I worked as a shop-clerk in Indianapolis for over a year. But there was a straw-boss over me named Crandall. He got to riding me. He rode everybody and they took it. But not me. One day I cooled him off and got canned. Same in Ohio. I worked in a chain shop and made pretty good money. But the boss didn't like me and began to give me the wrong end of the stick, so I told him off and quit. Them guys like you to be meek and mild, so they'll feel big. That was the trouble. I felt just as big as they did—bigger; even if they was the boss. . . . Pretty soon I was back working on the farm with Elmer. Elmer's steady. I ain't. I like to keep moving. I can't stand doing the same thing day after day. (90–91)

Roy recalls his father saying, "Roy's not like the rest of us. . . . He's restless and won't settle down," a trait, the father thinks, Roy got from his Uncle Will, who "couldn't stay in any one town over a day or so" and who, though "a good workman," ended up "just a bum" (4–5).

This restless energy that leads to a life of crime is shared by the main character in Burnett's first novel, *Little Caesar.* In a few short years Rico Bandello goes from being a yegg from Youngstown, Ohio, to the rising star of the Chicago mob world, having forced out his boss, Sam Vettori, and taken over his gang, run the gambler Little Arnie out of town to acquire his operation, then cut a deal with the Big Boy, John Michael O'Doul, for political protection that will allow him to take over the whole Northside from Pete Montana: "Rico lived at a tension. His nervous system was geared up to such a point that he was never sleepy, never felt the desire to relax, was always keenly alive. He did not average over five hours sleep a night and as soon as he opened his eyes he was awake. When he sat in a chair he never thrust out his feet and lolled, but sat rigid and alert. He walked, ate, took his pleasures in the same manner. What distinguished him from his associates was his inability to live in the present. He was like a man on a long train journey to a promised land. To him the present was but a dingy way-station; he had his eyes on the end of the journey. This is the mental attitude of a man destined for success."[2]

But if Rico in his twenties is unable to live in the present because his eyes are always on the future, Roy, prematurely old in his late thirties, is in the opposite fix. When Doc Parker tells Roy he's foolish to dream of marrying the innocent farm girl Velma and settling down, he reminds him of what John Dillinger said about men like himself and Roy: "He said you were just rushing toward death. Get yourself a hot young tommy you can keep moving with. And when they catch up with you, what does it matter?" (91). But Roy says, "Maybe I ain't got a future. But I got a present and that's what I'm interested in" (92).

Where Roy, with his animus against bosses but with all the qualities that make for a natural leader, reluctantly agrees to head the gang for the Tropico Springs job, Rico sets his sights on, and happily directs all his ruthless energy toward, becoming boss of the Chicago underworld, the universally acknowledged Mr. Big, with his picture in the papers, his name widely known and feared. But in *High Sierra* we are confronted not only with Roy's reluctance to be boss but also with the novel's problematic sense of who the boss really *is.* When Roy first arrives at the fishing camp, Babe Kozak argues that Roy's "not the boss no more than we are" (28), and similarly, when Red tells Louis Mendoza that with Roy "bossing things, we're a cinch," Louis says,

"Who said he was bossing things?" . . .
    "Nobody said so. He just is."
    "Like hell he is. Mr. M'Gann's the boss. Earle hasn't got a dime. He just works for M'Gann." (46)

According to Louis, M'Gann is the boss because he's put up the money for the heist, and Earle is a hired man just like them. But when the force of Roy's personality is brought to bear on Louis, he knuckles under, acknowledging that Roy is calling the shots. Yet after the robbery, when he takes the stolen jewelry to Big Mac's apartment and finds Mac dead of a heart attack, Roy, following Mac's written instructions in the event of trouble, ends up talking to a small-time fence named Art, who gives him the lowdown. Where Roy had thought Big Mac was the brains, putting up the money to spring him from prison and bankrolling the operation, Art tells him that Mac was broke and deeply in debt. Mac had simply overheard Louis shooting his mouth off one day about all the jewelry in the hotel during high season and how easy it would be to knock over. Mac took the idea for the heist to Ed Seidel, "the A-1 guy" (153) in L.A., who put up the money and was going to fence the jewelry, but with the heat after the robbery, Ed decides to take a run-out powder for Honolulu. Art tells Roy: "I guess you know that Max, in Kansas City, is the big noise behind this caper. He and Ed, that is; and Ed's out now. Mac was the engineer, that's all; and I'm strictly petty larceny with a cheap cut-in. Max's flying out. He got's guts and the heat won't scare him" (165). Though Max eventually arrives in L.A., Roy doesn't live long enough even to see him.

Trying to find the boss in *High Sierra* is like going through a box with a series of false bottoms, but throughout this regression of bosses Roy's attitude toward the idea of a boss remains constant, rising at the end to political statement. Roy asks Marie why, if he as a bank robber is called a criminal, the same isn't true of "a gypping banker; a crooked judge; coppers raking the community for a racket they can get a take on; a big-shot official selling jobs—stuff like that"? He continues: "A few guys have got all the dough in this country. Millions of people ain't got enough to eat. Not because there ain't any food, but because they got no money. Somebody else has got it all. O.K. Why don't all them people who haven't got any dough get together and take the dough? It's a cinch. A bank looks pretty tough, don't it? O.K. Give me a chopper and a couple of guys and I'll loot the biggest bank in the U.S.A. I'm just one guy. What could ten million do?" When Marie says they don't do it because "they're all scared" and "anyway, that's communism or something," Roy replies, "O.K. So what? Like in prison. A guy would get to talking like I am and some guy would yell: 'Communist!' and it would shut him up. But that don't scare me. Call it what you like. It's still good sense" (185).

III

In contrast, *Little Caesar's* Rico Bandello never saw a boss he didn't like—as long as he could push him aside and take his place. What is most striking about Burnett's first novel is how much it has in common with Fitzgerald's *The Great Gatsby*. It's as if Burnett's book, published four years after *Gatsby*, had separated the underworld portion of Gatsby's character and past (only implied in Fitzgerald's novel) from the naive, idealistic part, which drives his quest to regain Daisy Buchanan, and made the former the focus of *Little Caesar*. Nevertheless, the similarities between Gatsby and Rico are numerous. Each is marked by the same restless energy, a quality that Burnett characterizes in Rico's case as "the mental attitude of a man destined for success" and that Fitzgerald evokes in Nick Carraway's description of Gatsby "balancing himself on the dashboard of his car with that resourcefulness of movement that is so peculiarly American—that comes, I suppose, . . . with the formless grace of our nervous, sporadic games. This quality was continually breaking through his punctilious manner in the shape of restlessness. He was never quite still; there was always a tapping foot somewhere or the impatient opening and closing of a hand."[3]

This restless energy has served each man well, enabling him to rise quickly from his humble origins to wealth and visibility. Gatsby brags to Nick about his mansion, "It took me just three years to earn the money that bought it" (71), while Rico, after cutting a deal with the Big Boy to take control of the Northside, thinks admiringly of his own progress: "five years ago" I "wasn't nobody to speak of; just a lonely yegg sticking up chain-stores and filling-stations" (212–13). The goal of Gatsby's Horatio-Alger dreams is, of course, embodied by Daisy and the world of class and wealth she represents, a world symbolically evoked for him by Daisy's "beautiful house" in Louisville which had "a ripe mystery about it, a hint of bedrooms upstairs more beautiful and cool than other bedrooms, of gay and radiant activities taking place through its corridors and of romances that were not musty and laid away already in lavender but fresh and breathing and redolent of this year's shining motor cars and of dances whose flowers were scarcely withered" (116).

Gatsby had encountered this world before, "had come in contact with such people but always with indiscernible barbed wire between," yet with the war and the "invisible cloak" his officer's uniform had thrown over "a penniless young man without a past," Gatsby had found himself "in Daisy's house by a colossal accident," and "eventually he took Daisy one still October night, took her because he had no real right to touch her hand." He'd taken her "under false pretenses" by letting "her believe that he was a person from much the same strata as herself" (116). When the army shipped Gatsby overseas, Daisy "vanished into her rich house, into her rich, full life, leaving Gatsby—nothing" (117), and Gatsby set out to win his way back to the world Daisy represented, a quest that led him to Meyer Wolfshiem and his underworld activities as the only means for "a penniless young man" to reach that goal in three short years.

Like Gatsby, Rico too is fascinated by the world of high society but, as one would expect, in a much cruder fashion, more in keeping with his character's lack of any imaginative, idealistic component. Shown at one point reading a magazine story "about a rich society girl who fell in love with a bootlegger," Rico, says Burnett, "read everything he could find that had anything to do with society. He was fascinated by a stratum of existence which seemed so remote and unreal to him. The men of this level were 'saps' and 'softies' to him, but he envied them their women. He had seen them getting out of limousines at the doors of Gold Coast hotels. He had seen them, magnificently dressed, insolent, inaccessible, walking up the carpets under the canvas marquees. The doormen would bow. The women would disappear. Rico hated them. They were so arrogant and self-sufficient, and they did not know that there was such a person in the world as Rico" (78–79). Where Daisy "vanished into her rich house," the insolent and inaccessible society women "disappear" into the Gold Coast hotels that represent their lives' mysterious fullness, and the sense of the class barrier between observer and observed (that "indiscernible barbed wire between," in Nick words) is evoked by the bowing doormen who admit the arrogant, self-sufficient women but who would surely bar anyone who looked like a Youngstown yegg.

As Gatsby needed a mansion lavishly appointed and always filled with the brightest people at his parties to show Daisy that the man she'd loved in Louisville had become "a person of much the same strata as herself," so Rico, when he is about to gain ascendancy on the Northside, realizes he'll have to acquire trappings appropriate to his new position. Invited to dinner at the Big Boy's apartment, a signal honor in the gang world indicating that he's arrived, Rico has to wear a tuxedo for the first time in his life. Though he objects to the get-up, saying "All I need is a napkin over my arm," still, when he looks in the mirror, "the enormous white shirtfront, the black silk coat lapels, the neatly tied white tie dazzled him" (206–7). At dinner

> the magnificence of the Big Boy's apartment crushed Rico. He stared at the big pictures of old time guys in their gold frames; at the silver and glass ware on the serving table; at the high, carved chairs. Lord, why, it was like a hop dream.
>
> He shook his head slowly.
>
> "Some dump you got here," he said.
>
> "Yeah," said the Big Boy, glancing negligently about him, "and I sure paid for it." (207)

The Big Boy gives Rico a brief inventory of his apartment's choicest objects, along with their cost, each one more expensive than the last, and explains, "I got a spell about two years ago. I had a pot full of money and I thought, well, other guys that ain't got as much dough as I got put on a front, so why shouldn't I? Sure, I could buy and sell guys that's got three homes and a couple of chugwagons. So I got a guy down at a big store, . . . one of them decorators, to pick me out a swell apartment and fix it up A-1" (208). The tour Gatsby gives Daisy and Nick of his mansion on the afternoon Nick invites Daisy over for tea is only slightly less vulgar than the Big Boy's exhibition of his possessions—but only because Gatsby doesn't quote the price of everything. Inside they wander through "Marie Antoinette music rooms and Restoration salons" and what Nick calls "the Merton College Library," and then upstairs "through period bedrooms swathed in rose and lavender silk . . . , through dressing rooms and poolrooms, and bathrooms with sunken baths," and finally into Gatsby's own bedroom, where he opens two cabinets and displays "his massed suits and dressing gowns and ties, and his shirts piled like bricks in stacks a dozen high," then begins throwing the shirts on a table in front of his visitors, "shirts of sheer linen and thick silk and fine flannel . . . with stripes and scrolls and plaids in coral and apple green and lavender and faint orange with monograms in Indian blue" (71–72). And just as the Big Boy had "a guy down at a . . . store, . . . one of them decorators," furnish his apartment, so Gatsby also had professional help, not just with his mansion's decor, but with his wardrobe: There's "a man in England" who buys his clothes, sending "over a selection of things at the beginning of each season, spring and fall" (72).

Judging from one further shared detail in the descriptions of the Big Boy's apartment and Gatsby's mansion, one gathers the resemblance between the two scenes of vulgar display is no mere coincidence: In his inventory of classy items, the Big Boy tells Rico, "I got a library too and a lot of other stuff that ain't worth a damn. I was talking to a rich guy the other day and he said I was a damn fool to buy real books because he had a library twice as big as mine and dummy books. What the hell! If a guy's gonna have a library, why, I say do it right. . . . I got so damn many books it gives me a headache just to look at 'em through the glass. Shakespeare and all that stuff" (208–9). One can't help but recall the moment when Nick and Jordan Baker, wandering into Gatsby's library during one of his parties, find an inebriated guest "with enormous owl-eyed spectacles" examining the books and announcing they're "absolutely real—have pages and everything. I thought they'd be a nice durable cardboard" but they're "a bona fide piece of printed matter. It fooled me. This fella's a regular Belasco" (37–38) (referring to the Broadway producer David Belasco, renowned for the meticulous realism of his stage sets). Though Owl Eyes is amazed that the books are authentic, his comparison of Gatsby to Belasco still suggests that their reality doesn't tell us anything real about Gatsby's taste or intellect, that the library and its contents are a stage set in Gatsby's acting out a dream of class, an act that, as Owl Eyes notes appreciatively, Gatsby doesn't overplay: "It's a triumph. What thoroughness! What realism! Knew when to stop too—didn't cut the pages" (38).

Besides the larger similarities between *Little Caesar* and *The Great Gatsby,* there are several shared grace notes suggesting that Burnett clearly had Fitzgerald's novel in mind when writing his first book. For example, one of Rico's accomplices (whom he later kills to keep from squealing) enters a restaurant where "three Italians were playing cards at the table in back" while "up front a mechanical piano ground out 'The Rosary'" (22). "The Rosary" was a sentimental song from the 1890s, written by Ethelbert Nevin and Robert Cameron Rogers, that had regained popularity in the 1920s. Burnett's use of the song in this gangster milieu reminds us of the scene in which Nick goes to Meyer Wolfshiem's office, trying to get him to attend Gatsby's funeral. The secretary tells Nick that Wolfshiem's not in, but "this was obviously untrue for some one had begun to whistle 'The Rosary,' tunelessly, inside" (132). Wolfshiem's whistling this quasi-religious popular song is meant to evoke, yet again, that combined sense of vulgar sentimentalism and ruthless opportunism Fitzgerald had established for this character earlier on. As Gatsby explains to Nick when Wolfshiem becomes maudlin during lunch remembering his old friend Rosy Rosenthal's murder, "This is one of his sentimental days. He's quite a character around New York—a denizen of Broadway" and then adds, "He's the man who fixed the World Series back in 1919" (58). As evoked by Fitzgerald, American gangsters exhibit not so much the banality of evil as its sentimentality, a combination of sentiment and inhumanity suggested perhaps in Burnett's novel by its being a *mechanical* piano that plays "The Rosary" while the three men play cards. When Wolfshiem stops whistling "The Rosary" and responds to Nick's request about Gatsby's funeral, he once again becomes sentimental over a dead friend: "'My memory goes back to when first I met him'. . . . The hair in his nostrils quivered slightly and as he shook his head his eyes filled with tears" (133). But as a matter of business policy, Wolfshiem's not going to the funeral.

If the numerous similarities between *Little Caesar* and *The Great Gatsby* are intentional, then the comparison these similarities invite was doubtless meant to show that an underworld character who buys a mansion and gives lavish parties in an imaginative quest to recover the woman he loves and his own past is a fantasy whose opposing reality is a racketeer like Rico, a ruthlessly energetic gun thug for whom murder is not a moral but a business decision. As Burnett says of the diminutive, vain Rico, he "was a simple man. He loved but three things: himself, his hair, and his gun. He took excellent care of all three" (31). But perhaps the difference between Gatsby and Rico is also a function of their being two different types of underworld figure.

Where Rico is an Al Capone–type gangster, Gatsby is much more of a high-toned swindler and bootlegger, a perfect front man. Wolfshiem says that when he first met Gatsby, "I saw right away he was a fine appearing gentlemanly young man and when he told me he was an Oggsford I knew I could use him good" (133). And Tom Buchanan, who has Gatsby investigated, says, "I picked him for a bootlegger the first time I saw him" (104), though now, says Tom, he's into something so big that it makes "that drug store business" look like "small change" (105), a new racket that, judging from the telephone call Nick receives at Gatsby's home after his death, involves trafficking in stolen bonds.

Gatsby's two known underworld activities—bootlegging and stock swindling—were no doubt based on those of two real-life figures on whom Gatsby was modeled, Max Gerlach and Edward Fuller, both of whom lived in Great

Neck, Long Island, during the period the Fitzgeralds were there (fall 1922 to spring 1924). Gerlach was apparently a gentleman bootlegger or rumrunner fond of using the expression "old sport" in addressing his customers,[4] while Fuller, with his partner William McGee, ran a brokerage firm, which they systematically looted for several million dollars until they declared bankruptcy in June 1922. Fuller went through four trials in New York that were front page news before his final conviction, and "on the eve of his third trial, Fuller and his accomplices were arrested on a fresh charge" of running so-called bucket shops or phony brokerage offices, "hawking nonexistent stocks by telephone and preparing to form a new firm to issue worthless shares."[5] Further, Fuller was a known associate of the gambler Arnold Rothstein, the man reputed to have fixed the 1919 World Series and who was the model for Meyer Wolfshiem. Given Gatsby's drugstore bootlegging operation with Wolfshiem, one is tempted to see the detail of Rico's reading "a story about a rich society girl who fell in love with a bootlegger" (78) as Burnett's subtle acknowledgment of the way Fitzgerald's story had shaped by contraries the main character in Burnett's first novel.

IV

If, as I've suggested, the echoes of *Gatsby* in *Little Caesar* intentionally invite a comparison to demonstrate that a real gangster is an essentially one-dimensional character (someone like Rico, who doesn't drink or have any deep feelings for women, a "simple man" endowed with enormous energy and rigorously limited interests), a one-dimensionality created by stripping away from the equally energetic, driven figure of Gatsby his "extraordinary gift for hope, his romantic readiness" (6), his "gorgeous" imagination, and his hopelessly idealized love, then we can see that when Burnett, eleven years after *Little Caesar*, came to create a much more complex figure in the bank robber Roy Earle, he put back into *this* character many of the Gatsbylike qualities he had left out of Rico, the most important being the character's idealization of a woman whose longed-for possession holds the imagined promise of restoring the past and his former self.

Clearly, whatever Daisy was when Gatsby first met and fell in love with her, she had become, during the years of his lonely vigil, largely a function of his imagination, an ideal counter for that world of wealth and class that fired his boyhood ambitions, as well as for the dream of returning to that moment in the past when they'd parted, to his becoming again the man he was before his involvement in the rackets. When Nick warns Gatsby, "You can't repeat the past," Gatsby replies incredulously, "Why of course you can!" Nick says that Gatsby "talked a lot about the past and I gathered that he wanted to recover something, some idea of himself perhaps, that had gone into loving Daisy. His life had been confused and disordered since then, but if he could once return to a certain starting place and go over it all slowly, he could find out what that thing was" (86). But of course the real Daisy can't live up to Gatsby's imaginary image, and in the confrontation scene at the Plaza, when she refuses to tell Tom that she never loved him, Gatsby's fantasy falls apart.

When Roy Earle, during his lonely drive across country, first meets the Goodhues and Velma at a filling station in the Nevada desert, his nostalgia for the past and his dead sweetheart finds something living to attach itself to: "Such a powerful feeling of sadness came over him that he could hardly stand it. Jesus! A sweet kid like that with a gimpy leg. What was it about her face that attracted him so? . . . here he was with the bottom dropping out of his stomach because an Ohio hick had a red ribbon in her hair and a gimpy leg!" (17). That evening while he's trying to fall asleep, a picture of Velma suddenly springs to mind, and he thinks, "I thought I was dead inside; stir really fixes you up. But I feel just like I used to when I was a punk in overalls. . . . She looks like the girls I used to know when I was a punk. And then her grandparents. Just like my people. . . . They're not thinking what a so-and-so you are, or how much they can get out of you. You're just a human being to them" (19). So even though he's involved in preparing for the biggest caper of his life, Roy continues to see Velma and the Goodhues after they've settled in L.A., first arranging and then paying for the operation on her foot, hoping her feelings of gratitude will overcome any apprehension about their age difference (Roy is sixteen years her senior) when he proposes marriage. But before he allows Roy to pay for Velma's operation, Pa Goodhue says he has to tell him in good conscience that back in Ohio Velma was "running around with a divorced man" named Lon Preiser. Pa had given her an ultimatum that either Preiser had to marry her or he'd take her to California. Knowing how Roy feels about Velma, Pa tells him she's begun receiving letters from Preiser since arriving there and may still be in love with him. Ignoring this first hint that Velma's not the innocent, small-town girl he imagined her, Roy pays for the operation anyway, learning only later that Pa was right, that in effect he's fixed her up for another man.

After the robbery, Roy visits Velma and the Goodhues one last time, taking

Marie along to show Velma she's not the only fish in the sea, but finds that Preiser, already arrived from Ohio, is in the living room teaching Velma to dance and that they intend to be married. Not only is Velma no longer crippled, but her appearance has changed: She'd "been to the beauty parlor. Her coarse blond hair was arranged in symmetrical waves. She looked mighty cute and pretty. But to Roy this wasn't Velma at all. This was a blonde kid that you'd try to make quick or let alone. You'd never lie thinking about her at night. You'd never feel so sad over her you didn't know if you could stand it" (157). And with that the illusion of Velma passes for Roy, passes in imagery not as world-consuming as that which Fitzgerald gave Gatsby's disillusion—an "old, warm world" lost and "a new world, material without being real"—but only because Roy is a tougher sort than Gatsby, because there's a greater degree of self-consciousness in his disillusion, and because Roy has an alternative:

> Suddenly Roy didn't give a damn about Velma, or about Pa and Ma. He realized that they had never been real people to him at all, but figments out of a dream of the past. He began vaguely to understand that ever since the prison gate clanged shut behind him he'd been trying to return to his boyhood, where it was always summer and in the evenings the lightning-bugs flashed under the big branches of the sycamore trees and he swung on the farm gate with the yellow-haired girl from across the road while the Victrola on the porch played *Dardanella*. . . . Pa and Ma were replicas of his own folks merely, and Velma wasn't really Velma, a slim, ordinary little blonde, but the ghost of Roma Stover, the yellow-haired girl swinging on the gate. (158–59)

Roy is quickly reconciled to his disillusion because, during that final visit to Velma's, he's discovered whom he really cares for. He'd brought Marie along to make Velma jealous, to put her in her place, but when Marie, who'd worked in a dime-a-dance joint, cuts in on Velma and starts dancing with Lon Preiser, it's Roy who gets jealous. He realizes that though in his fantasy Velma seemed the type of wholesome, steadfast farm girl he'd known as a youth, in reality she was something of a tramp at heart, while Marie, the former taxi-dancer and sometime call girl, turns out to be a loyal, loving companion. And Roy sees that while he was dreaming about marrying Velma and acquiring a family, he'd actually been "collecting a family" (88) unawares, a family made up of Marie and Pard, the little homeless dog who had attached himself to Roy at the fishing camp. From the middle of the novel on, these two accompany Roy everywhere. He takes them along on the hotel robbery and on his subsequent evasive movements after the plan to fence the stolen jewelry begins to unravel.

Algernon, the black man who works at the fishing camp, had warned Roy when he saw Pard following him around that the little dog, whose three previous owners had died suddenly, was bad luck. And this begins to seem true once the robbery starts, because everything goes wrong. Roy has to shoot the night watchman at the hotel, then Louis Mendoza, the night desk clerk, who was supposed to remain behind after the robbery, loses his nerve and flees with Roy and the others. Roy, Marie, and Pard take one car, while Red, Babe, and Louis take the other. Babe, driving without lights, makes a wrong turn and collides head-on with an oncoming police car. Red and Babe are killed, and Louis injured. When Roy and Marie arrive at Big Mac's apartment in L.A. to deliver the jewelry, Roy finds Kranmer, a crooked cop who'd horned his way in on Mac's end of the operation, waiting there. Together they discover that Mac has died in his sleep, and Kranmer tries to take the jewelry away from Roy. Shots are exchanged, Kranmer is killed, and Roy wounded. He goes to Doc Parker to have his wound dressed, then he and Marie search for someone to fence the jewelry. They hide out in various seedy auto-courts outside L.A., waiting for Max to arrive from Kansas City, and their nerves begin to fray. Becoming increasingly superstitious, Marie blames Pard for their dilemma:

> "You know what Algernon always said. He was bad luck. Well, ain't he?" . . .
>
> "No," cried Roy. "Pard's got nothing to do with it. Blaming things on a poor little dog! Things were stashed up to go haywire and they did. That's all. Babe goes up the wrong road and he and Red get killed. Old Mac kicks off. A chiseling copper walks into one he's been breeding for a long time. Max starts out, his plane makes a forced landing on account of a storm, and he gets his arm busted. All on account of Pard. Nuts!" (172)

Though Roy vehemently rejects the notion that he's literally being "dogged" by fate, still it's Pard that ultimately trips Roy up. Having finally arrived in L.A., Max has Roy's cut ready, but that very morning the newspapers report that Louis Mendoza has identified Roy Earle as the surviving robber, who's traveling with a girl named Marie and a little dog named Pard. When the manager of their auto-court, who's seen the paper, calls Pard to see if he'll answer to that name, Roy overhears, grabs the manager, and leaves him tied up in their cabin. Roy then puts Marie and Pard on a bus to San Bernadino promising to rejoin them in a few days, after he's gotten his money from Max in L.A., but on the way in, short of money and low on gas, he's forced to stick up a drugstore, and the state police get on his trail and chase him up a mountain road, where he's surrounded. For all the times after the robbery (but before Roy was identified) when having Pard in the car with him and Marie provided a perfect cover for getting through police roadblocks, this last time Pard's presence gives Roy away (even though Roy had altered his appearance), setting in motion the events leading to his death.

Though it might seem that Algernon and Marie were right about Pard's being bad luck, the little dog turns out to embody Roy's fate in a different way than the notion of "luck" would imply. From the novel's start Burnett emphasizes Roy's loneliness, a crushing sense of isolation and depression that's worst at night, of separation from family and roots so acute that when Roy meets the homeless stray Pard, it's love at first sight, a mating of strays eventually repeated when Marie is admitted to this circle. Inasmuch as Pard mirrors and responds to something in Roy's own character, a need to mitigate loneliness by some form of companionship and affection, he does indeed represent Roy's destiny in that tragic sense of character as fate. And since the urgency of that need is in direct proportion to Roy's increasingly acute awareness of aging, his sense that it's one thing to be young and unattached but quite another to be old and alone, the stray mutt Pard becomes another evocation of Roy's life heading downhill, caught between a remembered rural world of family and friends and a later urban world of cronies and accomplices, the two extremes evoked in relation to Pard by Roy's memories of Sport, his Aunt Minnie's "mongrel farm dog" (3), harrying her geese, and of the mean chow that Roy and his wife, Myrtle, owned that bit John Dillinger.

Unlike the young, self-sufficient Roy, who seems not to have cared greatly about Myrtle or the chow (when Roy went to prison, Myrtle divorced him and married a cop), the aging Roy finds to his amazement that he cares deeply for Marie and Pard: "He heard Marie moving around in the kitchen, getting breakfast. A pleasant feeling of contentment stole over him. Damned if it wasn't nice to be lying there in bed with Pard sleeping on his feet and a smart kid like Marie moving about in the next room. 'Why hell,' he told himself, 'I never felt this happy when I was a married man. I'm getting old, I guess'" (82). But precisely because Roy has grown to care for Marie and Pard, he makes errors in judgment the younger, less emotionally needy Roy wouldn't have made. At the end, when he puts Marie and Pard on the bus to San Bernardino, trying to protect the only family he has, Marie becomes so upset at his not letting her stay that Roy gets flustered and hastily gives her a handful of cash, realizing only later that he hasn't left himself enough gas money to get back to L.A.

Through the novel's various moments that either question the necessity of bosses—ranging from Roy's reluctance to boss the gang, to his saying he became an outlaw because he couldn't "stand a boss," and finally his so-called communist suggestion that poor people should knock over the banks and become their own bosses—or else question who really is boss (not Roy but Big Mac, not Big Mac but Ed Seidel, not Ed Seidel but Max from Kansas City), the novel builds toward a climax that answers both. Trapped on the side of a mountain and surrounded by the police, Roy, keeping them at a distance with machine gun fire, hears someone shout,

> "You up there!. . . . Better give up. You got no chance in the world."
>
> In a sudden flash Roy saw the tiny death cells at Michigan City; remembered the way the lights used to flicker when they burned some guy. "No, thanks," he told himself. "I'm done right here. I know when my goose is cooked." . . .
>
> "Come get me, boys. There's plenty of you down there. What's the matter, yellow?"
>
> "Let's go get him!"
>
> "Keep your shirt on, Lou. He can't get away. I'm bossing this and I say we'll wait till the sheriff gets here." (213)

Significantly, in the novel's last scene (the place of greatest formal importance), an unnamed individual asserts, "I'm bossing this," and what he commands is that they wait till the real boss arrives. In effect he says that time is on their side just as surely as it's against Roy, that time is the real boss—an answer toward which the prematurely aging Roy has been working his way through the entire novel. For while it's one thing to know a truth intellectually, it's something else to realize it in your bones, to have lived long enough to know that the time ahead is less than the time that's past, to see, trapped on the side of a mountain, that you are literally "heading downhill," as Burnett says of Roy at the start, "toward an ambiguous destiny in the Far West" (1). This destiny is accomplished when the men surrounding him on the mountain side use up Roy's time, waiting till a deer hunter with a high-powered rifle arrives and fells Roy with a single shot. And with that, the answer to the other question, about the necessity of a boss, is implicitly given, for if time is the real boss, then the ultimate necessity associated with it—what the ancient Greeks called *ananke*

(Necessity) and understood as a deterministic chain of material causes actualized in and through time and associated with the concept of Fate—is each human being's death. Indeed, one can see in the events immediately leading up to Roy's end just such a relentless causal chain of misfortunes or missteps, the type of downward spiral that led one critic to see in Burnett's work the influence of European naturalist writers like Zola, who "recalled Greek tragedy in their focus on long, slow slides triggered by human weakness."[6]

That Roy is, in John Dillinger's words, a guy "just rushing toward death," is foreshadowed from the start—from the fatalistic aura of little Pard to the fact that during the first evening Roy spends with Velma they witness a meteor burning through the atmosphere, the proverbial falling star associated with someone's death. The meteor, "low in the sky and moving slowly eastward, parallel with the earth, was a huge flaming ball of green and white fire. . . . 'Look how slow it's moving and how bright it is,' said Velma. 'Do you suppose it will hit the earth?' She was standing close to Roy. He reached down and took her hand" (62). At the novel's end, Burnett uses this same image to describe Roy's sensations as he's hit by the fatal bullet: "He was falling down that black abyss. Suddenly a huge green and white ball of fire swept across in front of him and a hand reached out and took his hand. But the hand was not little and soft as it had been that other time. It was lean and firm. Marie! The hand checked his fall" (214).

If it's true, as the saying goes, that we live our lives forward but understand them backward, then the same moment that ends the forward progress of Roy's life is also his moment of supreme understanding of what meant most to him in that life, the lean hardness of reality versus the soft insubstantiality of fantasy or dream. And this movement in opposite directions is echoed by the falling star's "moving slowly eastward" while Roy is heading "toward an ambiguous destiny in the Far West," the proverbial connection between one's star and one's destiny being implicit in the balancing of these images. (Of course, anyone of Burnett's generation would have also been familiar with that euphemism for death common in the Allied trenches of World War I—"heading west," which is to say, being shipped home in a box.) Burnett puts the finishing touch on *High Sierra*'s theme of time, bosses, and necessity when he has the newspaper man Vince Healy, looking down at Roy's corpse, pronounce his epitaph: "Big-shot Earle! Well, well. Look at him lying there. Ain't much, is he? His pants are torn and he's got on a dirty undershirt. . . . *Sic transit gloria mundi*, or something" (214).

V

As Burnett created Roy Earle by putting back into this character some of the Gatsbylike qualities he'd excised in creating Rico in *Little Caesar,* so he created the two principal figures in *The Asphalt Jungle*—Doc Riemenschneider and Dix Handley—by dividing Roy's character traits and history between them. The novel, the first in a trilogy that includes *Little Men, Big World* (1951) and *Vanity Row* (1952), about the slow decline of a big city through crime and political corruption, begins when Doc Riemenschneider, fresh out of prison, arrives in an unnamed midwestern city looking for the bookmaker Cobby to put him in touch with the big-time lawyer Alonzo Emmerich. Doc's cell mate in prison, Joe Cool, had turned over to him the plans for a jewelry store robbery on condition that Doc get Emmerich to arrange a fix and have Cool's life sentence reduced. For Doc the robbery of Pelletier and Company will be "the final score, the last big one they all dreamed about. Mexico for him . . . Mexico City, where a man could live like a king with a hundred thousand in cold American cash. . . . Dark, dusky, sultry young Mexican girls . . . and nothing to do all day long under the hot Southern sun but chase them."[7] At Cobby's bookie joint, Doc notices that one of the horse players, Dix Handley, though owing Cobby money, refuses to let Cobby ride him about it. Impressed both by Handley's sense of personal honor and by the quiet menace of his bearing, Doc files away this impression for future reference.

Where Burnett has given Doc, as a big-shot ex-con fresh out of prison and immediately embarked on his last caper, one aspect of Roy Earle, he's given Dix Handley, who was born and raised on a Kentucky farm and who in his early fifties is filled with nostalgia for those days, another. A stick-up and strong-arm man who's fallen on hard times, Dix, "lying back on the bed" in his dingy furnished room, "would return to the past: that happy past which seemed like a dream and not a reality—though he'd lived through it; that pleasant time, completely removed from the ugly, inescapable, harsh uncertainties of the present. . . . He was a Jamieson, wasn't he?. . . . And hadn't both his grandfathers fought in the Southern army during the Civil War . . . ? Okay! So they were simple people—nothing fancy. . . . But real folks all the same, salt of the earth!" Where Dix's grandfathers had fought on the Southern side, both of Roy Earle's Indiana grandfathers had fought for the Union. And clearly, in making Dix a rural southerner in a large northern city, Burnett renders more individually complex both Dix's disaffection from the modern urban world and his shabby, futile efforts in that environment to retain his self-respect and the respect of others, to remember who he is, where he came from, and what his code is. He thinks of the past as a "time when no one knew him as 'Dixie' or 'Dix,' or laughed at his Southern accent, or called him 'you-all' . . . or took any attitude at all toward him except one of friendliness and respect" (22–23).

Cobby takes Doc to meet Emmerich, whose luxurious home and physical appearance impress Riemenschneider, a man who worships "only three things: wealth, power, and young girls" (42), the first two of which Emmerich seems to possess. But Doc finds something troubling in Emmerich's manner, "the weariness, the anxiety to make an impression, the false joviality. What was worrying this big, successful man?" (43). What neither Doc nor Cobby know at this point is that Emmerich, though putting up a big front, is almost bankrupt (like Big Mac in *High Sierra*), and consequently he jumps at the idea of being part of the jewelry store burglary. Cobby and Doc want Emmerich to supply the up-front money for the job, arrange to fence the jewels, give them their share of the proceeds, then afterward put in a fix for Joe Cool. What Emmerich intends to do, once the jewelry store has been robbed, is get them to trust him with the loot, then hop a plane, leaving behind his partners, his creditors, and his ailing wife. For him, as well as for Doc and Dix, the Pelletier job is that "big last one," which will allow him to start fresh. But Emmerich, who can't raise the up-front money, has to persuade Cobby to foot the costs as the price for being cut in on the take, warning him not to tell Riemenschneider about this deal because Emmerich has sensed that Doc suspects something's not quite right about this big-time lawyer.

Cobby and Doc select three men to accompany Riemenschneider on the job, men who'll be paid a straight salary in advance with no percentage of the loot—Louis Bellini to crack the safe, Gus Minisi to drive the car, and, against the misgivings of both Cobby and Bellini, Dix Handley as the strong-arm man in case there's trouble either during the burglary or after in collecting the money for the jewels. Burnett gives each of the secondary characters some overriding passion or obsession, some differentiating humor. Gus, a hunchback who runs a hamburger joint and who's the best "wheel man" in the city, loves cats and believes in absolute friendship for, and unwavering loyalty to, "right guys," of which "there were only three he'd make book on: Mike Miklos, Louis Bellini, and Dix Handley" (68–69). Gus's reputation as a stand-up guy and his support of Dix help convince Cobby and Louis that Dix should be part of the job. Louis, who works days for an electrical contractor (and some nights as the best "tool man" in the city), dotes on his wife and their new baby and only agrees to take part in the job because of the money he could put away for his family, his friendship for Gus, and because Dix owes him money that he can collect from Dix's fee after the burglary.

The four—Doc, Dix, Louis, and Gus—break into Pelletier's at night, Louis cracks the safe, and as they're about to get away with the jewelry, a night watchman comes in the back door and Dix overpowers him. In the struggle the watchman's gun goes off, and Louis is shot in the stomach. Gus drives Louis home, while Doc and Dix take the loot to Emmerich's place but find that he isn't alone. A crooked private detective named Brannom, who works for him, is there. When Emmerich tells Doc the money isn't ready yet, but that if Doc will leave the jewels with him, he'll get the money to him later, Doc smells a double-cross and refuses. Brannom pulls a gun, and there's a shoot-out (like that between the crooked cop Kranmer and Roy in *High Sierra*) in which Brannom is killed and Dix wounded. Fearing for his life, Emmerich promises to find Doc another fence for the loot, and Doc and Dix leave with the jewelry to hide out with one of Gus's friends. Meanwhile the police, putting the heat on, get a tip that leads them to Cobby. A sadistic cop beats him till he talks, and the cops pick up Gus and find when they go to Louis's place that he's died of the gunshot wound. The manhunt is on for Doc and Dix, and while they lie low, the wounded Dix's nostalgia for his family home and his desire to return there after twenty-five years becomes overwhelming. As Dix is looking out the window of their hideout at the "faintly glimmering stars. . . . A meteor streaked down toward the tall buildings, then suddenly went out like a spent burst from a Roman candle. Shooting star! It reminded him of home and long summer nights ages ago" (190).

The main difference between Roy and Dix is that Roy feels prematurely old at thirty-seven after spending six years in prison, a feeling compounded by his sense that the historical moment of his being a big-shot with the Dillinger gang has passed and that the jitterbugs he's leading think he's "a has-been," and Dix, in his mid-fifties and a veteran of World War I, is actually beginning to grow old. Cobby tells Doc at one point, "Dix is on the way out—a small-time stick-up guy" (100), and in a moment of self-appraisal Dix thinks, "I'm slipping, that's all. Not the man I used to be" (101). But where the Far West seemed to have a reinvigorating effect on Roy (with its outdoor regimen in the mountains, the dream of the twenty-two-year-old Velma, and the reality of the twenty-five-year-old Marie, not to mention the companionship of Pard), the big, decaying midwestern city only aggravates Dix's sense of decline: "Dix had a blinding desire to go home—to see all that lovely land again, maybe to stay. He felt a sudden and violent hatred of the city that throbbed and pulsated for miles in all directions beyond the thin walls of the bunkroom" (114).

Where Roy had Marie, the young, former taxi-dancer, as his girl, Dix has Doll, who works in a dive and has seen better days: "She was about thirty-five, and there were faint lines of weariness about her mouth and eyes. . . . The rough side of life was no mystery to her—she'd seen hardly anything else, as she'd been on her own for over twenty years; but she had managed to keep herself aloof from the sordid fatalism of her associates, and she had fought a constant, tough, but inconclusive battle against the long, easy slide down into the mire. But the struggle was telling on her" (25–26). The one thing she has to cling to is that "she was crazy about this big tramp" (27). Though at the start of the novel Dix wants to dump her, as the book progresses and he becomes increasingly preoccupied with the waste he's made of his life and with the idea of going home, she becomes something stable for him to hang on to.

When Doc and Dix have to leave their hideout, they head for Doll's place, but on the way they're braced by a cop and in the ensuing scuffle Doc's knocked out and Dix's gunshot wound is reopened. At Doll's place, Doc and Dix decide to split up. Doc plans to grab a cab, give the driver an address on the outskirts of the city, and then when he gets there offer the driver as much money as it takes to get him to drive to Cleveland. Dix, on the other hand, is determined to return to the family farm in Kentucky, and Doll volunteers to find a car if she can go with him. When Dix warns her, "I'm on the lam—wanted bad. You figuring on getting a stretch in some women's prison?" she says, "I don't care, Dix—as long as I can be with you" (218). Like Marie in *High Sierra*, who tells Roy, "Don't think you're going to shake me off so easy. I never been so happy in my life. I'm a different girl. I don't feel so much like a bum anymore. I feel clean" (144), Doll knows that without Dix her life won't be much different from prison. But unlike Marie, Doll accompanies Dix to the bitter end. When they arrive at his Kentucky farm, Dix, clearly dying from his wound, finds to his bewilderment that his family no longer owns the place and that his mother now lives in town with her other son, Woodford. They drive to his mother's house, where Dix is met by Woodford, the local lawman, who doesn't recognize Dix at first. Dix collapses, and they send for the same doctor who was present at his birth to attend him at his death. Dix thrusts a roll of bills into his brother's hand and says, "Over three thousand bucks there. . . . I want you to hang onto it for me. . . . Doll's got nothing. No people. No place to go. You look after her, Woodford. . . . No matter what I did, she didn't know anything about it. Law's got nothing on her—except she was with me." Lapsing into semiconsciousness, Dix drifts "away from them into another world . . . the pleasant world of the past" (266), evoked in two pages of boyhood memories drifting through his mind as Dix finally returns home.

Meanwhile, Doc betrays himself to the police through his own special character weakness, an obsessive attraction to young girls. Stopping at a roadside diner outside the city for something to eat, Doc and the cab driver stay there longer than they should while Doc plays records on the jukebox so he can watch a teenager dance. Eventually two passing motorcycle patrolmen spot Doc through the window and pick him up. At the same time the police are on Emmerich's trail and arrest him at his riverfront bungalow with his mistress, Angela. Phoning his wife from his study to tell her he's been arrested, Emmerich finds himself "wanting suddenly to tell her everything—all his errors, weaknesses, and follies; wanting above all to justify the erratic course of his life, and maybe even to gain a little sympathy. But it was no use. How could he make her understand? . . . He hung up quickly, then sat staring at the floor for a moment. An awful weariness had settled over him now, and suddenly he admitted to himself with unaccustomed candor that he'd been tired for years, bored with everything, moving through his life with automatic soullessness, like a clockwork robot" (253–54). He takes a pistol from his desk and shoots himself.

The basic structural resemblance of *High Sierra* and *The Asphalt Jungle* (like the echoes of *Gatsby* in *Little Caesar*) purposely invites a comparison that seems meant to point up the darkening of Burnett's fiction from the earlier to the later novel, meant to make the books' differences in era, setting, attitude, and mood stand out in greater relief. *High Sierra* takes place in either 1937 or 1938 and *The Asphalt Jungle* after World War II (and enough after for the Cold War to have already begun, as suggested by Riemenschneider's remark that "the Germans . . . are no longer the dogs to beat. They are beaten. Now it's the Russians" [44]). The difference between pre– and post–World War II America, between the world of the late thirties and the late forties, is embodied in the contrasting landscapes evoked in the books' titles: on the one hand, the frontierlike Far West of the Nevada-California desert and mountains, the luxury resort of Tropico Springs, and the raw, energetic desert town of L.A.

about to mushroom into a metropolis with the war—in effect, that golden land of promise so many Americans like the Goodhues flocked to during the Depression—and, on the other hand, the aging grimy industrial world of the Midwest, with its big-city decaying slums and rampant corruption, the slowly corroding buckle on the rust belt, with the difference between the two being played out in the contrasting outlooks and aspirations of Roy and Dix as each reacts to his situation at midlife.

Feeling a growing sense of his life as wasted ever since leaving home to pursue a criminal career and of his powers beginning to wane with age, each man finds himself increasingly consumed with nostalgia for his roots and rural past, and each has a Gatsbylike dream of recovering a former self associated with that past. Roy finds a way to bring the past back into the present by projecting the images of his first love and of his own family on Velma and the Goodhues, while Dix tries at the end to return physically to his past by going back home to his mother and brother. Though both are eventually disillusioned, Roy survives his misconception about Velma to accept whatever life and happiness he can find with Marie, no matter how brief, but Dix, like Gatsby, doesn't survive his discovery that you can't repeat the past or ever go home again, each of the three ultimately learning who the real boss is, because, though usually thought to be measured in hours, days, and years, time is really measured in loss.

Deadline at Midnight

Cornell Woolrich's *Night Has a Thousand Eyes*

I

Though critics often group Cornell Woolrich with hard-boiled writers like Hammett, Chandler, Cain, and Burnett, Woolrich's fiction is characterized by a quality present only by turns in the others' work. Woolrich is primarily a writer of suspense fiction, his trademark the creation of psychological terror so pervasive and paralyzing it seems almost more destructive than the thing feared, a type of story owing much to Poe, though not to the Poe of detective fiction but rather to tales such as "The Fall of the House of Usher." In the previous chapter we saw how Burnett in *High Sierra* and *The Asphalt Jungle* answered the question "Who's the boss?" for his two protagonists with the words *time* and *death*. Woolrich gives essentially the same answer in his work but with this difference: Roy Earle and Dix Handley experience the coercive force of time as a function of their own aging. They find themselves worn-out, middle-aged men in a young man's game of armed robbery or burglary, and they undergo time's ultimate coercion in the violent death that became their fate the moment they made the youthful decision to live by the gun, a fate sprung from choice and a choice sprung from character. In contrast, the typical Woolrich protagonist experiences time's coercive force because he or she foreknows the exact moment when time's ultimate sanction will fall on them or someone they care for. Woolrich's best work is about deadlines in the literal sense of the word, and as critics have noted, the typical Woolrich suspense mechanism is the race against time. The effect this exact foreknowledge has on a person's psyche, on his emotional and moral life, the devastating fear it creates, the hopeless sense of being trapped in a predestined series of events as the seconds slip away, is the psychological vein Woolrich mined with obsessive and consummate skill—indeed, with an obsessiveness, I would argue, largely rooted in Woolrich's sense of his own life.

II

Cornell George Hopley-Woolrich was born on December 4, 1903, in New York City, the only child of Genaro Hopley-Woolrich and Claire Attalie Tarler. Of mixed Latin and British descent, Woolrich's father was born in the state of Oaxaca in Mexico and was a Roman Catholic, the religion in which Cornell was baptized. As Woolrich's biographer Francis M. Nevins Jr. notes, Genaro was "either a civil engineer or a metallurgist" by profession,[1] and three years after Cornell's birth Genaro and Claire moved to Mexico. Claire was apparently unhappy in Mexico, and when the couple eventually separated (with Claire returning to the Tarler family in New York), young Cornell remained with his father in Mexico until he turned fourteen, when he too returned to New York and his mother's family.

In *Blues of a Lifetime,* a not entirely reliable memoir left unfinished at his death, Woolrich records two events from his years in Mexico that he felt significantly influenced the rest of his life. The first occurred when his grandfather George Tarler, on a visit to Mexico City, took the eight-year-old Cornell to see a performance of Puccini's *Madame Butterfly.* Noting its "lasting effect" on him, Woolrich describes the performance's "sudden, sharp insight into color and drama, that came back to the surface again years later when I became a writer."[2] But Woolrich's biographer Nevins suggests that the opera's dramatic situation also had a personal resonance for young Cornell and wonders whether "the luckless union of Cio-Cio San and Pinkerton" reminded him "of his own parents," whether he saw himself and perhaps got "an intimation of his own adult life in the figure of the couple's child, whose name is Trouble"

(7). What Woolrich, "a small boy in a foreign country," did experience in the opera was an intense sense of identification with the American naval lieutenant Pinkerton. He says, "I walked home on air" with "a secret dream, a secret pride": "I'm an American. I'm one of them. One of those" (25).

The second event from his years in Mexico, he says, occurred "one night when I was eleven and, huddling over my own knees, looked up at the low-hanging stars of the Valley of Anahuac, and knew I would surely die finally, or something worse. I had that trapped feeling, like some sort of poor insect that you've put inside a downturned glass, and it tries to climb up the sides, and it can't, and it can't, and it can't." Woolrich says that dating from that night "the sense of personal, private doom . . . had been in me all my life" (16). Whether or not this is an accurate account of something Woolrich experienced at age eleven, we do know that on at least one other occasion he gave a friend a different version of the circumstances surrounding this epiphany under the stars—which is only to say that *Blues of a Lifetime* may well be a memoir meant more to deliver the poetic truth of Woolrich's life than its factual details.

Though Woolrich left the manuscript of *Blues of a Lifetime* unfinished in 1966, two years before his death, he had previously used the stars in this same way (as a figure of fatalism and cosmic indifference) some twenty years earlier in *Night Has a Thousand Eyes* (1945), his best novel and the one he seems to have considered his most literary effort. Consequently, we can surmise either that the moment under the stars was so formative and influential for Woolrich that he made the image and the feelings associated with it central to his best novel, or that in writing the novel Woolrich found the perfect objective correlative for his sense of life and then decided to insert this figuration back into his own formative years. What makes the latter seem more than just a possibility is that Woolrich introduces the story of this moment under the stars in Mexico by giving instances of various habits, acquired as a young man in the 1920s, to show that "the path you follow is the path you have to follow; there are no digressions permitted you, even though you think there are" (14). Smoking and drinking are the two habits Woolrich mentions (both of which he practiced to excess all his life), even though he says he eventually realized he never really liked the taste of cigarettes or liquor. He says of the latter:

> It was as though I was either trying to cover up *from* something, or cover *up* something, or both.

It is a wrong thing and a bad thing to pervert yourself like this.... You destroy the you that was meant to be.... This is a form of suicide-in-life, and I committed it.

I would have been a great writer. I would have been a great and a good man. I would have left a name that would have gone down in the annals. And, speak it low, I would have led a happy life.

This credo of escape from responsibility, of fun and of the unserious, was in the atmosphere, the climate of the times ...; a whole generation ... shared it; but in others it waned ... and finally expired as the period that produced it passed away....

But in me it never did.... It was the perfect counterpoint to the sense of personal, private doom that had been in me all my life, ever since one night when I was eleven. (15–16)

Mark Bassett, the editor of *Blues of a Lifetime,* speculates that Woolrich's remark about his heavy drinking as an attempt either "to cover up *from* something, or to cover *up* something, or both" was a veiled reference to the fact that, as Woolrich's former sister-in-law claimed, he "had suppressed one key aspect of his personality—an inclination toward homosexuality," an aspect Bassett sees as explaining the "occasionally homophobic" quality of Woolrich's fiction (141n28). If Woolrich's feelings about this sexual inclination were what he'd tried to cover up *by* his drinking, then in the lengthy passage quoted above, his explicit admission of an excessive drinking habit may well be meant to cover up mentioning those feelings, turning his drinking, in effect, into a screen-image for that other habit. After linking his weakness for alcohol to the "unserious" atmosphere of the 1920s and then calling that atmosphere the "perfect counterpoint" to his "sense of personal, private doom" born under the stars, Woolrich proceeds to confirm the sexual subtext of his remarks about drinking by using this image of fate and the stars again later in *Blues of a Lifetime* to narrate his tragically unfulfilled "first-time love" for a working-class girl named Vera Gaffney.

Vera (Woolrich admits it's not her real name) had been introduced by a mutual friend, and Woolrich became enamored, even though there was an obvious class difference between them. Woolrich asks her to a fancy party, but she has nothing appropriate to wear. Vera, who works as a lady's maid, takes a fur coat from her employer without permission and goes to the party, where she becomes the hit of the evening. Afterward, Woolrich returns her to her front door, they kiss, and he realizes that she is his for the taking, but he says,

> I didn't want it to happen. I did, but I didn't. . . . I had this image of her. . . . There was a breathless springtime charm about her this way, a fragile sway she exerted over me, which would have been gone at a touch. Maybe a more heated, a more grown love would have taken its place. But only for a while. Then that would have gone too, as it always does in such cases. And nothing would have been left. . . . If you're not going to be idealistic at that age, you're never going to be idealistic. (57–58)

But when Woolrich misses seeing Vera the next day at their usual meeting place, he goes looking for her, only to learn that she's been arrested for taking the fur coat and sentenced as a minor to six months in a reformatory. Woolrich says he passed the building where she'd lived many times that winter and looked at the front door "longingly (not so much with love—for what did I know of love at nineteen? Or for that matter, what did I know of it at thirty-nine or forty-nine or fifty-nine?—as with some sense of isolation, of pinpointed and transfixed helplessness under the stars, of being left alone, unheard and unaided to face some final fated darkness and engulfment slowly advancing across the years toward me, that has hung over me all my life)" (63). Since versions of the Vera episode had appeared earlier in Woolrich's first novel *Cover Charge* (1926) and in chapter 8 of *The Black Angel* (1943), there remains, as with the earlier episode under the stars in Mexico, an ultimate uncertainty about whether a real incident from Woolrich's life had been turned into fiction before being recorded in his autobiography or whether fictional material from two of his novels (material that figured the fated loss of heterosexual love in his life as the loss of a young woman) was incorporated into his memoir. Suffice it to say, the thrust of the various incidents recorded in the autobiography is to portray most of Woolrich's character traits, habits, and inclinations as being predestined, not the result of free choice entailing personal accountability. When Woolrich said of his heavy drinking that the "credo of escape from responsibility," which he'd imbibed in the 1920s, had never left him, he spoke more truly and deeply than he perhaps realized.

Woolrich dates the Vera episode in *Blues of a Lifetime* to 1922–23, that is, to the period when, after his return in 1918 to New York, he was living in his grandfather's house on West 113th Street near Morningside Park. Woolrich finished high school in the city and then enrolled as a freshman at Columbia in the fall of 1921. His academic record at Columbia was abysmal, but the critic Jacques Barzun, who sat next to Woolrich in two classes (one in the English novel, one in creative writing) remembered Woolrich as being totally dedicated to becoming a writer: "Cornell gave me the impression that he had consciousness of being a second Scott Fitzgerald" (Nevins, 20). Barzun also recalled Woolrich as a shy, bitter young man in "revolt against circumstances and his own character and personality" and under the "domination" of his mother (19). Regarding Woolrich's considering himself a second Scott Fitzgerald, his biographer Francis Nevins notes the similarities in the two men's lives and careers: "Both were baptized as Catholics but rejected all religion. Both were below average height and wanted to be taken for macho men. Both entered college with the aspiration to be professional writers. Both were mediocre students and left school before graduation. . . . Both had their first novels published at almost identical ages. Each sought in his early fiction to capture the essence of the twenties. The first novel of each is a disjointed, disorganized potpourri of styles and motifs. . . . Each man was fascinated by the movies, longed for Hollywood success, and had bad experiences trying to write screenplays. Both were chain smokers and melancholy alcoholics, prone to self-destructiveness. Both tended to equate sex with defilement and love with something nobler than the body. . . . Each died prematurely, leaving unfinished a major novel that might have restored the reputation he had enjoyed in his prime" (20).

Leaving Columbia in 1925, Woolrich published his first novel, *Cover Charge,* in 1926 with Boni and Liveright, the firm that brought out Faulkner's first novel, *Soldier's Pay,* that same year and Hemingway's first American collection of stories, *In Our Time,* the year before. Over the next six years, Woolrich published five additional novels, most of them in the same Fitgeraldian, Jazz-Age vein. His second, *Children of the Ritz* (1927), was bought by the movies, and Woolrich moved to Hollywood in 1928 to work on the script, though he received no screen credit when the film appeared in 1929. In 1930 Woolrich suddenly married (eloping "on the spur of the moment," in the bride's words) Gloria Blackton, the daughter of J. Stuart Blackton, one of the founders of Vitagraph Studios, which later became part of Warner Brothers. The marriage (never consummated) lasted three months, whereupon Woolrich returned to New York to live with his mother.

Gloria's half-sister Marian told Woolrich's biographer that Cornell had left behind him a diary in which he "said many uncomplimentary things about our family, about Gloria," including "the thought that it might be a really good joke to marry this Gloria Blackton." But "the bulk of the diary . . . recounted a large number of homosexual encounters in 'sordid and dreadful detail'" (Nevins, 76). Marian claimed her half-sister had "a very strong streak of the maternal feeling in connection with her romances always," and Nevins speculates that if Woolrich's decision to marry Gloria wasn't just a cruel joke or a cover for his secret life, it was probably Gloria's maternal aspect that attracted him. At any rate, Woolrich seems to have felt that there was no point in finding a mother-substitute when his own mother was still available.

After returning to New York and following the sale of the family home, Cornell and his mother, Claire, moved in 1932 into an apartment in the Hotel Marseilles at Broadway and 103rd, where they lived until her death in 1957. Woolrich then moved into the Hotel Franconia and in 1965 to the Sheraton-Russell. Alone and drinking heavily during his last years, Woolrich virtually ceased being a writer, spending much of his time sitting in the hotel lobby watching people go by. In January 1968 Woolrich had a leg amputated because of gangrene resulting from an unattended foot wound. While in the hospital he apparently decided to renew the Catholic faith into which he'd been baptized, asking a priest to hear his confession and subsequently receiving communion, explaining to an acquaintance that he'd "reached the age where he was hearing 'Nearer My God to Thee'" (Nevins, 427). In the fall of 1968 he suffered a stroke and died on September 25, leaving his estate to Columbia University to establish a scholarship fund in his mother's name.

From 1930 on, when he returned to New York to live with his mother, most of the biographical data of the shy, reclusive Woolrich has to do with the publication of his fiction or its adaptation for film, radio, and television, which was extensive. Indeed, Woolrich probably had more of his fiction adapted to other media than any of the hard-boiled writers we've discussed. Among the films made from his works are Jacques Tourneur's *The Leopard Man* (1943), Robert Siodmak's *Phantom Lady* (1944), Harold Clurman's *Deadline at Dawn* (1946), John Farrow's *Night Has a Thousand Eyes* (1948), Alfred Hitchcock's *Rear Window* (1954), and Francois Truffaut's *The Bride Wore Black* (1968), to name only a few.

After the last of Woolrich's first group of novels, *Manhattan Love Song*, was published in 1932, Woolrich wrote one more, *I Love You, Paris*, for which, he says in *Blues of a Lifetime*, he was unable to find a publisher or a movie company interested in buying the screen rights: "My instinct told me very surely that this marked the ending of something or other in me. Call it being young, call it being completely carefree. Call it being wholeheartedly foolish, even" (94). Woolrich threw the manuscript in an ashcan, and over the next two years, in the very depths of the Depression, he set out to transform his subject matter in order to break into the pulp fiction market, a transformation driven by economic necessity and by the new mood of the times. Woolrich's first crime story, "Death Sits in the Dentist's Chair," appeared in *Detective Fiction Weekly*, August 4, 1934—for which he was paid one hundred ten dollars. Over the next six years he published stories in virtually all the major pulps, including *Argosy*, *Black Mask*, *Dime Detective*, and *Detective Fiction Weekly*, and in 1940 he brought out with Simon and Schuster his first novel using this new subject matter, *The Bride Wore Black*, inaugurating what is known as Woolrich's "black series"—*The Black Curtain* (1941), *Black Alibi* (1942), *The Black Angel* (1943), *The Black Path of Fear* (1944), and *Rendezvous in Black* (1948), the blackness of the titles evoking these books' generally fatalistic air.

So prolific was Woolrich in the decade between 1940 and 1950 that he also produced five other significant novels, four of which—*Phantom Lady* (1942), *Deadline at Dawn* (1944), *Waltz into Darkness* (1947), and *I Married a Dead Man* (1950)—were published under the pen name William Irish and the other —*Night Has a Thousand Eyes* (1945)—under the name George Hopley. During these years Woolrich also continued to publish stories and bring out collections of his short fiction, though after *I Married a Dead Man* the quality (and eventually the quantity) of his work declined. Though I focus in this chapter on Woolrich's best book, *Night Has a Thousand Eyes*, I want to begin by examining a story from the late 1930s that has been, over the years, among his most frequently anthologized and adapted and that critics consider in its subject matter and method to be archetypally Woolrichian.

III

"Three O'Clock," published in the October 1, 1938, issue of *Detective Fiction Weekly*, is, in the opinion of Woolrich's biographer Nevins, "the most powerful story he ever wrote" (120). Paul Stapp, the owner of a small watch-repair shop, after suffering a concussion, undergoes a disturbing mental change. Noticing various signs of a strange man's presence in his house while he's at work, Stapp ultimately convinces himself that his wife is having an affair. He was someone who "didn't bring his hates or grudges out into the open where they had a chance to heal" but "nursed them in the darkness of his mind . . . a dangerous kind of man."[3] It seemed to him that "he'd daydreamed of getting rid" of his wife "long before there was any reason to, that there had been something in him for years past now urging Kill, kill, kill. Maybe ever since that time he'd been treated at the hospital for a concussion" (65). Stapp plans to murder her by placing a time bomb in the basement, a bomb set to go off in the afternoon to kill his wife and her lover and so powerful that it will demolish the house as if by a natural gas explosion. For six weeks he's been bringing home the components unnoticed—"fine little strands of copper wire . . . and each time a very little package containing a substance that . . . if ignited . . . loose like that . . . it couldn't hurt you, only burn your skin" but "wadded tightly into cells, in what had formerly been a soap-box down in the basement, . . . that would be a different story" (66).

On the day he's chosen for the murder, he spends the whole morning in his shop working on an alarm clock for the bomb's timer, and as he's working, he reflects on something we've come to expect from men in hard-boiled fiction: "That was one good thing about being your own boss, operating your own shop, there was no one over you to tell you what to do and what not to do. And he didn't have an apprentice or helper in the shop, either, to notice this peculiar absorption in a mere alarm-clock and tell someone about it later" (68). The fact that Stapp, like Chandler's Marlowe, is his own boss and his own sole employee will come back to haunt him later. He leaves his shop at twelve-thirty and rides the bus home, knowing his wife will be out buying groceries. He attaches the alarm clock to the detonator on the explosive-filled soap-box in the basement and sets it for three. As he's preparing to leave, he hears footsteps above him on the first floor. He creeps up the basement stairs and is suddenly overpowered by two burglars who tie and gag him, carry him to the basement, and leave him trussed to a pipe with the fatal alarm clock in front of him but out of reach. When the burglars leave, Stapp's ordeal begins, one Woolrich describes in detail, using a device that would become a staple of his race-against-time stories:

> It was twenty-five to two now. His discovery of their presence, the fight, their trussing him up, . . . had all taken place within fifteen minutes.
>
> It went tick-tick, tick-tock; tick-tick, tick-tock, so rhythmically, so remorselessly, so *fast.* . . .

Eighty-five minutes left. How long that could seem if you were waiting for someone on a corner, under an umbrella, in the rain. . . . How short, how fleeting, how instantaneous, . . . when it was all the time there was left for you to live in . . .

No clock had ever gone this fast, of all the hundreds he'd looked at and set right. This was a demon-clock, its quarter-hours were minutes and its minutes seconds. . . .

Tick-tock-tick-tock-tick-tock. He broke it up into "Here I go, here I go, here I go." (76–77)

Endlessly inventive in making time palpable, in making the inexorable countdown an exquisite torture device, Woolrich alternates throughout the rest of the tale between the clock's ticking and periodic announcements of the time. But of course if the rest of the tale were just Stapp's helpless watching as the minutes slipped away, it would be no story at all. So Woolrich keeps giving Stapp chance after chance to be rescued and then, with increasing skill, keeps taking them away. First, Stapp hears his wife, returned from shopping, walking around just above his head, but he's gagged too tightly to make her hear. Yet even to have someone else in the house relieves a little "the awful lonesomeness" he'd felt, and his feelings about his wife undergo a sudden change: "He felt such gratitude for her nearness, he felt such love and need for her, he wondered how he could ever have thought of doing away with her—only one short hour ago. He saw now that he must have been insane to contemplate such a thing. Well if he had been, he was sane now, . . . this ordeal had brought him to his senses. Only release him, only rescue him from his jeopardy, and he'd never again . . ." (78).

Stapp hears his wife telephoning someone named Dave to tell him she's discovered her wristwatch and some cash missing from an upstairs bedroom. Stapp is overjoyed, thinking she'll now call the police, the house will be searched, and he'll be found. But Dave persuades her to look again and to call Stapp at his shop to see if he took them. As his wife calls the shop, Stapp goes through agonies, knowing that because he's his only employee there's no one in the shop to tell her he's gone home. Ten minutes later Dave shows up, and from their conversation it becomes clear Dave isn't his wife's lover but her brother, an escaped convict on the run who doesn't want the police called because they'll think he committed the burglary. Stapp's wife finally persuades

Dave they should tell Stapp about him and get his advice, and they leave for his shop. Again Stapp is plunged into despair, with only fifteen minutes left now: "He'd keep his eyes down and pretend the hands were moving slower than they were, . . . it blunted a little of the terror at least. The ticking he couldn't hide from. . . . Then he'd hold out as long as he could with his eyes down, but when he . . . would . . . raise them to see if he was right, it had gained *two* minutes. Then he'd have a bad fit of hysterics, in which he called on God, and even on his long-dead mother, to help him. . . . Then he'd pull himself together again, in a measure, and start the self-deception over again. . . . And so on, mounting slowly to another climax of terror and abysmal collapse" (84–85).

Playing a game of tension, release, and renewed tension with Stapp, Woolrich next has a meter reader from the gas company ring the front door bell. Stapp momentarily thinks he's saved because this is the one call "from earliest morning until latest night, that could have possibly brought anyone down into the basement." He gets a glimpse of the meter reader's legs through "the grimy transom . . . at ground level," and he thinks that all his "potential savior" has to do is "crouch down and peer in through it" (85) for him to be rescued. But clearly the meter reader doesn't expect anyone to be in the basement of a house where his repeated ringing hasn't been answered, and he leaves: "Stapp died a little. Not metaphorically, literally. His arms and legs got cold up to the elbows and knees, his heart seemed to beat slower, and he had trouble getting a full breath" (86). Stapp begins to hallucinate, but then the phone rings. Stapp's sure it's his wife, who hasn't found him at the shop and who's wondering if he's home by now, and he thinks that she'll let the phone ring for awhile and then hear the sound of a distant explosion and say, "It sounded as though it came from out our way" (87).

It's now nine minutes to three, and fate has one more teasing hope left for Stapp. He hears a mother calling her little boy outside, then sees a tennis ball hit the basement transom. Suddenly, a small child appears at the transom and leans over to pick up his ball. Even though Stapp can see the child's face clearly, for a long agonizing moment the youngster doesn't seem to see him, and then he does. Stapp wonders if the child will tell his mother, and he heaves a sigh of relief when the child says, "Mommy, look!" but when Stapp hears an impatient "Bobby, are you coming? I'm waiting" (89), his heart sinks. Again the child says, "Mommy, look! . . . Funny man tied up," but again the impatient adult voice, "inattentive to a child's fibs and fancies," replies, "Why that wouldn't look nice, Mommy can't peep into other people's houses like you can," and the child is suddenly "tugged erect at the end of its arm" (89–90) and disappears, leaving Stapp to feel he's being mocked "in his crucifixion" (90).

Using an image that looks forward (or perhaps backward) to that moment in *Blues of a Lifetime* when, under the stars in Mexico, he experienced a "trapped feeling, like some sort of poor insect that you've put inside a downturned glass" (16), Woolrich says that though Stapp "was more dead than alive by now," still "the will to live is an unconquerable thing" and "presently he started to crawl back again out of the depths of his despair, a slower longer crawl each time, like that of some indefatigable insect buried repeatedly in sand, that each time manages to burrow its way out" (90). As death approaches ever closer, Stapp enters a state in which he can't "*feel* anymore, terror or hope or anything else," a state in which "the protracted foreknowledge of death" has become "its own anaesthetic," for he is "in a state of death already," having fled down the "long dim corridors" of the mind "away from the doom that impended": "He was shaking all over from head to foot—not with fear, with laughter" (90–91), shaking so much that he doesn't even notice the clock's minute hand has gone past twelve.

In his best cinematic fashion Woolrich cuts away from the basement at this point and then cuts back four hours later as an ambulance attendant warns a policeman, "Don't take those ropes off him yet. . . . Wait'll they get here with the straitjacket first, or you'll have your hands full." Stapp's wife, apparently the one who'd discovered him, asks, "Can't you stop him from laughing like that? I can't stand it. Why does he keep laughing like that?" To which the ambulance intern replies, "He's out of his mind, lady." In a parting fillip, Woolrich has the policeman, noticing the soap box with the alarm clock attached, ask what it contains. "Nothing. . . . Just an empty box. It used to have some kind of fertilizer in it, but I took it out and used it on the flowers . . . I've been trying to raise out in back of the house" (91), says Stapp's wife.

IV

Though "Three O'Clock" exemplifies Woolrich's countdown-to-death scenario for generating suspense, the story's interest for us lies more in Woolrich's linking of Stapp's progressive psychological deterioration through his "protracted foreknowledge of death" to the author's own life-long "sense of personal, private doom" dating from his youthful realization under the stars that he "would surely die finally, or something worse," a link created through the shared image of a trapped insect struggling to free itself. And this progressive mental deterioration of a character through the terror-inducing foreknowledge of his own violent end is what in turn links "Three O'Clock" and *Night Has a Thousand Eyes* to the major influence on Woolrich's mature work, Poe's horror tales, and particularly, to that group known as "the dying woman" stories. In order to understand the extent of their influence on Woolrich's fiction, we must digress for a bit to examine the shared structure of "the dying woman" stories and give a reading of the most fully developed example of the group, "The Fall of the House of Usher," and its Freudian resonances.

These tales—"Berenicë" (1835), "Morella" (1835), "Ligeia" (1838), "The Fall of the House of Usher" (1839), and "Eleonora" (1841)—are all built around a structure of male/female doubling I described in my earlier book, *The Mystery to a Solution:*

> In its most general form, the dying woman story concerns a sensitive, often "artistic" young man (usually the story's narrator) whose precarious psychic stability is undermined by the illness and death of a woman to whom he is closely related. The nature of their relationship varies. Often the woman is the wife or betrothed of the young man as in "Morella" and "Ligeia," or a close relative (a twin) as in "The Fall of the House of Usher," or both as in "Berenicë" and "Eleonora" where she is the man's cousin and his betrothed. Sometimes the man and woman have been raised together in the same dwelling from childhood ("Berenicë," "The Fall of the House of Usher," "Eleonora"), and almost as frequently the man's unstable temperament is presented as an hereditary disposition embodied in and to some degree transmitted by the claustrophobic home.
>
> . . . the men in these tales find themselves emotionally bound (often inexplicably so) to women who are mortally ill and who, because of the life-threatening effect of their illness on the precarious mental state of their consorts, come to embody Death for these men. But while the women in these tales are weak in body, they are prodigiously strong in spirit, gifted with a power of will that enables them either to return from the grave in their own person (as in the case of Madeline Usher) or to return in spirit and take over another's body (as with Morella and Ligeia). . . . Moreover, in several of these stories the woman's strength of spirit manifests itself as an overmastering intelligence that reduces the man to childlike dependence, as if he were at his mother's knee. . . .
>
> The dying woman tends, then, to be coded as a mother-surrogate, and to the

extent this makes her an object of the man's desire, it also makes her, in a double sense, a threat to his life. On the one hand, since she serves as a kind of Psyche figure, the beloved woman's physical deterioration in the grip of a wasting illness mirrors (and thereby exacerbates) the man's psychic deterioration. On the other hand, as a mother figure the woman serves to keep the man in a state of childlike dependence, and since Poe's standard rite-of-passage scenario for depicting a character's progress from adolescence to maturity involves a symbolic death and rebirth, this arresting of the man in emotional immaturity by the mother figure is frequently depicted as a symbolic death without a subsequent rebirth, a living entombment in the womb of the family evoked either as a psychically incestuous union with a close relative or an inability to leave the ancestral home, or both....

It is to protect himself from being destroyed by the woman he desires that the man tries in several of these tales to rid himself of her terrifying presence by literally inflicting on her the living entombment she personifies for him. But with the woman's premature burial, a characteristic reversal occurs. As long as the dying woman is still alive, she represents death-in-life; but once she has been prematurely interred, she represents life-in-death, embodying the man's narcissistic obsession with survival enacted as the woman's real or hallucinated return from the grave to bring not life but madness or death.[4]

At the start of "The Fall of the House of Usher," the tale's unnamed narrator approaches the ancestral home of his boyhood companion Roderick Usher and is struck both by its gloomy aspect and by the way this impression is redoubled in the mirroring tarn at the mansion's foot, a hint of the narcissism that drives the tale's central character. The narrator, who hasn't seen Roderick in years, has come in response to Roderick's letter, which "gave evidence of nervous agitation": "The writer spoke of acute bodily illness—of a mental disorder which oppressed him—and of an earnest desire to see me, as his best, and indeed his only personal friend, with a view of attempting, by the cheerfulness of my society, some alleviation of his malady."[5] The narrator recalls that Roderick's family had always been noted "for a peculiar sensibility of temperament, displaying itself, through long ages, in many works of exalted art" (2:398–99). The "entire family lay in the direct line of descent," and given "the perfect keeping of the character of the premises with the accredited character" of the family, the two had become so closely identified "as to merge the original title of the estate in the quaint and equivocal appellation of the 'House of Usher'—an appellation which seemed to include, in the minds of the peasantry who used it, both the family and the family mansion" (2:399).

The narrator says that "the sole effect of my somewhat childish experiment—that of looking down within the tarn—had been to deepen the first singular impression" of gloom and of the mansion as an almost sentient being. He then proposes the psychological rule that will govern the rest of the tale: "There can be no doubt that the consciousness of the rapid increase of my superstition . . . served mainly to accelerate the increase itself. Such, I have long known, is the paradoxical law of all sentiments having terror as a basis" (2:399). Since the tarn mirroring the House of Usher (the dwelling but also the family) seems clearly meant to recall Narcissus's mirroring pool, and since the Narcissus scenario of gazing at one's own image to the point of fixation is clearly an extreme form of self-consciousness, it is significant both that the narrator describes his own *self-consciousness* "of the rapid increase" of his "superstition" as the accelerating agent of that terror-based sentiment and that he describes his looking into the mirroring tarn as a "childish experiment"— significant because both of these activities evoke aspects of narcissism.

The term *narcissism* first appears in Freud's writings in his 1910 monograph on Leonardo da Vinci, where he uses it to explain sexual object-choice in homosexuals. He says that in the cases of male homosexuals he's treated,

the subjects had had a very intense erotic attachment to a female person, as a rule their mother, during the first period of childhood, which is afterwards forgotten; this attachment was evoked or encouraged by too much tenderness on the part of the mother herself, and further reinforced by the small part played by the father during their childhood. . . . After this preliminary stage a transformation sets in. . . . The child's love for his mother cannot continue to develop consciously any further. . . . The boy represses his love for his mother: he puts himself in her place, identifies himself with her, and takes his own person as a model in whose likeness he chooses the new objects of his love. In this way he has become a homosexual. What he has in fact done is to slip back to auto-erotism: for the boys whom he now loves as he grows up are after all only substitutive figures and revivals of himself in childhood—boys whom he loves in the way in which his mother loved *him* when he was a child. He finds the objects of his love along the path of *narcissism,* as we say; for Narcissus, according to Greek legend, was a youth who preferred his own reflection to everything else.[6]

Since the object-choice in this narcissistic scenario is a "revival" of the subject's self "in childhood," it's not surprising that the narrator of "The Fall of the House of Usher" describes his looking into the mirroring tarn as a "childish experiment," nor surprising that, though he has not seen the narrator for many years, Roderick, in his "nervous agitation," has sent for someone who was one of his "boon companions in boyhood" (2:398).

Since what attracts Narcissus to his image in the pool in the Greek myth is his own youthful beauty, one aspect of the narcissistic personality is an intense fear and loathing of anything that threatens the beauty of youth—time and aging, illness and death. And that terror-based emotion, which the narrator experiences on looking into the mirroring tarn—an emotion whose rapid increase is accelerated by his consciousness of it (i.e., his self-reflection)—bears a striking resemblance to the condition in which the narrator finds his friend Roderick, a condition the narrator describes as "an habitual trepidancy"— something the narrator had been prepared for both by Roderick's letter and by "reminiscences of certain boyish traits" (2:402). Roderick describes his nervous affliction as "a constitutional and a family evil": "'I shall perish,' said he, 'I *must* perish in this deplorable folly. . . . I dread the events of the future, not in themselves, but in their results. I shudder at the thought of any, even the most trivial, incident, which may operate upon this intolerable agitation of soul. I have, indeed, no abhorrence of danger, except in its absolute effect—in terror. In this unnerved—in this pitiable condition—I feel that the period will sooner or later arrive when I must abandon life and reason together, in some struggle with the grim phantasm, FEAR'" (2:402–3).

Roderick tells the narrator that his nervous illness is linked to the influence on him of the family dwelling, "whence, for many years, he had never ventured forth," an influence "which some peculiarities" in its "mere form and substance" had "by dint of long sufferance . . . obtained over his spirit—an effect which the *physique* of the gray walls and turrets, and of the dim tarn into which they all looked down, had, at length, brought about upon the *morale* of his existence" (2:403).

But if the house's mirror-image in the tarn outside reflects the decaying state of the family home and by implication the declining state of the family, now reduced to its last two members, then a corresponding mirror-image inside the house shows Roderick his own declining condition every day and by that display accelerates it. He tells the narrator that the immediate cause of his nervous affliction is due "to the severe and long-continued illness—indeed to the evidently approaching dissolution—of a tenderly beloved sister—his sole companion for long years—his last and only relative on earth" (2:403–4). Roderick's twin sister, Madeline, suffers from "a settled apathy, a gradual wasting away of the person, and frequent although transient affections of a partially cataleptical character" (2:404). What Madeline's physical wasting away displays, outer for inner, is Roderick's own psychological deterioration, and on the evening of the narrator's arrival, Madeline succumbs "to the prostrating power of the destroyer" and takes to her bed.

Over the next few days the narrator tries unsuccessfully to raise Roderick's spirits, spending hours listening to his musical compositions, watching him paint (one picture in particular of an exitless, subterranean crypt), and hearing him render his poetic rhapsodies, one of which, entitled "The Haunted Palace," reveals to the narrator "a full consciousness on the part of Usher, of the tottering of his lofty reason on her throne" (2:406). The poem, which evokes a haunted dwelling as a metaphor for the human body inhabited by the spirit, leads to a discussion of Roderick's *idée fixe*—"the sentience" of inanimate things, in particular, "the gray stones of the home of his forefathers," which, "in the order of their arrangement, . . . above all, in the long undisturbed endurance of this arrangement, and in its reduplication in the still waters of the tarn," had led to the "condensation of an atmosphere" that exercised an "importunate and terrible influence which for centuries moulded the destinies of his family, and which made *him* what I now saw him" (2:408).

Suddenly one day Roderick announces that Madeline has died and that he intends to preserve "her corpse for a fortnight, (previously to its final interment,) in one of the numerous vaults within the main walls of the building" (2:409). Usher and the narrator carry Madeline's coffin down to the vault, and the narrator, remarking on the resemblance between Roderick and Madeline, learns they "had been twins, and that sympathies of a scarcely intelligible nature had always existed between them" (2:410). The narrator now tries to comfort Roderick in his grief but finds him becoming ever more distracted, as if "his unceasingly agitated mind was laboring with some oppressive secret, to divulge which he struggled for the necessary courage," until gradually the narrator finds himself beginning to be "infected" (2:411) by Roderick's state of mind.

Late one night, seven or eight days after Madeline's entombment, the narrator, unable to sleep, hears Roderick at his door and observes "a species of mad hilarity in his eyes—an evidently restrained *hysteria* in his whole demeanor." There is a storm raging outside, and Roderick throws open the window to show the narrator that "all the terrestrial objects" in the immediate vicinity are "glowing in the unnatural light of a faintly luminous and distinctly visible gaseous exhalation which hung about and enshrouded the mansion" (2:412), a gaseous exhalation Roderick seems to take as the physical medium of that atmosphere by which the house has moulded the destiny of his family and himself. Fearing for Roderick's sanity, the narrator tries to calm him, to distance him from his immediate surroundings by reading him a tale called the "'Mad Trist' of Sir Launcelot Canning" (2:413).

With the reading of this story Poe suggests the essential difference between Roderick, fixated in his childish narcissism, and his boyhood friend the narrator, who, though he describes his gazing into the mirroring tarn as a "childish experiment" and though he has even begun to feel himself infected by Roderick's narcissistic terror, is nevertheless stable enough, adult enough, to confront the fear of death and overcome it through rational reflection, a process symbolically evoked (rereflected, so to speak) in the story the narrator reads him. Caught in a tempest (like the one raging outside the house of Usher), Ethelred, the hero of the "Mad Trist," seeks admittance to the dwelling of a hermit and, receiving no answer to his knock and angered at such discourtesy, breaks down the door. At this point in the reading the narrator and Roderick hear "from some very remote portion of the mansion . . . what might have been, in its exact similarity of character, the echo . . . of the very cracking and ripping sound" (2:414) described in the story as Ethelred shatters the door.

Once inside the dwelling Ethelred finds not "the maliceful hermit" but "a dragon of a scaly and prodigious demeanor" guarding a palace of gold, "and upon the wall there hung a shield of shining brass with this legend enwritten—

Who entereth herein, a conqueror hath bin;
Who slayeth the dragon, the shield he shall win" (2:414)

Ethelred immediately fells the dragon with his mace, and the dragon in his death agony emits a dreadful scream. Once again the action of the tale is echoed by a distant "most unusual screaming or grating sound—the exact counterpart of what my fancy had already conjured up for the dragon's unnatural shriek" (2:414). Ethelred advances to claim the shield now freed from its enchantment, but as he approaches, the shield comes to meet him, falling "at his feet upon the silver floor, with a mighty great and terrible ringing sound," and at just that moment the narrator hears a "metallic, and clangorous, yet apparently muffled reverberation" (2:415).

Unnerved, the narrator rushes to Roderick and finds in his whole demeanor "a stony rigidity" (2:415) as Roderick whispers, "*We have put her living in the tomb.*" Roderick says that he has been aware of this for several days but dared not speak and that he understands the meaning of the echoes in Ethelred's tale: "the breaking of the hermit's door, and the death-cry of the dragon, and the clangor of the shield!—say, rather, the rending of her coffin, and the grating of the iron hinges of her prison, and her struggles within the copper archway of the vault." Roderick, deranged by the thought of his sister returning from the crypt to get him, cries out that at that very moment she stands outside the chamber door. Suddenly the door swings open, and there stands Madeline, with "blood upon her white robes, and the evidence of some bitter struggle upon . . . her emaciated frame" (2:416). Madeline totters for a moment and then, "with a low moaning cry," falls "heavily inward upon the person of her brother, and in her violent and now final death-agonies," bears him "to the floor a corpse, and a victim of the terrors he had anticipated" (2:417). Aghast, the narrator flees from the mansion, and as he does, that "barely-discernible fissure . . . extending from the roof of the building, in a zigzag direction, to the base," which he had noticed on first entering the house, suddenly widens with "a fierce breath of the whirlwind," and he sees through the crack "the full, setting, and blood-red moon" as the walls of the mansion collapse into the mirroring tarn at its foot, bearing with them the last two members of the family.

IV

Poe shaped the most significant imagery in "The Fall of the House of Usher" (as well as in the included tale of Ethelred and the dragon) by weaving together, with an uncanny sense of their psychological import, strands from two classical myths. Recall that in the story of Narcissus as it appears in book 3 of Ovid's *Metamorphoses* he is a youth of sixteen, who "might seem either boy or man," and is of such surpassing beauty that "many youths and many maidens sought his love; but in that slender form was pride so cold that no youth, no maiden touched his heart."[7] One day in the woods the nymph Echo sees Narcissus, is immediately attracted by his beauty, and tries to embrace him, but he spurns her love. Grief-stricken at his rejection, Echo wastes away until "only her voice and her bones remain: then, only voice; for they say that her bones were turned to stone." At last one of the many youths whose love he had scorned prayed to heaven: "So may he himself love and not gain the thing he loves!" (3:153). The goddess Nemesis heard "the righteous prayer" and contrived that Narcissus should come upon a woodland pool of clear unruffled water, and as he bends to drink, see his own image, immediately falling in love with what he takes to be a boy who lives within the pool. Lamenting that "by a thin barrier of water we are kept apart," Narcissus says, "When I have smiled, you smile back; and I have often seen tears, when I weep, on your cheeks. My becks you answer with your nod; and, as I suspect from the movement of your sweet lips, you answer my words as well, but words which do not reach my ears.—Oh, I am he! . . . I know now my own image. I burn with love of my own self; I both kindle the flames and suffer them" (3:157). Pining for a love that can never be consummated, Narcissus wastes away beside the pool (Echo doubling to the last his words of farewell to his image) until he is transformed into the eponymous flower.

Two things strike us immediately in the story of Narcissus: first, that it is the difference between the visual and the vocal orders which reveals to Narcissus that what he sees in the pool is a reflected image and not a three-dimensional body (i.e., he sees the image's lips moving in speech but he hears no words), and second, that Narcissus and Echo are linked in the myth as evocations of doubling in the visual and the vocal orders, respectively (Narcissus and his reflected image; Echo and her reiterated sounds). In "The Fall of the House of Usher" Poe counts on the reader's recalling this linking of visual and auditory doubling in the Narcissus myth when he has the sounds made by Roderick's mirror-image twin, as she breaks out of the crypt, echo the sounds of Ethelred breaking into the hermit's dwelling, slaying the dragon, and claiming the shield of shining brass. This echo effect is meant not only to underline the narcissistic relationship between Roderick and Madeline but also to suggest the opposing directions of Madeline's and Ethelred's activities; the sounds of Madeline breaking out of the crypt to frighten her brother to death (insofar as they counterpoint events in the "Mad Trist") are meant to evoke the hero Ethelred's actions as a symbolic breaking *into* the grave and a slaying of the monster of death.

In creating Ethelred's tale within the story of Roderick and Madeline, Poe joined to the Narcissus myth another Greek myth of opposite import—that of Perseus and Medusa. In the mythic past of virtually every culture there is at least one heroic figure whose actions seek to free mankind from the paralyzing fear of death, actions that characteristically involve either a descent into the earth or into the belly of a monster and a reemergence to show that death has been overcome, the flesh-eating monster slain. For example, Jesus invokes this traditional structure when he prophesies in Matthew 12:40 of his own burial and resurrection that "as Jonas was three days and three nights in the whale's belly; so shall the Son of man be three days and three nights in the heart of the earth." Culturally speaking, the overcoming of the fear of death becomes the great dividing line between childhood and maturity, and in many cultures the traditional form of the male initiation rite or rite of passage is a symbolic death and rebirth, "a ritual test," as I've noted elsewhere, in which an adolescent becomes an adult by demonstrating "his fearlessness of death, his understanding that death is not an end to life but the price of and portal to a higher form of life that one can never reach as long as one is afraid to pass through that narrow gate."

But this rite of passage is also "a means by which the community as a whole protects itself against the fear of death. By making the structure of the rite a symbolic death and rebirth, the community transforms death from a senseless alien force within whose grip man is essentially passive into a meaningful stage of human life, a stage over which man exercises active control through a ritual repetition."[8] By incorporating it into a ritual, the community makes death "subject to communal action," but more important, "what the structure of a symbolic death and rebirth ritually reenacts for the community . . . is not that the death of the child in a man necessarily leads to the birth of the adult, but rather that the state that follows real physical death is continuous with life, is another state of life in just the same way that childhood and adulthood are continuous states of life. The deepest significance of the rite-of-passage scenario is, then, not that it imprints the structure of a symbolic death and rebirth onto the passage from adolescence to maturity, but rather that by a kind of reverse transference it surreptitiously imprints upon physical death the sense of a passage between states of life" (186).

Among many primitive peoples, the male initiation rite traditionally involves as well the separation of adolescent boys from their mothers, while the ritual overcoming of the fear of death (the fear of the devouring womb/tomb of earth) often involves the boys' mastering the fear of the terrifying aspects of the feminine, or of the Great Mother, as the Jungian mythographer Erich Neumann styles the ancient matriarchal figuration of nature's fearful reproductive/disintegrative aspect. In his work on comparative mythology, *The Origins and History of Consciousness,* Neumann reads various recurring structures in ancient myths as symbolic accounts of the origin and development of human consciousness, of the progressive stabilization of the ego in the history of mankind. Indeed, he understands the archetypal heroic activity as the winning of this stabilization during the difficult passage from childhood to adulthood, and he reads the story of Perseus as a paradigm of this.

As Ovid recounts the story of Narcissus, the beautiful adolescent whose libido is fixated in an infantile object-choice (himself), in book 3 of the *Metamorphoses,* so in book 4 he tells the story of the heroic Perseus—recounts his slaying of the snake-haired Medusa (the sight of whose face has the power to turn "men and beasts . . . into stone" [3:233], that is, literally to petrify); his subsequent killing of the sea monster that threatens the maiden Andromeda; and his claiming of Andromeda as his bride. Perseus is able to kill Medusa because "he himself had looked upon the image of that dread face reflected from the bright bronze shield his left hand bore; and while deep sleep held fast both the snakes and her who wore them, he smote her head clean from her neck" (3: 233). Neumann points out that "Perseus has Hermes and Athene on his side, the tutelary deities of wisdom and consciousness. . . . Hermes presents him with a sword, and Athene lends him her brazen shield for a mirror, in which he can see the Medusa's head reflected and so is able to kill her."[9] As Narcissus's mirroring pool (which shows him an image of himself) represents the childish form of self-reflection, so Athene's brazen shield in Perseus's hands represents the adult form of reflective self-consciousness that reveals not himself but rather that Other from whose fearful sway he must free himself in order to become himself fully and stably. Neumann describes the Medusa's decapitated head as a "hideous death mask" (215), and Freud in his essay "The Medusa's Head" says that "this symbol of horror . . . worn upon her dress by the virgin goddess Athene" represents "the terrifying genitals of the Mother" and thus is appropriate for "a woman who is unapproachable and repels all sexual desires" (18:273–74). He adds, "Since the Greeks were in the main strongly homosexual, it was inevitable that we should find among them a representation of woman as a being who frightens and repels because she is castrated" (18:274), that is, decapitated. If the slaying of the Medusa frees Perseus from the fear of the terrifying aspect of the feminine (the mother's genitals), then his slaying of the sea monster in a hand-to-hand, life-and-death struggle would suggest his overcoming of the fear of death, and his winning the maiden Andromeda as his bride would then indicate, insofar as it is an adult object-choice, his successful passing of these two previous tests in the progress from adolescence to maturity.

Several details in the Ethelred story suggest that Poe had the Perseus myth in mind when he constructed the parabolic tale the narrator reads to Roderick as the latter's mind disintegrates under the terror of approaching death, a parable offering to Roderick, as a counter-example, the heroic overcoming of the very fears that are destroying him. In Ethelred's tale the hermit's dwelling (a dwelling with a lone occupant) is clearly meant to evoke another single-occupant enclosure (a coffin), an identification confirmed when Ethelred's shattering the hermit's door is echoed by the sound of Madeline breaking out of her coffin. And what Ethelred finds when he enters the dwelling is not the hermit but a dragon, the flesh-eating monster of the grave. Recall in this connection that among the ancient Greeks and Romans the limestone frequently used to construct stone coffins was called, respectively, *lithos sarkophagos* and *lapis sarcophagus,* literally, flesh-eating stone, from which the modern use of *sarcophagus* (flesh-eater) as a synonym for *coffin* derives. Ethelred slays the dragon, but unlike Perseus, who uses the shining brazen shield symbolizing adult reflective consciousness to kill Medusa, Ethelred *wins* the "shield of shining brass" for slaying the fear-inducing monster, as the verse engraved on the shield makes clear: "Who entereth herein, a conqueror hath bin; / Who slayeth the dragon, the shield he shall win."

Though the shining shield is transposed from being the *agent* of conquering the fearful figure in Perseus's myth to being the *reward* for slaying the monster in Ethelred's story (a characteristic transposition of means for end), clearly Poe has Perseus's shield in mind as an allusive background here, for when the metallic shield's falling to the floor in Ethelred's story is echoed by the sound of Madeline's "struggles within the copper archway of the vault," the narrator rushes to Roderick and finds that "throughout his whole countenance there reigned a stony rigidity." From Roderick's face of "stony rigidity" to Medusa's face able to turn those who look upon it to stone seems a short associative step, particularly when what induces this rigidity in Roderick is the sound of a once-beloved and now-terrifying woman breaking out of the crypt to drive him mad by bringing death to his doorstep, a woman he had wanted dead (because the sight of her gradual deterioration was killing him) but whom he didn't have the courage to kill. When Poe links in his tale the Narcissus myth with that of Perseus and Medusa as, respectively, the unsuccessful and successful versions of a young man's passage from adolescence to maturity, he seems to be reflecting the general sense of what the classical world understood was at issue in these myths. Neumann points out that Narcissus is one of a series of figures such as Horus, Hyacinthus, and Dionysus, who are "under the dominion of the all-powerful Mother Goddess," but also one of those youths who, like Pentheus, Hippolytus, and Adonis, are destroyed by her, for as Neumann says, "the Great Mother is their fate" (43).

That there is an incestuous attraction between Roderick and Madeline can be inferred from several details: first, in all Poe's other "dying woman" stories the woman is either the male figure's wife or betrothed; second, Roderick says of Madeline that "sympathies of a scarcely intelligible nature . . . had always existed between them;" and finally, for Roderick, trapped within the womb of the family home and doomed to a narcissistic object-choice, his sister functions both as a mirror-image of himself and as a substitutive mother figure (in the way that the opposite-sex sibling in incestuous attachments always serves as a substitute for the opposite-sex parent), a substitute for the mother whose sexually charged relationship to the male infant or young boy is the ultimate *cause*, in Freud's reading, of the narcissistic object-choice in the young man. That the "dying woman" scenario had a personal resonance for Poe can be judged from the fact that he'd married his thirteen-year-old first cousin, Virginia Clemm, whom he called "Sis," and that he lived for eleven years in a family unit composed of himself, his cousin/wife, and his beloved aunt/ mother-in-law, Maria Clemm, whom he called "Muddy." Poe's own mother, Eliza, had died of consumption when Poe was a small child, and though the "dying woman" stories were written before the onset of this same illness took Virginia Poe's life, still Virginia's health had always been delicate enough to make the possibility of this illness a constant danger. Moreover, Maria Clemm was perhaps Poe's most important surrogate mother figure. In a poem "To My Mother" (1849), he says of her:

> You who are more than mother unto me,
> And fill my heart of hearts, where Death installed you
>   In setting my Virginia's spirit free.
> My mother—my own mother, who died early,
>   Was the mother of myself; but you
> Are mother to the one I loved so dearly,
>   And thus are dearer than the mother I knew
> By that infinity with which my wife
>   Was dearer to my soul than its soul-life. (1:466–67)

As I observed in *The Mystery to a Solution*, "From what we know of Poe's life, he was a man whose relationships with women characteristically involved the need to be mothered. But to judge from his fiction, he was highly ambivalent about this need, at once wanting maternal care and affection from women and yet resenting it as an entrapment in childish dependency. Apparently, for Poe the reverse side of the need to be mothered was the fear of being (s)mothered, of being buried alive in the womb of the family" (231). And by as much as an "idealized prenatal condition" (the satisfaction and security of the womb) "had become associated in Poe's own life with the image of a dead mother," that association "linked the sleep of the womb with that of the grave and the goal of reunion with the means of reunion (the mother with Death). It is this deathly shadow that seems to fall across the women in Poe's life, a dark image of the dead mother as Mother Death superimposed on the living faces of the women he cared for. One might argue as well that his cousin Virginia ultimately surpassed his aunt Maria as a mother-substitute precisely by dying, by coming to resemble Poe's real mother in that most important of aspects" (232).

Given our reading of "The Fall of the House of Usher" and the relationship of this and the other "dying woman" stories to Poe's own life, Woolrich's evident attraction to Poe's work isn't surprising, nor are the significant resemblances between "Three O'Clock" and Poe's tale. In both stories a mentally unstable man is moved to take drastic action against a woman who dwells in his house, in one case a wife, in the other a beloved twin sister. One tries to prematurely bury his sister even though he knows her illness involves "transient affections of a partially cataleptical character" (2:404)—which is to say, he knows that what he takes for death may only be a seizure in which breathing, heartbeat, and pulse have become so shallow as to be undetectable, and yet he dispatches her to the crypt anyway because her continued presence has become so terrifying to his fragile, self-absorbed ego. In contrast, the other plans to destroy his wife, her suspected lover, and the family home in a single bomb blast. In each instance the man's intentions redound upon himself: in one case a quirk of fate traps Stapp within the destructive mechanism he's set in motion, and in the other Roderick is destroyed in accordance with that rule of narcissistic doubling that whatever violence you do to your double you do to yourself, as Poe makes clear in the double story "William Wilson" (1839), published one month after "Usher." But the most important resemblance, of course, between "Three O'Clock" and "Usher" is that this redounding of the men's deadly intentions back upon themselves involves their each being driven mad by terror from a more or less prolonged foreknowledge of their own deaths (with the final touch in Roderick's case that he is literally killed by fright)—a resemblance extending as well to the ingenuity with which Poe and Woolrich invent business to prolong and heighten the character's terror, for example, the sound effects that echo Ethelred's story and the numerous visitors to Stapp's house that raise and then dash his hopes of escape.

V

Before turning our attention to Woolrich's best novel, I want to look again for a moment at some of the things he tells us about himself in *Blues of a Lifetime,* and in particular, to read these in light of what we've said about "The Fall of the House of Usher," on the one hand, and what Freud has written about homosexuality in his essay on Leonardo da Vinci and about paranoia and persecutory complexes in his essay on Schreber, on the other. Recall that Freud's 1910 essay is titled "Leonardo da Vinci and a Memory of His Childhood" and that the memory Freud cites is from one of da Vinci's scientific notebooks, in which Leonardo accounts for "his preoccupation with the flight of birds as preordained by destiny" (11:84): "It seems that I was always destined to be so deeply concerned with vultures; for I recall as one of my very earliest memories that while I was in my cradle a vulture came down to me, and opened my mouth with its tail, and struck me many times with its tail against my lips" (11:82). (The German text of the quotation that Freud used was faulty regarding the name of the bird, translating the Italian word for *kite* as *vulture.*)

Noting that "what someone thinks he remembers from his childhood is not a matter of indifference" (11:84), Freud treats da Vinci's so-called memory as a childhood fantasy, reading the bird's tail (Italian *coda*) as a familiar "symbol . . . for the male sexual organ" (11:85) and its "beating about inside" the child's mouth as suggesting "an act of *fellatio*," and remarking further that Leonardo's fantasy resembles those "found in women or passive homosexuals" (11:86). As we noted earlier, Freud theorizes Leonardo's "homosexual attitude" was of that type in which "the future inverts" in earliest childhood "pass through a phase of very intense but short-lived fixation to a woman (usually their mother), and that, after leaving this behind, they identify themselves with a woman and take *themselves* as their sexual object. That is to say, they proceed from a narcissistic basis, and look for a young man who resembles themselves and whom *they* may love as their mother loved *them*" (7:145). Freud further theorizes that Leonardo repressed this homosexual attitude and sublimated his sexual energy into work—artistic work to begin with but, as he grew older, more and more into scientific research.

Freud observes that the first form of research in a human being's life is "the sexual researches of these early years of childhood," which are "always carried out in solitude" and which "constitute a first step toward taking an independent attitude in the world, and imply a high degree of alienation of the child from the people in his environment who formerly enjoyed his complete confidence" (7:197). Freud suggests that Leonardo's increasing devotion to scientific research and his waning artistic production amounted to a gradual turning away from an earlier form of sublimation in which he began by making "representations of his sexual objects" (Freud quotes Vasari to the effect "that heads of laughing women and beautiful boys . . . were notable among his first artistic endeavours" [11:133]), reached its high point in his depictions of women with enigmatic smiles (as in the Mona Lisa and in Saint Anne with the Madonna and Child—whom Freud interprets as images of Leonardo's mother), and then, as Leonardo's repression of his sexual tendencies became almost total, he further sublimated that sexual energy in a will to knowledge so extreme that it represents a distancing from, an objectifying of, his environment powerful enough to master that environment in direct proportion to his alienation from it, with the result that he seemed to lose interest in his artistic work and left many of his last paintings unfinished.

Freud notes that "the turning of his interests from art to science, which increased as time went on, must have played its part in widening the gulf between himself and his contemporaries. All the efforts in which in their opinion he frittered away his time when he could have been industriously painting . . . and becoming rich . . . seemed to them to be merely capricious trifling" (11:65). And to the extent that "the investigator in him," according to Freud, "never in the course of his development left the artist entirely free, but often made severe encroachments on him and perhaps in the end suppressed him," Leonardo himself seems to have been aware of this (and of his contemporaries' opinions on the matter), for Vasari records that in his final hours Leonardo, "having raised himself out of reverence so as to sit on the bed, and giving an account of his illness and its circumstances, yet showed how much he had offended God and mankind in not having worked at his art as he should have done" (11:64n).

Whatever one may think of Freud's attempt to psychoanalyze Leonardo four centuries after his death on the basis of several notebook entries, some sketchy biographical details, and an analysis of a couple of his paintings, nevertheless Freud's theory of the genesis of one type of male homosexual attitude (as initially set forth in the da Vinci essay) possessed a certain authoritative status in psychiatric circles during the years of Woolrich's adulthood. Whether Woolrich ever consulted a psychiatrist about his homosexuality or read Freud on the subject, we have no knowledge, but what we do know is that there are several striking, highly significant resemblances between Freud's account of da Vinci's homosexual attitude and what we know of Woolrich's life and what he tells us of that life in *Blues of a Lifetime.*

First, both da Vinci and Woolrich invoke a childhood memory to explain why an adult tendency in their characters was predestined by some early event that befell them: For da Vinci it's the memory of the bird that flew down into his cradle and put its tail in his mouth presented as a reason for his preoccupation with researching the flight of birds, and perhaps by extension, with research in general; and with Woolrich it's the memory of "the low-hanging stars of the Valley of Anahuac," which gave him "that trapped feeling, like some sort of poor insect that you've put inside a downturned glass," a memory that accounts for the "sense of personal, private doom" he'd felt ever since. While Freud doubts that da Vinci's is a "memory" at all, suggesting rather that it's a childhood fantasy of fellatio, we noted earlier that Woolrich's "memory" of the fatal stars in Mexico may well have been created out of whole cloth or at the very least reworked, since we know he'd given a friend, the author Lou Ellen Davis, a different version of this epiphany under the stars: "I remember him telling me that he was chasing a girl around a tree—it was a game, he wanted to kiss her—and he said he suddenly looked up—it was night—and he looked at all the stars and he thought: 'Gee, all the stars don't care, nobody cares,' and he ended the game" (Nevins, 7–8). If Woolrich's lifelong sense of fatalism coincided with his giving up this game of chasing a girl around a tree to kiss her—which is to say, with not finding women a sexual object-choice—then the subtexts of both da Vinci's and Woolrich's childhood memories would be the same, and the point of each memory would be to present in a more or less veiled manner each man's sexual orientation as something imposed on them by genetic inheritance or by events, something fated and not a matter of personal choice and thus personal responsibility.

As I noted earlier, Woolrich was, according to his sister-in-law, quite conflicted about his homosexuality, as is evident, I would argue, in the passage in *Blues of a Lifetime* immediately preceding his memory of the stars in Mexico, the passage in which he inveighs against his habits of excessive smoking and drinking acquired in the 1920s and persisting through a lifetime, habits that he felt had damaged him as a person and that, in Freudian terminology, represent a male fixation in infantile orality (the earliest form of sexual satisfaction caused by the erogenous stimulation of the infant's lips and mouth in sucking the mother's breast). Yet his choice of words and the vehemence of his response in condemning these two habits point perhaps to the habit whose mention he has suppressed; he says, "It is a wrong thing and a bad thing to pervert yourself like this." Certainly, the connotations and common usage of the verb *pervert*, which Woolrich surely knew, make it seem an odd choice to describe the harmful effects of simply smoking and drinking. If Woolrich has repressed an unnameable habit behind two nameable ones that serve as screens for it, then the return of the repressed occurs only three paragraphs later, in his "memory" of the fatalistic stars in Mexico with its homosexual subtext.

And just as Freud implies that the regret expressed by Leonardo on his deathbed (about not working at his art as he should have because he had presumably spent too much time on his research) may have lain behind Leonardo's earlier attempt to justify his preoccupation with studying the flight of birds by "remembering" a childhood event that had preordained this interest, thus absolving himself of the responsibility for having misspent his life on research rather then art, so too Woolrich, in a passage a couple of paragraphs before his memory of the stars in Mexico, expresses a similar regret about the way his life turned out versus what might have been expected. Had it not been for the excesses of the two habits that he mentions: "I would have been a great writer. I would have been a great and a good man. . . . I would have led a happy life" (15). This sense of regret as well as of the "personal, private doom" connected with his memory of the stars are the two emotions that pervade *Blues of a Lifetime*. And since what seems to be the common denominator with both Woolrich and Freud's da Vinci is the need to find that their sexual orientation is something beyond their control, the recovered or created "childhood memory" serves in both cases as a defense mechanism against guilt and regret.

In the da Vinci essay Freud raises the question of whether the homosexual attitude is innate or accidental, noting that "homosexual men . . . are fond of representing themselves, through their theoretical spokesmen, as being from the outset a distinct sexual species. . . . They are, they claim, men who are innately compelled by organic determinants to find pleasure in men and have been debarred from obtaining it in women" (11:98). Freud's position is that

"one must treat their theories with some reserve," a position he is almost compelled to take as a psychoanalyst, for if the homosexual attitude is something
genetically or biologically determined, psychoanalysis would be powerless to
affect it, but if it is something (or in some instances) determined by events of
early childhood, then psychoanalysis might have some scope for its activity,
and with that said, Freud immediately launches into his theory of the genesis
of the homosexual attitude based on the male homosexual cases he's treated,
a theory in which the unsatisfied mother takes "her little son in place of her
husband, and by the too early maturing of his erotism" robs "him of a part of
his masculinity" (11:117).

Clearly, from what we know of Woolrich's life, his close relationship with
his mother was something from which he seemed powerless to escape. There is
the testimony of his college friend Jacques Barzun about Woolrich being under
the "domination" of his mother, his marriage to a woman of a strongly mother-
ing type, Gloria Blackton (nicknamed "Bill"), his flight from his wife after three
months, and his return to his mother with whom he lived for the next twenty-
seven years in a New York hotel suite. Little wonder that Woolrich would be
attracted to a story like Poe's "Usher," whose main character, trapped in the
womb of the family home with a narcissistic mirror-image twin and mother-
substitute, interprets the influence, the "atmosphere," of the family home, as
the fate that "had moulded the destinies of his family, and which had made
him what I now saw him—what he was." But what Woolrich set out to do in
his fiction was transform "private doom" into a universal condition, a condition apparently so agonizingly felt by the author that he was able to transfer it
to the page with a minimal loss of intensity. There is thus one further aspect of
Woolrich's fatalism we must examine to appreciate the full effect of his fiction:
the sense that fate, in the cosmic backdrop it provides to man's petty strivings
and sufferings, is not just cruelly indifferent but is in some sense actively malevolent, persecutory, as if delighting in watching the insect under the downturned glass try to climb up the sides and fall back again and again.

In "Three O'Clock," we saw how the ceaseless insinuation and withdrawal
of the hope of rescue left Stapp feeling as if some unseen power were toying
with and torturing him, mocking him "in his crucifixion." And this expectation of fate's persecutory bias is a constant with the many Woolrich characters
wrongfully suspected or convicted of murder—Frank Townsend in *The Black
Curtain,* Scott Henderson in *Phantom Lady,* Kirk Murray in *The Black Angel,*
Quinn Williams in *Deadline at Dawn,* Bill Scott in *The Black Path of Fear*—as

well as with the women who love them. It's a constant as well for those characters whose lives are destroyed by an almost ironic intervention of fate that
brings sudden death to a loved one either at what should be a moment of
supreme happiness (as when Julie Killeen in *The Bride Wore Black* sees her
husband killed by a drunk driver as they're leaving the church on their wedding day) or by a means so wildly coincidental that it seems as if it must have
been calculated by some higher power (as when Johnny Marr, in *Rendezvous
in Black,* finds his fiancée lying dead in the town square, killed by a whiskey
bottle thrown out the window of a private plane by a drunk). Both Julie and
Johnny are destroyed by these events not just because their loved ones are
killed but because these deaths transform them into slightly mad, avenging
angels—hunting down the men in the hit-and-run vehicle and killing them
one by one in Julie's case, and tracking the men in the plane and then killing
the woman that each man loves most in Johnny's. (One might note here in
passing that the coincidental occurrences found so often in Woolrich's fiction
seem to spring from his sense that modern readers are never disappointed,
never feel cheated or manipulated, by coincidences that produce disastrous results, that it's only the Dickensian, fortuitous coincidences that solve problems
or create happy endings that modern readers balk at.)

If Woolrich dates his "sense of personal, private doom" from age eleven,
when he was living with his father in Mexico, and if we are correct in finding
in the alternate version of the episode he gave Lou Ellen Davis evidence of his
early awareness of his sexual orientation as a fate, then how did that personal
sense of a fateful sexuality become a general sense of being trapped within a
cosmic machinery (as figured by the stars) so indifferent to the human condition as to seem cruel, if not persecutory? The answer may well lie in what we
know of Woolrich's relationship with his father. While Freud theorizes the genesis of the homosexual attitude discussed in the da Vinci essay as lying in the
mother-son relationship, the resulting identification with the mother, which
makes the son take a feminine attitude toward young men resembling himself,
may also make him take a feminine attitude toward the father, as suggested in
Freud's essay on Dr. Schreber (12:58). As Woolrich's biographer Nevins points
out, Genaro Woolrich, the mining engineer, was by all accounts a very manly
figure, and Cornell's relationship with him "must have been intensely painful from the boy's perspective." Cornell told Lou Ellen Davis that "near where
they lived in South America there was a bigger kid, and that he paid this bigger
kid to let Cornell beat him up where Cornell's father could see it, that he gave

him money for this." Davis said that "Cornell wanted to impress his father with the kind of thing that *would* impress his father . . . here was this skinny, frail, very gifted, very artistic kid, and here was this macho guy, and the kid so wanted macho approval." Nevins notes that one of the recurring features of Woolrich's pulp tales from the 1930s was "an acid contempt for physical cowardice which at bottom," argues Nevins, was "a contempt for himself" (6).

Since all the evidence suggests that Woolrich was extremely conflicted about his homosexuality, it seems likely that if, on the one hand, he felt a feminine attraction to his father but, on the other, longed for Genaro's macho approval, he repressed that attraction in his father's case and set in motion the mechanism of paranoia Freud describes in the Schreber essay, a defense mechanism in which a repressed homosexual fantasy is projected outward as an external perception of enmity emanating from the object of the fantasy. This transformation of the subject's inner love for the other into the other's outer hatred of the subject protects the subject from the unacceptable attraction, and in the case in which the fantasy's object is a father or a father figure, this sense of the other person as an enemy bent on doing one harm has far-reaching effects. Freud argues that since in the Judeo-Christian tradition the primary image of God is as a father, a paranoid fantasy that has the father as its object tends to produce the sense that one "is being persecuted by powers of the greatest might" (12:48), by God or Fate. Mark Bassett records in *Blues of a Lifetime* that Woolrich once told the editor Martha Foley apropos of his searching for his own father that "a search for a father is a search for God" (144n2). The pathway leading from Woolrich's sense of the fatefulness of his homosexual orientation to a broader sense of the persecutory aspect of cosmic Fate would thus be suggested. But before going further we should note that, given both the conjectural nature of some of the details of Woolrich's biography cited in our discussion and the necessarily speculative character of the psychoanalytic reading of that material, the value of this critical approach and the psychological profile it draws of the author is ultimately a function of how much light it sheds on Woolrich's suspense fiction, and particularly, on the novel that is his most unremitting and most artistic examination of the persecutory aspect of Fate.

VI

Woolrich published *Night Has a Thousand Eyes* in 1945, and it was, as his biographer Nevins notes, his "longest and most ambitious" novel up to that point (310). Woolrich seemed to signal that he considered it something special by not publishing it under his own name, which had by this point become identified with the "black" series of novels, or under his other pseudonym, William Irish, but under a new pen name created from his two middle names, George Hopley. As in "Three O'Clock," the novel's plot turns around one character's knowing the exact time and ma....er of his own death. Indeed, so fond was Woolrich of this device that he used it in two earlier suspense novels, *Phantom Lady* and *The Black Angel,* but there the characters who share this "prolonged foreknowledge" of death are convicts awaiting execution for a murder they didn't commit. In both these previous books, however, the tantalizing race against time is ultimately won: in *Phantom Lady* the condemned character's girlfriend, after several dangerous adventures, finds the evidence to clear him, while in *The Black Angel* it's the character's wife who puts herself in peril to save her man. But in *Night Has a Thousand Eyes* the race against time is not won, and the whole effect of the novel is to leave us feeling at the end that the character's fate couldn't possibly have been altered, no matter how skillful or frantic the efforts had been to avoid it.

The novel begins with police detective Tom Shawn walking home one night after work, along the embankment of the river that runs through his city. He notices a five-dollar bill on the sidewalk, and as he continues walking, another and another, then a diamond ring, next a lady's handbag with its contents scattered on the ground. Following this trail, Shawn sees a young woman standing on the parapet of a bridge: "Her head was tilted slightly upward, not downward. She was covering her eyes, as if the stars blinded her. It was against them her hand was backed in shelter, and not against the water below."[10] Shawn grabs the young woman to keep her from jumping, but she tells him, "You should have let me get away from them. I wanted to go down deep, where I can't see them shining, and they can't see me" (12). The young woman, "no more than twenty" (13), is attractive and expensively dressed, and Shawn's initial sense is that she has everything to live for. Shawn takes the young woman, whose name is Jean Reid, to an all-night restaurant to calm her and find out why she wanted to kill herself. Feeling that by stopping her attempt at suicide fate has thrust her care into his hands, Shawn thinks, "Now I've got to finish it, and save her" (19)—and it doesn't hurt that he feels sexually attracted to her, either. For the novel's next hundred pages, Jean, sitting at a table in the restaurant, tells Shawn her story, a story that begins with the words "There was a time when I wasn't afraid—" (23).

Saying she's the daughter of a wealthy importer named Harlan Reid and that she lives with her father in the family mansion outside town, Jean explains:

> God put it into our hearts that we should love our fathers, and God put it stronger into the hearts of daughters than of sons. But then God forgot to give us anything that would take away the pain that love can sometimes bring. Above all, God permits us to look backward but God has forbidden us to look forward. And if we do, we do so at our own risk. There is no opiate that can precede the pain; only one that can follow, called time.
>
> I lost my mother when I was two, and so I never really knew her. It was always just my father, my father and I. Sometimes I think that is the strongest of all loves; the full strength of natal love, to which has been added all the aspects of romantic love but a forbidden few. That is the way it has always been with us, and maybe it is not good, but still we should not have been punished this way. (23–24)

Woolrich, like many hard-boiled fiction writers, often reworked previously published short stories for the plots of his novels. In the story he turned into *Night Has a Thousand Eyes*—"Speak to Me of Death," published in *Argosy* (Feb. 1937)—the heroine, Ann Bridges, is the *niece* of the wealthy man whose death has been predicted, and in changing this relationship to the closer one of father and only daughter in the novel, Woolrich was able not only to increase the heroine's anxiety level over a sole parent's fate but also perhaps to make that relationship a vehicle (with roles and genders reversed) for emotions Woolrich felt regarding his closeness with his own mother. When Jean Reid characterizes what she feels for her widowed father, the only parent she's known since the age of two, as "the strongest of all loves; the full strength of natal love, to which has been added all the aspects of romantic love but a forbidden few," her sense of a perhaps inappropriate piggybacking of romantic love on natal love—the sort of thing Freud had in mind when he said in the da Vinci essay that the unsatisfied mother takes "her little son in place of her husband" and causes "the too early maturing of his erotism"—leads her to concede "maybe it is not good, but still we should not have been punished this way," thus linking her father's individual fate as well as the novel's overall sense of fatalism to an overpowering parental attachment.

The foreknowledge of her father's fate forms the core of the novel's action and of Jean's explanation to Shawn of her suicide attempt. She tells him that several months earlier at a dinner party she and her father, discussing his plans to fly to the West Coast, had been overheard by one of the maids, Eileen McGuire. Eileen had come to Jean's room later that night and warned her that her father mustn't make the return trip from San Francisco by plane because it would crash and he'd be killed. Eileen says that a friend of hers with the gift of second sight told her this, but Jean laughs it off, feeling the maid's been drinking. Her father leaves on his trip to San Francisco, and while he's gone, Eileen keeps warning Jean about the return flight until Jean finally becomes so fed up she fires Eileen. However, the warnings have begun to work on her mind, and at the last minute she tries to phone her father at the San Francisco airport to tell him to take the train home, but the plane has already left. Jean then goes through agony waiting for his return or for news, and the next day the radio announces the plane has crashed in the Rockies with no apparent survivors. Jean is devastated, not just by the loss of her father but by what the foreknowledge of that death tells her about the real state of the universe:

> When you were four or five, and you went to Sunday school for the first time, they told you all about God. You'd never heard of Him before. But you weren't frightened. Because that was positive. That was walls about you. That was a roof over your head. Now you're twenty. And now you're frightened, frightened sick. Because this is negative. This takes the walls away, and takes the roof from over your head. You're alone now and naked and very small against the night wind.
>
> They don't know. They can't know.
>
> They did. Someone did. (53)

But then a telegram from her father arrives saying he'd changed his plans and is returning by train.

When Harlan Reid gets back and Jean tells him of the plane crash being foretold, they go to visit Eileen McGuire to learn the name of the friend who'd foreseen Reid's death, and she reluctantly introduces them to the man who lives in the apartment upstairs, a man named Jeremiah Tompkins, who has been a friend of the family ever since he and Eileen's mother and father were children. Both Jean and her father are let down by Tompkins's ordinary, somewhat shabby appearance, but Woolrich's physical description of Tompkins seems more of an inside joke than anything else, since in many respects it's a description of Woolrich himself: "He was thin and scrawny, almost to the point of emaciation. His cheeks were gaunt, his neck was like a gnarled stem supporting his head, his bared arms were bony and whipcorded by their own leanness. . . . His eyes were blue, and dull. They expressed mildness. . . . Over them were sandy brows, incapable of etching any very great expression on his face, perhaps because of their coloring. . . . His hair was reddish gold, and very fine, and growing thin" (85).

Though Jean and her father have ostensibly visited Tompkins to thank him for warning them about the plane, Harlan Reid has another unspoken motive that Tompkins immediately voices for him: "You've come here to show me up, to teach your daughter a lesson. So that she'll stop thinking on it" (87). But Tompkins says he wants nothing from them, not thanks, not money, only to be left alone. And he warns Reid never to come back: "Go back to your fine house, and your dinner guests with diamond watches at their knees, and your broker, and your buying of shares. And try not to run down any little girls getting there" (89). Jean and her father leave, but during the course of that evening and the next day every one of the events Tompkins had so casually mentioned comes to pass—a little girl almost hit by Reid's car, surprise dinner guests that include a woman who has used a wristwatch to hold up her stocking because her garter has broken, and Reid's broker calling to tell him to dump a stock but Reid deciding instead to buy more, hoping it will continue to go down and thus disprove Tompkins's remark. When the stock reverses direction and soars, the once skeptical Reid is convinced, and against Tompkins's advice, he goes back again to ask questions about a business deal. The deal succeeds on the basis of Tompkins's answers, and Reid returns again and again, ignoring Tompkins's warning that knowing the future will ultimately bring him sorrow. On Reid's last visit to Tompkins, he asks about a long-term business venture he's contemplating and whether it will turn out well or not. Tompkins tells him it doesn't matter because Reid won't be around in six months, when the venture concludes. Reid is aghast and asks how much time he has, and Tompkins tells him, "Three weeks from now. . . . On the seam between the fourteenth and fifteenth of June. At midnight on the stroke." And when he asks how, Tompkins says, "You will meet your death at the jaws of a lion" (119). When Reid tells Jean what Tompkins said, he asks, "Is it wrong to be so afraid, Jean?" and she thinks, "It's human not to be able to bear knowing when you are to die" (124).

At this point Jean's flashback narrative ends, and the peculiarly persecutory aspect of fate in Woolrich's universe takes center stage as Reid, knowing the exact time and manner of his death and yet having to live for a certain period with the fear and hopelessness this foreknowledge brings, begins to disintegrate, unable to leave the house and sometimes unable to leave his own room. Jean also becomes infected by this fatalistic despair, even to the point of attempting suicide to free herself of having to watch her beloved but panic-stricken father suffer a thousand deaths before the last one. Of course, in real life there *are* situations in which people know well in advance the exact time and manner of their deaths, and as we noted, Woolrich used one of these in two previous novels with men on death row awaiting execution. There are also instances where people know in advance the *approximate* time and manner of their deaths, as when someone is diagnosed with a terminal illness. But neither of these is Reid's case; he's healthy, he's not on death row, he has everything to live for, and yet he's going to die. And what the near miss by a falling beam is to Flitcraft, an event that "felt like somebody had taken the lid off life and let him look at the works" (66), the prediction of his death "at the jaws of a lion" is to Reid: the foreknowledge of an event that, by any rational standard, could only be the result of a series of random occurrences, except that this very foreknowledge undercuts the sense of the accidental, making the event seem something intended by a higher-than-human, malevolent power.

Certainly, knowing the exact time of his death causes Reid's paralyzing fear but also his knowing that the predicted manner of death must by its very nature be violent, painful, terrifying, and must come upon him by surprise. All this makes it impossible for Reid to take the advice he'd given Jean as a child, advice Jean had related to Shawn at the beginning of her narrative in characterizing the closeness of her bond with her father. Jean said that she was eight or nine before she learned that "there was something different" about her (a childhood memory of "difference" that may well have been suggested by the author's own childhood memory of the stars in Mexico, whose subtext, as we've argued, was the discovery of "something different" about himself). One day on the playground a little girl said to Jean, "You're beastly rich" (24). Jean denied it, but the little girl insisted, and that evening Jean had asked her father, "What does it mean, when you're rich?" He'd said:

> "Listen close. And tomorrow don't remember this. But remember it some other day, when you're eighteen or you're twenty. You'll need it more then. It means you'll have a hard time of it. It means you'll always be a little lonely. Reaching out, with no one there to clasp your hand. It means no one will ever love you. And if they do, you won't be able to tell if it's meant for you alone. It means you'll have to be careful. There will be traps laid."
>
> "What do I have to do?" I asked, sucking in my breath.

"There is only one thing you can do. Act as though you didn't know. Act—
and live, and think—as though you weren't rich. And then maybe the world will
let you forget it." (24–25)

Reid's advice evokes great wealth as its own fate, and certainly in the novel
his wealth functions as a counterpoint to his predicted death, a symbol of all
the richness of life that makes the thought of losing of it so tragic and fearful, of all the buyable security that keeps so many of the preventable causes of
death at a distance. But of course the ultimate fate of every human being is
death. We all know this in the abstract, and past a certain age most of us realize
this in a particular way. Yet if life requires a condition of hope, no matter how
flimsy, in order to flourish or even persist, that is, some sense of an indefinite
future, then any advance knowledge of its precise temporal limit erodes that
sense and with it the grounds of hope. In order to still function with such
knowledge, one must either relocate one's hope to a life after death (which no
one in Woolrich seems ever to consider) or act, as Reid tells his daughter about
being rich, "as though you didn't know. Act—and think and live—as though
you weren't" going to die at a predicted moment. It's advice Reid can give but
can't take when the death is his own. Indeed, this parallel between great wealth
and death as fates is underlined when Reid's remark to the young Jean that being
rich "means you'll always be a little lonely" is echoed later by Jean herself when,
on returning to Tompkins's apartment to verify the prediction of her father's
death she says, "He's waiting for me downstairs. . . . I better go back to him. He's
alone," and Tompkins replies, "We're all alone. . . . Every one of us" (120). Re-
joining her father, she thinks, "Nobody can help you when you're dying" (122).

With Jean's flashback narrative completed, Shawn immediately takes
charge. He suggests they go to Shawn's boss Lieutenant McManus, the head
of the Homicide Bureau, because the prediction of Reid's death "is killing him
just as surely" (132) as any conventional method of murder. In persuading Jean
to meet McManus, Shawn represents him as a father figure who still possesses
the ability to act effectively, in contrast to her own father. Indeed, in describing
him, Shawn states more explicitly than in any of the novels we've discussed so
far the boss-as-better-man principle:

"I work for someone who's smarter than I am, who knows more than I do. That's
why I'm working for him, instead of him for me. . . . He's a wiser man than I am,
and he's older, more experienced. . . . "

"You like your boss, don't you?"

"I think he's swell," he said simply. . . . "He's got a kid of his own, a daughter. . . . We'll go and talk to him a little while. . . . It'll be like talking to your own—" He quickly checked that word as he saw her face shadow. (129)

On hearing the situation, McManus immediately treats it as an elaborate con or extortion scheme (even though Tompkins has rejected all Reid's offers of money), a scheme in which Tompkins has set out to convince Reid and Jean of his clairvoyant powers in order to make one big killing with his prophecy of Reid's death, which McManus feels sure Tompkins will take back if Reid offers him enough cash. McManus assigns seven detectives to work full time on the case for the next three days before the prediction is slated to be fulfilled. He assigns three of them to check on certain facts Tompkins had told Reid during the course of his visits over several months, facts McManus wants his detectives to show Tompkins could have known by normal means, saying "If we can hang plausibility" on his having learned them in that manner, "we've saved a man's mind from dying" (133). He assigns one detective to shadow Eileen McGuire, who he suspects may be Tompkins accomplice; another to check on all lions within a five-hundred-mile radius of the city, in zoos, traveling circuses, animal acts, and to warn all their handlers to keep a close watch on them the next three days; and finally, two detectives to install a listening device in Tompkins apartment and monitor it around the clock for the next seventy-two hours. McManus tells Shawn to have Jean bring him to the Reid mansion as a house guest who'll be staying there for a while, and with that all the preparations to thwart the prediction are in place.

From this point on, Woolrich keeps cutting back and forth between parallel actions (on the one hand, the activities of McManus's detectives on their various assignments; on the other, those of Shawn, Reid, and Jean sequestered in the Reid mansion), while constantly drawing our attention to the fact that time is running out. Arriving at the Reid house, Shawn notices there are two large carved-stone lions outside the front door and for a moment considers suggesting they be removed but doesn't. When Jean gives him a tour of the house he notices that in the conservatory on each side there is a "ceiling-high stained glass window . . . set into the blank wall" and lit from behind by electric lights. Jean tells him her grandfather, who built the house, had the windows brought over from an abbey in England, and Shawn notes that the windows in "each leaded subdivision" bear "the head of some mythological or heraldic animal—a unicorn, a griffin, a wild boar, a lion, a phoenix" (140).

Taking Shawn in to meet her father for the first time, Jean warns, "There'll be a number of clocks in there, he can't surround himself with enough of them," and when Shawn objects, she says, "He's more frightened without them. He's afraid it's going faster, slipping away from him. The imagination, you know, is always more terrible than the reality" (142)—the ground rule of all suspense fiction. Shawn finds Reid, who'd been an energetic, successful businessman, already reduced by fear to a shadow of himself. Though Jean introduces Shawn as a friend visiting for a few days, Reid immediately recognizes that he's a policeman and asks if Shawn can help him. Before he can answer, Reid signs a blank check and tells Shawn he can fill in any amount for himself if only he'll save him. Trying to hide his irritation at Reid's collapse of will, Shawn says, "Why don't you get yourself a little courage? You're not only doing this to yourself, you're doing it to others," and Reid replies, "It's so easy to be brave, when you've got a slack of forty years. Try it when you've got less than forty-nine hours" (147).

While things have gotten off to a shaky start at the mansion, McManus's detectives have been busy. In balancing the parallel actions inside and outside the Reid home, Woolrich employs a technique similar to that in "Three O'Clock": Shawn, Jean, and Reid, confined for fear or safety's sake within the mansion, are the novel's equivalent of Paul Stapp trapped in his basement, while the detectives pursuing their leads are the equivalent of the characters in "Three O'Clock" who periodically raise Stapp's hope of rescue only to dash it again—the detectives' work continually seeming to promise some logical solution to Tompkins's prediction but with that promise never fulfilled.

As McManus's men carry out their assignments, the sense of fatalism grows. First, the former maid, Eileen McGuire, a timid soul who thinks she's interfered with the impersonal mechanism of fate in warning Jean about the plane, feels that sooner or later she'll be ground up by that mechanism. Her feelings of guilt and impending doom increase once she becomes aware that she's being shadowed by the police, and after a long day of wandering about the city with a policeman tailing her, she cracks and takes poison in the ladies' room of a movie theater, killing herself. Back at the Reid mansion Shawn has his hands full fighting Reid's complete paralysis of will, fighting the "death in him" (213), and trying to keep Jean and himself from becoming infected with the "fear of fear" (217). When Jean has trouble sleeping, Shawn offers to sit by her bedside until she falls asleep, and Jean thinks, "The child and her protector. The child and her big brother. . . . Now I can sleep, you're here. There always should be someone older, wiser, stronger than I am" (185). Though this brother-sister imagery combined with the claustrophobic setting of the Reid mansion recalls "Usher," the attraction between Shawn and Jean seems headed for a more romantic conclusion.

The next day, Reid's last, the three of them go out to watch the sunset. Complaining, "It rushes downward so fast," Reid holds "out his hands toward it, making a circle of them that did not quite join, as if trying to hold it fast between them, get it to stay. . . . It must have slipped through his grasp, little by little, escaping irretrievably downward; for they saw him convulsively expand and contract his hands several times, the way a clumsy person would fumble trying to hold onto a slippery ball that has just been thrown to him. Then they came together, palm to palm, over emptiness" (196). If the brother-sister imagery in the claustrophobic mansion recalls Poe, then this scene of Reid stretching out his hands to a distant light as an expression of desire recalls another of Woolrich's major influences, Fitzgerald's *The Great Gatsby* and the scene in which Nick Carraway sees Gatsby standing out on his lawn one night stretching out his hands toward the green light at the end of Daisy's dock, reaching for something he's lost and seeks to recover, as opposed to Reid, who's trying to hold on to something he's losing.

In the meantime, the detectives assigned to bug Tompkins's apartment have spent a day and a half listening to Tompkins moving around in his room by himself, but at two-thirty on the night before Reid's predicted death Tompkins has a surprise visitor, a man who the reader later learns is Reid's stockbroker, Walt Myers. It becomes clear from their conversation that Myers had learned about the information Tompkins provided Reid for business deals and also that Reid eventually believed everything Tompkins predicted. When he'd found that Tompkins had foretold Reid's death, Myers apparently visited Tompkins and in the course of that visit had gotten him drunk, then tricked him into endorsing one of the many checks Reid had sent him but that Tompkins had never cashed. Myers apparently altered the amount on the check from five hundred dollars to five thousand and now uses that altered check to try to blackmail Tompkins into calling Reid and telling him that he's had another vision, that the prediction of Reid's death is not so certain as it was and that Reid's prospects would be improved if he'd make Tompkins the beneficiary on his will after Jean, thus allying Reid's fate with Tompkins's. Tompkins, who's clearly had no part in this scheme, refuses, and Myers draws a gun, threatening his life. Tompkins tells Myers that he'll never live to enjoy Reid's money, that he has even less time than Reid because there are two police detectives, named Sokolsky and Dobbs, in the apartment above listening to every word he's been saying. Myers thinks Tompkins has set him up and tries to kill him. The detectives in the apartment above, hearing the shots, rush out onto the landing in time to see Myers, gun in hand, running down the stairs. When Sokolsky orders him to stop, Myers takes a shot, and Sokolsky fires back, killing him. As Sokolsky is standing over Myers's body at the foot of the stairs, Tompkins comes down and walks past him heading for the front door. Sokolsky orders him to stop as well, then fires a warning shot over his head, but Tompkins says, "You can't do anything to me with that. It isn't my time yet" (235) and keeps walking. At point-blank range Sokolsky pulls the trigger three more times, but each time the gun misfires, and Tompkins walks out the door and vanishes into the night. He wanders the streets for a while and then phones McManus to turn himself in.

On the evening of the day Reid is slated to die, Shawn and Jean, trying to dispel the growing tension in the house and distract her father, engage him in various after-dinner games. First Shawn tries playing cards with Reid, but that's a flop. Then Jean brings out a small roulette wheel and suggests the three play, saying it was a game her father was fond of in his younger days. Jean volunteers to be croupier, suggesting they only bet on red or black and on odd or even, winner take all. They place their bets—Reid, black, odd; Jean, red, even; Shawn, black, even. Reid wagers with thousand-dollar packets of money taken from his study safe, Jean with her jewelry, and Shawn with a packet of money lent him by Reid. Shawn wins and leaves his money on black, even. Jean spins the wheel again and Shawn wins, and he keeps winning until Reid has lost all his packets of money and Jean all her jewelry, and she drops out. Reid takes out his checkbook and bets all the money he has in the bank, and again Shawn wins. He wants to end the game and give back his winnings, but Reid says, "This little wheel runs true to the other, bigger one. You think this is just a wooden gambling wheel. It isn't; it's my wheel of life. I've got to win just once, before it's too late. I want a sign from it; then that'll mean—I've got to keep on playing . . . until I get one" (247).

Though the language in this passage reminds us of Walter Huff's gambling-wheel image for the insurance business in *Double Indemnity* (Huff says, "You think it's a business, don't you, just like your business, and maybe a little better than that, because it's the friend of the widow, the orphan, and needy in time of trouble? It's not. It's the biggest gambling wheel in the world"),[11] Huff and

Reid invoke the image for different purposes: Huff to illustrate that buying insurance is like making a bet and that the insurance company is the house, the professional who knows the odds over the long term and never makes a sucker bet; while Reid uses the image to assert the existence of chance, of randomness, in human events, of a principle capable of interrupting the pre-ordinations of fate. But Reid, who wants another spin of the wheel and a sign that chance can break the grip that fate has on him, is running out of things to bet. He writes out a deed to the house, which he and Jean sign, and wagers it on "red, the color of life" (246) against everything Shawn has won playing black. But Shawn wins again. In desperation Reid, with seemingly nothing left to wager, suddenly looks at Jean. Shawn realizing what Reid has in mind says, "You're going mad. . . . It's time to stop." But Reid says, "You don't know you love her, but I do. She doesn't know she loves you, but I do" (248). Reid says that all he's wagering is Jean's hand in marriage and that Shawn can refuse it if he chooses, but Shawn agrees, as does Jean, and they spin the wheel again. Of course Shawn wins, and Reid now takes out his birth certificate and puts it on the table, saying "On the red to win." But Shawn objects, "What'll I meet it with? It's a hypothetical bet. This wheel can't affect it. If I win, how can I take it? If I lose, how can I give it up to you—when I haven't got it in the first place?" (250).

This exchange, highlighting the difference between being and having, leads immediately to an unequivocal demonstration on Shawn's part that a man's work is his being. Reid says that he must have one last spin of the wheel:

"I want my sign. . . . This wheel can give it to me. This wheel can save me. There's still time. If I win, I've saved it. If I lose—"

"And what do I bet against it? This?" Shawn swept the accumulated winnings off the table edge onto the floor.

"Haven't you anything that you value? There must be something. Every man has something. Something that you want to lose as little as I want to lose—what I am staking." (250–51)

Jean doesn't say a word, doesn't help Shawn out, because "she wanted to learn what the highest thing in life to Shawn was; or if he had any such thing at all." Shawn admits that there is something that means more to him than anything else but that he doesn't "go around putting it down on gambling tables." Yet when Reid pleads, "I'm dying. . . . That's my life, there, on the red," Shawn responds by putting "his badge down, on the black," and Woolrich comments, "The symbol was complete" (251). They spin the wheel, and Shawn wins.

Meanwhile, the last of the detectives reports to McManus that a lion has escaped from a carnival and that there's evidence the chain on the cage's door had been tampered with. The lion is at large, and though this raises the hope of finding some explainable human agency in the Reid affair, this too will be taken away when the detective later reports that the lion cage was tampered with by a man plotting to kill his wife but who was himself killed instead and the lion subsequently tracked down and shot. By this point the countdown at the Reid house has reached the final fifteen minutes, and Reid, though still breathing, is "spiritually . . . dead already" (273). Shawn and Jean have become so unnerved by the wait and by the roulette game in which Reid continually lost that Shawn feels "they'd never forget this night, the two of them, no matter what else happened for the rest of their lives. . . . They were getting scars on their souls, the sort of scars people got in the Dark Ages, when they believed in devils and black magic. Scars that would never completely heal. . . . When it got dark, when other nights came, when other fears came, there would be twinges" (274).

Then, as the clock begins to sound twelve, the telephone outside the locked living room rings, and Shawn goes to answer it, leaving Jean alone with her father. It's McManus saying, "It's over. We've beaten the rap. The guy's saved. Tompkins just committed suicide in his cell" (277). As Shawn hangs up he hears Jean scream, "Hold him! He's gone out of his mind!" and Reid rushes out the living room door and down the darkened hall. Shawn, after looking in the living room to make sure Jean's all right, gives chase. Panic-stricken, Reid suddenly turns into the conservatory, and Shawn hears a crash of glass. When he arrives, the room is pitch black, and when he turns on the lights he sees Reid standing upright against one of the stained-glass windows: "He was headless, or seemed to be; he ended at the neck. Jagged teeth of thick, splintered glass held his craned neck in a vise, formed a collar, had pierced his jugular. His head was on the other side, had been rammed through the leaded pane to the space where the lights were. You could see the dark shadow that was his life blood running down the inside of the lighted pane." As the clock strikes twelve, Shawn notices that the panel Reid had "aimed himself unerringly at, in his blind headlong flight, with the room pitch-black around him . . . was that of the lion rampant. Its mane and rabid eyes and flat feline nostrils still showed undestroyed above his gashed neck, as though it were swallowing him bodily. And for fangs now, instead of painted ones it had those jagged incisors of glass, thrusting into his flesh from all sides of the orifice he himself had created." As Tompkins had foreseen, Reid was dead "by the jaws of a lion" (278).

Later that same night McManus and Shawn discuss Reid's death, and Shawn witnesses his father figure admit that he'd been essentially powerless to protect Jean's father from a death foretold and that he now feels helpless to explain its cause. McManus says the medical examiner's report will give the cause as "a severed jugular," but "'what'll I say, what'll I put down, that's what I'm wondering. Death by accident. Death while of unsound mind. Murder by mental suggestion. Death by decree of—' He turned speculative eyes toward the windows, where the draperies were now thrown wide, and restless twinkles simmered across the face of the sky" (279). McManus goes back over all the facts of the case and then says that he wishes Shawn had never brought Jean to him in the first place, wishes he'd never heard of the whole thing, and he bets that Shawn wishes he "never walked along the river that night." To which Shawn replies, "I had to. . . . That was where I was to walk, there wasn't any other place" (284). McManus leaves, and Shawn walks back toward the house to find Jean: "It was cool and quiet and dark. He wasn't afraid but he felt very small, very unimportant. He felt as though there were no longer any need to worry about what happened to him, whether for good or ill; that was all taken care of from now on, that was all out of his hands. It was a strange feeling, a light feeling, as though something heavy had dropped off your back" (285). In many ways this moment seems to be the emotional climax of the novel, but what are we to make of it within the psychic economy of the novel's author? Is this lightness Shawn feels the ultimate result of the heavy weight of one's personal responsibility for, as well as the consequences of, one's actions being dropped into the abyss of fate?

VII

In *Night Has a Thousand Eyes* Woolrich shaded the hard-boiled suspense fiction he'd produced in the "black series" of novels over into a type of philosophical/psychological "What-if?" fiction influenced by Poe's terror stories (and certainly the plot of *Night Has a Thousand Eyes* is no more outré, to use a favorite word of Poe's, than that of "Usher" or any other of the "dying woman" stories). Like Poe, Woolrich focuses on achieving a unity of emotional effect in his fiction, on creating a more or less (and often, very much less) realistic objective correlative to certain darker psychological states, on presenting hypothetical situations (with enough of a veneer of realism to satisfy the hardboiled fiction reader) in which the individual psyche begins to break down and the grimmer elements of the human condition come through. If, as I've suggested, the fatalism that pervades *Night Has a Thousand Eyes* represents Woolrich's attempt to embody on a cosmic level his "sense of personal, private doom" first experienced under the stars in Mexico when he realized he'd "surely die finally, or something worse," and if we are further correct that his sexual orientation was what he experienced as his personal fate, then many of the choices Woolrich made in plotting the novel become clearer.

Woolrich had inherited from the hard-boiled fiction tradition a sense of the desirability of both becoming one's own boss and being one's own sole employee (as Paul Stapp states in "Three O'Clock") and the principle of the boss as the better man (which Shawn voices in telling Jean about Lieutenant McManus). But in *Night Has a Thousand Eyes* Woolrich constructs a plot in which two bosses (Reid, the owner of his own import/export business, and McManus, the head of the Homicide Bureau), the former a father, the latter a father and a father figure, are both defeated by fate—Reid unable to stave off his predicted death, and McManus unable to explain and thus deflect that prediction. Given that during Woolrich's lifetime he must have experienced again and again in American society the sense that someone of his sexual orientation could not possibly be "the better man," and further, that he must have been conscious from a fairly early age of a certain masculinity deficit in the eyes of his macho father (hence his paying a larger boy to let Cornell beat him up where his father could watch), we can see that in plotting *Night Has a Thousand Eyes* Woolrich set out not just to beat the boss or defeat the father, not just to show that neither is the better man, but rather to call into question the whole category of "the better man." In effect, Woolrich seems to be saying that if his sexual orientation (determined either biologically or by childhood events) is his fate in life and that if in the eyes of his society that orientation means he could never be considered "more manly" in any sort of comparison, then he means to show that all men share a fate in terms of which no one can be the better man, and more, that if anyone doubts the unmanning effect of death, let him consider the way a person's prolonged foreknowledge of his own demise can disintegrate his psyche through a fear that eventually turns to blind panic and ends in madness.

We can also see that the image created by the book's title—of the fateful stars as eyes watching the actions of the fated—an image repeated again and again in the novel, combines, on the one hand, the connection between the stars and fate (i.e., the notion that one's fate is determined by the arrangement of the stars and planets at the exact moment of one's birth) and, on the other, the connection between the stars as malevolent (because indifferent) observers of human suffering and that persecutory sense of cosmic surveillance, of homosexual paranoia, that, in Freud's reading, leaves its victim constantly aware of being under the gaze of a menacing father or father figure become the All-Father. Indeed, given the abiding influence of Fitzgerald on Woolrich's work, one might almost see this image of the stars being the thousand eyes of night as a further development of the painted eyes of Dr. T. J. Eckleburg in *The Great Gatsby,* that figure of the unseeing all-seeing eye of God derived from the notion of conscience as the introjected gaze of the father.

At the novel's end, when Shawn puts down on the roulette table his badge as the thing he values most in life, Woolrich affirms the sense, inherited from the tradition of hard-boiled fiction, that a man's work is his being. It's no wonder, then, that in *Blues of a Lifetime* Woolrich's ambivalence about (not to say distaste for) his own life and his life's work seem about equal. The memoir's opening chapter, titled "Remington Portable NC69411," begins as an ode to his first typewriter (to which he had dedicated his first suspense novel, *The Bride Wore Black),* and then details his early biography and his decision to become a writer. He says of the typewriter: "The love of a man for a machine. I never loved women much, I guess. Only three times, that I'm fully aware of. And each time I got more or less of a kick in the jaw, so there wasn't much incentive to go ahead trying more frequently. . . . I was born to be solitary, and I liked it that way" (4). In the unfinished memoir's fifth and final chapter, "The Maid Who Played the Races," Woolrich recounts how, when he was staying in a hotel in Seattle on a visit during the 1960s, one of the chambermaids who was making up his room asked him what he did for a living, and when he said, "I'm a writer," the maid, given how short and slightly built Woolrich was, apparently misunderstood the word as "rider," immediately asking him for an inside tip on the races. Woolrich says,

> I think I must have been secretly flattered at being mistaken for a racehorse rider, one of those small but wiry men who crouch low over their mount's neck and fly down the stretch at breakneck speed and sometimes take a spill.

All my life I've admired the active and physically competitive callings and wished that I had been equipped by nature to take up one of them instead of entering into the one that did come to me. . . . I used to say to myself, in my early days before the mold had hardened about me, "You only live it once, so why not live it as a man, not as a mole?"

So, it wasn't that I wanted to impress this elderly chambermaid. . . . It was myself that I wanted to impress, I think, far more.

I thought: let me feel big for a moment or two, let me feel good, let me glow. Let me feel like someone who does something for a change. Let me feel like the sort of man I used to think when I was a boy I was surely going to turn into some day. . . . How often have I ever been taken for a bike racer or a coxswain or a racing crewman—or a jockey? How often will I be again? Enjoy it for a second.

Any pleasure I ever got from my writing was never pleasure as a *man*. I don't know if I can make this clear or not. What got the pleasure was a selfless thing, a shadowy thing, a bloodless, bodiless hand poised over a row of typewriter keys. But to be mistaken for a jockey for a moment, that was pleasure as a *man*. (127–28)

When Woolrich based the clairvoyant Jeremiah Tompkins's physical description so closely on his own, he may have been motivated, consciously or not, by a further spiritual resemblance between Tompkins's attitude toward his gift of second sight (he feels it's a fateful power that's trapped and doomed him) and Woolrich's attitude toward his own gift as a writer. Woolrich's biographer, Mike Nevins, once remarked in conversation that all his research had left him with the sense that the one constant factor in Woolrich's adult life, as well as in his attitude toward his writing, was self-hatred, and to the extent that that is an accurate assessment, we can see why the types of issue Woolrich inherited from hard-boiled fiction had an immediate personal resonance for him and, further, see how these issues ultimately allowed him to turn self-hatred into art, to turn, in Emerson's phrase, a fate into a power, making that material his own in his special mix of universal fear and universal fate, of persecution and preordination, which reached its high point in *Night Has a Thousand Eyes*.

A Puzzle of Character

I

A look back over the books and authors we've discussed so far reveals several patterns in the development of hard-boiled fiction in the 1930s and '40s. As we noted, the genre began with the work of detective-story writers in the twenties (most notably Dashiell Hammett) and reached a high point in Hammett's career with the 1930 publication of *The Maltese Falcon,* a work that would serve as a model for Raymond Chandler's fiction over the next two decades. The Hammett style of hard-boiled detective story positioned itself, according to Chandler's 1944 essay "The Simple Art of Murder," as a more realistic, and thus in literary terms more serious, alternative to the form as it had developed in England, France, and America in the later nineteenth and early twentieth centuries, a tradition that originated with Poe's invention of the detective genre in the 1840s. Poe's three Dupin stories—"The Murders in the Rue Morgue" (1841), "The Mystery of Marie Rogêt" (1842–43), and "The Purloined Letter" (1844)—established the tradition of what I have called elsewhere the analytic detective story,[1] a narrative whose structure and emotional dynamic turn upon the analysis of clues and the deductive solution of a crime—though in the Dupin stories it's often more the appearance of analysis and deduction than the reality.

The tradition of analytic detective fiction that grew out of Poe's tales ultimately included authors such as Wilkie Collins, Arthur Conan Doyle, Israel Zangwill, Gaston Leroux, Jacques Futrelle, E. C. Bentley, Dorothy Sayers, Agatha Christie, S. S. Van Dine, Rex Stout, and Ellery Queen, to name only a few of Hammett's more prominent predecessors or contemporaries. As the analytic detective story developed in the first three decades of the twentieth century, it came to be governed more and more by what was known as the "fair play" method of composition, the notion that, as Willard Huntington Wright (who wrote the Philo Vance novels under the pseudonym S. S. Van Dine) put it, "the reader must have equal opportunity with the detective for solving the mystery," and to that end "all clues must be plainly stated and described" and "the culprit must turn out to be a person who has played a more or less prominent part in the story."[2] With the fair-play method the story's battle of wits between detective and criminal became in effect a battle of wits between reader and author, a contest to see whether the reader, who'd been given equal access along with the detective to the clues in the case, could arrive at the correct solution to the mystery before the detective revealed it at the story's close. And the test of an author's skill was the ingenuity with which he prolonged this battle of wits while still being able, without cheating, to surprise the reader at the story's conclusion, a surprise best achieved, as Wright says, by the answer to the mystery already being present "in the printed word, so that if the reader should go back over the book he would find that the solution had been there all the time if he had had sufficient shrewdness to grasp it" (*TAMS*, 40).

Several essays published in the 1920s by prominent practitioners such as R. Austin Freeman, Willard Huntington Wright, and Dorothy Sayers made explicit the necessity of the fair-play method in analytic detective fiction, Freeman noting that "the tacit understanding of the author with the reader" in this kind of story "is that the problem is susceptible of solution by the latter by reasoning from the facts given; and such solution should be actually possible."[3] But what also seems clear in these critical examinations is that the fair-play method rested upon a basic understanding of the detective novel as not falling "under the head of fiction in the ordinary sense" but belonging rather "in the category of riddles," of its being "in fact, a complicated and extended puzzle cast in fictional form," as Wright argues, a fictional form whose "structure and mechanism" resemble those of "a cross-word puzzle" with its solution depending "wholly on mental processes—. . . the fitting together of apparently unrelated parts" (*TAMS*, 35–36).

Many of these 1920s essays were prefaces to anthologies of detective stories, collections meant to give readers a historical overview of the genre and thus demonstrate the superiority of the modern fair-play stories to earlier works that depended for their effect on sensationalism or trickery. These prefatory essays characteristically set out to defend the genre against the charge of being literarily worthless, of being fiction not meriting an intelligent adult's attention. And the defense as a rule involved a dual argument: On the one hand, the essayists contended that the genre's "most devoted adherents," as E. M. Wrong noted, "are found principally among the highly educated,"[4] an argument meant to address (particularly in Britain) the social-class objection that, as Austin Freeman framed it, detective fiction was "produced by half-educated and wholly incompetent writers for consumption by office boys, factory girls, and other persons devoid of culture and literary taste" (*TAMS*, 7). This form of the argument frequently ended with a list of detective fiction's famous fans, names ranging from Abraham Lincoln to T. S. Eliot.

The second prong of the argument proposed a lowering, or at the very least an adjustment, of literary expectations regarding the genre because of structural features peculiar to the analytic detective story, in effect, proposed a special generic category for this type of writing, as when Wright suggested that it should be classed in the category of "a complicated and extended puzzle cast in fictional form." Thus, Dorothy Sayers, in her introduction to *The Omnibus of Crime* (1929), argued that analytic detective fiction "does not, and by hypothesis never can, attain the loftiest level of literary achievement. Though it deals with the most desperate effects of rage, jealousy, and revenge, it rarely touches the heights and depths of human passion."[5] Since the main thrust of these stories involves the analytic solution of a mystery (a dynamic requiring a certain objectivity), Sayers argues, "a too violent emotion flung into the glittering mechanism of the detective-story jars the movement by disturbing its delicate balance. The most successful writers are those who contrive to keep the story running from beginning to end upon the same emotional level, and it is better to err in the direction of too little feeling than too much" (*TAMS*, 102)–which is simply Sayers's way of saying that analytic detective fiction is essentially a plot-driven genre with a low tolerance for or interest in fully developed characters. Indeed, the only character who tends to be developed at all in an analytic detective story is the detective himself, and the fullness of this development is often simply a function of an individual detective's becoming an ongoing figure in story after story. Even then, figures such as Dupin, Sherlock Holmes, Hercule Poirot, Philo Vance, and Nero Wolfe tend as characters to be little more than congeries of odd traits and idiosyncratic behaviors, designed either to emphasize a devotion to analysis and deduction so complete that it has led them to ignore social conventions and the normal affairs of everyday living or else to emphasize their status as amateurs, dilettantes, connoisseurs—persons possessed of specialized interests and the sort of arcane knowledge oddly suited to crime detection.

II

I have focused on these essays from the 1920s because they are the immediate predecessors of, and provide the intellectual underpinnings for, the fullest critical and historical treatment of the genre produced up to that time, Howard Haycraft's *Murder for Pleasure: The Life and Times of the Detective Story*, published in 1941, the genre's centennial year. A survey of the genre from its beginnings in Poe up to the year 1940, Haycraft's book follows the critical line laid down by Freeman, Wrong, Sayers, and Wright. Though noting that at present "one out of every four new works of fiction published in the English language belongs" to the category of detective fiction and that "no less a qualified authority than Mr. Somerset Maugham has recently ascribed this state of affairs to the fact that 'the serious novel of to-day is regrettably namby-pamby'"[6] in comparison, Haycraft nevertheless refuses, in spite of the genre's wide readership and Maugham's upscale approval, to set his sights too high in discussing the genre, saying he's "endeavored at all times to consider" it "only for what it is—a frankly non-serious, entertainment form of literature" that possesses "its own rules and standards . . . and at its best has won the right to respectful consideration on its own merits" (*MFP*, xi–xii). Having sufficiently lowered the reader's expectations, Haycraft divides the genre's history by periods and geography, characterizing each in a phrase in his table of contents:

I.   Time: 1841—Place: America (Genesis) [Poe]

II.   The In-Between Years (Development) [Gaboriau, Collins, Dickens]

III. Profile by Gaslight (Renaissance) [Doyle]

IV.   England: 1890–1914 (The Romantic Era) [Freeman, A. E. W. Mason, Chesterton, Bentley, Bramah, et al.]

V.   America: 1890–1914 (The Romantic Era) [Green, Futrelle, Rinehart, Post, et al.]

VI.   The Continental Detective Story [Leroux, Leblanc, et al.]

VII.   England: 1918–1930 (The Golden Age) [Freeman, Sayers, Christie, Crofts, et al.]

VIII.   America: 1918–1930 (The Golden Age) [Van Dine {Wright}, Hammett, Queen, Biggers)

IX.   England: 1930–(The Moderns) [Allingham, Blake {Day Lewis}, Innis {Stewart}, Marsh, Carr, et al.)

X.   America: 1930–(The Moderns) [Stout, Gardner, Eberhart, et al.].

Haycraft's designation of the period 1918–30 in England and America as the "Golden Age" makes his take on the genre's development clear. According to Haycraft, after the detective story's beginnings in the 1840s with Poe and the occasional use of detective elements by fiction writers such as Collins and Dickens during the 1860s and '70s, the analytic detective story form per se only gained widespread popularity in English in the late 1880s, with the Sherlock Holmes tales. Then, in the period 1890–1914, the often-blurred distinction between the analytic detective genre and the pure mystery genre, a distinction that depends for Haycraft on whether a tale's solution "is accomplished by incident (mystery story) or deduction (detective story)" (*MFP*, 87), began to sharpen through R. Austin Freeman's "pioneer insistence on the fair-play method" in his tales of Dr. John Thorndyke. Describing Freeman as "a Modern before the Moderns" (70), Haycraft sees the widespread acceptance of the fair-play method by detective fiction writers as one of the things that put the gold in the succeeding "Golden Age" (1918–30)—that and an increased sense of realism in the genre, "a trend toward a more credible form and style" (112). The English writers of this period whose work Haycraft discusses at length are the group dubbed by "the British press" the "Big Five" (125), namely, Sayers, Christie, Freeman, Crofts, and Bailey, and the Americans he focuses on from this same period are Van Dine [Wright], Hammett, and Ellery Queen [Frederic Dannay and Manfred B. Lee]. For our purposes the most interesting part of Haycraft's treatment of these American writers is his comparison of Van Dine and Hammett and thus, implicitly, of analytic and hard-boiled detective fiction.

Gauged against the advances in detective fiction made in England by the Big Five in the years immediately after World War I, "the American detective story," says Haycraft, "stood still, exactly where it had been before the War. Suddenly, in 1926, came the long-overdue 'break,' with the publication of *The Benson Murder Case,* the first of the epochal Philo Vance novels by 'S. S. Van Dine'. . . . Overnight, American crime fiction came of age" (*MFP,* 163). *The Benson Murder Case* was, for the first few weeks after its publication, "principally a succès d'estime among the chosen few . . . but gradually the word spread that something unusual had happened in the detective story," and when the second Philo Vance book, *The "Canary" Murder Case,* appeared in 1927, the book "broke all modern publishing records for detective fiction." As succeeding Vance novels were adapted for films, both silent and talking, Van Dine's detective became "for a few years, the best known fictional sleuth on the globe" (166).

As Haycraft explains, Wright, during a long convalescence from illness in the early 1920s, amassed "a library of nearly two thousand volumes of detective fiction and criminology," and his study of these convinced him that "the highly individual technique of the detective story had suffered from poor execution in America, thereby limiting its field of appeal" (*MFP,* 164–65). Consequently, "he determined to write tales aimed at a higher stratum of the public than had previously been accustomed to read them. (This was exactly the same decision which had been arrived at by the better English writers a few years earlier)." Wright decided to publish his novels under the pseudonym S. S. Van Dine, because, as he says, "I rather feared ostracism if I boldly switched from esthetics and philologic research to fictional sleuthing" (165).

A palpable sense of class distinction pervades Wright's and Haycraft's remarks, recalling the tone of Austin Freeman's comment cited earlier that the detective story was "apt to be dismissed contemptuously . . . as a type of work produced" by the "half-educated and incompetent . . . for consumption by office boys, factory girls, and other persons devoid of culture" (*TAMS,* 7). Following the example of "the better English writers" such as Sayers and Christie, whose books combined elements of the British class-conscious novel of manners with analytic detective fiction (the sort of upstairs/downstairs atmosphere of the so-called English country house school of mystery writers, which Robert Altman so nostalgically parodied in the film *Gosford Park*), Wright set out to inject a similar interest for, and sense of, "the higher stratum" of society into the American detective story.

On the one hand he achieved this, explains Haycraft, through "the brilliant plot-work of the initial novels . . . , the great literacy with which they were written, matching the hero's—at first—impressive learning; and a high degree of verisimilitude, so carefully worked out in every detail that in the early years numerous uncritical readers thought the cases had really occurred" (*MFP*, 166). But on the other hand, he created his stories' upper-class aura by basing his first two novels on famous contemporary murders linked to high society.

The Benson Murder Case drew on the June 1920 murder of Joseph Bowne Elwell, the greatest bridge player of his time, known as the "Wizard of Whist." Elwell, who gave bridge and whist instruction to the wealthy, numbered among his former pupils the Vanderbilts and the king of England. Besides authoring textbooks on bridge, Elwell made large sums of money gambling on cards and horseracing, owned a stable of racehorses, dabbled in Florida real estate, and was reputed to have dealt in bootleg liquor. He was also, in the phrase of the day, a notorious "chicken-chaser," pursuing married and unmarried women alike. Shot in the head from close range with a .45 automatic, Elwell's body was discovered by his housekeeper inside his locked Manhattan home in the West Seventies.[7] In a 1952 article, Ellery Queen pointed to *The Benson Murder Case* as the inspiration for Queen's own detective story career: "Wright determined single-handedly to lift the American detective story out of the literary slums, give it a bath and a suit of modish clothes—and an education! . . . With the publication of *The Benson Murder Case,* the back-alley American detective story crossed the tracks to sign a long-term lease in the most reputable part of town" (Goodman, 212).

Similarly, *The "Canary" Murder Case* was, as Haycraft says, "another roman à clef based on the 'Dot' King murder" (*MFP*, 165). A former Ziegfeld Follies chorus girl and companion of various society playboys, King was found chloroformed to death in her plush Manhattan apartment on March 15, 1923. Clues in her apartment led the police to one J. Kearsley Mitchell, wealthy son-in-law of Edward B. Stotesbury, "Philadelphia bank partner of J. P. Morgan and president of the Philadelphia Rubber Works Company,"[8] and the reputed sole arbiter of Philadelphia's Four Hundred. Mitchell admitted being with King on the night of the murder but he had an alibi for the time of death. Like the murder of Elwell, the King case was never solved.

For all their good qualities, Wright's novels suffered, in Haycraft's opinion, from "a heavy pretentiousness and lack of humor," Vance's erudition growing in succeeding books "thin and wearisome" until "even its 'snob appeal' eventually faltered" (167). By the time of Wright's death in 1939, "much of Vance's popularity had evaporated," and yet Haycraft ends his evaluation of Wright on a high note: "In a few short years he had become the best known American writer of the detective story since Poe; he had rejuvenated and re-established the genre in his native land; and his name and that of his sleuth will endure—for all their joint pretentious faults—among the immortals of literature" (168).

Haycraft then turns his attention to Hammett, introducing his discussion of the "acknowledged founder" of the hard-boiled detective story by comparing him to Wright, who is "essentially . . . an adapter and polisher of other men's techniques," while Hammett is "a *creator* of the first rank . . . who brought something really new" to detective fiction (*MFP*, 168–69). Noting that whereas the Vance novels were American "in the narrow sense" of "their milieu and subject matter; . . . yet in method and style . . . departed no whit from the well established English tradition," Haycraft says that "Hammett's lean, dynamic, unsentimental narratives created a definitely *American style* . . . distinct from the accepted English pattern. (. . . So separate and so distinct . . . that to this day certain short-sighted formalists refuse to admit that they are detective stories at all!" (169). Describing *The Maltese Falcon* as Hammett's "zenith" and "one of the all-time high points" in the genre, he notes that this novel is "the only contemporary detective story to date to be included in the carefully selected Modern Library series" (170).

Haycraft understands that a large part of the originality of Hammett's work stems from his actually having worked as a private detective, thus being a far different sort of author from Wright, whom he had earlier characterized as "something of an exotic and a poseur" (*MFP*, 168). Yet when Haycraft tries to explain what Hammett's "startling originality" consists in, he must admit the novels "virtually defy exegesis even to-day." Instead, he gives his broad impressions of Hammett's work: "As straightaway detective stories they can hold their own with the best. They are also character studies of close to top rank . . . and are penetrating if often shocking novels of manners as well. They established new standards of realism in the genre. Yet they are as sharply stylized and deliberately artificial as Restoration Comedy, and have been called an inverted form of romanticism. They were commercial in inception; but miss being Literature, if at all, by the narrowest of margins" (171).

Haycraft sees Hammett's strengths quite clearly, but he doesn't articulate the major difference between Hammett's hard-boiled fiction and the analytic detective story tradition he examines in *Murder for Pleasure* (particularly that of the fair-play-method writers of the "Golden Age" with whom he groups Hammett): namely, the virtual indifference in Hammett's first three novels to matters of analysis and deduction. Even though Haycraft draws a sharp contrast between Hammett's work and Wright's, one can imagine, reading Hammett's 1927 review of Wright's *The Benson Murder Case* in the *Saturday Review of Literature*, that the contrast couldn't have been sharp enough to suit Hammett. Noting that Philo Vance's "conversational manner is that of a high-school girl who has been studying the foreign words and phrases in the back of her dictionary," Hammett pronounces Vance "a bore when he discusses art and philosophy, but when he switches to criminal psychology he is delightful . . . he manages always, and usually ridiculously, to be wrong."[9] Hammett then lists the novel's mistakes in ballistics and police procedure, and the review becomes an obituary. The tendency to compare Hammett's work to Wright's became even more pronounced (and perhaps even more galling to the hard-boiled novelist) when Hammett's last novel, *The Thin Man*, was made into a movie in 1934. The actor who played Nick Charles—William Powell—had also played Philo Vance in a series of earlier films, and one of the trailers for *The Thin Man* showed Powell (dressed as the dandified Vance) in split-screen interviewing himself (dressed as Nick Charles) about his new role.

III

Haycraft's version of the detective story tradition is significant for our purposes because Raymond Chandler's 1944 essay "The Simple Art of Murder," in which he tries to define the difference between Hammett's type of fiction and the mainstream of the analytic detective story, addresses itself specifically to Haycraft's work and the authors he canonizes. Beginning with the disclaimer that he doesn't intend to maintain that the detective story "is a vital and significant form of art" precisely because "there are no vital and significant forms of art; there is only art, and precious little of that," Chandler contends that because of the detective story's special requirements "good specimens of the art are much rarer than good serious novels."[10] In order to throw Hammett's originality into greater relief, Chandler first turns his attention to "the ladies and gentlemen of what Mr. Howard Haycraft (in his book *Murder for Pleasure*) calls the Golden Age of detective fiction," authors who, Chandler says, "really get me down." Noting that Haycraft considers the Golden Age as extending from 1918 to 1930, Chandler contends that it still persists, inasmuch as "two-thirds or three-quarters of all the detective stories published still adhere to the formula the giants of this era created . . . and sold to the world as problems in logic and deduction" (*TAMS*, 226).

He then critiques a novel from the English detective story's "Golden Age" that Haycraft praises, A. A. Milne's *The Red House Mystery*, a book Chandler describes as "an acknowledged masterpiece of the art of fooling the reader without cheating him" (*TAMS*, 226). That Milne is the creator of the beloved Winnie the Pooh books buys him nothing once Chandler starts dismantling *The Red House Mystery* using the same approach Hammett had employed in his review of *The Benson Murder Case*. Briefly summarizing the novel's plot, Chandler notes that "however light in texture the story may be, it is offered as a problem in logic and deduction. . . . If the problem does not contain the elements of truth and plausibility, it is no problem; if the logic is an illusion, there is nothing to deduce," and consequently, says Chandler, "the whole thing is a fraud" (227). Chandler then proceeds to list all those aspects of a coroner's inquest and of a standard police murder investigation that Milne is either ignorant of or else had to ignore in order to make his story work. Leaving not a stone upon a stone in Milne's *Red House*, Chandler proceeds to demolish the plausibility of Bentley's *Trent's Last Case* and individual detective novels by Freeman Wills Crofts, Dorothy Sayers, and Agatha Christie, describing Hercule Poirot as "that ingenious Belgian who talks in a literal translation of school-boy French" (230). But Chandler's harshest words are reserved for Van Dine's Philo Vance, who he says is "probably the most asinine character in detective fiction" (230). Chandler concludes that over its history the analytic detective story "has learned nothing and forgotten nothing" and that the great difficulty with such novels is that "they do not really come off intellectually as problems" or "come off artistically as fiction" (230–31).

Objecting to the inherent dishonesty of this type of detective story, Chandler says that "the poor writer is dishonest without knowing it, and the fairly good one can be dishonest because he doesn't know what to be honest about," giving as an example of the latter the analytic genre's conventional use of a complicated or exotic murder method that baffles "the lazy reader" and police alike. He explains that the police "know that the easiest murder case . . . to break is the one somebody tried to get very cute with" and adds, "if writers of this fiction wrote about the kind of murders that happen, they would also have to write about the authentic flavor of life as it is lived. And since they cannot do that, they pretend that what they do is what should be done. Which is begging the question—and the best of them know it" (*TAMS*, 231).

As Haycraft had used Van Dine as a contrast to demonstrate Hammett's originality, so Chandler uses Sayers, apparently because he considers her one of "the best of them," who knew she was begging the question. He begins by dismissing her dictum in the first *Omnibus of Crime* that the detective story "does not, and by hypothesis never can, attain the loftiest level of literary achievement" because it is a "literature of escape" and not a "literature of expression" (*TAMS*, 231). Rejecting her categories as "critics' jargon," Chandler claims that "*all* reading for pleasure is escape, whether it be Greek, mathematics, astronomy, Benedetto Croce, or *The Diary of the Forgotten Man*. To say otherwise is to be an intellectual snob, and a juvenile at the art of living" (232).

Describing Sayers's introduction to the first *Omnibus of Crime* as an "essay in critical futility," Chandler contends that "what was really gnawing at her mind was the slow realization that her kind of detective story was an arid formula which could not even satisfy its own implications. . . . If it started out to be about real people (and she could write about them—her minor characters show that), they must very soon do unreal things in order to form the artificial pattern required by the plot. When they did unreal things, they ceased to be real themselves   Dorothy Sayers's own stories show that she was annoyed by this triteness. . . . Yet she could not or would not give her characters their heads and let them make their own mystery" (*TAMS*, 232–33). The analytic detective story tends to be artistically dishonest, Chandler argues, precisely because as a plot-driven narrative (and a specialized kind of plot at that) it forces its characters to "do unreal things." Chandler's notion of the direction in which the detective story should move looks toward a more character-driven narrative, in which the figures in the novel are given their heads and "make their own mystery." But if this means jettisoning the puzzle component, then in what direction can detective fiction as a genre move? Chandler seems to suggest that the detective story, less the element of analysis and deduction, would tend to become more a novel of manners, a direction that Sayers herself had predicted in the introduction to the first *Omnibus of Crime*. And the person Chandler believed had most clearly initiated this movement was Hammett.

Contending that Hammett was the most visible member ("the only one who achieved critical recognition") of a group that "tried to write realistic mystery fiction," Chandler notes that "a rather revolutionary debunking of both the language and material of fiction had been going on for some time," a debunking Hammett applied to the detective story's "heavy crust of English gentility and American pseudo-gentility" (*TAMS*, 233), bringing to the genre "a sharp, aggressive attitude to life" embodied in a specifically American linguistic style. He wrote, says Chandler, for people who "were not afraid of the seamy side of things. . . . Violence . . . was right down their street" (234). With *The Maltese Falcon* Hammett showed that the detective story could be "important writing" (235); while in *The Glass Key,* the novel Hammett thought was his best, he achieved within the resources of the genre "an effect of movement, intrigue, cross-purposes and the gradual elucidation of character, which is all the detective story has any right to be about anyway" (236). But Chandler refers only obliquely or in passing to the theme Hammett touched on in the two Continental Op novels and made central to *The Maltese Falcon* (a theme that was to run through all the Marlowe books)—the conflict between the detective's professional and personal lives as he tries to earn a living and stay true to his code, an action that almost always involves the detective's attempt to become and stay his own boss. In addressing Sayers's comment that the detective story can't ever reach the highest level of literary achievement because its material isn't important enough, Chandler acknowledges that "a more powerful theme will provoke a more powerful performance. Yet some very dull books have been written about God, and some very fine ones about how to make a living and stay fairly honest" (231–32). And later, in giving his generic description of the hard-boiled detective, Chandler again obliquely evokes the subject that he'd found in Hammett's work: "He is a relatively poor man, or he would not be a detective at all. . . . He will take no man's money dishonestly . . . and his pride is that you will treat him as a proud man or be very sorry you ever saw him" (237).

Emphasizing the detective's sense of personal and professional honor as well as his independence, Chandler then describes the detective's manner of speech as an embodiment of these traits, implicitly defining as well the linguistic style Hammett brought to the detective story: "He talks as the man of his age talks, that is, with rude wit, a lively sense of the grotesque, a disgust for sham, and a contempt for pettiness. . . . He has a range of awareness that startles you, but it belongs to him by right, because it belongs to the world he lives in" (*TAMS*, 237). Chandler suggests that the "sharp, aggressive attitude to life" inherent in hard-boiled fiction, and embodied in the detective's speech, belonged to the world Hammett had lived in as a Pinkerton detective and that when Hammett's health failed he made "a living by writing something he had first hand information about," something with "a basis in fact . . . made up out of real things." This immediately distinguished him from the tradition of genteel detective writers in England and America: "The only reality the English detective writers knew was the conversational accent of Surbiton and Bognor Regis. If they wrote about dukes and Venetian vases, they knew no more about them out of their own experience than the well-heeled Hollywood character knows about the French Modernists that hang in his Bel-Air chateau. . . . Hammett took murder out of the Venetian vase and dropped it into the alley" (234). But if Hammett's sharp, aggressive attitude and language had come to him from the world he'd lived in as a Pinkerton detective, then Chandler, as his disciple, could claim that he too had been schooled in a working world (the California oilfields of the 1920s) almost as rough and morally ambiguous as the demimonde through which Hammett had plied his trade as a Pinkerton, both of them coming to detective fiction from no-nonsense businesses rather than from the world of high journalism or popular humor writing, as had so many analytic detective writers.

IV

If what Hammett achieved in creating hard-boiled detective fiction (and what Chandler built on, following Hammett's lead) was to move detective writing from the realm of puzzle fiction more in the direction of the novel of manners by jettisoning the logic-and-deduction element to allow greater depth of characterization, then the various conventions and plot devices Poe had created in the Dupin tales served in effect as a kind of reverse template for shaping the conventions of this new offshoot of the detective genre. Recall for a moment some of the things Poe originally introduced: *first,* the figure of the detective as an amateur whom the police consult whenever they encounter an especially baffling case; *second,* the sedentary detective, sedentary because as a pure reasoner he is content (or else constrained, as with Ernest Bramah's blind detective Max Carrados or Borges's convict detective Don Isidro Parodi) to exercise his powers on clues gathered by, or observations made by, others (as in "The Mystery of Marie Rogêt," in which Dupin does nothing more than read various newspaper accounts of the case, indicating to his friend, the tale's unnamed narrator, the significant clues pointing to a solution); *third,* the detective's sidekick or legman (e.g., Dupin's unnamed companion, Holmes's

Dr. Watson, Poirot's Captain Hastings, Wolfe's Archie Goodwin, to name a few), a figure who serves to gather information for the sedentary detective but whose real purpose is to allow the author to explain the detective's thought processes through a dialogue with this character, who is, in consequence, often made slow on the uptake; *fourth,* a police officer (e.g., Dupin's Prefect, Holmes's Inspector Lestrade, Poirot's Chief Inspector Japp, etc.) who brings to the detective's attention cases defying solution through the usual official methods, smooths his way by granting official sanction, and whose confusion often serves as a humorous foil to the detective's intellect; *fifth,* the exotic, complex, or bizarre murder method (almost a given in any genre whose original story has an orangutan as the killer)—what Sayers in the first *Omnibus of Crime* calls "the unexpected means" when she suggests methods for writers just starting out: "poisoned tooth-stoppings; licking poisoned stamps; . . . stabbing with a sharp icicle; electrocution by telephone; . . . hypodermic injections shot from air-guns; . . . guns concealed in cameras" (one that Hitchcock in fact used in his film *Foreign Correspondent*) (*TAMS,* 107); and *sixth,* the final confrontation in which the culprit is revealed and the correctness of the detective's deductions verified. As for the types of plot that became standard in the analytic detective genre, Poe invented two of the best: the locked-room problem in "The Murders in the Rue Morgue" and the hidden-object problem in "The Purloined Letter."

As I said, in striving for greater realism, Hammett turned away from analytic-deductive plots in favor of character-driven narratives resembling novels of manners, but since Hammett's detective stories began as popular fiction appearing in what were essentially men's magazines, he had to find another plot element that would be as interesting and appealing to his male audience as the puzzle aspect of analytic detective fiction. And this element was the conflict between the professional and the personal, between work and relationships, in the detective's life. What this theme necessarily entailed was that the detective as amateur could have no place in hard-boiled fiction. Clearly, he would have to be a working professional, trying simultaneously to make a living, stay honest, and remain independent in thought and action. And once the detective's amateur status was gone, most of the other conventions Poe originated had to fall away as well.

Of course, the notion of the detective as a sedentary deductive genius to whom the police bring baffling cases was false not only to the kind of dull, patient legwork that forms the core of private investigators' business but also to the true relationship between a private eye and the police. Hammett's Continental Op and Sam Spade both know that when it comes to solving crimes the cops have as much brain power as they do and many more resources. When Spade is called to the scene of Miles Archer's murder and his friend Sergeant Tom Polhaus briefs him on what he thinks happened, then asks Spade if he wants to look at the body, Spade says, "No . . . you've seen him. You'd see everything I could."[11] Chandler is particularly scathing in "The Simple Art of Murder" about the convention of the police seeking out the help of a brilliant amateur, remarking that in Milne's *The Red House Mystery* the detective, "an insouciant gent . . . with a cheery eye, a cozy little flat in London, and that airy manner" isn't "making any money on the assignment, but is always available when the local gendarmie loses its notebook. The English police seem to endure him with their customary stoicism; but I shudder to think of what the boys at the Homicide Bureau in my city would do to him" (*TAMS*, 229).

In *The Maltese Falcon* there is clearly no love lost between Spade and Lieutenant Dundy, and one of the ongoing elements in the Marlowe books is the often strained relationship between a private investigator and the police, even though Marlowe himself had previously been part of law enforcement as an investigator for the district attorney's office. Thus, in *The Big Sleep*, when Marlowe turns over Carol Lundgren for the murder of Joe Brody to Hollywood police Lieutenant Cronjager at a late night meeting in the district attorney's home and then explains how he hadn't reported the previous murder of Arthur Gwynn Geiger, which was the motive for Lundgren killing Brody, Cronjager snarls, "I love private dicks that play murders close to the vest. . . . So all you did was not report a murder that happened last night and then spend today foxing around so that this kid of Geiger's could commit a second murder this evening."[12] Cronjager's angry and wants to take it out of Marlowe's hide, but when he realizes the DA and his chief investigator Bernie Ohls are on Marlowe's side, he says, "I'm one against three here. . . . I'm a homicide man. If this Geiger was running indecent literature, that's no skin off my nose. But I'm ready to admit it won't help my division any to have it washed over in the papers. What do you birds want?" (105). Marlowe wins this round, but he knows that even though Cronjager will get the credit in the newspapers for having arrested Lundgren, there'll always be a check mark by Marlowe's name in Cronjager's memory and sooner or later he or someone else in the Hollywood division will get even.

Knowing that they have no advantage over the police in investigative skill or scientific resources, Hammett's and Chandler's detectives see their only leverage as a greater independence of action when it comes to accepting or rejecting clients, bending the law for their clients' benefit, and not having to make their findings public or turn over all their information to the police— that, and perhaps in the case of Spade and Marlowe, a deeper understanding of human psychology and greater acting skill (something John Huston makes much of in his film version of *The Maltese Falcon*).

Once one does away with the sedentary detective, one of the reasons for the sidekick or legman vanishes. And since the other major reason for this character is to give the reader access to the detective's thought processes through a dialogue with his assistant, then in the Continental Op stories and novels as well as in the Marlowe books, where the detective is the first-person narrator and thus gives the reader immediate access to his thinking, there's no need for any explanatory dialogue with a sidekick. (*The Maltese Falcon* is, of course, narrated in the third person precisely to deny the reader access to Spade's thoughts [specifically, to his certainty almost from the start that the only person who could have enticed Archer up a dark alley with his gun on his hip and his overcoat buttoned was a beautiful young woman, i.e., Brigid O'Shaughnessy] and by thus denying such access, to make the climax, in which Spade tells Brigid that he may love her but he's going to send her over for Archer's murder, more striking.) Moreover, since the most extreme form, as represented by the Marlowe novels, of the effort to become one's own boss also involves being one's own sole employee, that is, a lone wolf, there is an obvious thematic reason for the Watson-type figure not having made the transition to hard-boiled detective fiction. Finally, regarding the convention of exotic murder-methods, Chandler is as acerbic as he was about the police seeking help from gifted amateurs, noting that the kind of people who actually commit murders do it "with the means at hand, not with hand-wrought duelling pistols, curare, and tropical fish" (*TAMS*, 234).

If the conventions and devices of hard-boiled detective fiction represent a negation of those Poe established in the Dupin stories (so that Poe's is in effect a reverse influence on the work of Hammett, Chandler, and others), there is still an aspect of hard-boiled fiction for which Poe represents a direct, positive influence—and that is in the area of motive. As I suggested earlier, Poe's notion of "perverseness" as presented in "The Black Cat" and "The Imp of the Perverse," the notion that there exists a principle in the human psyche bent on vexing the self by making it perform acts the conscious mind identifies as being in the self's worst interests, seems clearly present in Hawthorne's story "Wakefield," which is the immediate precursor of the Flitcraft episode in *The Maltese Falcon* and present again in Cain's *Double Indemnity* when Walter Huff decides to help Phyllis murder her husband even though all his experience and shrewdness tell him he shouldn't—not to mention the fact that the narrative form of "The Imp of the Perverse" and "The Black Cat" (a first-person account of his crime written by a murderer awaiting punishment) is reproduced in both *Double Indemnity* and *The Postman Always Rings Twice*.

Before leaving the issue of Poe's influence (both negative and positive) on hard-boiled fiction, we should note one further connection between Poe's Dupin stories and the recurrent conflict between the professional and the personal faced by Hammett's and Chandler's detectives. After reading the Dupin stories, the Goncourt brothers described them in an 1856 journal entry as "a new literary world" bearing "signs of the literature of the twentieth century—love giving place to deductions . . . the interest of the story moved from the heart to the head . . . from the drama to the solution."[13] If we were to translate the Goncourts' terms *love, heart,* and *drama* into the more prosaic twentieth-century phrase *personal relationships* and their *deductions, head,* and *solution* into the term *mental work* (i.e., the sort of work associated with a profession, the sort of work done by people with the leisure, background, and inclination to read detective stories for relaxation), then this movement in the story's interest from heart to head, from love to work, which the Goncourts thought foreshadowed the literature of the twentieth century, was thematized by Hammett and Chandler, was given in effect its dramatic form within the genre as the struggle between work and love in their detectives lives. But even more significantly, since Spade and Marlowe always resolve this conflict in favor of the professional over the personal, the ultimate direction of the movement in the story's interest remains the same (from heart to head) as that detected by the Goncourts in the Dupin tales, so that for all the differences of the analytic detective genre from the hard-boiled, Poe as the originator of the former remained in one sense the overarching influence on the latter.

V

If hard-boiled fiction first began as a new type of detective story, it soon spread to the form that Haycraft, in *Murder for Pleasure*, called "the 'inverted' detective story" (*MFP*, 148), that is, "psychological studies of murder" that examine "'the events leading up to the crime' as seen and felt by the participants" (147). Haycraft singles out as a prime example of this in England Francis Iles's novel *Before the Fact* (1932), the work Hitchcock turned into his 1941 film *Suspicion*. Noting that though "the idea of the inside-out crime novel was not, per se, particularly new: Mrs. Belloc Lowndes, among others, had achieved a very considerable success with it a decade or more earlier," Haycraft says that Iles (the pen name of A. B. Cox, who also wrote detective novels under the name Anthony Berkeley) achieved in his inverted detective fiction something that came close to "the true 'melodrama of the soul'": "Not many 'serious' novelists of the present era, in fact, have produced character studies to compare with Iles's internally terrifying portrait of the murderer in *Before the Fact*" (147–48). Haycraft notes that in the preface to his 1930 detective novel *The Last Shot* Berkeley had argued that "the detective story is in the process of developing into the novel with a detective or crime interest, holding its readers less by mathematical than by psychological ties. The puzzle element will no doubt remain, but it will become a puzzle of character rather than a puzzle of time, place, motive, and opportunity" (147). Haycraft implies that Cox began publishing his inverted detective stories under the name Francis Iles the next year to pursue this goal. Indeed, one wonders if Cox had been influenced in his decision to make his narratives more character-driven by the success of *The Maltese Falcon* in 1930.

Of course, the two American authors we've discussed whose work falls into the category of inverted detective stories are James M. Cain and W. R. Burnett. In his two best books, *Double Indemnity* (1936) and *The Postman Always Rings Twice* (1934), Cain produces character studies of killers. Exhibiting that same "sharp, aggressive attitude to life" embodied in a terse, colloquially American speech Chandler identified as the essence of Hammett's style, Cain's "tough-guy" fiction involves as well a pervasive bleakness of spirit, of being trapped by circumstances, a dog-eat-dog quality that mirrored the feelings of American men in the depths of the Great Depression—though of course someone like Walter Huff is trapped as much by his own character flaws as by his environment.

In contrast, Burnett's Dillinger-era bank robber Roy Earle in *High Sierra* and the small-time strong-arm man Dix Handley in *The Asphalt Jungle* seem trapped less by the economic woes of a particular decade in American history than by the whole direction of twentieth-century American life, by the country's shift from a largely rural to a largely urban populace, a move that displaced the two farm boys Earle and Handley, ultimately forcing them to confront the loss not just of the world of their youth but of their own youthful vigor as middle-aged men in a young man's game of violent crime. Though people get killed in both *High Sierra* and *The Asphalt Jungle,* these novels are clearly not inverted murder mysteries, for the killings are unplanned, occurring only because something went wrong with a robbery or its aftermath. Burnett's type of inverted detective story, with its inside view of the careful planning and execution of a heist and its subsequent unraveling, belongs, properly speaking, to the subgenre of the "caper" story.

In Cain's and Burnett's inverted detective novels, the conflict between the main character's professional and personal life remains a constant, but the outcome of that conflict is inverted as well, as Walter Huff and Roy Earle both let personal attachments overrule professional codes and long years of experience with disastrous results, a not unpredictable outcome given that the effort to become and stay one's own boss (which had characterized both Spade and Marlowe) undergoes its own inversion as Walter Huff tries to beat the boss and Roy Earle tries to avoid bossing a gang of young, inexperienced punks only to find that time is the real boss.

VI

With both Cain and Burnett the inverted detective story continues the Hammett-originated movement of taking detective fiction more in the direction of the novel of manners "with a detective or crime interest," more in the direction of high-art fiction. But this raises the question of which American high-art writers of the twenties, thirties, and forties should writers like Hammett, Chandler, Cain, and Burnett be compared with or judged against? Which (if any) of these high-art novelists do the hard-boiled writers resemble? And did the former influence the latter or vice versa? From the 1940s on, the most frequently offered answer to the first of these questions was Hemingway. Chandler says in "The Simple Art of Murder" that there's nothing in Hammett's work that's "not implicit in the early novels and short stories of Hemingway. Yet for all I know, Hemingway may have learned something from Hammett, as well as from writers like Dreiser, Ring Lardner, Carl Sandburg, Sherwood Anderson and himself" (*TAMS*, 233). Yet four years earlier Chandler had taken an oblique shot at Hemingway in one of his patented wisecracks. In *Farewell, My Lovely* Marlowe calls a policeman (who keeps repeating everything Marlowe says) "Hemingway" until the cop finally asks,

"Who is this Hemingway person at all?"

"A guy that keeps saying the same thing over and over again until you begin to believe it must be good."

"That must take a hell of a long time," the big man said. "For a private dick you certainly have a wandering kind of mind. Are you still wearing your own teeth?"[14]

Whereas Chandler admits a resemblance in style and attitude between Hammett and Hemingway and raises the question in which direction the influence ran or whether it ran in both, Cain and Burnett each goes out of his way to deny Hemingway's influence on his work. In 1942 Burnett wrote, "Although a cry of 'Hemingway' was raised when my books began to appear, I was but little influenced by him. I was influenced mostly by European writers, by way of translation. . . . I formed my present style after a long study of Merimée, Flaubert, and Maupassant; also Pío Baroja, an unappreciated (in this country) Spanish writer and Giovanni Verga, a little known Italian author . . . whose short stories are better than those of Chekhov or Maupassant."[15] In openly acknowledging the effect of several older European masters on his work, Burnett establishes his claim in terms of literary culture to be dismissive of a contemporary American influence such as Hemingway's. And in this same vein Cain, in his 1946 preface to *The Butterfly,* explains away any superficial stylistic resemblance to Hemingway:

I owe no debt, beyond the pleasure his books have given me, to Mr. Ernest Hemingway. . . . Just what it is I am supposed to have got from him I have never quite made out, though I am sure it can hardly be in the realm of content. . . . He writes of God's eternal mayhem against Man, a theme he works into great, classic cathedrals. . . .

I . . . write of the wish that comes true, for some reason a terrifying concept . . .

Nor do I see any similarity in manner, beyond the circumstance that . . . each of us shudders at the least hint of the highfalutin, the pompous, or the literary. We have people talk as they do talk, and as some of them are of a low station in life, no doubt they often say things in a similar way. . . . We each cut down to a minimum the *he-saids* and *she-replied-laughinglys,* though I carry this somewhat further than he does. . . .

I grant, of course, that even such resemblances between Mr. Hemingway and myself do make for a certain leanness in each of us . . . and might be taken, by those accustomed to thinking in terms of schools, as evidence I had in some part walked in his footsteps.[16]

But Cain points out that being more than six years older than Hemingway, he had "done a mountain of writing, in newspapers and magazines, including dialogue sketches, short stories, and one performed play" before Hemingway "appeared on the scene at all," and that he'd already established his own style in the short story "Pastorale," written in 1927, before he'd first read Hemingway "when *Men Without Women* appeared in 1928" (354). Cain implies that any stylistic resemblance between his and Hemingway's writing was a function of their shared background in journalism, though in his lengthy denial of influence he seems to protest too much. Yet this may simply be a case of Cain feeling, as Chandler had said of Hammett and hard-boiled fiction, that in all literary movements there is always some one individual "picked out to represent the whole" (*TAMS*, 233), and since this one individual clearly appeared, by the time of Cain's writing in 1946, to be Hemingway, the strenuousness of Cain's denial probably reflects his determination not to be swept up into this process "by those accustomed to thinking in schools" (354). Earlier in this same preface Cain had emphatically stated, "I belong to no school, hardboiled or otherwise" and had denied any Hammett influence as well.

If we put aside any stylistic "similarity of manner" between Cain and Hemingway due to their both having worked as reporters, then Cain's sense that he owed nothing to Hemingway in "the realm of content" seems accurate. Inasmuch as Cain's best writing confronts the conflict between the main character's professional life and his personal lusts, a struggle that is won by the latter and that involves as well an effort to outwit or do away with the boss, then in terms of its content Hemingway's fiction could have had little effect on Cain, for the mundane reality, the attractions and demands, of a man's normal working life or career have virtually no presence in Hemingway's writings.

If one considers just those Hemingway works that have survived best, works that seem to have engaged his imagination most fully, these are all set at times (vacations, sabbaticals, leaves, convalescences) or in the midst of activities (big-game safaris, fishing trips, fiestas, volunteer service) coded as *nonwork*. Though Jake Barnes in *The Sun Also Rises* is a foreign correspondent for a newspaper service, one gathers from the first third of the book that his duties consist largely in drinking in various Parisian cafes. Of course, the novel's principal action takes place during his vacation in Spain, where Jake goes fishing in Burguete, attends the fiesta in Pamplona, and goes swimming at San Sebastian, joined most of the time by people as unencumbered by work as himself. And where Hemingway's first novel is set during its main character's vacation, his best novel takes place during *its* hero's sabbatical: Robert Jordan of *For Whom the Bell Tolls* is on leave from his job as a Spanish instructor at the University of Montana to fight in the Spanish Civil War, periodically wondering whether the fighting will go well enough for him to return to his position when his sabbatical is over, or whether the university will take him back at all since he'd fought on the Communist side. In Hemingway's other wartime novel, *A Farewell to Arms,* the action takes place during a time that's equally "in parenthesis" in its main character's life.

In *The Green Hills of Africa,* a sort of nonfiction novel *avant la lettre* in which Hemingway sets out "to see whether the shape of a country and the pattern of a month's action, can, if truly presented, compete with a work of the imagination,"[17] the character "Hemingway" hunts big game by day and pontificates at the campfire by night. An Austrian visitor to the camp asks Hemingway to tell him about American writers, and in the course of presenting a brief history of American literature he says, "All modern American literature comes from one book by Mark Twain called *Huckleberry Finn* . . . it's the best book we've had. All American writing comes from that. There was nothing before. There has been nothing as good since" (22).

It seems only appropriate that the bard of twentieth-century-American-male perpetual adolescence, the singer of that fierce wish to grow old without ever having to grow up, should invoke Huck Finn as the patron saint of his ongoing theme and Twain's novel as the source from which "all modern American literature" flows. For clearly Hemingway is twentieth-century America's great writer of stylistically sophisticated, highly mannered "boys' stories," narratives whose "you-can't-fool-me-'cause-life's-a-bitch-and-then-you-die" tone of rueful yet self-congratulatory knowingness has an enormous appeal for adolescents of all ages. And all those narratives, with their times, settings, and activities so obviously coded as *nonwork,* make clear what the *Huckleberry Finn* component in modern American literature amounted to for Hemingway, for if to the childish or adolescent mind, work is one great marker of adulthood, then avoiding work, playing hooky from its constraints and responsibilities, seems to that mind one way to keep from growing old.

VII

As I suggested in the chapter on Cain, it's not Hemingway's work (as so many contemporary critics of both writers thought) that Cain's work resembles in terms of content, but Fitzgerald's, a writer who, in terms of style, Cain resembles not at all. Given that the lilt and lyricism of Fitzgerald's prose makes reading Cain seem like getting a telegram, still—be it Gatsby's willingness to toss away his meteoric but shady success for an attachment to a woman or Dick Diver's sacrificing his brilliant medical career by committing the cardinal sin of marrying a psychiatric patient or Monroe Stahr's risking losing control of his movie studio for the love of a woman who's a physical reincarnation of his dead wife—these narratives are, in terms of subject matter, the closest structural match in modern American high-art fiction for Walter Huff's actions in *Double Indemnity*. Nor should we underestimate the influence of *The Great Gatsby* on hard-boiled and inverted detective fiction generally, for if, as we saw, the hard-boiled detective narrative, in seeking greater realism, developed by moving the story away from being a puzzle in logic and deduction more in the direction of the character-driven novel of manners, then there already existed in 1925 a widely popular, American high art novel of manners "with a crime interest," written by someone of Cain's own generation, to serve as a model for this development, a novel whose main character was an underworld figure and whose action culminated with a hit-and-run death whose perpetrator was never caught and a murder/suicide whose true circumstances were never made public.

Though Cain and Fitzgerald had many friends in common in New York, the two had apparently never met until they were both working as screenwriters at M-G-M in 1937. As Cain's biographer tells the story, Fitzgerald stopped by Cain's office in the writer's building one morning to say hello and welcome him to the lot. Cain said thanks and Fitzgerald left, but "then Cain got to thinking that was hardly any way to treat the great Scott Fitzgerald," so at noon he went to Fitzgerald's office and invited him to lunch at the commissary. Cain says that during lunch he tried to make conversation but that Fitzgerald didn't say a word, and finally, after paying the check, Cain excused himself and left: "Later, someone who knew Fitzgerald—John O'Hara, Cain recalled—told Cain that Fitzgerald probably figured 'you were pitying him for being a has-been and had invited him to lunch for that reason.' Whatever it was, Cain said, it was the most uncomfortable hour he ever spent in his life. He never saw Fitzgerald again."[18]

But that wasn't the end of his involvement with Fitzgerald. In 1945 Paramount tapped Cain to work on the screenplay for *The Great Gatsby*, a film that was to star Alan Ladd and Betty Field as Gatsby and Daisy. Even though Cain, according to his biographer, "always thought *Gatsby* 'claptrap'" and Fitzgerald's writing "all diction, cadence and accent" (Hoopes, 376), clearly someone at Paramount thought there was enough similarity between Fitzgerald's novel and the sort of thing Cain did best to make the pairing appropriate. One of the suggested changes to the novel that Cain came up with (which explains why Cain was dropped from the project) was "a new ending in which Gatsby would be thought to have been killed in the famous automobile accident that kills the girl friend of Daisy's husband. 'Attending his own funeral and anticipating . . . the enormous crowd he thinks will be there, he stands behind a tree in the rain,' as Cain describes the scene in his treatment, 'to discover that only two or three people even think it necessary to show up.' One who does . . . show up is a gum-chewing, former Gatsby girl friend from the Midwest, who (unlike Daisy) really loves him. . . . She recognizes him and leads 'him off to a new life and fade-out. This, however, naturally needs thought, as well as the tricky accident,' Cain concludes" (377).

In the mid-1950s Cain would run up against *The Great Gatsby* yet again when he sent a play he'd written, *The Guest in 701*, to his Hollywood agent H. N. Swanson, who had also been Fitzgerald's Hollywood agent. Swanson thought the play's hero Tenny "a kind of Jay Gatsby—very rich and in love with another man's wife—and recommended that Cain go back and reread Fitzgerald's novel" (Hoopes, 466). And when Cain later reviewed Budd Schulberg's novel about Fitzgerald, *The Disenchanted*, in the *New York Times Book Review*, he was asked by the editor to revise his review "for being too rough on Fitzgerald," whom he'd taken to task "particularly on the score of workmanship" (470). Cain's biographer explains, "Cain always felt that Fitzgerald did not rewrite enough and that '*Gatsby* could have been a great book . . . and it wasn't, through sheer sloth'" (470–71). In his Preface to *The Butterfly* Cain had been lavish in his praise of Hemingway's work (calling it "a Matterhorn of literature" in comparison with which his own work was only "a foothill" [Pref., 355]) while denying any debt of influence to Hemingway in either content or "similarity of manner" (353). If Cain's appreciative treatment of Hemingway is an instance of an author's willingness to acknowledge the talent of a contemporary with whom he feels no significant similarity and no debt of influence, then one wonders whether, given the number of times during his career Cain had to confront *The Great Gatsby,* his opposite treatment of Fitzgerald suggests Cain's sense of both a similarity of content with Fitzgerald's work and a debt.

With Burnett, on the other hand, the numerous resemblances between *The Great Gatsby* and *Little Caesar* noted earlier are so patent it's as if Burnett were consciously inviting the reader to appreciate the verisimilitude of his gangster Rico Bandello in comparison with Fitzgerald's bootlegger and stock swindler Jay Gatsby. And when it comes to Cornell Woolrich, the Fitzgerald influence on his career is even clearer—from the remark of his college classmate Jacques Barzun that Woolrich was conscious "of being a second Scott Fitzgerald,"[19] to Woolrich's biographer's listing of the numerous similarities between the two authors' lives and careers, to Woolrich's early novels such as *Cover Charge* (1926) and *Children of the Ritz* (1927), overtly Fitzgeraldian works in both style and content. In the early 1930s, when Woolrich turned to the more popular and lucrative hard-boiled suspense fiction for which he's best known, he was able to combine what was left of Fitzgerald's influence with Poe's in creating psychological terror stories.

As to the similarity of Hammett's and Chandler's work to Fitzgerald's or any Fitzgerald influence there, we can see that if their hard-boiled fiction represented the American detective novel's development in the direction of a character-driven novel of manners, a sort of American equivalent of the English upstairs/downstairs "country house" school of novel with its emphasis on class differences in speech and behavior but minus the puzzle element of the plot, then *The Great Gatsby,* published before either Hammett or Chandler had begun writing, also served as both model and encouragement for the course they were to set for the detective story. And particularly so for Chandler, since Gatsby's meteoric rise from his humble origins in the Midwest to his position in the East, hobnobbing with old and new money on Long Island, as well the kind of social and linguistic gaffs the lower-class Gatsby made in these upper-class surroundings, is precisely the stuff Chandler works with when he has the middle-class Marlowe move across the social strata from high to low and back again, taking the rich and powerful down a peg if they get too hoity-toity and verbally raising an eyebrow at the more egregious behavior of the lower orders. Further, there's a clear similarity between Gatsby and Marlowe as regards the inner idealism each man maintains, the former while engaged in his shady work and the latter in traversing various sordid environments. In Nick Carraway's judgment Gatsby had preserved his "single dream"[20] and his "extraordinary gift for hope," preserved his "romantic readiness" uncorrupted by the "foul dust" that "floated in the wake of his dreams" (6). And Chandler evokes Marlowe again and again as a sort of battered knight-errant who, though traversing the "mean streets . . . is not himself mean, who is neither tarnished nor afraid. . . . He must be, to use a rather weathered phrase, a man of honor, by instinct, by inevitability, without thought of it, and certainly without saying it. He must be the best man in his world and a good enough man for any world" (*TAMS*, 237).

A certain similarity of tone also links the writing of Fitzgerald, Hammett, and Chandler, one Chandler described as "rude wit, a lively sense of the grotesque, a disgust for sham, and a contempt for pettiness." It's the tone I hear in that passage where Nick attends his first party at Gatsby's house and a drunken young woman begins to sing a song she's decided is "very, very sad," weeping as she sings: "The tears coursed down her cheeks—not freely, however, for when they came into contact with her heavily beaded eyelashes they assumed an inky color, and pursued the rest of their way in slow black rivulets. A humorous suggestion was made that she sing the notes on her face whereupon she threw up her hands" (42). A tone I hear again at that moment in *The Maltese Falcon* when Sam Spade, meeting Joel Cairo in the lobby of his hotel after Cairo'd been grilled by the police all night, says, "Let's go some place where we can talk," and Cairo replies, "Please excuse me. . . . Our conversations in private have not been such that I am anxious to continue them"—something of an understatement given that during each of their two previous conversations Spade had struck him and taken away his gun. Spade tries to convince Cairo that on the last occasion he'd behaved this way to play along with Brigid O'Shaughnessey because she's the only one who knows where the falcon is. Cairo says, "You have always, I must say, a smooth explanation ready." To which Spade replies, "What do you want me to do? Learn to stutter?" (100). And you can hear it again in Marlowe's remark in *The Big Sleep* (when he tries unsuccessfully to break open the front door of Geiger's house after hearing gunshots) that he should have remembered "the only part of a California house you can't put your foot through is the front door" (30) or in his calling the police detective in *Farewell, My Lovely!* "Hemingway."

Indeed, with Marlowe the wisecrack gets raised to the status of a peculiarly American art form, the embodiment, the verbal emblem, of that "sharp, aggressive attitude toward life" Chandler thought was the essence of hard-boiled fiction. And the tone's there again in those omnipresent Marlovian similes, as, for example, when Marlowe at the start of *Farewell, My Lovely!* describes the huge and loudly dressed Moose Malloy walking down Central Avenue in L.A. ("not the quietest dressed street in the world") looking "about as inconspicuous as a tarantula on a slice of angel food" (1). The remark's wit lies in its double reversal of the reader's expectations: the image of something black standing out against a white background being used to evoke the way a white man stands out walking down a street in a black neighborhood and then the second reversal (of a black stereotype), by having the white man attract attention because he's more garishly dressed than the black people around him. Marlowe's similes are not just commentaries on the "mean streets" he walks down in doing his job, they're the ways this intelligent man brings his sordid, threatening environment under verbal control, the way he makes the "mean streets" mean. Similarly, Spade's comeback to Cairo "What do you want me to do? Learn to stutter?" is more than just a smart remark: its deeper resonance—that Spade could easily give a different dramatic reading of his words that would seem less pat and more convincing—subtly points to the fact that all the major characters in *The Maltese Falcon*, including Spade, are acting, each playing a role meant to fool and thus gain the upper hand on the other characters.

Hammett's resemblance to Fitzgerald seems closest, however, in *The Thin Man*, where one feels that the detective or crime interest of the novel has begun to slip below the horizon. In setting out to portray a modern marriage (based on the relationship of Hammett and Lillian Hellman) through the characters of Nick and Nora Charles, Hammett essentially abandoned the hard-boiled detective genre he had created and turned more toward a comedy of manners, in which Nick and Nora's sophisticated mating is played out against the background of the New York "smart set" during the final months of Prohibition, played out with sexual broad-mindedness, clever repartee, and cocktails mixed with a dash of mystery. Since Nick Charles has retired as a working private detective five years before the story opens, the professional/personal conflict is absent from the start, his relationship to the case being more that of the gifted amateur of analytic detective fiction than a hard-boiled private eye.

Hammett biographer Richard Layman notes that, unlike Nick Charles, Hammett's earlier detectives "were serious, single-minded men who would never allow their social lives to intrude upon their work. They were successful not because of their brilliant analytical skills, but because they followed every clue and intelligently considered all the evidence."[21] Hammett's earlier detectives "went hunting evidence," while "in *The Thin Man* the evidence comes to Nick Charles" (141–42), and Nick's ultimate solution of the murders, "based on . . . facts, guesses, and instinct" (143), involves one of those final gatherings of suspects in which damaging admissions are elicited and the murderer made to reveal himself—the sort of ending one would expect in an analytic detective story. Indeed, it seems as if once Hammett had decided that this novel was going to be more about the relationship of Nick and Nora than about the solving of murders, he in effect jettisoned all those realistic aspects of detective work he'd brought to hard-boiled fiction and fell back on the conventions of the analytic genre to handle the detective part of the plot. Worst of all, as Layman points out, Nick Charles "withholds clues from the police as well as the reader—a defect Hammett objected to loudly when he found it in the work of others" (141). As Nick goes about solving the murders in *The Thin Man,* with Nora tagging along, he moves in an "alcoholic haze," to use Layman's words, through a world of high-classed New York apartments and hotel suites, nightclubs, and speakeasies and through an atmosphere as breezy and brittle as one of Gatsby's parties.

It seems only appropriate that Hammett's last novel was published in the same year, 1934, as Fitzgerald's *Tender Is the Night,* and the structural resemblance between the two books is noteworthy—each is the story of a man who marries an heiress and of the effect the wife's money has on his career. Nick Charles retires from his job as a private detective to manage his wife's fortune, though what the reader sees is that Nick mostly drinks and loafs, while Dick Diver reduces his brilliant work as a psychiatrist to being his mentally disturbed wife's doctor, finally feeling more like her kept man, and begins to fall apart, with an ever-increasing use of alcohol as the only anesthetic for his pain and humiliation.

There is one further resemblance between the two novels that attended their appearance in 1934, as each book pushed the limits of sexually explicit language. Where Hammett's earlier detective novels had tested the limits of depicting mayhem, in *The Thin Man* he evidently set out to be as explicit about sexuality as he'd previously been about violence, as explicit as he thought his publisher and the contemporary reading public would allow. This ultimate test of limits in the novel occurs at the end of chapter 25, when Nora asks Nick, after he'd had a scuffle with one of the female suspects in her apartment:

"Tell me the truth: when you were wrestling with Mimi, didn't you have an erection?"

"Oh, a little."

She laughed and got up from the floor. "If you aren't a disgusting old lecher," she said. (Layman, 145)

Hammett's biographer Layman notes that while *Redbook* censored the passage when they serialized the novel, "Knopf decided to capitalize on it. On January 30, 1934, the publisher took an ad in the *New York Times* boldly declaring: 'I don't believe the question on page 192 of Dashiell Hammett's *The Thin Man* has had the slightest influence upon the sales of the book. It takes more than that to make a best seller these days. Twenty thousand people don't buy a book within three weeks to read a five word question.' The statement was signed by Alfred Knopf, and it did not prevent the Canadian government from banning the sale of the novel in Canada" (145).

The equivalent stretching of linguistic proprieties in Fitzgerald's novel occurs during a confrontation among Dick, Nicole, and Tommy Barban when Nicole announces her intention to leave Dick for Tommy, and Tommy warns Dick, "Let it be understood that from this moment . . . I stand in the position of Nicole's protector until details can be arranged. And I shall hold you strictly accountable for any abuse of the fact that you continue to inhabit the same house." To which Dick replies, "I never did go in for making love to dry loins."[22] Unlike Knopf, Fitzgerald's publisher, Scribner, didn't try to make the novel a *succès de scandale* on the basis of this one line, and indeed two years after the novel's appearance Fitzgerald had second thoughts about it. Writing to Bennett Cerf in August 1936 about making revisions in the text for a possible Modern Library edition of *Tender Is the Night,* Fitzgerald said, "There is not more than one complete sentence that I want to eliminate, one that has offended many people and that I admit is out of Dick's character: 'I never did go in for making love to dry loins.' It is a strong line but definitely offensive."[23] Like virtually all the changes Fitzgerald considered making in *Tender Is the Night* after the book's lukewarm reception, changes contemplated during a period when his faith in his own talent was at a low ebb and he had become increasingly dependent on alcohol, the deletion of this line from the novel would have been a mistake. Fitzgerald's sense that the line is out of character for Dick is precisely the point; the remark suggests how much Dick's character has deteriorated, how much the innate gentlemanliness that had characterized him at his best has cracked under the progressively humiliating sense of his own emasculation.

If, as I contend, the work of the hard-boiled fiction writers I've discussed bears only a surface resemblance in written style to Hemingway's writings while showing a deep structural resemblance to Fitzgerald's fiction, thus suggesting a Fitzgerald influence, then one well might ask whether there's any resemblance to, or influence of, the work of the other member of the "big three" of contemporary American high-art fiction—William Faulkner. After all, unlike Fitzgerald and Hemingway, Faulkner actually wrote detective stories— the novel *Intruder in the Dust* (1948), the short stories and novella collected in *Knight's Gambit and Other Stories* (1949)—as well as being a friend and drinking buddy of Hammett's and co-writing the script for Howard Hawks's screen version of Chandler's *The Big Sleep*. And yet with all these points of connection, there seems to be little resemblance between hard-boiled fiction and Faulkner's work. There are at least three reasons. First, hard-boiled fiction mainly tends to be a big-city genre in setting and attitude, while Faulkner's work is simply too rural, too regional to be an influence in this area. The only part of Faulkner's work that has, to my way of thinking, anything resembling a hard-boiled urban atmosphere is the segment of *Sanctuary* in which Popeye and Temple are in Memphis and Popeye murders Red at the roadhouse. But while this may have something of the atmosphere, it's not written in a hard-boiled narrative style; for, to cite the second reason, hard-boiled fiction bears stylistically a certain family resemblance to the type of tabloid reporting of the twenties and thirties that provided the real-life equivalent of the crime and murder stories the genre thrived on—terse, straightforward prose, colloquial American speech, slang, all characterized hard-boiled fiction, and nothing could be further from Faulkner's type of narrative, by turns Baroque, lyrical, stream-of-consciousness, run-on. Finally, and most importantly, the kind of detective story Faulkner wrote wasn't the hard-boiled variety but the older, analytic type. He has an ongoing detective (the county attorney Gavin Stevens) who has an official capacity as prosecutor but is strictly an amateur at detective work. Stevens has a sidekick (his nephew Chick Mallison) who sometimes does legwork for his uncle but more often is responsible for getting him involved in a case and who is always there to let Gavin think out loud about the investigation. And since the plots of all the Gavin Stevens detective stories are of the old logic-and-deduction variety (and handled for the most part rather perfunctorily), there would have been little in Faulkner's detective fiction Hammett or Chandler could have felt an affinity for.

Of course, in comparing hard-boiled writing to American high-art fiction of the 1920s, '30s, and '40s, we inevitably confront the fact that the former falls into the category of "popular fiction." Chandler said in "The Simple Art of Murder" that he doubted "Hammett had any deliberate artistic aims whatever; he was trying to make a living by writing something he had first hand information about" (*TAMS*, 234). This opposition between "artistic aims" and selling enough books to make a living suggests the usual assumption about popular fiction: that to have a widespread readership an author can't cast his work at too high a level. And yet if writers like Faulkner, Fitzgerald, and Hemingway clearly wanted to make a living from their books, it seems equally clear that the hard-boiled fiction writers we've discussed, all of them serious professional craftsman, wanted to write novels as skillfully and powerfully made as their talents and the specialized constraints of these stories permitted. When Fitzgerald published *The Great Gatsby*, a novel of manners whose protagonist was an underworld figure, and when Hammett soon after began moving the detective story toward a character-driven novel of manners with a crime interest, they shared a common thematic ground: the conflict between work and love in the lives of American men, played out as a struggle to become or stay boss in both spheres.

I take second place to no one in my admiration for *Gatsby* (though I think *Tender Is the Night* a greater, more heartbreaking novel and Dick Diver a more tragic figure), and yet I think *The Maltese Falcon* in its own way is as perfect a book as *Gatsby*. It doesn't have *Gatsby*'s elegiac lyricism, as a hopelessly idealized love overwhelms the protagonist's meteoric but sinister career, but it has an edge sharp as a knife when Spade's professionalism cuts loose a once-in-a-lifetime woman with the words, "If they hang you I'll always remember. . . . If I send you over I'll be sorry as hell—I'll have some rotten nights—but that'll pass" (223, 227). And though Chandler's *The Big Sleep* or Cain's *Double Indemnity*, Burnett's *High Sierra* or Woolrich's *Night Has a Thousand Eyes* never quite rose to *The Maltese Falcon*'s level of excellence, still they are, each in a different way, prime examples of how good hard-boiled fiction can be.

VIII

The hard-boiled writing we've discussed forms one part (perhaps the earliest) of a larger category of popular fiction (doctor novels and lawyer novels are the other segments that come immediately to mind) whose readership has remained constant and widespread throughout the last two-thirds of the twentieth century, a type of fiction in which the reader's interest is engaged first of all by being given inside information about a specialized field of work (and usually a field with some analytic or deductive component, as, for example, in either a doctor's diagnosis or a lawyer's strategy in arraying the facts of a case, a component that gives "detective" work pride of place among these professions) and then, secondarily, by the conflict that develops in the life of the protagonist between his dedication to this work and its code, on the one hand, and his personal relationships, on the other. But one should also note that while there are doctor novels aplenty, there are generally no dentist novels; lawyer novels but no certified-public-accountant novels; detective novels but no process-server novels, for a type of fiction whose dramatic interest is based on the conflicting attractions of one's work and one's personal life must necessarily focus on types of work that are interesting, rewarding, or demanding enough to make the competition between the two believable and thus to make it understandable that, for example, Marlowe could choose being a detective and his own boss over marrying an attractive heiress with whom he might be in love.

This type of story tends to belong more to the realm of popular fiction than high art, tends not to deal with the big questions (life's value and meaning, the existence of a moral order in the universe, the over-reachings of the Faustian self) in the biggest way but with middling questions of the workaday world: the emotional trade-off between job and family or the place that work has in establishing a sense of self, creating gender definitions, or the dynamics of relationships—finite questions with answers. For in these detective or doctor or lawyer novels there are generically expected conclusions—a solution to a mystery, or a diagnosis and cure, or a verdict—which is to say, finite answers; while the big questions of life are often not finite or decidable and the type of fiction that raises them often considers raising them an end in itself.

A further aspect to consider in comparing high-art and popular fiction as regards the hard-boiled writers we've discussed is the different mechanisms by which the visibility of each is maintained. In the case of high-art fiction the mechanism is canon-formation and the academy, that is, the designation of certain works as classics to be read and taught in high school and college as the necessary cultural luggage of an educated person; while in the case of hard-boiled fiction a different mechanism has been instrumental in keeping these works read more than three generations after their first appearance. And that, of course, is that each of the books we've focused on was turned into a first-rate Hollywood film in the 1940s, constituting a group of movies that helped set the standard for the film noir genre, whose first (black-and-white) cycle continued for almost twenty years, to the end of the 1950s. And even when the second (color) cycle of film noir began in the 1970s, the hard-boiled novels of the thirties and forties were still well represented. There were remakes of both *Farewell, My Lovely!* (1975, directed by Dick Richards) and *The Big Sleep* (1978, directed by Michael Winner), as well as films such as Lawrence Kasdan's *Body Heat* (1981), in effect an adaptation of Cain's *Double Indemnity,* and the Coen brothers' *Miller's Crossing* (1990), a reworking of Hammett's *The Glass Key.* The fact that film versions from both cycles are regularly replayed on cable movie channels, as well as being available on cassette and DVD, has been the major means of continually reintroducing the work of these hard-boiled writers to new generations of readers.

The sort of mass-media visibility current authors seek through flogging a new book on television talk-shows is to a degree what the hard-boiled fiction writers, whose novels were turned into distinguished noir films, have enjoyed for the past sixty years. One need only scan the most widespread form of popular fictional narrative in America—the hour-long drama series on network television—to see how much the same theme that runs through these hard-boiled novels still dominates. Whether they're cop/detective shows (e.g., *NYPD Blue*), doctor shows (e.g., *ER*), or lawyer shows (e.g., *The Practice*), or some combination of these (cop/lawyer: *Law and Order;* doctor/detective: *CSI, Crossing Jordan;* cop/doctor: *Third Watch*), the formula remains the same: The viewer is given an insider's take on an interesting line of work, its specialized "business" and mores, its peculiar demands, and then shown how different characters balance the stresses of this work against their private lives as they try to retain some measure of control in both spheres. The virtual omnipresence of this theme in hour-long television drama series means that when younger viewers see a film like *The Maltese Falcon* they're already attuned to the kind of struggle Spade goes through in staying true to his code and turning over his love, Brigid, to the cops.

That film noir adaptations have been the main mechanism for introducing the hard-boiled genre to new generations of readers doesn't mean that hard-boiled writers haven't on their own undergone some degree of literary canonization in recent years. Where Howard Haycraft in 1941 pointed with pride to the fact that *The Maltese Falcon* was the only detective novel to that date to be included in the Modern Library series, we might note that the current Library of America series (which bills itself variously as "the only definitive collection of America's greatest writers" or as being "dedicated to preserving America's best and most significant writing") includes two volumes of Hammett's novels and stories, two of Chandler's, and two volumes devoted to hard-boiled fiction (*Crime Novels: American Noir of the 1930s and 40s* and *Crime Novels: American Noir of the 1950s*). Cain's *The Postman Always Rings Twice* and Cornell Woolrich's *I Married a Dead Man* appear in the first of these two volumes, along with works by Horace McCoy, Edward Anderson, and Kenneth Fearing, while novels by Jim Thompson, Patricia Highsmith, and Chester Himes are included in the second. (One might note in passing that these works by Cain, Anderson, Fearing, Thompson, Highsmith, Woolrich, and McCoy all had noir film adaptations, and that except in the case of the last two authors, each of the novels included in the Library of America volumes has been filmed twice, so that one gets a clear sense of how much back-pressure the excellence and popularity of these book's film adaptations exercised on the selection process for the two volumes, a sense confirmed by the presence of the phrase *American Noir* in their subtitles). However, this degree of literary canonization hasn't yet translated, as far as I can tell, into a corresponding presence of hard-boiled fiction titles on required or recommended reading lists in colleges or high schools or by these works being regularly taught in college English departments, so the odds today are still that any young reader's first acquaintance with hard-boiled fiction will come as a result of having seen one or several of the movies made in the 1940s from these books.

The mechanism of having had a novel turned into a first-rate film should theoretically benefit, in terms of that novel's greater visibility for future readers, a work of high-art fiction as much as it does a work of popular fiction. The only difficulty is that modern American high-art novels seldom get translated into first-rate films. Indeed, if one considers just the high-art novelists that we've invoked here for comparison purposes, then the films made from their fiction are almost uniformly disappointing. The only first-rate movies from their works are Sam Wood's 1943 version of Hemingway's *For Whom the Bell*

Tolls, scripted by Dudley Nichols; Clarence Brown's 1949 film of Faulkner's *Intruder in the Dust,* adapted by Ben Maddow; and Elia Kazan's 1976 version of Fitzgerald's *The Last Tycoon,* from a screenplay by Harold Pinter. In contrast, both sound versions of *The Great Gatsby* are a mess, though the 1949 black-and-white film directed by Elliott Nugent with Alan Ladd as Gatsby is less of a mess than the 1974 color film directed by Jack Clayton with Robert Redford as Gatsby, while Henry King's 1962 film of *Tender Is the Night* gives the word *disaster* a new meaning, with its casting of the inert Jason Robards Jr. as the charming Dick Diver. The number of bombs made from Faulkner's works is even longer, from Douglas Sirk's 1957 *The Tarnished Angels* (based on Faulkner's *Pylon*), through Martin Ritt's 1958 *The Long Hot Summer* (based on *The Hamlet*) and his 1959 *The Sound and the Fury* (with Yul Brynner as Jason Compson) to Tony Richardson's *Sanctuary* (based on that novel and on *Requiem for a Nun*), the only relief in this sequence of Faulkner screen adaptations being Mark Rydell's 1969 pleasant but slight film of *The Reivers.*

The big winner in the turkey-film sweepstakes, however, is clearly Hemingway: Both Frank Borzage's 1932 version and Charles Vidor's 1958 version of *A Farewell to Arms* are failures, while John Sturges's 1958 *The Old Man and the Sea,* from a screenplay by Peter Viertel, manages to turn the old fisherman Santiago into more of a Disney character than he is in the book, even with Santiago being played by Spencer Tracy. Henry King's 1952 *The Snows of Kilimanjaro* is simply plodding, while his 1957 *The Sun Also Rises,* with a Peter Viertel script, stars Tyrone Power, Errol Flynn, and Ava Gardner in roles they might have been the right age for (though not the right personalities) twenty years earlier. Martin Ritt's 1962 *Ernest Hemingway's Adventures of a Young Man* (based on some of the Nick Adams stories), with a screenplay by A. E. Hotchner, is a waste of time, while Franklin Schaffner's 1977 version of *Islands in the Stream* makes a hodge-podge of a movie from a hodge-podge of a book. I haven't included in this list of botched Hemingway screen adaptations either Howard Hawks's 1944 *To Have and Have Not,* from a screenplay by Jules Furthman and William Faulkner, or Robert Siodmak's 1946 *The Killers,* scripted by Anthony Veiller, because both of these excellent films are essentially Hemingway films in name only. The former takes only its title, the main character's name and his job as a charter fishing boat captain, his alcoholic helper Eddie, and the client who tries to beat him out of his hire from the first thirty or so pages of Hemingway's novel, while the rest of the film is in effect another Warner Brothers attempt (like Michael Curtiz's 1944 *Passage to Marseilles*) to capitalize on the popularity of Curtiz's 1943 *Casablanca* by casting Bogart in a story about the conflict between Vichy and Free-French elements in a French colony (Martinique this time, rather than French Morocco), with Hoagy Carmichael as the piano playing entertainer in Harry Morgan's hotel rather than Dooley Wilson in Rick's café. Similarly, Veiller's script for Siodmak's *The Killers* uses Hemingway's short story only for the opening sequence, in which the two hit men wait for Ole Andresen in the diner, and then creates an entirely original work for the rest of the film.

In trying to account for the relative lack of success of films adapted from works by these high-art fiction writers, we could say that the novels were simply too long and complex to be successfully reduced to dramatizations running ninety minutes or two hours, or that the fiction involved a level of psychological interiority difficult to treat visually, or that the more time that had elapsed between the novel's appearance and the film adaptation, if it conferred classic status on the novel, made the film adaptor more reluctant to tamper with the book (and the audience's expectations) and thus made the job more difficult. Any or all of these are plausible explanations, but what really concerns us here is why hard-boiled popular fiction spawned so many first-rate film adaptations in comparison, a question we will try to answer in the next chapter by examining the way in which the hard-boiled novels we've discussed were turned into films.

SEVEN

Hard-Boiled Fiction and Film Noir

I

In examining the films made in the 1940s from the hard-boiled novels we've discussed—movies representing some of the best examples of film noir I intend to avoid for the most part the sorts of well-worked-over arguments the analysis of this subject typically generates: as, for example, whether film noir is a movie genre like the Western, the musical, or the gangster picture; or whether instead it's defined by a certain visual style, a style (rooted in German Expressionism and in the 1930s French films of Carné, Duvivier, Guitry, and others) that involved the use of chiaroscuro, deep focus, and visually unsettling camera angles and that was achieved through a combination of lighting, set design, faster film, and camera placement; or whether film noir is defined by a set of recurrent themes and motifs (e.g., "the pervasive atmosphere of corruption, crime, psychopathology and evil; the constant resort to gratuitous violence; the omnipresence of the returning veteran; the importance of the oneiric in structure and substance"),[1] or by a tone, attitude, or mood (described variously as skeptical, cynical, fatalistic, or existential) as regards life in America in the 1940s and '50s.

Each of these approaches to defining the essence of film noir has produced intelligent and informative results, yet each has its drawbacks. Thus, for example, one difficulty in considering film noir a movie genre is, as R. Barton Palmer has argued, that "because *noir* film remained, during its brief but spectacular history, an invisible category of Hollywood production," it can't be "identified through the industrial discourse relating to its production, promotion, and consumption" as can the Western.[2] Film noir is "essentially a scholarly discovery" (Palmer, 141), a category created by critical retrospection. Virtually none of the studio executives, directors, writers, or actors who made these movies in the 1940s and '50s would have even heard of the term *film noir;* rather, they would simply have described this type of picture as either a detective story, murder mystery, thriller, or crime drama. Consequently, there could have been no self-conscious *institutional* awareness that motivated the making of these films as a specific genre. On the other hand, when it comes to considering visual style or mood or tone as the defining aspect of film noir, the difficulty arises that any one of these can be transgeneric, which is to say that no one of these by itself will always define a film as noir. Thus, for example, while John Huston's 1941 *The Maltese Falcon* is one of the earliest and best examples of the genre, Orson Welles's 1941 *Citizen Kane,* to my way of thinking, clearly is not, because it lacks a central crime element, not a noir film in spite of its chiaroscuro lighting, deep focus, disturbing camera angles, and generally skeptical tone—even though its look influenced the visual style of noir films at RKO and even though Welles went on to direct or appear in notable examples of the genre, such as *The Stranger, The Third Man,* and *Touch of Evil.*

Indeed, most contemporary studies of film noir as a genre or of individual noir films usually employ some combination of the approaches or terminology mentioned above (genre, visual style, recurring story motifs, recurring tone or mood). And even if, as one critic has remarked, there tends to be a certain "critical vagueness as to specifics" in these studies, still the noir "label has helped in the revaluation of a large number of neglected films,"[3] helped by focusing attention on these examples of an unself-conscious genre that thrived for some twenty years in its black-and-white cycle and that comprised some three hundred movies.

II

Though there may be disagreement about certain aspects of film noir, there seems to be one point on which no one disagrees—that the widespread popularity of hard-boiled fiction in the 1930s and '40s had prepared an audience for this film genre, an audience that was accustomed to crime narratives with a skeptical, cynical, or fatalistic tone, and further that many of the earliest and best noir films were adaptations of hard-boiled novels. As Paul Schrader notes, "When the movies of the forties turned to the American 'tough' moral understrata, the hard-boiled school was waiting with preset conventions of heroes, minor characters, plots, dialogue, and themes. Like the German expatriates, the hard-boiled writers had a style made to order for film noir; and, in turn, they influenced noir screenwriting as much as the Germans influenced noir cinematography."[4] And Robert G. Porfirio contends that "the hard-boiled school of fiction" was "a source . . . without which quite possibly there would have been no *film noir*."[5] Indeed, as several scholars have noted, the French film critics who invented the genre's very name coined it by analogy with the well-known book-publishing venture the Série Noire (edited by Marcel Duhamel for Gallimard), which brought out French translations of contempo rary crime fiction, including works by the principal hard-boiled writers.

In this chapter I focus on what happened to the narratives of the novels previously discussed when they were adapted for the screen (what deletions or additions were made and to what effect) and, conversely, on the influence these adaptations had on the shaping of the noir genre. The first thing to recall is that each of the five novelists we've dealt with worked at one time or another writing screenplays in Hollywood, worked there for varying durations and with differing degrees of success, ranging from Woolrich (who was in Hollywood for three years but never earned a screenwriting credit) to W. R. Burnett, whose screenwriting career lasted for more than thirty-five years and whose string of hit movies garnered him two Academy Award nominations along the way, overshadowing to some degree his success as a fiction writer. The Hollywood careers of Hammett, Chandler, and Cain fall somewhere in between these extremes, with Chandler being the most successful of this trio. All five of these writers were used to having their fiction adapted for the screen and, with the exception of Woolrich, were also used to adapting their own or others' fiction for film.

The two movies that form the best starting point for our discussion, Raoul

Walsh's *High Sierra* and John Huston's *The Maltese Falcon,* opened in January and October 1941, respectively, and are linked by the presence on both projects of Huston, who collaborated with W. R. Burnett on the screenplay for the former and wrote the screenplay and directed the latter. *High Sierra* was not the first time Burnett and Huston had worked together on a script (Burnett, Huston, and Tom Reed did the screenplay for Universal's 1932 *Law and Order,* starring Huston's father Walter, from Burnett's novel *Saint Johnson,* though Burnett's work was uncredited), nor would it be the last (they would collaborate on the script for Huston's 1950 film *The Asphalt Jungle,* from Burnett's novel, with Burnett's screen work again uncredited). The importance of *High Sierra* and *The Maltese Falcon* for our purposes is not simply that they are both excellent films adapted from hard-boiled novels but also that there's probably only one American film generally considered noir that was released earlier than these two—Boris Ingster's 1940 *Stranger on the Third Floor,* an RKO B-picture (screenplay by Frank Parsons) whose expressionist sets and lighting, nightmare sequences, and "condemned-wrong-man" plot point to things to come at RKO. Neither *High Sierra* nor *The Maltese Falcon* has, in terms of set design, lighting, or camera work, a particularly noir look. They look for the most part like what they are—standard, studio-made Warner Bros. movies. Instead, the noir quality of these films is more a function of mood and motif—the weary toughness, rebellious individualism, and ultimate fatalism of Roy Earle in *High Sierra,* and the professional scepticism, not to say cynicism, of Sam Spade confronted with an attractive, dangerous woman as a client in *The Maltese Falcon.*

Besides its level of quality and the fact that it launched Humphrey Bogart's career as a leading man, *High Sierra* is significant in illustrating the way the critically retrospective genre of film noir evolved out of two earlier, industry-recognized genres: the gangster film and, to a lesser extent, the Western. Clearly, the two are related, both having to do with violence, one with nineteenth-century American outlawry (or other threats to domestic peace), and the other with twentieth-century lawbreaking. W. R. Burnett had written fiction and worked on screenplays in both genres before he and Huston did the script for *High Sierra.* There was his uncredited work on Edward L. Cahn's 1932 Western *Law and Order* for Universal, as well as William Wyler's 1940 *The Westerner* for United Artists, and his collaboration on the screenplay for Howard Hawks's 1932 gangster film *Scarface: Shame of a Nation* for United Artists.[6] Of course, the success of Mervyn Leroy's 1930 film of Burnett's novel *Little*

Caesar from Warner Bros., the film that made Edward G. Robinson a star, launched the first cycle of gangster talking-films in the early thirties, a cycle that included, to name only a few, William Wellman's 1931 *The Public Enemy* (Warner Bros.), Hawks's *Scarface,* and Rouben Mamoulian's 1931 *City Streets* (Paramount), from an original story line by Dashiell Hammett.

Films of this early cycle were what Andrew Bergman has called "success tragedies,"[7] stories of the meteoric rise and fall of an underworld figure. Arguing that "Americans were attracted to outlaws during the Depression's most wrenching years" because their stories "reinforced some of the country's most cherished myths about individual success," Bergman contends that "only gangsters could make upward mobility believable" during the 1930s (Bergman, 6–7). The protagonists of these films were dark versions of Horatio Alger heroes, with the energetic over-reaching that caused their rise also precipitating their sudden downfalls. Indeed, one could trace a genealogy of the underworld "success tragedy" running from Fitzgerald's *The Great Gatsby* to Burnett's novel *Little Caesar* to the screen version of this novel and then to Burnett's screenplay for *Scarface* and most of the other early thirties gangster films.

By the time Burnett and Huston collaborated at Warner Bros. on *High Sierra,* which began shooting in July 1940, the studio had established a virtual hegemony in the gangster genre by having under contract the actors most frequently associated with these roles—Edward G. Robinson, Paul Muni, James Cagney, George Raft, and Humphrey Bogart. Bogart, who played Roy Earle in *High Sierra,* was not the first actor tapped for the role. The studio had offered it to Muni, who turned it down, then to George Raft, who also declined. Raft had refused the role because he thought it would hurt his career to die in a film, so the part was eventually offered to Bogart who, during the four years he'd been under contract to Warner Bros., had made something of a specialty of dying on screen.

Recall that Bogart, who had been a Broadway actor, first came to Hollywood in the early 1930s, made a few films that went nowhere, and then returned to Broadway, where he landed the role of the Dillinger-type outlaw Duke Mantee in Robert Sherwood's 1935 play *The Petrified Forest.* The play was a hit, and when it was bought by Warner Bros. they signed the play's star, Leslie Howard, to repeat his role in the film. The studio cast Edward G. Robinson as Mantee, but Howard, who'd become good friends with Bogart during the play's run, refused to appear in the film unless Bogart also reprised his role. Bogart got the part, the movie was a success, and Warner Bros. put Bogart under contract. In the twentieth-eight Warner movies he appeared in between *The Petrified Forest* (1936) and *High Sierra* (1941), Bogart occasionally played leads in B-films but more usually second leads in A-films (often as the heavy), to Robinson four times, Cagney three times, and Raft twice, and he died, usually on screen and violently, in twelve of those twenty-eight films. Consequently, Bogart would have had no misgivings about how his character's being shot down by police at the end of *High Sierra* would affect his career. Though Bogart was the male lead and the film's success moved him up a notch in the studio's pecking order, he didn't get top billing in *High Sierra;* that went to Ida Lupino, who played Marie Garson.

Though *High Sierra* presents itself essentially as a gangster film, its mainly outdoor setting in the mountains and high desert of Southern California (the location shooting for the film was done in the Big Bear Lake and Lake Arrowhead regions) and its climactic car chase and cornering of Roy on a mountain side give the movie the feel of a Western as well, a feeling enhanced by the film's elegiac evocation of Earle as the last of the old-time outlaws, a bank robber who, during his days with Dillinger, had been protected by country folk whose farms had been foreclosed by banks, protected in much the same way that Jesse James was shielded by farmers whose lands had been taken by the railroads. (Recall that two years before the appearance of *High Sierra* Henry King's *Jesse James,* a big-budget color film hit from Twentieth-Century Fox starring Tyrone Power and Henry Fonda as Jesse and Frank, had presented a highly sympathetic portrait of the outlaw brothers doing battle with the railroads. Further, the Old-West-outlaw quality of the Roy Earle character was made explicit in 1949, when Warner Bros. remade the film [again directed by Raoul Walsh] as a Western called *Colorado Territory,* starring Joel McCrea in the Bogart role and Virginia Mayo in the Lupino role.)

One of the big differences between *High Sierra* and the gangster films of the early thirties such as *Little Caesar, Public Enemy,* and *Scarface* is that the main characters in those movies, unlike Roy Earle, had all grown up in the city. Indeed, the danger of big-city life leading boys into crime was the subject of several late thirties films, such as William Wyler's *Dead End* (1937) and Michael Curtiz's *Angels with Dirty Faces* (1938), both Warner movies and both with Bogart in a supporting role as an adult gangster who gets killed. But Roy's origins are in a more innocent rural world, and the film's nostalgic, not to say elegiac, tone regarding the passing of an era in Roy's life and, by extension, the passing of an older, simpler time in American life made it mesh easily with one of the Western's characteristic scenarios—the necessary passing away of the Old West as the frontier became domesticated.

Bosley Crowther, in his review of the film in the *New York Times,* sensed a certain self-reflexive quality in its theme, saw it as an elegy not just to the passing of an era in the history of American crime but also to the passing of an era in American film—the waning of the gangster film genre itself: "We wouldn't know for certain whether the twilight of the American gangster is here. But Warner Brothers, who should know if anybody does, have apparently taken it for granted and, in a solemn Wagnerian mood, are giving that titanic figure a send-off befitting a first-string god in the film called *High Sierra.*"[8] The importance of *High Sierra* in the development of film noir stems in part from its being a transitional work, a film that, though growing out of the thirties gangster genre, is a more or less self-conscious farewell to that genre, a farewell achieved through the film's creation of a new type of central character. In March 1940 John Huston wrote the movie's producer, Hal Wallis, to make a pitch for the film's maintaining the spirit of Burnett's novel, that "strange sense of inevitability that comes with our deepening understanding of his characters," a pitch that the book not be turned into a standard Warner's gangster film but rather be "done with real seriousness—the seriousness that Burnett deserves."[9]

A few days earlier the movie's associate producer, Mark Hellinger, had also written to Wallis praising the possibilities inherent in the book's "superb romance between the man and the crippled girl" as well as "the basic character of a man who was born a farmer . . . and wound up as the last of the Dillinger mob . . . of a tough girl who is willing to die for the unattainable love of the strangest of men. . . . All I ask, Hal, is that you find me someone who has just half the enthusiasm I hold for this grand yarn." That someone was John Huston, and, as Bogart's biographers A. M. Sperber and Eric Lax note, Huston proposed "a revolutionary idea to the studio: Rather than write the conventional screenplay pre-narrative treatment, which inevitably led to heavy rewrites that in turn made the original all but unrecognizable, why not bypass the treatment and, for once, base the screenplay on *the book?*" (Sperber, 120). Wallis agreed, and the book's author was signed to co-write the script with Huston under Hellinger's supervision. As a result, the film was remarkably faithful to the novel, retaining what Huston had called the book's "strange sense of inevitability" born of "our deepening understanding" of Burnett's characters, and though not everything in the novel would be present in the film, virtually everything in the film is taken from the novel.

If *High Sierra* marked the beginning of the end for the gangster genre so popular in the 1930s and the start of what would become film noir, then it is not without significance that this transition in genres directly paralleled the transition in Humphrey Bogart's career at Warner's from playing supporting roles in gangster pictures to playing male leads in some of the most important noir films. Indeed, of the five movies made from the hard-boiled novels we've discussed, Bogart starred in three, and I would argue that the development of Bogart's screen persona simultaneously influenced and was influenced by the development of film noir in a crucial way. The screen persona of any movie star is constituted both from a composite of his or her most successful film roles (those roles most appealing to the audience and those the actor seems to have inhabited most fully) and from elements in the actor's own physical, psychological, and emotional personality.

Of course it's the meshing of aspects of the fictive character with qualities in the actor's self that creates the audience's sense of a role fully inhabited, and when Bogart played the lead in *High Sierra* the creation of the ongoing Bogart star persona drew upon, for the characterization of Roy Earle, elements from two of his best previous roles—the hunted, Dillinger-style outlaw Duke Mantee in *The Petrified Forest* and the doomed gangster Baby Face Martin in *Dead End*. The latter in particular added a deeper resonance to Bogart's portrayal in *High Sierra*, for just as Earle, after his release from prison, visits what had once been his family's farm in Indiana and then later, on his drive west, becomes involved with Ma and Pa Goodhue (Elizabeth Risdon and Henry Travers) and their granddaughter (Joan Leslie) because they remind him of his own parents and of his childhood sweetheart, so Baby Face Martin at the start of *Dead End* made his own sentimental journey back to his old neighborhood on Manhattan's East Side to see his mother (Marjorie Main) and his childhood girl friend, Francey (Claire Trevor). Each character's exercise in nostalgia ends disastrously. In *High Sierra* the farmer who owns the old Earle place becomes frightened and unfriendly when he realizes his visitor is the notorious bank robber, and subsequently Roy's dreams of recovering his past are shattered by Velma's turning out not to be the innocent farm girl he thought; while in *Dead End* Martin's mother greets him with a slap across the face and calls him a murderer, and he finds that his old girl friend has ended up as a streetwalker.

Roy Earle's resemblance to two of Bogart's more memorable previous roles as Mantee and Martin would have given the film's audience something like a ready-made sense of the character's personal history and psychology, a sense that they already knew at the start the type of person Earle was because they knew the type of role Bogart played best. And given this preexisting sense of the character, the casting of Bogart allowed for a deepening of his portrayal of Earle, allowed the actor to play to and against the audience's expectations about a "Bogart" role. As we said, given Bogart's earlier Warner films, particularly those in which he played the heavy to Cagney, Robinson, or Raft, audiences expected Bogart to die on screen, and usually to die like a rat pleading for his life. Of course, he does die at the end of *High Sierra*, but Walsh's spectacular staging of the car chase through the Sierras and Earle's last stand, cornered by the police on a mountainside, turns Earle's death into a kind of apotheosis of the doomed antihero continuing to resist to the end. (Walsh would employ this ending—the criminal trapped and killed in a high place—at least twice more in films he directed: in *White Heat* [1949], in which the psychotic killer Cody Jarrett [James Cagney], chased to the top of a propane storage tank by the police, enacts his determination not to be captured by firing his pistol into the tank and dying in a fiery explosion after uttering the line, "Made it, Ma, top of the world!" and again in the 1949 *Colorado Territory*, in which the aging outlaw takes refuge from a pursuing posse by climbing up to an ancient Indian cliff dwelling and is picked off by a marksman with a telescopic rifle.)

When I try to put into an image the difference between forties American film noir and the thirties noir films made in France by directors like Carné, Duvivier, and Guitry, I always compare the ending of *High Sierra* (with Bogart brandishing a machine gun and taunting the cops, "Come and get me, buddy") to the ending of Carné's *Le Jour se lève* (1939), when Jean Gabin, an accused murderer trapped in an apartment and standing off the police, reprises in flashback the events leading to his present situation. The film's end occurs as Gabin realizes the full hopelessness of his predicament, and as the camera pulls back out the apartment window, the sound of a single gunshot is heard. The Sierras framed against the sky versus the claustrophobic apartment, the last outlaw resisting to the end versus the trapped killer taking his own life, the camera watching as Earle is shot and rolls down the mountain versus the camera withdrawing its gaze as if ashamed to watch Gabin's final act—those oppositions not only suggest the difference in mood and attitude

between American and French noir films but also point to what would become some of the key ingredients in the Bogart persona as it began to take
shape in *High Sierra.*

If, as I've said, *High Sierra* is a crucial transitional work both between film
genres and within Bogart's career, this is largely because the character of Roy
Earle, as written for the screen by Huston and Burnett and embodied by Bogart, began the work of humanizing the gangster figure in a new way, ultimately allowing the more forceful and exciting aspects of the gangster to be
transferred to the noir antihero, but without making it obligatory that he be
punished for those traits by having to die on screen. The sympathetic outlaw
Roy Earle dies so that the often unsympathetic private eye Sam Spade (Bogart's next role) may live. Roy's nostalgia for the world of his rural origins and
his consequent attachment to the Goodhues and his paying for the crippled
Velma's operation, his psychological vulnerability after years spent in prison,
his awareness of his aging and of his best days being behind him as he leads
a gang of young punks, the crushing sense of loneliness that attracts to him
strays as lost and alone as he is—all these qualities create the sense of someone who is first a human being and only secondarily a criminal. Such is the
audience's feeling for Roy by the end of the film that his death at the hands
of the police (a punishment demanded by the Hollywood Production Code),
while it might give the appearance of justice, has an emotional effect more of
cosmic injustice, of a man trapped and killed by blind forces.

One of the more moving exchanges between Roy and Marie in the film
occurs when Roy wants to send Marie back to Los Angeles before he, Red (Arthur Kennedy), and Babe (Alan Curtis) rob the Tropico Springs Hotel. Saying
she has no one in L.A. to return to, Marie reminds Roy what he'd said earlier
"about prison and the way you kept from going crazy by thinking all the time
about a crash-out" and adds, "I been trying to crash out ever since I can remember." Her previous crash-out of the dance-hall came when she took up
with Babe Kozak because she "thought Babe was a right guy": "I guess I was
never really hooked up with any guys that wasn't wrong so I had nothing to go
by . . . till I met you." This sense—that whether or not one has spent time in jail
one's life can itself be a kind of prison—is given voice again at the film's end
when Marie, kneeling by Roy's body, asks the newspaperman Vince Healy (Jerome Cowan), "Mister, what does it mean when a man crashes out?" Healy replies, "Crashes out? That's a funny question for you to ask now, sister. It means
he's free." It's a funny question not only because Roy is dead and Marie is likely

headed for jail but because Marie had certainly known in that earlier exchange with Roy what "crashing out" meant. Clearly, having Marie ask Healy here what the phrase means is the screenwriters' way of evoking Roy's death as the ultimate release from the prison of his life, a prison that Marie is still in. So the film fades out with a close-up of Marie cradling the little dog Pard in her arms and repeating the word *free.*

If the sense of existence as a prison is embedded in Roy Earle's character, so is his determination to remain his own man, to resist that imprisonment to the end. The Bogart persona that starts to evolve in *High Sierra* is very much a rebel bent on going his own way—smart, tough, skeptical if not cynical, a man who knows his work and how to get things done even if that means stepping over the line, a man with few illusions but with his own code who knows that finally the game of life can't be won but still must be played well, and withal a man (and here's where something in Bogart's own emotional and physical make-up added a special element to the persona) who responds to life with a certain lonely determination deeply tinged with sadness. Virtually everyone who knew Bogart at all well remarked on this last quality. Edward G. Robinson, who had acted with him in so many films and who, over the course of their careers at Warner Bros. had seen their positions as leading and supporting actors reversed, summed it up this way: "For all his outward toughness, insolence, braggadocio, and contempt (and those were always part of the characters he played, though they were not entirely within Bogie), there came through a kind of sadness, loneliness, and heartbreak (all of which were very much a part of Bogie the man). I always felt sorry for him—sorry that he imposed upon himself the facade of the character with which he had become identified."[10]

Similarly, Mary Astor, who co-starred with Bogart in two Huston films, noticed, according to his biographers, "an element of sadness about Bogart that was all too visible beneath the blustery surface. 'Bogey looked at the world, at his place in it, at movies, at life in general,' she wrote in an unedited draft of an essay, 'and there was something about it that made him sick, contemptuous, bitter. And it showed. He related to people as though they had no clothes on, and no skin for that matter'" (Sperber, 156–57). The writer-director Richard Brooks recalled an occasion in the early 1950s when he'd asked Bogart why he was so unhappy, and when Bogart denied this, Brooks replied,

"You sure *seem* unhappy. Why do you knock yourself? You're always putting yourself down. You do it with humor, but nevertheless you do it."

Bogart's answer came quickly. "Well, I expected a lot more from me. And I'm never going to get it." (466)

And Julie Gibson, an actress and publicist, who'd known Bogart in Rome when he was working on John Huston's *Beat the Devil* (1954), remembered him as "one of the most melancholy people she ever met . . . 'a very sad man'" (477).

Whatever its source, that sadness became part of the Bogart persona, a melancholy counterpoint to the persona's toughness and rebellious insolence. It seemed the price the noir hero paid for the loneliness of going his own way, a loneliness that in hard-boiled detective fiction usually resulted from the detective's choosing his work over his love. Indeed, in each of the three films that mainly established the Bogart persona—*High Sierra, The Maltese Falcon,* and *Casablanca*—Bogart's character sends the woman he loves away at the end. In *High Sierra,* after Roy's picture appears in the newspapers as one of the hotel robbers, he puts Marie and Pard on a bus to San Bernadino to get them out of harm's way while he drives into Los Angeles to collect his money from the fence. In the book Roy is trapped by police on the way to L.A. and killed; he never sees Marie again and the reader never learns what becomes of her. But in the film Huston and Burnett have Marie, as her bus passes through a small town, overhear a news broadcast on a loudspeaker outside a radio store saying that Roy has been cornered by the police. She gets off the bus and returns to find him. But when Marie, still carrying Pard in a wicker hamper, shows up that evening at the police cordon surrounding the mountain, the newspaperman Vince Healy recognizes her and turns her in. At dawn the police call to Roy, giving him a last chance to surrender. When Roy shouts back, Pard hears his voice and begins running up the mountainside barking. Realizing that if Pard is there Marie must be too, Roy stands up and shouts, "Marie," and the sharpshooter on the cliff fells him with a single shot.

Whereas Roy had sent Marie away to keep her from going to prison, Sam Spade in *The Maltese Falcon* sends Brigid (Mary Astor), the woman he's made love to and may even be in love with, to prison or worse for Archer's murder, and in *Casablanca* Rick Blaine sends Ilsa Lund (Ingrid Bergman) away on the Lisbon plane with her husband, Victor Lazlo (Paul Henreid), as Rick goes off to join the Free French. Earlier in the film Captain Louis Renault (Claude Rains), seeing Rick send his former girlfriend Yvonne home by herself, had remarked, "How extravagant you are, throwing away women like that! Someday they may be scarce." Clearly, the three roles that made Bogart a star and that, by the time *Casablanca* won the best picture Oscar for 1943, made him the king of the Warner's lot, roles in which Bogart "threw women away," added to the Bogart persona the sense not only that his tough exterior often masked a sentimental or idealistic core but also that he possessed an interior toughness able to sacrifice personal desires to a professional code or political ideal. These roles created precisely the sort of persona suited to the personal/professional conflict that drove the hard-boiled fiction so many noir films were based on.

III

Earlier I suggested that the character of Roy Earle as written by Huston and Burnett and acted by Bogart began the work of humanizing the gangster figure to create the noir antihero. The need for this new type of hero, a good bad guy who fights on our side, reflected Hollywood's sense that the epithet *gangster* had, by the late 1930s, acquired an even more sinister referent in the realm of world politics. Following Nazi Germany's annexation of Austria in 1938, the Roosevelt administration began characterizing the dictatorial regimes in Germany, Italy, and Japan as "international gangsters"—rhetoric that became even more intense once the war in Europe began. For example, Harold Ickes, Roosevelt's Secretary of the Interior, in an "I am an American" day speech in New York's Central Park in May 1941, spoke of the millions of "liberty-loving people" in the lands the Germans had overrun as having "the will to destroy the Nazi gangsters." And FDR himself, in his fireside chat of December 9, 1941, called the Japanese attack on Pearl Harbor "the climax of a decade of international immorality," adding that "powerful and resourceful gangsters have banded together to make war upon the whole human race." Responding to this description by FDR, Hitler in his speech of December 11 to the Reichstag declaring war on the United States said: "I will pass over the insulting attacks made by this so-called President against me. That he calls me a gangster is uninteresting. After all, this expression was not coined in Europe but in America, no doubt because such gangsters are lacking here." (Hollywood's most explicit characterization of Hitler in this way was John Farrow's 1944 *The Hitler Gang*, in which the rise of the dictator and his cronies was depicted as a band of ruthless political mobsters seizing control not of a city [as Capone had of Cicero, Illinois] but of an entire nation.)

If one Hollywood response to this image of the Nazis was to create a figure tough and ruthless as a gangster, who in defending freedom could fight dirty

against dirty fighters, then Warner Bros., the studio that had virtually created the thirties screen image of the American underworld and whose head,
Jack Warner, was a friend and supporter of FDR, seemed determined to show
Roosevelt's "international gangsters" what they were up against in tangling
with the real American article. Though there is no explicit reference to the international situation in Huston and Burnett's screenplay for *High Sierra*, there
certainly is in Burnett's novel. At one point after the robbery, while Roy and
Marie are waiting around for Roy's cut from the fence, they go out to a "little
dine-and-dance joint." Roy, sitting in a booth reading the newspaper, suddenly
slaps his hand on the table: "Them Japs!" he said. "They're going to ask for it
till they get it. Just like the Germans. Guys that go around with chips on their
shoulders always get 'em knocked off. . . . That's the way the Kaiser done and
look what happened to him. England holds off till she can't get out of fighting
no longer; then she really goes to town. I've known guys like that. And you
better look out for 'em. They're the worst kind." Marie, an isolationist, replies,
"You and your Japs. What do you think I care about Japs and Germans and
all that hooey! I care about you and me and having some fun; that's all I care
about."[11]

Given the subtext of world events to the evolution of Bogart's noir antihero
from the gangster roles he'd previously played, it's significant that in his next
film, Huston's *The Maltese Falcon,* two of the principal villains, Kasper (Casper
in the novel) Gutman and Joel Cairo, are both played by foreign-born actors
(Sydney Greenstreet and Peter Lorre, respectively), neither of whom speaks
with an American accent; significant as well that Gutman's name is of Ger-
manic origin, that both he and Cairo have recently arrived in San Francisco
from the Orient, and that Peter Lorre's most memorable series of roles in Hollywood films prior to his appearance in *The Maltese Falcon* was as the Japanese
Mr. Moto. Keep in mind the dates of these two films' appearance in relation to
international affairs: Burnett wrote the novel *High Sierra* during 1939 (the year
the war in Europe began); in March 1940 *High Sierra* was published, France
fell in June of that year, the filming of *High Sierra* started in July, the battle of
Britain was raging in August, and in September a ten-year alliance between
Germany, Italy, and Japan was signed forming the Rome-Berlin-Tokyo Axis;
High Sierra premiered in January 1941, the filming of *The Maltese Falcon* began
in June, the film premiered in October, the Japanese attacked Pearl Harbor in
December, whereupon the United States entered the war.

Whatever subliminal associations American audiences might have made between the foreign villains Bogart battled in *The Maltese Falcon* and the "international gangsters" at large in the world, this link was made explicit in Bogart's next film, Vincent Sherman's *All Through the Night* (1942), a comedy-mystery in which Bogart plays a big-time New York gambler named Gloves Donahue, who, surrounded by assorted Damon Runyonesque characters acted by Frank McHugh, William Demarest, Jackie Gleason, and Phil Silvers, becomes involved in thwarting a Nazi sabotage ring planning to blow up a battleship in New York harbor. One of the Nazis is played by Peter Lorre and the ringleader by Conrad Veidt (whom Bogart will do battle with again in *Casablanca*, with Veidt playing Major Strasser). Though the character of Gloves Donahue is not, strictly speaking, a gangster, he *is* an underworld figure who gets wrongly accused of a murder Lorre has committed and must track down the real killer while being pursued by the police. This pattern of having a shady character with the street smarts, toughness, and no-holds-barred attitude of the underworld take on Axis gangs of saboteurs is varied slightly in another 1942 Bogart movie, John Huston's *Across the Pacific*. Bogart plays Rick Leland, an army intelligence agent who masquerades as a court-martialed and embittered ex-army officer willing to sell out the secrets of the U.S. defenses of the Panama Canal to the highest bidder. He books passage on a Japanese ship headed for Central America in order to infiltrate a sabotage ring planning to bomb the canal. Leland ultimately foils the sabotage plot and captures the head Japanese agent (Sydney Greenstreet).

With Peter Lorre as a Nazi saboteur opposite Bogart in one 1942 film and Sydney Greenstreet as a Japanese saboteur opposite him in another, any regular moviegoer of that period looking back on *The Maltese Falcon* and the events of that December could hardly have failed to sense the international-gangster aura of its two foreign villains. Interestingly enough, Dashiell Hammett, recalling some of the real-life figures on whom he had based characters in *The Maltese Falcon*, remarked that Gutman's "original" was a man he had once followed in Washington when he was working as a Pinkerton detective prior to America's entry into World War I, a man "suspected of being a German spy."[12]

IV

The Maltese Falcon was, of course, the first film John Huston directed, and in writing the screenplay he followed the same procedure he'd used in

adapting *High Sierra,* working directly from the novel without an interme-
diate treatment and trying "to follow the book rather than depart from it,"
the result being that virtually all the dialogue in the film (with a few minor
and one major exception) is taken from the novel. Warner, which originally
bought the screen rights to Hammett's novel in 1930, had filmed it twice prior
to Huston's version, once in 1931 as *The Maltese Falcon,* directed by Roy del
Ruth and starring Ricardo Cortez and Bebe Daniels, and again in 1936 as *Satan
Met a Lady,* directed by William Dieterle and starring Bette Davis and Warren
Williams. The 1931 version (which was subsequently renamed *Dangerous Female* by the studio to avoid confusion with the more successful Huston film)
had been relatively faithful to the novel and done well at the box office, while
the 1936 version, which was played for comedy, had departed from the book
and was, according to rumor, Bette Davis's least favorite film. When Huston
came to choosing a project for his first outing as a director he turned to a
novel he admired to which the studio already owned the rights and which he
felt "had never really been put on screen" (Sperber, 149). Given the success of
High Sierra, Huston wanted Bogart for the role of Sam Spade, but the studio
first offered it to George Raft, who turned it down because he didn't feel it
was an important picture and didn't want to trust his career to a first-time
director. Both Bogart and the female lead, Mary Astor, were as enthusiastic
as Huston about filming *The Maltese Falcon* as close to the novel as possible,
with the result that the first two American noir films to achieve both critical
and commercial success clearly exhibited the centrality of hard-boiled fiction's
language, tone, and worldview to the new film genre.

Though in making *The Maltese Falcon* Huston concentrated on the profes-
sional/personal conflict that forms the core of the novel, he also emphasized
another recurring plot element possessing a special appropriateness for its
screen dramatization: the book repeatedly calls attention to its characters' theatricality, to their continual playacting as they try to take advantage of whom-
ever they're dealing with, a theatricality that Spade, who may be the best actor
among them, often points out with self-conscious relish. For example, on the
day after Archer's murder, when Brigid admits to Spade that her real name is
not Wonderly or LeBlanc but O'Shaughnessey and that the story she'd first
told him and Archer "was just a story," Spade says, "We didn't exactly believe
your story. . . . We believed your two hundred dollars. . . . you paid us more
than if you'd been telling the truth and enough more to make it all right."[13]
Saying that she can't tell Spade what the affair is about, she asks him to trust

her because she needs his help so badly, but Spade, clearly enjoying her ability to keep playing a role even though she's been caught in a lie, critiques her acting, "You won't need much of anybody's help. You're good. It's chiefly your eyes, I think, and that throb you get in your voice when you say things like, 'Be generous, Mr. Spade.'" Brigid replies that "the lie was in the way I said it, not at all in what I said. It's my own fault if you can't believe me now." Admiring this skill of continuing to adjust her performance as one lie after another is exposed, Spade says, "Ah, now you *are* dangerous" (Luhr, 41).

Spade's commentary on Brigid's dramatic talents continues in a later scene in her apartment when he asks, "You aren't exactly the sort of person you pretend to be, are you? . . . The schoolgirl manner, you know, blushing, stammering, and all that." When she says, "I haven't lived a good life. I've been bad, worse than you could know," he replies, "Yeah, well that's good, because if you actually were as innocent as you pretend to be, we'd never get anywhere" (Luhr, 50). At this point, Spade, springing a surprise, mentions that he's just spoken with Joel Cairo, hoping it will rattle Brigid enough to let something slip. Instead Brigid stands up, goes to the fireplace, stokes the fire with a poker, runs her hand along the mantel and the coffee table, goes to another table, where she gets a cigarette from a box, lights it, and then sits down—all of which Spade watches with an appreciative grin before he says, "You're good; you're very good." When Brigid asks what he and Cairo talked about, Spade says that Cairo offered him five thousand dollars for the black bird. Brigid stands up, and Spade says, "Er, you're not going to go around the room straightening things and poking the fire again, are you?" (51).

Spade's evident appreciation of acting talent isn't confined to Brigid, however; it extends to his own abilities as well. In the scene in which he meets Gutman in his hotel room the first time, Spade, feigning anger because Gutman won't tell him what the falcon is, throws down his glass, smashing it on the coffee table, then shouts that if Gutman doesn't keep the boy Wilmer out of his way he'll kill him, and before storming out delivers an ultimatum that Gutman has until five o'clock to decide whether he's in the deal or out. The next shot shows Spade walking down the hotel corridor, putting his hat on, taking out his handkerchief and wiping his face, then grinning appreciatively as he looks down at his hand that's still shaking. Clearly, Spade's a method actor in advance of his time.

Huston's decision to foreground the novel's constant awareness of its characters' theatricality affected both the movie's preproduction and filming. The sets for *The Maltese Falcon* were constructed to emphasize the seedy realism of Spade's world, being, in the words of the Warner's publicity department, "real rooms and offices with real ceilings . . . no familiar catwalks, blazing lights overhead" (Sperber, 154). Certainly the natural lighting these real rooms with real ceilings entailed gave the film exactly the kind of grim, claustrophobic feeling Huston wanted for his story, but such fully constructed sets also served his directorial aims in two other ways. First, rooms with real ceilings were needed to accommodate Huston's plentiful use of low-angle shots, shots that necessarily involved showing part of the ceiling. (Indeed, such low-angle shots looking upward seem like the cinematic equivalent of what Raymond Chandler called the "up-from-under look" that characters in his novels often give people either when they want to observe them without directly engaging the other's gaze or when they're telling a lie and don't want to look the other person in the eye.)

The real ceilings also fitted in with Huston's method of subtly violating the invisible fourth wall of the theatrical space so as to call attention to the fact that it *is* a theatrical space. Thus, at the end of the film's opening sequence, after Brigid has told her story to Spade and Archer and has left their office, the camera pulls back to show the two detectives sitting at their desks on opposite sides of the frame (a shot that also shows part of the office's ceiling), but one senses that to make this shot wide enough the camera had to be pulled back beyond where the office wall behind the camera must be (a sense of a violated boundary the viewer probably only notices on a second viewing, when he has become familiar with the office's layout). To underline this bit of theatricality, the camera then points down toward the floor to show the shadow of "Spade and Archer" cast by the lettering on a window, one name above the other, the letters right side up and reading left to right. But since we have already seen during the preceding sequence the position of both the office windows bearing the lettering, the viewer is struck by the clear impossibility of either window casting the shadow in this manner, struck by the realization that only a window in the ceiling (or a lighted cut-out) directly above the shadow could have produced it. This concluding dramatic flourish leads directly into the next scene, which shows the violent dissolution of that partnership (Miles Archer's murder) and prepares us for Spade's return to the office the morning after and his unsentimental erasure of his partner when he tells Effie, "Have Miles's desk moved out of the office and have 'Spade and Archer' taken off all the doors and windows and, er, have 'Samuel Spade' put on" (Luhr, 39).

Huston again calls attention to the same wandering fourth wall in a later scene, when the mortally wounded Captain Jacobi, bearing the falcon, collapses on the couch in Spade's office. This couch, shown in an early sequence in which Spade puts the unconscious Joel Cairo there after knocking him out, has its back flush against that fourth wall, yet in two separate shots in the later sequence with Jacobi, Huston positions the camera behind the couch, far enough back to show part of the couch's back, and shoots over the dead captain's shoulder as Spade examines the corpse.

In Spade's apartment the set's construction again underlines the characters' self-conscious role-playing. The only windows in the living room are set within a bay whose entrance resembles a proscenium arch with the window curtains at its rear, an arrangement that codes the interior space behind those curtains (the living room) as a stage. This coding is made explicit in the scene of Spade and Brigid's first meeting with Cairo, when the police unexpectedly knock at the door. Closing the sliding doors to the living room, Spade answers the front door, where he finds Lieutenant Dundy (Barton MacLane) and Sergeant Tom Polhaus (Ward Bond). Spade says they can't come in, but while they're arguing, they hear the sounds of a scuffle inside and Cairo calling for help. The police enter and find Cairo, blood trickling from a wound on his forehead, struggling with Brigid. On the spur of the moment Spade concocts an outrageous story that the struggle and the cry for help were part of a gag to razz the cops, a story that makes Dundy lose his temper and hit Spade. With that, Spade has won the battle of wits, and the police leave. But in claiming that Brigid and Cairo's struggle and Cairo's call for help were a dramatic performance staged for the police, Spade not only evokes the room, with its proscenium arch, as a stage, but also points toward the other, more earnest dramatic performance that will take place there as soon as the police and Cairo leave and Spade begins questioning Brigid about the falcon. Sitting on the couch set within the alcove's arch and with the curtains at her back, Brigid purports to tell Spade everything she knows about the black bird, and Sam replies, "You *are* a liar." Brigid happily admits that she's "always been a liar," and Spade asks, "Was there any truth at all in that yarn?" To which Brigid, smiling, answers, "Some. Not very much" (Luhr, 60).

The film's thematizing of theatricality is so complete it pervades even the smallest details. In that earlier scene when Spade searches Joel Cairo's wallet after knocking him out, he finds a ticket for that evening's performance at the Geary Theatre, and when Spade and Brigid decide to meet with Cairo later that same evening, Spade telephones the theater box office to leave a message. Similarly, when Spade leaves his office building after his first meeting with Cairo, he is shown walking along a street with the marquee of the Bailey Theatre visible behind him. Aware that he's being followed, Spade continues along the block and turns into the entrance to the Palladium Theatre to let the person tailing him (Gutman's gunman Wilmer Cook [Elisha Cook Jr.]) pass so that Spade can get a look at him. A shot of a poster in front of the theater shows that the play being performed there is *The Girl from Albany,* perhaps a sly reference to the fact that when Brigid, using the name Ruth Wonderly, had first hired Spade, she'd told him, "I'm from New York" (Luhr, 28).

One is hardly surprised to learn that Huston didn't shoot *The Maltese Falcon* in the "customary money-saving method of filming batches of unrelated scenes using the same set" but rather "shot the script in sequence" (Sperber, 158), that is, as if it were a play. Nor surprised that for his final flourish, Huston makes Spade's last line of dialogue in the film (a line not contained in the novel) an allusion to one of the most famous instances of theatrical self-reflexiveness in English drama. When Sergeant Polhaus picks up the statue of the falcon to take it along as evidence, he says to Spade, "Heavy. What is it?" And Spade replies, "The, uh, stuff that dreams are made of" (Luhr, 103). The allusion, of course, is to Prospero's speech in act 4, scene 1 of *The Tempest,* where, after magically calling up spirits who enact a wedding masque in honor of Ferdinand and Miranda, Prospero concludes the masque's performance with this speech:

> Our revels now are ended. These our actors,
> As I foretold you, were all spirits, and
> Are melted into air, into thin air.
> And, like the baseless fabric of this vision,
> The cloud-capped towers, the gorgeous palaces,
> The solemn temples, the great globe itself—
> Yea, all which it inherit—shall dissolve
> And, like this insubstantial pageant faded,
> Leave not a rack behind. We are such stuff
> As dreams are made on, and our little life
> Is rounded with a sleep.

Just as the actors performing the masque were spirits conjured by his magic art out of thin air, so too by implication are the characters in *The Tempest* simply actors in a drama conjured by poetic art out of Shakespeare's imagi-nation—with the further sense that life itself is a dreamlike drama rounded by the twin sleeps of womb and tomb, its hopes, fears, and desires seeming ultimately as "baseless" and "insubstantial" as visions in a dream, a figure that recalls Jaques's "All the world's a stage" speech in *As You Like It* (2.7.139) or Macbeth's line that life is "a poor player / That struts and frets his hour upon the stage / And then is heard no more" (5.5.24).

In responding to Polhaus's question about the falcon's substantiality, its heaviness, Spade's allusion to Shakespeare resonates on at least two different levels. First, as Spade's last line of dialogue it suggests that the various deceptive guises the characters have adopted during the course of the story, their playact-ing, constituted a play within a larger play (*The Maltese Falcon*), both of which are now ended. Second, in replying to a query about the statue's heaviness with an allusion to the dreamlike insubstantiality of life and the world, Spade suggests that the goal animating these characters' role-playing, the dreamlike stuff they were made of, had been precisely their belief in the statue's weighti-ness, their dream that it was a substance (gold) heavier than lead. But since the audience knows by the time Spade delivers his Shakespearean allusion that the statue *is* lead, then the linking of the notion of ending a play whose actors' motivations are the "stuff dreams are made on" with the image of the sleep of death that rounds "our little life" immediately calls up other Shakespearean echoes linking sleep, death, and lead (a material often used in the Elizabethan era for coffins), such as the phrase "death counterfeiting sleep with leaden legs" from *A Midsummer Night's Dream* (3.2.364–65) or Richmond's "I'll strive, with troubled thoughts, to take a nap, lest leaden slumber peise [weigh] me down tomorrow," spoken on the night before the battle of Bosworth (*Richard III*, 5.3.104–5). This association of the leaden statue with death carries over into the film's final shot, in which the elevator's grated screen closes in front of Brigid's face, then the elevator drops through the floor and the glass darkens, suggesting the fall through a trapdoor in a gallows. The film's narrative, end-ing with this sequence, fades into one final self-consciously theatrical flourish as the acting credits, titled "The Players" and listing the characters' names with their corresponding actors, are flashed on the screen and the soundtrack sud-denly shifts from Adolph Deutsch's dark, foreboding musical score to the kind of bright, up-tempo overture music played for an audience to leave a theater.

If, as I've argued, Huston's film foregrounds the novel's subtext of theatri-cality, then one naturally asks, "To what purpose?" The foregrounding seems meant not simply to place the book's dramatization in that tradition (evoked by the Shakespearean allusion) of self-reflexive dramatic pieces involving a play within a play or even within a modernist tradition of reflexivity in the arts (of works that self-consciously examine the conditions of their own artificiality) but rather to demonstrate how important the theatrical component of self-representation is to self-formation in the modern world, and then specifically, to examine what in Spade's self and in his chosen profession makes the two such a close fit, what makes his choice of his work over Brigid seem the inevitable one of *self* preservation (and not just in the sense that if he chose Brigid he couldn't be sure, as he tells her, "you wouldn't put a hole in me someday" (Luhr, 99). In a previous chapter, I noted that what the former Pinkerton Hammett saw as the essence of the detectives he created was precisely that they are *private* in several senses of the word—not just private citizens without public police responsibilities, or detectives privately employed by individuals often to keep the results of an investigation, or even the fact one's being conducted, from ever becoming public, but more especially, private in their need to conceal their motives or identities from others in order to do their job.

In other words, for a Hammett-style private eye the core of his professional work is usually some form of acting. Moreover, his not being bound by police responsibilities means that one of the roles he frequently plays (and sometimes all too much in earnest) is of someone with ambiguous ethical or legal standards. Spade assumes this latter role when he accepts a retainer from two clients with conflicting interests. Gutman calls Spade on it during their first meeting, asking which one he's there representing, adding, "It'll be one or the other." But when Spade replies, "I didn't say so," and Gutman asks, "Who else is it?" Spade says, "There's me," and Gutman laughs, "That's wonderful, sir, wonderful. I do like a man who tells you right out he's looking out for himself. Don't we all? I don't trust a man who says he's not" (Luhr, 67). Spade uses the conflict of interest both between Brigid and Cairo and with his own self-interest to convince Gutman that his services are for sale to the highest bidder. It's an act convincing enough to make plausible Spade's later performance, when he's being held at gunpoint by Gutman, Wilmer, and Cairo in his apartment and begins bargaining with them for the falcon, saying that part of his price for turning it over is having "a fall guy" for the police. Clearly relishing his own mental agility and acting skill in pitting his opponents against one another, Spade performs his part with such bravura that he's ultimately able to disarm them.

In the climactic sequence between Spade and Brigid the essentially theatrical nature of his work becomes an ongoing subtext of their conversation. When Spade tells Brigid how she sexually lured Archer up a dark alley, then "put a hole through him," and she replies, "Oh, why do you accuse me of such a . . . ," Spade immediately accuses her of acting, "This isn't the time for that schoolgirl act! We're both of us sitting under the gallows!" (Luhr, 96). But of course with that last statement (pretending they're both still in this together), Spade himself is acting out the charade that she needs to tell him everything because they've "got only minutes to get set for the police" (95). However, once she admits killing Archer and Spade makes it clear that he's turning her in, Brigid realizes exactly what Spade's professional skill amounts to, realizes that if Spade felt Archer "had too many years experience as a detective to be caught like that by a man he was shadowing up a blind alley" (96) but that he'd have gone up that alley with a beautiful woman, then Spade must have suspected her from the start, and consequently his romancing her had been an example of his dramatic expertise. She says, "You've been playing with me, just pretending you cared, to trap me like this. You didn't care at all. You don't love me" (97). Though Brigid's use of the phrase "playing with me" suggests at first she means "toying with me," her next phrase, "pretending you cared, to trap me," makes clear the sense of "play" she has in mind, and it's that sense Spade takes up when he replies, "I won't play the sap for you. I won't walk in Thursby's and I don't know how many others' footsteps" (98). Spade acknowledges the essentially theatrical nature of private detective work when Brigid asks him if he'd have turned her in "if the Falcon had been real and you'd got your money?": "Don't be too sure I'm as crooked as I'm supposed to be. That sort of reputation might be good business, bringing high-priced jobs and making it easier to deal with the enemy" (100). Given the extent to which the subject of acting informs the film's lengthy climactic sequence, Spade's final line, with its Shakespearean allusion, seems particularly appropriate considering that Huston said the line was "Bogart's idea" (Sperber, 163), the actor in effect commenting on his character's self-conscious role playing.

V

As Bogart gave the best and most memorable (though not the first) portrayal of Hammett's Sam Spade on film, so he also gave the best and most memorable (though not the first) film portrayal of Chandler's Philip Marlowe in Howard Hawks's 1946 *The Big Sleep*. In 1941 Chandler had sold the screen rights for *Farewell, My Lovely* to RKO and for *The High Window* to Twentieth-Century Fox. In 1942 RKO turned the plot of *Farewell, My Lovely* into the film *The Falcon Takes Over,* one of the studio's series of "Falcon" B-pictures starring George Sanders, and that same year Twentieth-Century Fox used the plot of *The High Window* for the film *Time to Kill,* one of its "Michael Shayne" series starring Lloyd Nolan. As Chandler biographer Tom Hiney notes, the success of Billy Wilder's film of Cain's *Double Indemnity,* with its screenplay by Chandler and Wilder, had drawn attention to Chandler's fiction and "raised Philip Marlowe's stock in Hollywood." Wilder's *Double Indemnity* "was groundbreaking enough, in censorship terms, to make the possibility of a more faithful Marlowe adaptation now appear feasible."[14] In 1944 Warner Bros. bought the screen rights to *The Big Sleep,* while RKO decided to cash in on the interest in Chandler's work by doing a second film adaptation of *Farewell, My Lovely,* this time as an A-picture titled *Murder My Sweet,* directed by Edward Dmytryk from a screenplay by John Paxton and starring Dick Powell.

Powell was the first actor to portray Marlowe on film, and Dmytryk's 1944 *Murder My Sweet* was the first American movie to bring together all the various features that are now associated with the term *film noir*—a hard-boiled crime drama told in voice-over and flashback (a technique that would soon become a staple of noir films) by a skeptical, not to say cynical, narrator and filmed in a visual style that makes full use of chiaroscuro lighting and subjective camera work (as when Marlowe is knocked unconscious or drugged and the screen registers his altered mental state as a visual distortion created either by an optical special effect or by expressionistic set design). But if, as one critic has remarked, *Murder My Sweet* represents the first appearance of "the fully realized *noir* look" in American film as well as the first screen appearance of Marlowe,[15] still Howard Hawks's *The Big Sleep* has always enjoyed a greater reputation than Dmytryk's film, and Bogart's portrayal of the detective in comparison with Powell's has always seemed more serious and substantial, creating in effect the definitive Marlowe. Chandler himself summed up the difference in a 1946 letter to a friend: Bogart is "so much better than any other tough-guy actor that he makes bums of the Ladds and the Powells. As we say here, Bogart can be tough without a gun. Also he has a sense of humor that contains that grating undertone of contempt. . . . Bogart is the genuine article."[16]

The difference in the two actors' portrayals of Marlowe can be accounted for in part by Bogart's having come to the role from a decade of playing tough guys, while Powell came to it from a decade of starring in musical comedies. Indeed, Powell's success in the role was partly a function of its allowing him to demonstrate a new, unexpected, and more mature aspect of his acting talent, an aspect that became part of his persona and enabled him to complete, in Powell's words, his "ten-year effort to escape musicals" (Hiney, 150). But another and more important factor contributed to the difference between Bogart's and Powell's performances as Marlowe: Dmytryk's film, in attempting to be more faithful to the feel of the Chandler novel, sought to reproduce something of the immediacy of the book's first-person narrator through Marlowe's voice-over of the flashback—the flashback being in effect the narrative technique that explains the need for, and thus the presence of, the voice-over as Marlowe tells his story to the cops. And since the voice-over gives the audience immediate access to the detective's thoughts, the film's narrative monologue contained a virtually unlimited supply of Marlowe's patented wisecracks and "exaggerated similes" from the book, with the result that Powell's Marlowe comes across as a lighter character than Bogart's, as a character too easily satisfied with a quip or a one-liner. Though Chandler had seen Bogart's skeptical sense of humor as containing a "grating undertone of contempt," Powell's wisecracks only manage a sort of ongoing comic exasperation. Chandler himself had given extensive instructions on how to play Marlowe's wisecracks in a 1948 letter to Ray Stark, who was planning a radio series about the detective. He pointed out that Marlowe is "a first-person character" and that such characters can often give "an offensively cocky impression. . . . To avoid that you must not always give him the punch line or the exit line. . . . Howard Hawks . . . remarked to me when he was doing *The Big Sleep* that he thought one of Marlowe's most effective tricks was just giving the other man the trick and not saying anything at all. That puts the other man on the spot. A devastating crack loses a lot of its force when it doesn't provoke any answer, when the other man just rides with the punch. Then you either have to top it yourself or give ground" (*Papers*, 94–95).

Hawks began filming *The Big Sleep* from a screenplay by William Faulkner, Leigh Brackett, and Jules Furthman in October 1944, the same year that *Double Indemnity* and *Murder My Sweet* were released. According to Hawks, Jack Warner, wanting to reteam Bogart and Bacall in another film after the success of Hawks's *To Have and Have Not,* had asked the director if he had a story in mind, and Hawks said he did, a story "something like *Maltese Falcon.*"[17] But in the three years that elapsed between his playing Sam Spade and Philip Marlowe, two important changes had occurred in Bogart's career and life that were to affect *The Big Sleep*'s screen adaptation. First, appearing in *Casablanca* opposite Ingrid Bergman, the former tough guy had became a major romantic star. Audiences now expected him to be alive at the end of a picture and also to get the girl (even though he'd nobly refused to take Ilsa away from her husband). Second, while filming Hawks's *To Have and Have Not* from February to May of 1944, Bogart met and fell in love with his co-star, the eighteen-year-old former New York model and first-time film actress Lauren Bacall. The pairing of Bogart and Bacall made the film a hit because their off-screen chemistry carried over into their performances, though, according to Hawks, his establishing the pattern of their on-screen chemistry had come first and led to the real-life romance. As he recalled it, Bacall "was a little girl who, when she became insolent, became rather attractive." So Hawks told Bogart, "'We are going try an interesting thing. You are about the most insolent man on the screen and I'm going to make a girl a little more insolent than you are. . . . she's going to walk out on you in every scene.' . . . So as every scene ended, she walked out on him. It was a sex antagonism."[18]

While the second film teaming of the two progressed, Bogart was in the process of bringing his marriage to his third wife, the actress Mayo Methot, to an end and planning to marry Bacall once his divorce was final. Principal photography on *The Big Sleep* finished in mid-January 1945, and Bogart and Bacall were married that May. Bacall had been under personal contract to Hawks prior to *To Have and Have Not,* and after the film's success Warner Bros. had bought her contract in a deal brokered by the agent Charles Feldman and rushed her into another picture, a film adaptation of Graham Greene's *The Confidential Agent* (opposite Charles Boyer), which went into general release while *The Big Sleep* was still going through sneak previews for GI's in the Pacific. After the glowing reviews for Bacall in *To Have and Have Not,* her universally bad reviews in *The Confidential Agent* seemed likely to nip her career in the bud. Charles Feldman, who felt that a second flop would finish Bacall, considered her role in *The Big Sleep* "hardly more than a bit part that had been beefed up through a few post-production retakes" (Sperber, 322). As Bogart biographers Sperber and Lax tell it, in November 1945 "Feldman wrote a long letter to Jack Warner, outlining a way to protect both his client and the studio's financial stake in her future. What he proposed were entirely new, one-on-one scenes with Bogart and Bacall, loaded with provocative banter. He wanted to highlight the 'insolence' that had endeared Bacall to both the critics and the public" (322–23). Warner agreed, and Philip Epstein, one of the writers of *Casablanca,* was brought in, and he and Hawks wrote new scenes and rewrote others, and shooting began again in January 1946. Among these new scenes was the lengthy exchange between Bogart and Bacall in which the two rate each other's romantic possibilities in horse-racing imagery, in effect a series of double entendres culminating in Bogart's appraisal of Bacall, "Well, I can't tell till I've seen you over a distance of ground. You've got a touch of class, but uh . . . I don't know how . . . how far you can go" and Bacall's reply, "A lot depends on who's in the saddle."

When *The Big Sleep* was released in August 1946, it was an enormous hit, and Bogart and Bacall became a surefire combination at the box office. But there is another version of why Feldman had asked Warner for the retakes—that Martha Vickers, who played the nymphomaniac little sister, Carmen Sternwood, had stolen the picture from Bacall. As Chandler told a friend in a 1946 letter, "*The Big Sleep* has had an unfortunate history. The girl who played the nymphy sister was so good she shattered Miss Bacall completely. So they cut the picture in such a way all her best scenes were left out except one. The result made nonsense and Howard Hawks threatened to sue to restrain Warners from releasing the picture. After long argument, I hear it, he went back and did a lot of re-shooting" (*Papers,* 67–68).

Clearly, then, from its beginning the film version of *The Big Sleep* had been mainly conceived as a starring vehicle for Bogart and Bacall meant to capitalize on their romantic chemistry from *To Have and Have Not.* Hawks himself had thought of *To Have and Have Not* as essentially a love story, with all the *Casablanca*-like business of sneaking a French Resistance leader into and out of Vichy Martinique as only "a secondary plot," providing "an excuse" for some "marvelous" scenes (Bogdanovich, 24). Hawks would later say that the plot of *The Big Sleep* "didn't matter at all," that "neither the author, the writer, nor myself knew who had killed whom. It was all about what made a good scene," and his "main idea was to try and make every scene fun to look at" (25–26). The frequently told story is that neither Hawks nor the screenwriters knew for sure if Owen Taylor (the Sternwood's chauffeur, who'd killed the pornographer

Arthur Gwynn Geiger after Geiger had photographed the drugged and naked Carmen Sternwood) had been murdered and, if so, who had killed him, and that Hawks had wired Chandler to ask and Chandler had said he didn't know. Whether Chandler's reply was serious or simply a joke, the novel purposely leaves the question of Taylor's death undecided between two possibilities— either Taylor committed suicide by driving his car off the Lido Pier or he was knocked unconscious by Joe Brody, who then set the car's hand throttle and ran it off the pier. The novel's refusal to decide one way or the other may well have been Chandler's hard-boiled way of avoiding the pat neatness of tying up all the loose ends in the manner of analytic detective fiction.

However, the real confusion in the film's plot resulted from the rewriting and retakes done to beef up the love story between Bogart and Bacall, rewriting that gives greater credence to Chandler's version of the reason the retakes were done. The film's uncertainty as to who killed whom centers on the identity of Rusty Regan's murderer. In the book it is clear: Regan, who's married to the older Sternwood daughter, Vivian, is killed by his sister-in-law, Carmen, during one of her epileptic seizures, a killing motivated by Regan's having rejected Carmen's amorous advances. But in the film's concluding sequence, when Marlowe and the elder Sternwood girl, whose name has been changed in the film from Vivian Regan to Vivian Rutledge, confront the gambler Eddie Mars in Geiger's house, the hurried dialogue gives the impression that Marlowe thinks either Mars or his gunman Canino may have killed Regan (perhaps because Regan was involved with Mars's wife) and then that Mars convinced Vivian that Carmen had killed him during one of her seizures in order to blackmail Vivian. When Marlowe fires a shot and then forces Mars out of the house, Mars's gunmen outside, who've been told to shoot the first person out the door, kill their boss by mistake. But Chandler's version of how that final scene came about is revealing. In a 1946 letter he says that Hawks and he had "planned together in talk" a "wonderful scene":

> At the end of the picture Bogart and Carmen were caught in Geiger's house by Eddie Mars and his lifetakers. . . . Bogart knew that she was a murderess and he also knew that the first person out of that door would walk into a hail of machine gun bullets. The girl didn't know this. Marlowe also knew that if he sent the girl out to be killed, the gang would take it on the lam, thus saving his own life for the time being. . . . So he put it up to God by tossing a coin. . . . If the coin came down heads, he would let the girl go. He tossed and it came down heads. The girl

thought this was some kind of a game to hold her there for the police. She started to leave. At the last moment, as she had her hand on the doorknob, Marlowe weakened and started for her to stop her. She laughed in his face and pulled a gun on him. Then she opened the door an inch or two and you could see she was going to shoot and was thoroughly delighted with the situation. At that moment a burst of machine gun fire walked across the panel of the door and tore her to pieces. The gunmen outside had heard a siren in the distance and panicked and thrown a casual burst through the door just for a visiting card—without expecting to hit anyone. I don't know what happened to this scene. Perhaps the boys wouldn't write it or couldn't. . . . All I know is it would have been a hair-raising thing well done. (*Papers*, 68)

Chandler wrote this letter in May 1946, before he had seen the finished version of the film, not knowing that the scene had in fact been made, but with significant changes, which satisfied both Charles Feldman's and Chandler's versions of why the reshooting was done. In the finished version of this sequence, Marlowe, instead of being alone in Geiger's house with Carmen while Mars and his henchman are waiting outside, as Chandler had imagined it, is inside the house with Vivian (Bacall) when Mars enters for the final confrontation. This version cuts Martha Vickers out of what would have been (if Carmen had been machine gunned, as Chandler described) a "hair-raising" scene—indeed, perhaps the most memorable in the film and one that might well have been the making of her career—while providing yet another scene in which Bogart and Bacall interact, outwitting Mars and ending up together at the final fade-out, as Vivian declares her love for Marlowe and the music of composer Max Steiner's love theme swells over the sound of approaching police sirens.

If the pattern exhibited in this scene—the building up of Bacall's role and of the love story with Bogart, and the reduction of Vickers's part—holds true for most of the reshooting and editing, still we should note that the first part of that pattern was already present to some degree in the original script. For example, in the novel Vivian Sternwood is married to Rusty Regan (who Marlowe and the General think is missing but who Vivian knows is dead), while in the film she is divorced from a man named Rutledge—a change that keeps the film's romantic involvement of Marlowe and Vivian from appearing to be an adulterous affair. Since Bogart was planning a divorce to marry his young co-star, the studio as well as the two actors wanted to avoid any taint of scandal that might make the divorce messy, damaging the actors' careers and *The Big Sleep*'s box office. Consequently, though the change of Vivian's last name and of her status from married to divorced would have been prompted partly by the Hollywood Production Code's restrictions against adulterous liaisons ending happily, it was probably also influenced by a desire not to have the fictional involvement of Marlowe and Vivian resemble too closely the real-life situation of the actors playing them.

Though the romantic relationship between Marlowe and Vivian is a core element in the film version of *The Big Sleep*, in the novel the strong physical attraction between the two, expressed mainly through insolent flirtation and sexual innuendo and used for the most part by Vivian to distract Marlowe from his inquiry, has run its course two-thirds of the way through the book. Indeed, the only woman whose memory seems to haunt Marlowe at the novel's end with anything like romantic longing is Eddie Mars's wife, who'd saved Marlowe's life when he was being held prisoner by two of Mars's thugs, Canino and Art Huck. But just as Vivian had been put into the film's final scene rather than Carmen, so Vivian was added to this scene, in which Marlowe is handcuffed and tied up by Canino in the house behind Art Huck's garage—added so that he can be freed, not by Mars's wife, who'd been hiding there, but by Vivian, the woman he's attracted to and is slated to end up with.

As we noted earlier, a large part of the film's legendary confusion derives from the hurried conversation between Marlowe and Eddie Mars during their final confrontation in Geiger's house:

> *Marlowe:* Regan's dead all right. . . . It was Carmen, wasn't it? How'd it happen, Eddie?
> *Mars:* You mean she didn't tell you . . .
> *Marlowe:* I asked you how it happened . . .
> *Mars:* Well, Carmen liked Regan . . .
> *Marlowe:* But he liked your wife. He said no to Carmen. She gets mad when anybody says that, I've seen her that way. Go on.
> *Mars:* She was pretty high. By the time it was over she didn't remember much about it.
> *Marlowe:* Yeah, I've seen her that way too. Then you hid the body, Eddie.
> *Mars:* You can't prove that . . .
> *Marlowe:* It'll be just as bad for you if I prove it to myself. Then you started

blackmailing Mrs. Rutledge by telling her what Carmen had done. How did you prove to *her* that Carmen had done it. Go ahead, prove it to me.

Mars: You've seen Carmen when she's that way.

Marlowe: Sure I have, have you?

Mars: Well, how do you suppose . . .

Marlowe: Then why didn't you know her when you walked in here that day, tell me that. You're pretty smart, Eddie, but I've been waiting for this one.

Mars: What you gonna do about it.

Marlowe: I told you you were smart. You walked in here without a gun. You were gonna sit there and agree to everything just like you're doing now. When I went out that door, things were gonna be different. That's what those boys are doing out there. Everything's changed now, Eddie, because I got here first.

In suggesting that Rusty Regan was killed by Mars or Canino rather than, as Mars claims, by Carmen, the film tries to solve at a single blow several difficulties posed by the rewriting and reshooting and by the demands of the Hollywood Production Code. On the one hand, if Mars is a cold-blooded killer, then Marlowe's forcing him out the front door to be machine gunned by his own men is to some extent justified. On the other, if Carmen didn't kill Regan, then Vivian is not an accessory after the fact (as she is in the novel, when she calls on Eddie Mars to dispose of Regan's body after Carmen tells her what she's done), so that in terms of the Code Vivian doesn't have to be punished at the film's end. And that final conversation between Marlowe and Mars, designed as it was to muddy the waters about who killed Regan, in effect frees Vivian from any taint of criminal complicity, thus permitting a happy ending to her and Marlowe's romantic involvement.

Marlowe's final exchange with Vivian (after Mars has been killed, Marlowe has phoned the police, and they are waiting in Geiger's house for the cops to arrive) muddies the waters even further:

Marlowe: I don't know yet what I'm gonna tell 'em, but it'll be pretty close to the truth. You'll have to send Carmen away—from a lot of things. They have places for that. Maybe they can cure her. It's been done before. We'll have to tell your father about Regan, I think he can take it.

Vivian: You've forgotten one thing—me.

Marlowe: What's wrong with you?

Vivian: Nothing you can't fix.

In the novel, after getting Vivian to admit that Carmen killed Regan, Marlowe gives Vivian three days to leave town, take Carmen with her, "and see that she's watched every minute" (215), or else he'll go to the police and it will all come out. In letting the criminally insane Carmen get away, Marlowe is motivated not by any love for Vivian (their flirtation is long since past) but by his private detective's code of loyalty to and respect for his client, the ailing General, who would certainly die if he learned that his younger daughter had killed his best friend. But in the final exchange from the film, Marlowe's decision not to tell the cops the whole story and have Vivian send Carmen to an asylum raises the question of whether Marlowe himself wholly believes the story he's going to tell the police (that Mars, not Carmen, killed Regan) and, further, whether he's bending the truth out of professional loyalty to the General or because he's in love with Vivian. Where Huston's *The Maltese Falcon* sticks about as close to Hammett's novel as a film adaptation can, Hawks's version of *The Big Sleep,* which was thought of as a love story from its inception, never really foregrounds the professional/personal conflict in Marlowe's life, and the film's ending raises the possibility that Marlowe does for Vivian what Spade wouldn't do for Brigid—let a personal relationship influence his professional behavior.

We can judge what Chandler felt about the changes the screen adaptation made in his book from a 1947 letter written after he'd seen the film's reshot version: "The really good detective picture has not yet been made. . . . *The Maltese Falcon* came closest. The reason is that the detective in the picture always has to fall for some girl, whereas the real distinction of the detective's personality is that, as a detective, he falls for nobody. He is the avenging justice, the bringer of order out of chaos, and to make his doing this part of a trite boy-meets-girl story is to make it silly" (*Papers,* 80–81). In a 1949 letter Chandler describes the detective story as "a tragedy with a happy ending," noting that "modern outspokenness has utterly destroyed the romantic dream on which love feeds," that love simply "cannot exist against a background of cheese cake and multiple marriages": "The peculiar appropriateness of the detective or mystery story to our time is that it is incapable of love. The love story and the detective story cannot exist, not only in the same book—one might almost say the same culture" (117), a sentiment that seems to echo what the Goncourt brothers thought was the peculiarly twentieth-century element in Poe's Dupin stories. And in an undated note from his notebook, Chandler reminds himself why this is: "Has anyone ever said clearly that what is wrong with the modern family, or modern marriage" is that there are "no longer any kind of people who are not in some sense *cornered*. The lawyer may love his wife and children, but his true love is the law. What a man *does* to live is all. Like the house, the mistress, the drunken orgy, the perversion even, marriage is only a convenient arrangement. A man of this age really lives (and dies) for his work" (228–29).

EIGHT

Hard-Boiled Fiction and Film Noir, Continued

I

When Paramount Pictures contacted Chandler in 1943 to ask if he'd be interested in collaborating on the screenplay of Cain's *Double Indemnity* with the film's director Billy Wilder, Chandler got his chance, for his first venture in screenwriting, to work on adapting a book embodying his sense that the detective story and the love story "cannot exist . . . in the same book—one might almost say the same culture"—albeit embodying this in an inverse detective story and in what Chandler would have considered a tale of lust rather than love. In a 1946 letter noting that "the love story proper has little or nothing to do with lust," Chandler says that "the synthetic stallions like James Cain have made a fetish of pure animal lust which honester and better men take in their stride, without literary orgasms, and which the middle classes seem to regard as a semi-respectable adjunct to raising a family."[1] But if adapting Cain's novel was to offer Chandler the opportunity of demonstrating the mutual exclusivity of love and detection in the same story, he had to come up with a screenplay that would get past the Hays Office, the industry's self-regulatory agency that administered the Hollywood Production Code.

When Cain and his agent had originally shopped the screen rights of *Double Indemnity* around the Hollywood studios in 1935 with an asking price of $25,000, there was great interest in the book, but the studios all wanted to wait for "the Hays Office report on the story" before deciding. However, when the report came back with a first sentence that began "Under no circumstances in no way shape or form . . . ,"[2] no studio would touch the book. When Wilder decided eight years later to try to film *Double Indemnity* for Paramount, he counted on the fact that in the third year of World War II the Hays Office was likely to be less shocked by Cain's tale of violence. The screen rights were bought for $15,000, and Wilder's first choice of a collaborator was his longtime writing partner Charles Brackett, but Brackett refused and told Wilder the story was "disgusting"[3]—Brackett likely knowing in advance how difficult it would be to get the screenplay past the censors. Wilder then wanted James Cain, but Cain was working on a picture at another studio. When Wilder asked the film's producer, Joseph Sistrom, if he knew another writer who wrote like Cain, Sistrom gave Wilder a novel by Chandler, whom Wilder had never heard of, and the director's enthusiastic response was ultimately to initiate a collaboration on the Cain film that was as stormy as it was successful.

Clearly, Wilder chose Chandler as a collaborator not just because Chandler's skeptical, hard-boiled writing style fit the kind of film Wilder intended to make but also because Chandler, who had never written for the screen before, wouldn't be as daunted as a veteran screenwriter like Brackett about the difficulties of getting the kind of script Wilder wanted approved by the Hays Office. An experienced screenwriter, Wilder had collaborated with Brackett on the scripts for Ernst Lubitsch's *Bluebeard's Eighth Wife* (1938), Mitchell Leisen's *Midnight* (1939), Lubitsch's *Ninotchka* (1939), Howard Hawks's *Ball of Fire* (1942), and his own *The Major and the Minor* (1942), to name only the high points—screenplays in which he had honed the edge of his gift for writing comic sexual banter. But with *Double Indemnity* Wilder wanted, as he told an interviewer at the time, "to set Hollywood back on its heels. . . . Even my own studio said I was crazy to attempt it" (Hoopes, 333).

As a young man growing up in his native Austria, then as a freelance journalist in Berlin in the 1920s and as a screenwriter for the German studio UFA working under the producer Erich Pommer in the early '30s, Wilder had become enamored of all things American—American dances, popular songs, films, and especially American colloquial speech and slang (the last two an enthusiasm he clearly shared with Chandler). Wilder arrived in the United States in January 1934 (Zolotow, 52) in response to a wire from Joe May, a producer at Columbia pictures whom Wilder had known when May was a filmmaker in Germany, and went to work for May, first at Columbia and then at Fox. After teaming with Brackett and writing a series of hit films, Wilder turned to directing as the only way to keep other directors or actors from tampering with his scripts.

Double Indemnity was Wilder's third Hollywood film as a director, and in writing the screenplay he and Chandler had tried, as Chandler said in a 1944 letter to Cain, to get "an emotionally integrated story . . . on the screen in the mood in which it was written" (*Papers*, 41). But, as Chandler also said in his letter, Cain's dialogue in the novel posed a difficulty: "Nothing could be more natural and easy and to the point on paper, yet it doesn't quite play. We tried it out by having a couple of actors do a scene right out of the book. It had a sort of remote effect that I was at a loss to understand." Noting that on paper Cain's "unevenly spaced hunks of quick-moving speech hit the eye with a sort of explosive effect" so that "you read the stuff in batches, not in individual speech and counterspeech," Chandler said that "on the screen this is all lost, and the essential mildness of the phrasing shows up as lacking in sharpness. They tell me that is the difference between photographic dialogue and written dialogue. For the screen everything has to be sharpened and pointed and wherever possible elided" (*Papers*, 41).

Of the many alterations Chandler and Wilder made in adapting Cain's novel perhaps the first and most obvious was changing the names of the two main characters—Walter Huff became Walter Neff (according to Fred Mac-Murray, the actor who played this role, the "name was Walter Ness in the first version of the script" but "then they found out that there was an insurance guy over in Palos Verdes named Walter Ness so Billy changed it to Neff" [Zolotow, 116]), and Phyllis Nirdlinger became Phyllis Dietrichson (Barbara Stanwyck). Since most of Wilder's best-known work in Hollywood prior to *Double Indemnity* had been in light comedy, these name changes no doubt reflected Wilder's concern that the names Huff and Nirdlinger (particularly the latter) had a comic ring and might give audiences either an initial misimpression of the film's genre or provoke a laugh where none was appropriate.

The screenplay's first major structural change from the novel was to shift Huff's first-person narration from something written (the notarized confession he must send Keyes as part of their deal for giving Huff a head start in escaping from the police) to something spoken (the Dictaphone recording of an "office memorandum" Neff makes for Keyes "to set you right," as he says, "about one thing you couldn't see" in the Dietrichson case "because it was smack up against your nose"). Bleeding from a shoulder wound, Neff had gone back to his office to make his confession after having been shot by Phyllis, whom he'd then killed. The making of the recording becomes the realistic premise for and framework of the film's voice-over and flashback narration, with the latter being periodically interrupted whenever the film switches back to show Neff at his desk speaking into the Dictaphone and growing progressively weaker from blood loss as his narration continues. (As noted earlier, the success of two 1944 movies employing the voice-over/flashback technique—Dmytryk's *Murder My Sweet* and Wilder's film—along with the prevalence of first-person narration in many hard-boiled novels turned into noir films, was to make this type of screen narration a staple of the genre.)

In terms of characterization, the changes Chandler and Wilder made in turning the novel's Walter Huff into the film's Walter Neff were minimal, but the changes to the novel's principal female character, Phyllis Nirdlinger, were substantial. Recall that in the book Phyllis is initially presented as a bored, potentially adulterous wife who wants to get rid of her husband for the insurance. But as the story continues, Phyllis's mental instability becomes increasingly clear, until near the end, when Keyes uncovers evidence that she probably killed Nirdlinger's first wife and five other patients under her care as a nurse, has tried to kill Huff, and plans to kill Nirdlinger's daughter, Lola, he pronounces her the worst "pathological case" he's "ever heard of"—"an out-and-out lunatic."[4] None of the pathological component in Phyllis's character makes it over into the Phyllis Dietrichson of the film, and though the Dietrichson's daughter, Lola (Jean Heather), believes that Phyllis, who had been her mother's nurse, was responsible for the first Mrs. Dietrichson's death, there is never any suggestion that Phyllis is a psychopathic serial killer. Rather, she is simply a ruthless, opportunistic woman like *The Maltese Falcon*'s Brigid O'Shaughnessey, the characteristic noir femme fatale.

This change in Phyllis's character in the film also alters the character of Lola's boyfriend, Nino Zachette (Sachetti in the book). Recall that in the novel Sachetti is the son of a doctor whose practice and life had been ruined when three children in the sanatorium he owned died suddenly of pneumonia. Sachetti suspects the children were killed by Phyllis, her motive being, as Keyes later theorizes, that she stood to inherit property from one of the children and had simply killed the other two to make it look like a case of negligence rather than murder. So Sachetti, say Keyes, "elected himself a one-man detective agency" (Cain, 116) and tried to keep an eye on Phyllis, whom he had known through his father, but when he met Phyllis's new stepdaughter, Lola, he fell in love with her. After Nirdlinger's suspicious death, Sachetti stopped seeing Lola and started wooing Phyllis to entrap her. For the screenwriters this whole Sachetti backstory became irrelevant once Chandler and Wilder decided to jettison Phyllis's psychopathic-killer aspect, and thus the film's Zachette (Byron Barr) is simply a surly young man who happens to be Lola's boyfriend. In the book Huff comes to believe not only that Sachetti and Phyllis are having an affair during the period after Nirdlinger's murder (when Phyllis is under surveillance and Huff and Phyllis must avoid seeing each other) but also that Sachetti and Phyllis may have been involved even before Huff met her, and that they had simply used Huff and his insurance expertise to murder her husband. Huff also wants Sachetti out of the way because he's fallen in love with Lola, and she still loves Sachetti. So Huff decides to kill Phyllis and frame Sachetti for the crime. But the plan backfires because Phyllis strikes first, shooting Huff while he's waiting for her in Griffith Park, and the frame Huff had arranged, instead of entrapping Sachetti for Phyllis's murder, entraps him for Huff's shooting and makes the police think Lola is his accomplice. It's the prospect of Lola's being given the third degree by the cops that moves Huff to confess Nirdlinger's murder to Keyes.

However, in the film, where Zachette doesn't carry this baggage of being the sanatorium owner's son out to clear his father's name, the reason he drops Lola and takes up with Phyllis after Dietrichson's death, according to Lola, is that they simply "had a fight" and she's "not seeing him any more." But in their last scene together, when Neff accuses Phyllis of two-timing him with Zachette, she says, "He came here the first time just to ask where Lola was. I made him come back. I was working on him. He's a crazy sort of guy, quick-tempered. I kept hammering into him that she was with another man, so he'd get into one of his jealous rages, and then I'd tell him where she was. And you know what he'd have done to her, don't you, Walter." Phyllis claims she'd only been using Zachette as a means to do away with Lola to prevent her from voicing her suspicions about the death of the first Mrs. Dietrichson. But Neff isn't buying it: "You got me to take care of your husband, and then you got Zachette to take care of Lola, and maybe take care of me too, and then somebody else would have come along to take care of Zachette for you. That's the way you operate isn't it, baby." And Phyllis says, "Suppose it is, Walter. Is what you've cooked up for tonight any better?" Because of course Neff is planning to kill Phyllis and pin it on Zachette, and as he goes around the living room closing the windows and drawing the drapes, Phyllis, who's hidden a pistol under the cushion of her chair, pulls it out and shoots Neff in the shoulder. As he stands there waiting for her to finish him off, he says, "What's the matter? Why don't you shoot again? Maybe if I came a little closer?" But as he walks toward her, she still doesn't shoot. He takes the gun, she puts her arms around his neck, and Neff says, "Don't tell me it's because you've been in love with me all this time." Phyllis replies, "I never loved you, Walter. Not you, or anybody else. I'm rotten to the heart. I used you, just as you said. That's all you ever meant to me—until a minute ago. I didn't think anything like that could ever happen to me." Saying "I'm sorry, baby. I'm not buying," Neff holds her close and shoots her twice.

Clearly, the weakest part of the book is its ending: Phyllis's and Huff's presumed double suicide by jumping overboard at night in mid-ocean from the ship carrying them to Mexico (I say "presumed" because, while Huff's narrative contemplates the deed, his writing must obviously break off before it's actually accomplished). However, their suicide, presented as the only way out once they know they've been recognized and that the police will be waiting for them when the ship arrives, produces an ending whose overwrought, melodramatic quality is at odds with, and thus to some degree betrays, the preceding narrative's hard-edged precision. In terms of character psychology, Huff's having become infected with Phyllis's madness seems the only halfway-plausible explanation for the novel's ending, but the film's final encounter between Neff and Phyllis, which substitutes for the book's punishment of the guilty pair, has its problems as well: the film's viewer is asked to believe that after having shot Neff once, Phyllis, who says she'd never loved Walter or anybody else, realizes maybe she did love him, and stands still while he takes the gun and kills her, a situation that gives *volte-face* a new meaning.

Indeed, the only explanation I can give for the shape of this final encounter is that Chandler and Wilder, in trying to stay true to the spirit of the novel's ending, imagined this scene as a substitutive equivalent of an extended double suicide, that is, that Phyllis, deciding the game is up once Walter and she have turned on each other and Walter intends to kill her, wounds him, then lets him kill her, leaving Walter to face the consequences of his bullet wound, a wound he won't be able to hide or explain without the truth coming out and his ultimately going to the gas chamber. And this substitutive double-suicide subtext would thus also account for the oddness of the film's opening premise: that the wounded Neff returned to his office after killing Phyllis to record his lengthy confession for Keyes—almost as if he wanted to bleed to death or be caught. Moreover, if Neff realized he was finished once Phyllis had shot him, that would also explain the unselfishness of his actions immediately after killing Phyllis, actions meant to protect the woman he really loves, Lola. Knowing Zachette was due to visit Phyllis on the night of the murder, Neff had planned to pin her murder on him, but instead he waits outside the house after the killing and as Zachette approaches warns him not to go in, not to believe what Phyllis had said about Lola not loving him, and tells him to leave immediately and call her. If clearing Zachette is also part of Neff's motive for returning to his office to record his confession, it's simply his way of making amends to Lola for having killed her father by saving the man she loves.

From these instances the method Chandler and Wilder used in adapting Cain's book becomes clear: In aiming to keep the novel's overall feel, they identified the principal characters' emotions and intentions in the book's key episodes, those crucial to its dramatic arc, and then tried to remain faithful to these. If this could be achieved in a dramatic and visually satisfying way by using incidents or dialogue from the book, then they did so, but if not (and the shortening and tightening of the action as well as the excision of the element of insanity from Phyllis's character often meant they couldn't), they created a new objective correlative for these emotions and intentions. Sometimes these actions or conversations were entirely original with the screenwriters, resembling moments or speeches in Chandler's novels or Wilder's previous screen work, as when Neff and Phyllis meet for the first time, a scene that combines the "meet-cute" structure Wilder was familiar with from his earlier screenwriting work in sophisticated comedy for Lubitsch, with the sort of double entendre and sexual banter Chandler used in virtually every encounter between Marlowe and Vivian Regan in *The Big Sleep*. But often they created new scenes for the film by taking elements or images from different parts of the book, moving or combining them, or putting them to a different use. Thus, for example, the idea of having Neff record his confession as an office memorandum on his Dictaphone, the idea of making this the realistic frame for the film's voice-over and flashback, was clearly suggested by the scene in the book (also included in the film) in which Neff, trying to find out how much Keyes knows, goes into Keyes's office at night and listens to his Dictaphone recording of a memorandum telling the company president he doesn't agree with his suggestion to put Neff under surveillance.

This method of adaptation created a work, according to Wilder's biographer, that "as a whole was almost entirely a reconstruction" but seemed more like "a totally new aesthetic experience, although if you see it . . . and you think of Cain's novel (in memory only) you may think the film is a faithful translation of the novel. And, says Wilder, that is just the way it should be" (Zolotow, 119). Certainly Chandler and Wilder's script aimed to create a greater number of suspenseful moments than those the book contained, moments allowing Wilder to show that Hitchcock wasn't the only director who could play with his audience's emotions. Indeed, the novel has only one moment of suspense that makes it into the film—the scene in which Neff, impersonating the murdered Dietrichson (Tom Powers), boards the train and goes to the rear observation platform to jump off only to find he's not alone, that there's a man sitting there and that he's got to figure out a way that's not too suspicious to get him to leave. But Chandler and Wilder immediately top this when, after Neff has leapt from the train and he and Phyllis have put Dietrichson's body by the tracks, they get into her car to leave and it won't start. Here's the way it's described in the script:

> The starter grinds, but the motor doesn't catch. She tries again. It still doesn't catch. Neff looks at her. She tries a third time. The starter barely turns over. The battery is very low. Phyllis leans back. They stare at each other desperately. After a moment Neff bends forward slowly and turns the ignition key to the OFF position. He holds his left thumb poised over the starter button. There is a breathless moment. Then he presses the starter button with swift decision. The starter grinds with nerve-wracking sluggishness. Neff twists the ignition key to ON and instantly pulls the hand-throttle wide open. With a last feeble kick of the starter, the motor catches and races. He eases the throttle down and slides back into his place. They look at each other again. The tenseness of the moment still shows in their faces.[5]

Not all of the details in this description make it onto the screen, but enough do so that, as Fred MacMurray recalled, it was "the most successful scene in the picture." He also remembered that when he was trying to start the car Wilder "kept saying, 'Make it longer, make it longer,' and finally I yelled, 'For Chrissake Billy, it's not going to hold that long' and he said, 'Make it longer,' and he was right. . . . It held—that was how much the audience was involved in the story" (Zolotow, 116).

If by "the most successful scene in the picture" MacMurray meant the most suspenseful, then many viewers might disagree, preferring instead the sequence in which Neff receives a phone call in his apartment from Phyllis after her meeting with Norton, asking if it's safe to come up. He says yes and hangs up the phone. An instant later the doorbell rings, and it's Keyes, who's dropped by to say "there's something wrong with that Dietrichson case" (Wilder, 85). As Keyes continues to talk, the suspense mounts. Phyllis is shown in the hall outside approaching the apartment's front door. She's just about to knock when she hears the voices of people inside approaching the door, and she quickly steps aside. As the door opens, she hides behind it, and Neff stands with his hand on the doorknob talking to Keyes, who's walking down the hall toward the elevator. Phyllis grasps the doorknob on her side and pulls it slightly toward herself, so that Neff knows she's there and that he's got to stay out in the hall talking until Keyes gets on the elevator. Wilder tweaks the viewer's nerves again by having Keyes walk back toward Neff asking for a match and Neff goes to meet him to keep him as far away from the door as possible. Neff lights his cigar, the elevator arrives, and Keyes leaves. But of course it's a scene that only works because a detail's been rigged to create suspense—an apartment front door that opens outward into a hall rather than inward into the apartment, something I've never seen—and no one else has either. But the scene is so well crafted and so tense that audiences almost never notice.

Chandler and Wilder found yet another way of extending the suspense of the scene on the train's rear platform to a moment later in the film by having Keyes bring in the man from the observation platform who'd seen Neff impersonating Dietrichson and then asking Neff to sit in on their meeting. All during the scene Neff tries not to betray any emotion, to make his interaction with Jackson (Porter Hall) as affectless as possible, but toward the end of the scene Jackson begins to look intently at Neff and asks him if he's ever been to Oregon, where Jackson lives, or ever been trout fishing in Klamath Falls. The suspense mounts as Jackson tries to remember why Neff looks familiar and then suddenly the tension is released when Jackson says, "I've got it! It's the name. There's a family of Neffs in Corvallis," to which Neff replies, "No relation."

Besides excising the element of mental instability from Phyllis's character, Chandler and Wilder make one other major change to a principal figure from the book, transforming Barton Keyes, who's an important but fairly undelineated character in the novel, into a more fully realized role, worthy of Edward G. Robinson. This involves not only writing new scenes for Keyes (e.g., when he interviews Jackson in his office with Neff present) but also providing new bits of business for scenes that *are* in the book (e.g., the way Keyes personifies the sort of hunches he gets about suspicious insurance claims by referring to "the little man" inside him who "ties knots in my stomach" every time a phony claim comes along). The most significant enlargement of Keyes's character comes, however, in his relationship with Neff, which is even more clearly one of mentor and protégé, of surrogate father and surrogate son in the film, the recurrent visual symbol of their mutual regard and affection being Neff's striking a match on his thumbnail to light Keyes's cigar.

(The image of lighting or sharing a cigarette functioned in many Hollywood films of the Production Code era as a visual tag for heterosexual attraction or involvement, the association being the postcoital cigarette. Thus, for example, in Irving Rapper's *Now, Voyager* [Warner Bros., 1942] Paul Henreid memorably puts two cigarettes in his mouth, lights one, and gives the other to the woman he loves [Bette Davis]. In Hawks's *The Big Sleep* we see behind the opening credits a man and a woman in silhouette; the man lights the woman's cigarette, both are smoking and then the woman lays her cigarette in an ashtray on the table in front of them, the man places his cigarette beside hers, the ashtray and the two cigarettes remaining visible in the lower left hand corner of the frame for the remainder of the credits; and then again, behind the closing credits, the ashtray with its two smouldering cigarettes is shown, suggesting that the man and woman are now otherwise engaged in an activity for which the image of the phallic cigarette burning in the concave receptacle is a metaphor.)

The repeated image of Neff lighting Keyes's cigar sets up the final shot of the film: Having collapsed from loss of blood as he tried to leave the insurance company's office, Neff lies at the door while Keyes, who's phoned for an ambulance, leans over him. Neff tells him that the reason Keyes didn't figure this case out was that "the guy you were looking for was too close. He was right across the desk from you." Keyes says, "Closer than that, Walter." At this point the stage direction in the script reads, "The eyes of the two men meet in a moment of silence," then Neff jokingly but not in jest replies, "I love you too" (Wilder, 120). Neff then takes a cigarette out and puts it in his mouth, but he's too weak to strike the match, so Keyes takes the match, strikes it on his thumbnail, and lights Neff's cigarette—fade out.

Perhaps the single most important scene Chandler and Wilder wrote in enlarging Keyes's character and deepening his relationship with Neff occurs midway through the picture, when Keyes tells Neff that he'd like him to become his assistant in the claims department. Clearly, the point of the scene is that Keyes is anointing him as his professional heir and thus explicitly making a judgment about Neff's dedication to his work. Keyes says the job he's offering him "takes brains and integrity . . . and more guts than there is in fifty salesmen." When Neff demurs on the grounds that he's a salesman and doesn't want a desk job, Keyes goes into an impassioned defense of investigative work, comparing it to the work of a surgeon (recall in this connection that detective, doctor, and lawyer are the three professions of choice for staging the conflict between the professional and the personal): "To me a claims man is a surgeon, that desk is an operating table, and those pencils are scalpels and bone chisels. And those papers are not just forms and statistics and claims for compensation. They're alive, they're packed with drama, with twisted hopes and crooked dreams. A claims man, Walter, is a doctor and a blood-hound and a cop and a judge and a jury and a father confessor, all in one." Keyes interrupts his speech to answer a phone call, then hands the phone to Neff, saying "There's a dame on your phone."

It's Phyllis calling to tell Neff that Dietrichson has decided to leave that evening by train for his college reunion at Stanford and that their plan has to be put into effect in a matter of hours. In the voice-over that introduced this scene, Neff had said that "maybe those fates they say watch over you had gotten together and broken" Dietrichson's "leg to give me a way out." But with Phyllis's phone call he suddenly commits himself to going through with the murder, and the brilliance of the script at this point is the way it places Neff's decision to choose the personal over the professional right in the middle of Keyes's paean to work, professional integrity, and dedication to a code, and then, for an added touch, the way Keyes follows this up immediately with an explicit warning about letting personal emotion overrule professional procedure. Keyes asks Neff why he doesn't settle down and get married, and Neff asks, "Why don't you, for instance?" Keyes says he "almost did once—a long time ago," and then in a personal reminiscence suggesting how close he feels to Neff, Keyes recalls that his fiancée had already bought her wedding dress, they'd picked out a church, and Keyes was on the way to buy the ring when he suddenly got one of his hunches that something was wrong. To which Neff replies, "So you went back and started investigating her. That it?" As Keyes begins to recite the list of damaging things he discovered about his fiancée, Neff interrupts him: "I get the general idea. She was a tramp from a long line of tramps." The scene ends with Neff telling Keyes he's not interested in the job as his assistant, and Keyes replying with a typical Marlovian wisecrack: "I picked you for the job, not because I think you're so darn smart, but because I thought you were a shade less dumb than the rest of the outfit. I guess I was all wet. You're not smart, Walter. You're just a little taller" (Wilder, 58).

Chandler and Wilder's script originally had a different last scene for the film from the one viewers are familiar with. After Neff collapses at the insurance company's door and Keyes has told him that an ambulance and the police are on the way, the scene ends, and the next one opens in the witness room of the gas chamber at San Quentin. Neff is brought into the chamber, sees the witnesses and Keyes through the window, nods to Keyes, and then the guards strap Neff in a chair with his back to the window. The execution begins, and the camera, shooting from inside the chamber above Neff's head "towards the spectators standing outside . . . , Keyes in the center," shows the gas floating up between the camera and the spectators, and "Keyes, unable to watch, looks away" (Wilder, 122). Neff is pronounced dead, and the spectators leave, the script's final stage direction being "Keyes slowly walks into the sunshine, stiffly, his head bent, a forlorn and lonely man" (123), almost a description of the later Marlowe or of Chandler in his last years. The execution scene, which was virtually wordless, was actually shot at a cost of $150,000 (a replica of the San Quentin gas chamber having been built at the studio), according to Wilder's biographer. Everyone at the studio thought it was terrific, but after many viewings Wilder decided, says Zolotow, that it was "too strong" and "out of key," so "against Chandler's wishes" (Zolotow, 118), he scrapped the scene and substituted the ending we know, with Keyes's last line "Closer than that, Walter" and his lighting Neff's cigarette. Wilder was to say later that the two best scenes he ever shot were the original ending of *Double Indemnity* and the original opening of *Sunset Boulevard* (the gas chamber sequence and the morgue sequence, respectively [168–69]), and that neither made it into these films' final versions.

In spite of their stormy collaboration on the script (Chandler would say that working with Wilder had taken years off his life, and Wilder for years afterward would become apoplectic at the mention of Chandler's name), they produced a brilliant screenplay, which Wilder turned into a critical and commercial hit, a film like Huston's *The Maltese Falcon* and Hawks's *The Big Sleep,* which ends up on everyone's top-ten list of Hollywood movies from its golden age. *Double Indemnity* was nominated for seven Academy Awards in 1944: best picture, director, screenplay, actress, cinematography, score, and sound. But it won none, the award for best picture as well as best director going to Leo Mc-Carey's *Going My Way*. Wilder always attributed his film's loss to the fact that both *Double Indemnity* and *Going My Way* were Paramount pictures and that the studio had thrown its entire support behind McCarey's heart-warming comedy rather than Wilder's noir film (in those days studio employees who were members of the Academy of Motion Picture Arts and Sciences were expected to vote as a bloc for the picture the studio was pushing for the Oscar). Wilder also thought Paramount's decision not to support his film was their way of trying to repair their relationship with the Hays Office for having made the film in the first place. Whatever the decision of the Academy, *Double Indemnity* has long ago won the only award worth winning, the award only time bestows. The film gave its two leading actors (MacMurray and Stanwyck) the best roles of their careers and Edward G. Robinson the best supporting role of his. Predictably enough, Fred MacMurray, whose work up to that point had been in light comedy, had never wanted to play Walter Neff, fearing the role would "ruin his happy-go-lucky image," but Wilder finally badgered him into it, and the studio "suddenly let him play it" in order to "punish him," to "cut him down to size," for having fought "with the studio over his new contract" (Zolotow, 117–18). Instead of ruining his image, the role added a new dimension to MacMurray's screen persona. He went on to star in several more noir films, and he worked with Wilder again in what would be the best supporting role of *his* life, in *The Apartment* (1960).

As we've seen, the noir genre was an important stepping-stone in many Hollywood careers. It gave John Huston his first chance to direct with *The Maltese Falcon* as well as another of his best films, *The Asphalt Jungle*, in 1950. It allowed Humphrey Bogart as a contract player at Warner Bros. to move from leads in B-pictures and second leads in A-pictures to playing leads in A-pictures and then to being the biggest star at his studio. It allowed Dick Powell to change the direction of his acting career from musical comedy to serious drama, with the role of Philip Marlowe in *Murder My Sweet*, and then to add additional careers in directing and producing, with the 1952 noir film *Split Second*. And it significantly enlarged the range of Fred MacMurray's screen persona, while it took Robinson's in a different direction.

II

In his autobiography Edward G. Robinson says that when he was offered the role of Barton Keyes, a role he described as "the third lead" in the picture, he "debated accepting it" but reasoned, "at my age it was time to begin thinking of character roles, to slide into middle and old age. . . . I was never the handsome leading man; I could proceed with my career growing older in roles that would grow older, too."[6] After playing Barton Keyes, some of Robinson's best roles were to be not just as older men but as men facing the fact of their own aging, like Professor Richard Wanley in Fritz Lang's 1944 *The Woman in the Window*, the film Robinson starred in immediately after *Double Indemnity*. Robinson plays a happily married man who, through a chance encounter, becomes involved with a beautiful woman (Joan Bennett) and with murder. Early in the film Wanley, who's already described himself as "a middle-aged man," discusses their time of life with two friends the same age, saying "We're three old crocks. . . . I hate this stolidity, the stodginess I'm beginning to feel. To me it's the end of the brightness of life, the end of spirit and adventure."

In a similar vein the character Robinson plays in Fritz Lang's 1945 *Scarlet Street*, the meek little cashier Christopher Cross, is an unhappily married man whose only enjoyment in life comes from the paintings he does in his spare time. His predicament is summed up at the start when another man his age says to him, "When we're young, we have dreams that never pan out, but we go on dreaming." By one of those unlucky chances that were a staple of noir films, Cross becomes involved with a beautiful, unscrupulous young woman (again played by Joan Bennett)—a woman to whom he says, "I'm old enough to be your father"—falls in love with her, is ultimately driven to kill her once he discovers her treachery, and then lets another man go to the electric chair for the murder, while he survives as a ruined man, a homeless derelict. Indeed, even in the role of Johnny Rocco, the deported mob boss in John Huston's 1949 *Key Largo* (in which Robinson again plays "third lead," this time to Bogart and Bacall), a role that gave him a chance to recapture some of the power of those earlier gangster characters that had made him a star, Robinson once again plays someone trying to act as if things haven't changed, as if the times haven't passed him by. But it is in the role of John Triton, the clairvoyant in John Farrow's 1948 *Night Has a Thousand Eyes*, that Robinson gives his deepest and most moving performance from this stage of his career, as "a lonely and forlorn man" (to use Chandler and Wilder's description of Barton Keyes after Neff's execution) confronting both his own aging and the fate that has pursued him for most of his life.

If one were to arrange the noir films we've been discussing along a scale running from those with scripts that made the fewest alterations in their adapted novels to those that made the most, then clearly Huston's *The Maltese Falcon* and Walsh's *High Sierra* would be at the "least-altered" end of the scale, Hawks's *The Big Sleep* and Wilder's *Double Indemnity* somewhere in the middle, and Farrow's *Night Has a Thousand Eyes* at the "most-altered" end, for the screenplay of Farrow's film, written by Barré Lyndon and Jonathan Latimer, shifts the entire focus of the book, making the clairvoyant (a peripheral character, Jeremiah Tompkins, in the novel) the film's central figure. Both Lyndon and Latimer were experienced screenwriters by the time they worked on *Night Has a Thousand Eyes.* Lyndon, an English playwright, had come to Hollywood in 1941 to write the screenplay for Henry Hathaway's *Sundown* from his own magazine serial, and he would go on to write the scripts for, among others, John Brahm's psychological thrillers *The Lodger* (1944) and *Hangover Square* (1945) and Henry Hathaway's *The House on 92nd Street* (1945) before working with Latimer on Woolrich's novel. He would subsequently work on the screenplays for DeMille's *The Greatest Show on Earth* (1952) and Byron Haskin's *The War of the Worlds* (1953).[7]

In contrast, Latimer was from the American Midwest and had come to screenwriting from a background in journalism and hard-boiled detective fiction. In the 1930s he wrote several novels featuring an often-inebriated private detective named Bill Crane. Several of the novels were made into films, and Latimer began writing for the movies in 1939. Before working on *Night Has a Thousand Eyes* he wrote or collaborated on the screenplays for, among others, Roy Del Ruth's *Topper Returns* (1941); Stuart Heisler's *The Glass Key* (1942), from the Hammett novel; Irving Pichel's *They Won't Believe Me* (1946); and John Farrow's *The Big Clock* (1947), from the Kenneth Fearing novel. During his long career Latimer worked on screenplays for ten of Farrow's films as well as adapting or writing over ninety scripts for the Perry Mason television series. Latimer had settled in La Jolla, California, in 1938, and after service in the navy in World War II, he returned there, where he became friends with Raymond Chandler, another La Jolla resident.[8]

In making the clairvoyant the central figure in the film, Lyndon and Latimer's screenplay opts for the character in the novel with the greatest dramatic potential. Recall that in the book the central figures are Jean Reid and police detective Tom Shawn, who struggle to prevent the death that has been fore-seen for Jean's father, Harlan, and that the effect of their progressive failure to protect him is a mounting sense of inescapable doom. But since their ever-in-creasing helplessness and passivity were unlikely to play well on the screen, the screenwriters' decisions—to foreground the clairvoyant, to give him both a personal stake in the lives of the people whose deaths he foresees and a nagging sense that his previsions somehow bring about the events they predict—were clearly intended to increase dramatic tension by centering the film's conflict within this character's psyche. Indeed, the screenwriters may also have been influenced in their decision about the central character by an excellent 1935 British film called *The Clairvoyant,* starring Claude Rains and Fay Wray and directed by Maurice Elvey, about a fake mind-reader who performs in English music halls and who discovers during one performance that in the presence of a strange young woman, who apparently channels the power of second sight for him, he can foresee the future.

Farrow's film begins with a view of the Los Angeles railroad yards at night. Elliot Carson (John Lund) is searching for his fiancée, Jean Courtland (Gail Russell). He finds her gloves on the ground, then her purse with its contents scattered about, and then he sees her on a catwalk over the tracks preparing to jump in front of an approaching train. Carson prevents her from commit-ting suicide and takes her to a restaurant, where they meet John Triton, who had told Carson where to find Jean. In typical noir fashion (voice-over and flashback), Triton then tells Carson and Jean how he first became aware of his powers of second sight and the history of his connection with Jean and her father. In the 1920s Triton was part of a mind-reading act in vaudeville with his fiancée, Jenny (Virginia Bruce), and his best friend, Whitney Courtland (Jerome Cowan). While performing his trick mental feats one night in a small town in Louisiana, Triton suddenly has a vision that an audience member's child is in danger, and he tells the child's mother to go home immediately. The act continues, and Triton dismisses the incident, but after the show the child's parents return to the theater to tell him their small son had gotten hold of some matches, set his bed on fire and been burned, and that they'd taken him to the hospital and now want to ask Triton if the son will be all right. Triton says he doesn't know. After that incident Triton's visions come again at odd moments. On one occasion he sees that a certain horse will win a race or a certain stock will go up. Whitney Courtland bets on the horse and buys the stock, and he, Triton, and Jenny share in the profits.

Then one rainy afternoon in Wichita, Triton is leaving the theater when a newsboy asks him how the St. Louis Cardinals will do that year; Triton says that if their pitching holds up they'll be right up on top, but suddenly he has a vision that the newsboy will be run down by a car that day. He starts to warn him about crossing streets but doesn't, thinking that in telling people what he foresees he somehow sets in motion a mechanism that makes the events come true. Instead, he impulsively gives the boy money so he can go to Triton's evening show, hoping this will keep him off the streets. But the boy is so excited by his sudden windfall that he takes off at a dead run to tell his mother and is struck by a car and killed. Triton begins to realize that, though he can foresee tragic events, he can't intervene to alter them or, rather, that his intervention becomes part of the chain of events that makes the prediction come true. That evening during his performance he has yet another vision in which he sees that if he and Jenny marry they will have a child and Jenny will die in childbirth. To protect Jenny from this, he decides to leave without saying a word, separating himself from those close to him and from his former life. But before going he gives Courtland one last tip on investing in the Comanche Hills oilfield in Oklahoma, knowing that this will make his fortune and that Courtland will take care of Jenny.

Triton takes the first train heading west, gets off in a deserted gold mining town in Arizona, and stays there for the next five years. During those years Courtland marries Jenny, and later Triton sees in a newspaper obituary that Jenny has died in childbirth. He also sees in a newspaper article that the wealthy oilman Whitney Courtland has moved his headquarters to Los Angeles and that he lives there with his young daughter, Jean. Explaining that he'd simply become too lonely living in the deserted town, Triton moves to Los Angeles, "drawn," as he says, "by a strange sort of compulsion to be near the only friend I had on earth." But once there he never makes contact with Courtland, preferring to live and work in obscurity; he never "risks fate," as he says, by trying to see Courtland and his daughter, except on one occasion, when he reads in the paper that Jean is making her debut and he stands in the crowd outside a hotel to get a glimpse of Jean and her father as they enter for the debutante ball. They pass without seeing him, but as they pass Triton suddenly has a hazy vision of airplane wreckage. He dismisses it, but three months later the vision comes into sharp focus when he hears on the radio that wealthy oilman Whitney Courtland is flying his own plane from New York to Los Angeles trying to break the transcontinental speed record. Triton goes to the Courtland mansion to tell Jean that she must contact her father and stop the flight. He persuades Jean to call the Kansas City airport, where Courtland is due to stop to refuel, and tell Courtland that John Triton says he's had a vision of a plane crashing. Jean calls, but Courtland's plane has already left. Triton slips away without saying anything more.

The next morning Jean and Elliot Carson show up at Triton's shabby furnished room. Courtland's plane is overdue, and Jean wants to know if Triton can tell them where it is. Triton says he had a vision of it crashing in the mountains, and then he suddenly stares at Jean and says, "You have a maid, a thin, dark girl." Jean replies, "Yes—Edna," and Triton says, "Well, get rid of her before your brooch, your sapphire . . . " He pauses, then says, "It doesn't matter. It won't make any difference." Before Jean can ask what he means, a news bulletin on the radio interrupts them announcing that the wreckage of Whitney Courtland's plane has been found by forest rangers near Gallup, New Mexico, and that Courtland is dead. Jean and Carson abruptly leave, but Jean returns to see Triton a week later to tell him that her sapphire brooch and her maid Edna have disappeared, "just as you said they would." Then Jean says, "I remember you said it wouldn't make any difference. You meant I was going to die, didn't you?" When Triton's silence confirms her suspicion, she asks, "How soon and where?" And when he replies, "Within a few days, at night, under the stars," Jean faints, and Triton finishes his voice-over and flashback narration.

Clearly, it was Jean's despair at the prediction of her death that had led her to attempt suicide, but Triton, after having narrated the events that led up to his sending Carson to save her, pleads with Carson to help him again in preventing her death. Carson asks what Triton wants him to do, and Triton says that if he could only see more clearly the place where Jean lay dead in his vision, then they could keep her from ever going there. Carson says he'll do what he can, and he and Jean leave the restaurant. But suspecting that Triton is a con man, Carson calls the police and has an interview with special prosecutor Melville Weston (Roman Bohnen), who calls in police Lieutenant Shawn (William Demarest). Shawn gives several plausible alternative explanations of how Triton could have known some of the things he predicted, and he reveals that Courtland's plane crash wasn't an accident, that the aircraft had been tampered with.

Carson, along with Shawn and several policemen, go to Jean's home to guard her. They find Jean there, as well as three of her father's business associates who are trying to settle his affairs—her father's secretary, Richard Vinson

(Richard Webb); his lawyer, Mr. Myers (Luis Van Rooten); and a Mr. Gilman (John Alexander), president of Midtide Oil, with which Courtland's company was planning a merger. They also find that Jean has invited Triton to stay in the house until the predicted time of death has passed, since Triton thinks that he's the only person who might be able to save her. Lieutenant Shawn agrees to let Triton stay if he remains in his room at night with armed policemen outside. Later that evening, in his room, Triton has another prevision while gazing at his image in a mirror, a series of disjointed images, and when Carson comes to see him, he tells him the details: "I saw a flower crushed under a heel, a sudden hot wind that shook the windows, a vase shattered on the floor, and I heard a voice saying, 'There's no danger now.' And then I saw her again lying under the stars and by her . . . something I don't understand at all, something that looked like the feet of a lion. Why, I know this sounds ridiculous but I saw them clearly, big front paws with curved talons almost touching her head." Triton had also seen when Jean's death would occur: "Tomorrow night, as the clock strikes eleven." And he says he saw one more thing, about himself, but "that's not important."

In the meantime, Jean is asleep in her bedroom, and we see a figure in dark silhouette approach her bed with a pillow, press it down over her face, and try to smother her. She struggles and screams, and her screams bring Shawn and Carson running. Meanwhile Triton leaves his room, telling the two police guards that something's wrong. One of the policemen draws his gun and warns him to halt, but Triton keeps walking. The cop pulls the trigger twice, the gun doesn't fire, but as soon as Triton is out of sight the gun goes off. Triton walks into Jean's bedroom as Carson and Shawn are asking her what happened. On seeing Triton out of his room, Shawn accuses him of having tried to smother Jean, arrests him, and sends him downtown to jail in the custody of the two policemen who'd been guarding him. The next day special prosecutor Weston has two experts in parapsychology interview Triton. Triton tries to convince them and Weston that his previsions are real and that he must be allowed to return to Jean before eleven o'clock that night: "This gift which I never asked for and I don't understand has brought me only unhappiness. Over a period of twenty years at various times I have foreseen tragic occurrences, and no matter what I did I couldn't prevent them coming true. . . . Why was this gift given to me and why was this other power withheld, this power to turn evil into good. . . . This is my only chance, my last one. There is a possibility that this time I . . . I may disrupt this chain of events . . . , defy fate and save Miss

Courtland." Finally, by predicting the suicide of a person being held in the jail, Triton convinces Weston to take him back to Jean's home, and they leave.

Back at the Courtland mansion, several of Triton's predictions—a flower crushed under a heel, a sudden wind that shakes the windows, a vase shattered on the floor—have already come true, and Jean, Carson, and Shawn have gathered in the living room waiting for eleven o'clock. There is a movement, unnoticed by the room's occupants, behind the floor-to-ceiling drapes in one corner next to a grandfather clock; a hand slides from behind the drapes and moves the minute hand on the clock ahead five minutes. When the clock sounds eleven, Jean, Carson, and Shawn all breathe a sigh of relief, and Jean tells Carson she'd like to be alone for a moment in her secret place in the garden. She leaves the room and goes down into the garden just as Triton and Weston enter the front door. Shawn tells them that everything is fine, the predicted hour is past, and Jean is safe, but Weston, looking at his watch, says that it's still two minutes to eleven, and Triton rushes off to find her.

Jean is in the garden standing on a terrace looking down at the city lights far below when Mr. Gilman steps out from behind some ferns, revealing, as he pushes the ferns aside, the concrete statue of a lion with massive paws. As he approaches Jean from behind, the clock from a distant steeple begins to chime eleven. Jean turns just as Gilman says, "There's no danger now," and Jean says, "A voice saying . . . 'There's no danger now'—he must have meant . . . " Suddenly, Gilman grabs Jean and tries to throw her off the terrace, but Triton comes rushing up and knocks Gilman down. The policemen, who've been running after Triton, misinterpret what's happening, and the cop whose weapon had failed to fire the night before shoots Triton and kills him. Jean tells them that Triton hadn't been trying to kill her but had saved her from Gilman. Courtland's lawyer, Mr. Myers, who'd also come running into the garden, tells the police that Gilman would have stood to make a fortune if the merger of his and Courtland's companies fell through, as it would have if Courtland and Jean, his heir, both died. Someone notices that a letter has fallen out of Triton's coat, a letter addressed to Carson. He reads it aloud: "When you read this, I will be lying at your feet, killed by the revolver that failed to fire last night. No one is to blame. My death was as certain as the other events I saw in my mirror. Some of you who have just seen me die will doubt me, will believe these events to have been contrived by me. Or you may call them a series of weird coincidences. But I know that you, Carson, and some of the others will not dismiss them so easily. My own strange fate must make you ponder for a moment, must make you realize that there are things on earth still hidden from us, secret things, dark and mysterious." As the letter ends, the camera pans upward to the starry skies and Victor Young's haunting musical score swells to a crescendo.

John Farrow's film version of *Night Has a Thousand Eyes* was neither a critical nor a box-office success when it appeared in 1948, and in his autobiography Robinson dismissed the movie as "unadulterated hokum that I did for the money" (Robinson, 254), but over the years it has become something of a noir classic. The film's power is a function of Farrow's taut direction, of Robinson's and Gail Russell's moving performances, and of what Lyndon and Latimer's script made out of Woolrich's novel. With a different central character, the film has a different emotional dynamic from the novel, one focused on the paradoxical condition of a superhuman gift (second sight) that becomes a curse. John Triton (a name with a certain mythological ring) reminds one of an ancient figure like Cassandra, King Priam's daughter, who had been given the gift of prophecy by Apollo to win her love, but who, once the god turned against her, saw the gift become a two-edged sword when no one believed what she foretold. In Triton's case, he is suspicious of his power from the start; he doesn't understand how it works or why it came to him. And even when his previsions are profitable (as with the winning racehorse or the stock tips), bringing him, Jenny, and Courtland much-needed funds, he feels, as does Jenny, that accepting the winnings resulting from his gift implicates him in the disasters it foretells, that he can't benefit from the good things without bearing responsibility for the bad or at least responsibility for not having prevented disastrous events of which he had foreknowledge. As he tells the two parapsychologists, he doesn't understand why this gift was given to him and "this other power withheld, the power to turn evil into good." But when he foresees Jean's death, he knows he has to make a decision: "There had to be some way to avert the tragedy that I'd seen. My running away, my not speaking hadn't saved Jenny. Now I wondered if I should try the other course—challenge fate." But what Triton foresees in that final vision (the one full of details such as the crushed flower, the broken vase, etc.) is his own death, and what he understands is that he *can* successfully challenge fate and prevent Jean's death, but only at the price of dying in her place.

One of the things that makes the film so moving is how completely Robinson inhabits the role of Triton, the role of a lonely, reclusive, aging man who has been progressively deprived of a life—the companionship of his best friend, the love of the woman he was going to marry, and the child they would have had. (Indeed, some critics have suggested that Robinson's performance as a man who tells the truth and yet is met with skepticism and disbelief was emotionally informed by his own experiences in 1947–48 trying to combat both the Hollywood blacklist and accusations of his own "intensive affiliation with Communist front organizations" [Robinson, 256]).

But what accounts for most of the film's power is the way it evokes and manipulates the feeling of the uncanny. In his 1919 essay "The 'Uncanny,'" Freud says that "if psycho-analytic theory is correct in maintaining that every affect belonging to an emotional impulse, whatever its kind, is transformed, if it is repressed, into anxiety, then among instances of frightening things there must be one class in which the frightening element can be shown to be something repressed which *recurs*. This class of frightening things would then constitute the uncanny."[9] Freud says that we can "recognize the dominance in the unconscious mind of a 'compulsion to repeat' proceeding from the instinctual impulses and probably inherent in the very nature of the instincts—a compulsion powerful enough to overrule the pleasure principle, lending to certain aspects of the mind their daemonic character and still very clearly expressed in the impulses of small children" and further that "whatever reminds us of this inner 'compulsion to repeat' is perceived as uncanny" (Freud, 17:238). The uncanny affect associated with this compelled repetition "recalls the sense of helplessness experienced in some dream-states" (237)—and, I would also add, recalls the sense of helplessness that is our earliest, deepest, and most anxiety-ridden experience of life, the infant's total helplessness either to control his environment or even exercise motor control of his own body.

Drawing a parallel between the general mental development of the human race from primitive times to the present and a contemporary individual's mental development from infancy to adulthood, Freud says that his analysis of the uncanny leads us "back to the old, animistic conception of the universe" held by humans in primitive times:

> This was characterized by the idea that the world was peopled with the spirits of human beings; by the subject's narcissistic overvaluation of his own mental processes; by the belief in the omnipotence of thoughts and the technique of magic based on that belief; by the attribution to various outside persons and things of carefully graded magical powers. . . . It seems as if each one of us has been through a phase of individual development corresponding to this animistic

stage in primitive men, that none of us has passed through it without preserving certain residues and traces of it which are still capable of manifesting themselves, and that everything which now strikes us as 'uncanny' fulfills the condition of touching those residues of animistic mental activity within us and bringing them to expression. (Freud, 17:240–41)

This sense that the uncanny attaches to "impressions that seek to confirm the omnipotence of thoughts and the animistic mode of thinking in general, after we have reached a stage at which, in our *judgement,* we have abandoned such beliefs" (Freud, 17:241n1) recalls Tom Shawn's remark in the novel, after the terrible night when Reid died, that he and Jean "were getting scars on their souls, the sort of scars people got in the Dark Ages, when they believed in devils and black magic,"[10] and Lieutenant Shawn's remark in the film when several of the details Triton had foreseen have come true, "You know, my old Irish grandmother used to tell stories about banshees and leprechauns and blind singers with second sight. I always used to think she was kidding, but now I'm beginning to wonder."

Lieutenant Shawn's remark suggests that the events he's witnessed have made him uncertain about which worldview to believe, his adult realistic one or the childish animistic one imbibed at his grandmother's knee. Freud points out that the psychiatrist E. Jentsch, in a 1906 paper on the uncanny, had ascribed "the essential factor" in "the feeling of uncanniness to intellectual uncertainty," the uncanny being mentally disorienting, "something one does not know one's way about in" (Freud, 17:221). This sense of an uncertainty between two worldviews evokes a pervasive doubleness that Freud associates with the uncanny, beginning with its very name in German. He notes that the word for the "uncanny," *unheimlich,* is the opposite of the word for "what is familiar" or homely, *heimlich;* but he also notes that "among its different shades of meaning the word '*heimlich*' expresses one which is identical with its opposite," for *heimlich* can mean both "what is familiar and agreeable" and "what is concealed and kept out of sight," and this second meaning coincides with Schelling's sense of the *unheimlich* as what "ought to have remained secret and hidden but has come to light" (220–25). Freud adds that *heimlich* is a word whose meaning "develops in the direction of ambivalence" (226) and that "the uncanny [*unheimlich*] is something which is secretly familiar [*heimlich-heimisch*], which has undergone repression and then returned from it, and that everything that is uncanny fulfills this condition" (245). Thus, the mental doubleness (the intellectual uncertainty) associated with the feeling of the uncanny corresponds to a linguistic doubleness Freud finds in the German names, which in turn corresponds to an emotional doubleness, or ambivalence, experienced by the adult self when confronted by the recurrence of something secret and familiar that has been rendered unfamiliar by repression. Because this recurrence—the return of the repressed—is involuntary, capable of overruling the will and the pleasure-principle, it creates ambivalence by reawakening in the adult mind a sense of childish helplessness in the face of this uncertainty.

Among the factors "which turn something frightening into something uncanny" (Freud, 17:243), Freud lists animism, magic, the figure of the double, the castration complex, the omnipotence of thoughts, man's attitude to death, and involuntary repetition—the last three being those most obviously associated with Triton's situation. First, Triton thinks of his previsions as instances of his own thought's power to cause the events they envision. Second, since the most significant of Triton's previsions concern the deaths of those he loves, man's ultimate helplessness before the universal human fate is evoked by Triton's powerlessness not only to alter the events he foresees but even to prevent his visions from coming. And third, just as the coming of his previsions is involuntary and repetitive, so too the events that occur in his mind's eye are automatically, that is, involuntarily, repeated in the real world, this latter form of repetition representing a kind of temporal doubling. And it is with doubling, and in particular with the figure of the double, that an uncanniness from a deeper and less obvious source makes itself felt in the film.

Citing Otto Rank's work on "the theme of the 'double'" and the figure's connection "with reflections in mirrors, with shadows, with guardian spirits, with the belief in the soul and the fear of death," Freud notes that "the 'double' was originally an insurance against the destruction of the ego, an 'energetic denial of the power of death,' as Rank says; and probably the 'immortal' soul was the first 'double' of the body. The invention of doubling as a preservation against extinction has its counterpart in the language of dreams" as well as in the ancient Egyptians' desire "to develop the art of making images of the dead in lasting materials. Such ideas, however, have sprung from the soil of unbounded self-love, from the primary narcissism which dominates the mind of the child and of primitive man. But when this stage has been surmounted, the 'double' reverses its aspect. From having been an assurance of immortality, it becomes the uncanny harbinger of death" (Freud, 17:234–35).

Noting that "the idea of the 'double' does not necessarily disappear with the passing of primary narcissism," Freud contends that as the ego develops, an agency is formed "to stand over against the rest of the ego" with "the function of observing and criticizing the self and exercising a censorship within the mind" (i.e., the conscience), "an agency . . . able to treat the rest of the ego like an object," and that this agency "renders it possible to invest the old idea of a 'double' with a new meaning and to ascribe a number of things to it—above all, those things which seem to self-criticism to belong to the old surmounted narcissism of earliest times" (235). He adds that "when poets complain that two souls dwell in the human breast, and when popular psychologists talk of the splitting of people's egos, what they are thinking of is this division (in the sphere of ego-psychology) between the critical agency and the rest of the ego, and not the antithesis discovered by psycho-analysis between the ego and what is unconscious and repressed. It is true that the distinction between these two antitheses is to some extent effaced by the circumstance that foremost among the things that are rejected by the criticism of the ego are derivatives of the repressed" (17:235n2).

In this latter passage Freud outlines the psychological mechanism of splitting and doubling that creates the figure of the double, and particularly the figure as it takes shape in literature. A division is created in the self when the ego, through the self-criticizing agency of the conscience, treats "the rest of the ego like an object" in order to censor or suppress those aspects of behavior that are felt to be incompatible with the adult ego, aspects that are childish, animistic, brutal, shameful, etc. This congeries of rejected traits, tendencies, desires becomes in effect an "other" self in relation to the ego, a dark self as opposed to the ego's bright self, a slave to its master. And because among these rejected traits, the foremost are those derived from the repressed, this antithetical self has as well an unconscious component, one whose content is endowed with that instinctual compulsion to repeat inherent in repressed material. In the form that double stories in literature characteristically take, this compulsion to repeat, this return of the repressed, occurs when a mentally unstable individual projects this suppressed/repressed antithetical self outward either onto a hallucinated or an imaginary figure, for example, a shadow or mirror image (as in the case of Poe's male-male double story "William Wilson") or onto another person who in some way resembles or is related to the unstable individual (as in the case of Poe's most fully developed male-female double story, "The Fall of the House of Usher," whose influence on Woolrich's novel we examined earlier). The mentally unstable person experiences this externally projected antithetical self as threatening, as that unfamiliar/familiar "other" that returns and tries to reverse the master/slave relationship by asserting its independence from, and then its mastery over, the ego. Characteristically, a struggle ensues in which one or the other is defeated and destroyed, but since these two are halves of the same person, the destruction of one ultimately means the destruction of both.

One of the first things Triton tells us about his previsions, those images of future events that suddenly arise unbidden in his mind, is that he doesn't know where they come from, whether from outside or inside the self, and that he can neither will them to come nor will them to stop. If they come from outside, their source is something more powerful than the self, and if they come from inside, their source is a part of the self beyond the control of the will or the conscious mind. In either case these previsions rob the ego of its self-mastery, and Triton's uncertainty as to whether this is an internal or external power corresponds to the psychic mechanism in which the split occurs inside the self but is then projected outside and embodied.

In order to comprehend how completely the figure of the double structures Triton's story, we must consider one further observation of Freud's about this figure in literature. He says that what gets incorporated into the figure of the double is not only material that is "offensive . . . to the criticism of the ego" but "also all the unfulfilled but possible futures to which we still like to cling in phantasy, all the strivings of the ego which adverse external circumstances have crushed, and all our suppressed acts of volition which nourish in us the illusion of Free Will" (Freud, 17:236). With this in mind, consider Triton's situation at the time of his first previsions. He is part of a male-male-female triangle of which the other two members are his best friend, Whitney Courtland, and his fiancée, Jenny, and when the previsions start to come, their results begin to sort themselves in an odd way, that is, all the fortunate results are welcomed and taken advantage of by Courtland while all the unfortunate results weigh ever more heavily on Triton's conscience. The effect of this psychic power, which overrules Triton's will and divides its results this way, makes Triton and his best friend each other's antithetical doubles. This situation becomes even clearer when Triton leaves to save Jenny, for then Courtland, made rich by Triton's tips, proceeds to usurp the rest of Triton's life by marrying the woman he loved and fathering the child that would have been his.

Once the viewer understands the doubling between Triton and Courtland,

Triton's explanation of why, after having lived as a recluse for five years, he decided to move to Los Angeles when he read that Courtland had relocated the headquarters of his oil company there takes on a new significance. Triton says that he'd been "drawn by a strange sort of compulsion to be near the only friend I had on earth." As he tells Jean and Carson,

> It was a lonely life, but it was pleasant to be near Court and his daughter. I read about them in the papers, and in my room where I ate and slept and worked, I could go to the window and see the skyscraper he built—the Comanche Building. Only once in all that time did I risk fate by going near either of you. That was three months ago. It was the night of your debut at the Mayfield Hotel. . . . I watched you leave the limousine and walk towards the doors holding tight to Court's arm, and for a moment it was almost as though the twenty years had never been, as though it was Court and Jenny going into the hotel—and then just as you disappeared, something happened. I had a fleeting glimpse of wreckage, the wreckage of an airplane. It was a faint impression, blurred and hazy like a double-exposed negative.

That Triton is drawn "by a strange sort of compulsion" to be near his double is just what one would expect given that the unconscious, instinctual "compulsion to repeat" drives the repressed antithetical self to return. And what Courtland represents for Triton is the life Triton might have had, had he not experienced his gift as a curse. For Triton, Courtland embodies all those "unfulfilled but possible futures to which we still like to cling in phantasy, all the strivings of the ego which adverse external circumstances have crushed." And surely it is significant that when Triton catches a glimpse of Courtland and Jean outside the hotel, the image seems to turn into one of Courtland and Jenny, one that evokes the full measure of what Triton has lost to his friend, the latter image seeming to bleed through or be superimposed on that of Courtland and Jean, thus focusing our attention on the final image with which Triton describes his prevision. Since the double is often experienced as "the uncanny harbinger of death," it is not surprising that when Triton risks seeing his double again after almost twenty years, he immediately foresees the plane wreck that will kill Courtland; nor is it surprising that this prevision involves Triton in a chain of events inevitably leading to his own death as well. And it is surely no coincidence that the language the screenwriters give Triton to describe the visual quality of foreseeing his double's death depicts that image as being "blurred and hazy like a *double-exposed* negative" (my italics).

The emotional affect associated with the double is, as I've said, ambivalence, with the figure being "an assurance of immortality" in the original state of "primary narcissism," which "dominates in the child and in primitive man" but reversing its aspect "when that stage has been surmounted" (Freud 17:235), both in the human race and in the individual, and becoming something fearful, a threatening, alienated part of the self. Certainly this ambivalence should alert us to a possible doubleness in Triton's motives when he decides to "risk" seeing his double again after twenty years. For though Triton calls Courtland "my best friend on earth" and though Courtland may represent for Triton the living embodiment of what could have been Triton's future, the cherished "might-have-been" to console him in his self-imposed loneliness, yet Courtland is also the figure who usurped Triton's life. Indeed, it would be odd if Triton, while feeling affection for his friend, didn't also feel a certain resentment (conscious or not), didn't experience an ambivalence that would both make him want to see that friend again and make him willing to risk what might happen to his double as a result of that seeing.

We know what does happen as soon as Triton sets eyes on him. Indeed, when Triton tells Jean and Carson that he'd had this glimpse of a plane's wreckage three months before the actual crash, Carson asks, "Look, if you saw all this three months ago, why did you wait?" And that is our question, too. One would think that even if the original vision of the wreck was blurred and hazy, as Triton says, still his knowledge of what his visions had portended in the past, particularly in regard to those close to him, ought to have moved him at once to tell his friend what he'd foreseen. He couldn't have been deterred by fear that Courtland wouldn't believe him, for if there was one person living who knew the efficacy of his predictions, it was Courtland. One wonders if perhaps Triton was motivated by the same timidity or passivity, the same desire not to get caught up in an involuntary chain of events, that had moved him not to speak in the case of the newsboy and then not to speak and run away in the case of Jenny. Just as the splitting up of the results of Triton's visions had previously caused the benefits to accrue to Courtland and the guilt to Triton, so this division had paralleled a split between the two men's characters. Courtland's response to Triton's gift had been to take action: he'd bet on the horserace, bought the stocks, invested in the oilfield; while Triton's reaction had been, as we said, essentially passive, a kind of paralysis of the will faced with these involuntary visions in which he first kept silent about what he'd seen and then abandoned all contact with human beings during the five years he'd lived as a recluse.

If we are right in thinking the film encourages us to speculate about Triton's ambivalence in waiting three months before trying to warn Courtland about the plane—indeed, in waiting till the very evening when Courtland tries to beat the transcontinental speed record (a time perhaps unconsciously determined so as to allow him both the excuse that he tried to save his double and yet the virtual assurance that his effort will fail)—then this questioning of motives is empowered by, and of a piece with, Carson's, Shawn's, and Weston's efforts during the film's second half to find a rational (albeit criminal) explanation for Triton's predictions. Recall that in the novel, the subplot of Harlan Reid's embezzling broker, Walter Myers, trying to blackmail Jeremiah Tompkins into serving as his cat's-paw in a scheme to get control of Reid's estate, a scheme that would have ultimately required both Reid's and Jean's death, is introduced precisely to validate the cops' (and our) uncertainty about whether Tompkins's second sight is real or part of a con game. In the film, the subplot of Gilman's involvement in the sabotage of Courtland's plane and his subsequent attempt to smother Jean serves the same purpose but with this further effect: that, within a scenario of doubling, the cops' and our own uncertainty about whether Triton's gift is real or fake reenforces the uncanniness of that other intellectual uncertainty, between an animistic and realistic worldview.

What results from Triton's seeing Courtland again after twenty years and his failure to warn his friend about what he'd foreseen certainly accords with the notion of Triton's ambivalence, his unconscious resentment of the man who'd usurped his life, for Courtland's death allows Triton to begin reclaiming that life by becoming in effect Jean's surrogate father, even to performing the supreme parental act of giving up his life to save hers. And as Triton begins to fill the father role vacated by Courtland's death, a sort of reversal-into-the-opposite characteristic of double stories occurs, which is to say, that once Triton takes the place of his double, he begins to move from a passive to an active role regarding his gift. He says that once he'd foreseen Jean's death, he knew there was "a decision" he "had to make": "My running away, my not speaking hadn't saved Jenny." So he decides to "try the other course—challenge fate."

While much of the uncanny effect of the film derives from the splitting and doubling between Triton and Courtland and from the intellectual uncertainty between a realistic and an animistic worldview created by Triton's previsions, there is yet another manifestation associated with the latter in the film. As an uncanny feeling can be caused by our uncertainty as to whether an inanimate object might be animated by a spirit, so it can also be caused by our uncertainty as to whether an animate being might only be a physical mechanism, such as a life-sized mechanical doll or an automaton (Freud's example of this from literature being the figure of Olympia in E. T. A. Hoffman's tale "The Sand Man"). In the film, Jean and Carson discuss at one point her sense of the inevitability of Triton's prediction. Carson urges her to resist such feelings, but Jean says, "If it's to be, there's nothing we can do about it." He replies, "I hate this . . . this terrible resignation. It's as though you were half-dead already, you're like a, well, like an automaton playing a part." And she says, "An automaton wound up for forty-eight hours" (the time left before the moment of her predicted death). Of course, the uncanny uncertainty evoked here isn't about whether Jean is a real human being or a wind-up automaton, but rather about the possible illusoriness of a prime indicator of human animation (of whether a being has a soul or not)—free will. If a human being's freedom of action isn't real, if everything a person does or endures is determined in advance, is simply an involuntary repetition of a preset pattern, then for all practical purposes a human being *is* an automaton, and Jean's resignation to the inevitability of Triton's prediction, her refusal to actively resist it, evokes this condition for Carson.

From everything we've said, one would judge that either or both of the film's writers were well acquainted with Freud's works. Two of Lyndon's most successful prior screenplays (*The Lodger* and *Hangover Square*) were for psychological thrillers, while Latimer's first Bill Crane detective novel, *Murder in the Madhouse* (1935), had psychiatrists as principal characters. Further, Hitchcock's 1945 film *Spellbound,* with its good psychiatrist (Ingrid Bergman) and its evil psychiatrist (Leo G. Carroll), its Freudian analysis of dream imagery, and its dream sequences designed by Salvador Dali, suggests the extent to which Freudianism was au courant in 1940s Hollywood, while Anatole Litvak's *The Snakepit,* which appeared in 1948 (the same year as *Night Has a Thousand Eyes*), suggests the extent to which mental illness had become a trendy subject for films. Although the two scientists Weston invites to question Triton are parapsychologists rather than psychiatrists, one of the explanations they offer for his often-convincing power of prophetic behavior is that he's so strongly delusional he's able to infect others with his fantasies—a judgment more psychiatric than otherwise.

III

That *Night Has a Thousand Eyes,* unlike the other films we've discussed in this chapter, was not particularly successful when it first appeared raises the question of whether the initial reaction of audiences and critics was affected by a confusion about its genre. Though it's clearly a noir film in many respects, some recent viewers, apparently seeking a more precise description of its special quality, have taken to designating its genre as "*noir* science fiction." One senses that it's the film's suprarational aspect this designation means to evoke, and yet it ultimately seems to me as accurate to call *Night Has a Thousand Eyes* a work of noir science fiction as it would be to use this term for a work such as *Oedipus Rex* (with its series of mind-boggling coincidences in the working out of an inexorable fate). Nevertheless, one understands why the "science fiction" label would come to mind given the era in which Farrow's film appeared, an era in which Hollywood produced some of the best movies ever made in this genre.

These movies generally fell into three main groups: The first were films about extraterrestrial beings (usually hostile) coming to earth—for example, Christian Nyby's 1951 *The Thing (From Another World),* produced by Howard Hawks; Robert Wise's 1951 *The Day the Earth Stood Still;* Jack Arnold's 1953 *It Came from Outer Space,* written for the screen by Ray Bradbury; Byron Haskin's 1953 *The War of the Worlds,* with a script by Barré Lyndon; William Cameron Menzies's 1953 *Invaders from Mars;* and Don Siegel's 1956 *The Invasion of the Body Snatchers.* The second were films about humans traveling in outer space–for example, Kurt Neumann's 1950 *Rocketship X-M,* Irving Pichel's 1950 *Destination Moon,* Rudolph Maté's 1951 *When Worlds Collide,* and Fred M. Wilcox's 1956 *Forbidden Planet;* and the third, about the dangers of atomic weapons or the side effects of radiation—for example, Gordon Douglas's *Them!* and Jack Arnold's *The Incredible Shrinking Man,* as well as both *Rocketship X-M* and *The Day the Earth Stood Still.* Generally speaking, the first group grew out of, and played upon, both the Cold War paranoia about alien forces at work among us and the post–World War II upsurge in UFO sightings; the second paralleled the period of America's early experiments in adapting captured German rocket technology to space travel; and the third reflected Cold War fears about nuclear testing in the atmosphere and a thermonuclear Armageddon. But Farrow's film predates the earliest of these science fiction movies, and its narrative lacks any appreciable "scientific" theme or motif that would lead to its being grouped with these films. (There are, of course, the two scientists from the university whom Weston calls in to question Triton, but their questioning amounts to nothing, and the scene only exists to serve as a delaying action, heightening the suspense over whether Triton will make it back to the Courtland mansion in time to save Jean.)

I would argue that the association of a film like *Night Has a Thousand Eyes* with the 1950s Hollywood science fiction genre resulted from looking back at Farrow's film through the lens of three of the most popular, best-written, and intellectually intriguing series in television history—Rod Serling's *The Twilight Zone* and *The Night Gallery,* and *The Outer Limits.* All three were composed of episodes that were either straightforward science fiction tales, tales of the uncanny like Farrow's film, or a combination of the two, and this intermingling of the two types of narratives undoubtedly influenced a retrospective categorization of *Night Has a Thousand Eyes* as noir science fiction.

But if I'm reluctant to categorize Farrow's film with this term, so too would I be to call it "*noir* fantasy fiction," a label linking it to films it has even less in common with than the sci fi movies of the fifties. In discussing Woolrich's novel, I employed at one point the term *noir philosophical/psychological fiction* to describe its subgenre, namely, a type of fiction that alters one condition of reality, then creates a more or less realistic narrative based on that alteration in order to render the familiar world of experience suddenly unfamiliar, allowing us to reexperience the familiar as if for the first time—in effect, to grasp the inherent strangeness of the human condition, of reflective self-consciousness, of space-time, etc. Similarly, Lyndon and Latimer's script for Farrow's film creates a narrative in which the sudden, unexplained recrudescence, within a modern setting, of a power associated with an earlier, animistic worldview gives the audience a renewed access to the type of fatalism that animated ancient drama. (Indeed, it was not without reason that I invoked *Oedipus Rex* earlier to suggest the fatalistic effect of the film.) Such an intention on the screenwriters' part would not be surprising given that some of the most influential works of literary modernism had sought this sort of reaccess: for example, Faulkner's greatest novels—*The Sound and the Fury, Light In August,* and *Absalom, Absalom!*—which chronicle the decline of the Compson or Sutpen families (as if the curse of Southern slavery were like the curse on the house of Atreus) or evoke the doom that dogs Joe Christmas, Joanna Burden, and Gail Hightower as a result of something done by each of their grandfathers, are clearly in this vein. (According to the Americanist Charles Anderson, Faulkner told him in conversation that he reread the Greek tragedies once a year to this end.) And Eliot's so-called mythical method, discerned in Yeats's poetry and in Joyce's *Ulysses* and employed by Eliot in *The Waste Land,* also sought to recapture in modern scenarios the dramatic power of individuals reenacting ancient fated patterns.

If the dramatic force of Farrow's movie derives from its giving a modern audience an uncanny sense of the return of a surpassed or repressed fatalistic worldview (a kind of psychic ghost from the past), and if, therefore, the film has little in common with science fiction movies of the 1950s, then what films does it resemble? I can think of at least four that can be grouped with it in terms of uncanny affect, one that appeared before the Farrow film and three after. The first film is Lewis Allen's 1944 *The Uninvited,* the first serious ghost story done by a Hollywood studio, from a screenplay by Frank Partos and Dodie Smith and based on the novel *Uneasy Freehold,* by Dorothy Macardle. Like Farrow's film, it was a Paramount production, and one of its stars, Gail Russell (who plays Stella Meredith in Allen's ghost story), would go on to play Jean Courtland in Farrow's movie; while the composer of its musical score, Victor Young, would also write the music for *Night Has a Thousand Eyes* (the score of *The Uninvited* perhaps being best remembered for producing the popular song "Stella by Starlight"). The second is Jack Clayton's 1961 *The Innocents* from Henry James's "The Turn of the Screw," with a screenplay by William Archibald and Truman Capote, whose uncanniness is not a function of its simply being a ghost story but rather of the viewers' intellectual uncertainty as to whether the ghosts on screen are supposed to be real or are the hallucinations of an emotionally disturbed governess. The third film is Nicholas Roeg's 1973 *Don't Look Now,* with a screenplay by Allan Scott and Chris Bryant from a story by Daphne Du Maurier. Like *Night Has a Thousand Eyes,* Roeg's film is a tale of psychic prevision that reaccesses the ancient sense of a person's fate being predetermined (with the attendant possibility of its being foreseen). And the fourth is Irvin Kershner's 1978 *The Eyes of Laura Mars,* with a script by John Carpenter and David Zelag Goodman, in which the strange psychological connection between a Helmut Newton–type high fashion photographer (who specializes in scenes of mayhem) and a serial killer (who uses her photos as blueprints for his murders) develops into an uncanny psychic connection between the two as she is suddenly able to see through the killer's eyes as he stalks her friends and finally herself. It is to this small group of films with the power to create a sense of the uncanny that *Night Has a Thousand Eyes* by rights belongs.

Afterword

We've come a certain distance together since my questioning of an obsessive annual rereading of Hammett's *The Maltese Falcon* began this study, a starting point that ultimately led into an examination of a twentieth-century popular (not to say pulp) fiction genre whose origin was in a different kind of detective story, one that would eventually give birth to a novel of manners with a detective or crime interest. What began essentially as a men's genre—these hard-boiled detective stories first appeared in pulp magazines like *Black Mask*—was to become, when the novels were adapted for the screen in the early 1940s, a genre that increasingly appealed to women as well. With actresses as forceful as Mary Astor and Barbara Stanwyck portraying shrewd, dangerous women capable of outwitting, sexually manipulating, or killing the men they dealt with, these films presented, during the war years, an image of empowerment that had a special resonance for female viewers, many of whom were taking over jobs on the home front previously reserved for men. And in recent years, as more and more women have pursued careers in the business world, the underlying theme of so much hard-boiled fiction, concerned as it is with bosses and with balancing the demands of the office and home, has been as meaningful for female readers as for male.

In examining the conflict between the professional and the personal as it structures the narratives under discussion, I've characterized it at various moments as a conflict between work and love, but one can also see in retrospect that, particularly with Hammett's and Chandler's detectives, their work *is* their love, and that by as much as their work is that special *doing* that constitutes their *being*, this conflict between professional and personal is effectively one between love of self and love of another. One's sense of this becomes even clearer when we consider that Hammett and Chandler, in choosing to stage this conflict within the life of a private detective, were prompted not only by the need to make the professional activity interesting and glamorous enough for the conflict between the professional and the personal to be a real one capable of going in either direction but also by the fact that private detective work served as an ideal figuration for the professional choice both Hammett and Chandler had actually made in their lives: the decision to leave working in the business world as salaried employees in order to support themselves as fiction writers.

Hammett himself had explicitly drawn the analogy between detective work and detective writing in an exchange between the Continental Op and the writer Owen Fitzstephan in *The Dain Curse*. When the Op objects to Fitzstephan's becoming too inquisitive about the details of a case, the writer asks, "Are you—who make your living snooping—sneering about my curiosity about people?" and the Op replies that they're different because he does his snooping "with the object of putting people in jail, and I get paid for it, though not as much as I should." To which Fitzstephan retorts, "That's not different. . . . I do mine with the object of putting people in books, and I get paid for it, though not as much as I should" (22). As we noted earlier, the difference between the two is the way in which each gets paid: One is a salaried employee of a large agency, and the other is his own boss, owns the product of his labor, and receives a royalty for its use. To the extent that a person's own writing expresses the best of what he is mentally and emotionally—constitutes a written simulacrum of the self, a corpus of work that is the writer's other body, able to survive his death—then the level of devotion to, and satisfaction derived from, the work of creating a written self (a product with which the author has a more intimate relationship and owns more completely and inalienably than any mere physical work of his hand) seems the ultimate form of a *doing* that constitutes one's *being*. This ideal of a total commitment to the work of self-creation, to the work of making in words the best of their own being, which Hammett and Chandler had both found in becoming writers after leaving the business world, was to be embodied in the slightly less idealized, workaday-professional commitment of their detectives, Spade and Marlowe, and then thematized in the narratives of their adventures.

Of course, the beginning of a new branch of detective fiction in Hammett's and Chandler's narratives neither supplanted nor brought to a close the analytic detective story tradition from which hard-boiled fiction had originally differentiated itself. That older tradition of logic-and-deduction, puzzle narratives still remained, and remains today, as viable and popular a form in detective fiction as ever. But in substituting for the puzzle element in the older detective story form the theme of trying to become and stay one's own boss, with its resulting conflict between the detective's professional and personal lives, Hammett and Chandler gave the newer form a relevance to the lives of Americans that has kept hard-boiled fiction an appealing narrative genre through the century of its birth and well into the next.

Notes

O N E : "Where Their Best Interest Lies": Hammett's *The Maltese Falcon*

1. Dashiell Hammett, *The Maltese Falcon* (New York: Vintage, 1972), 64; hereafter cited in the text.
2. Sigmund Freud, *The Standard Edition of the Complete Psychological Works of Sigmund Freud*, 24 vols., trans. James Strachey et al. (London: Hogarth Press, 1955–78), 18:16.
3. Steven Marcus, "Dashiell Hammett and the Continental Op," in *The Critical Response to Dashiell Hammett*, ed. Christopher Metress (Westport, CT: Greenwood Press, 1994), 194; hereafter cited in the text.
4. Jean Pierre Chartier, "The Americans Are Making Dark Films Too," in *Perspectives on Film Noir*, ed. R. Barton Palmer (New York: G. K. Hall, 1996), 25–27.
5. Robert G. Porfirio, "No Way Out: Existential Motifs in Film Noir," in Palmer, *Perspectives on Film Noir*, 120.
6. Charles Gregory, "Living Life Sideways," in ibid., 155.
7. Nathaniel Hawthorne, *The Complete Short Stories of Nathaniel Hawthorne* (Garden City, NJ: Doubleday, 1959), 75; hereafter cited in the text.
8. Edgar Allan Poe, *Collected Works of Edgar Allan Poe*, 3 vols., ed. Thomas Ollive Mabbott (Cambridge: Belknap Press of Harvard University Press, 1969–78), 2:723; hereafter cited in the text.
9. F. Scott Fitzgerald, *The Great Gatsby*, ed. Matthew J. Bruccoli (New York: Cambridge University Press, 1991), 119.

T W O : Being Boss: Chandler's *The Big Sleep*

1. Frank MacShane, *The Life of Raymond Chandler* (New York: Penguin, 1978), 34; hereafter cited in the text.
2. Dashiell Hammett, *The Maltese Falcon* (New York: Vintage, 1972), 30.
3. Dashiell Hammett, "The Girl with the Silver Eyes," in *The Continental Op*, ed. Steven Marcus (New York: Vintage, 1975), 128.
4. Dashiell Hammett, *Red Harvest* (New York: Vintage, 1972), 59.
5. Dashiell Hammett, "The Assistant Murderer," in *Nightmare Town*, ed. Kirby McCauley et al. (New York: Knopf, 1999), 132.
6. Dashiell Hammett, *The Dain Curse* (New York: Vintage, 1972), 29; hereafter cited in the text.
7. Dashiell Hammett, "The Gutting of Couffignal," in *The Big Knockover*, ed. Lillian Hellman (New York: Vintage, 1972), 34.

8. Raymond Chandler, *The Big Sleep* (New York: Vintage, 1976), 7–8; hereafter cited in the text.

9. Raymond Chandler, "The Simple Art of Murder," in *The Simple Art of Murder* (New York: Ballantine, 1977), 20; hereafter cited in the text.

10. Raymond Chandler, *The Long Goodbye* (New York: Ballantine, 1973), 298; hereafter cited in the text.

11. Wallace Stevens, "The Noble Rider and the Sound of Words," in *The Necessary Angel* (New York: Vintage), 36.

12. Raymond Chandler, *Playback* (New York: Ballantine, 1978), 76; hereafter cited in the text.

13. Thomas Hiney, *Raymond Chandler: A Biography* (New York: Grove Press, 1997), 257; hereafter cited in the text.

14. Dashiell Hammett, *The Thin Man* (New York: Vintage, 1972), 6; hereafter cited in the text.

15. Ernest Hemingway, *The Sun Also Rises* (New York: Scribner's, 1926), 245.

16. F. Scott Fitzgerald, *Tender Is the Night* (New York: Scribner's, 1934), 161–62.

THREE: Beating the Boss: Cain's *Double Indemnity*

1. James M. Cain, *Three by Cain: "Serenade," "Love's Lovely Counterfeit," "The Butterfly"* (New York: Vintage, 1989), 355; hereafter cited in the text as "Pref."

2. Frank MacShane, *The Life of Raymond Chandler* (New York: Penguin, 1978), 101.

3. Roy Hoopes, *Cain: The Biograpghy of James M. Cain* (Carbondale: Southern Illinois University Press, 1982), 213; hereafter cited in the text.

4. James M. Cain, *Double Indemnity* (New York: Vintage, 1978), 17; hereafter cited in the text.

5. Edgar Allan Poe, "The Imp of the Perverse," in the *Collected Works of Edgar Allen Poe*, 3 vols., ed. Thomas Ollive Mabbott (Cambridge: Belknap Press of Harvard University Press, 1969–78), 3:1220.

6. James M. Cain, *The Postman Always Rings Twice* (New York: Vintage, 1978), 118; hereafter cited in the text.

7. Edgar Allan Poe, "The Black Cat," in *Collected Works*, 3:852.

8. F. Scott Fitzgerald, *The Last Tycoon* (New York: Scribner's, 1941), 28; hereafter cited in the text.

9. Ibid., 163. The sentence also appears in *The Notebooks of F. Scott Fitzgerald*. ed. Matthew J. Broccoli (New York: Harcourt, 1978), 58, item 428, and it appears as "I once thought there were no second acts in American lives" in Fitzgeralds's essay "My Lost City," in *The Crack-Up*, ed. Edmund Wilson (New York: New Directions, 1962), 31.

10. Matthew J. Bruccoli, *Some Sort of Epic Grandeur: The Life of F. Scott Fitzgerald* (New York: Harcourt Brace Jovanovich, 1981), 349.

11. Ernest Hemingway, *A Moveable Feast* (New York: Bantam, 1970), 188–89.

12. Dashiell Hammett, "The Gutting of Couffignal," in *The Big Knockover*, ed. Lillian Hellman (New York: Vintage, 1972), 34.

F O U R : Who's the Boss? W. R. Burnett's *High Sierra*

1. W. R. Burnett, *High Sierra* (New York: Bantam, 1950), 7; hereafter cited in the text.
2. W. R. Burnett, *Little Caesar* (New York: Carroll & Graf, 1986),132–33; hereafter cited in the text.
3. F. Scott Fitzgerald, *The Great Gatsby,* ed. Matthew J. Bruccoli (New York: Cambridge University Press, 1991), 51; hereafter cited in the text.
4. Matthew J. Bruccoli, *Some Sort of Epic Grandeur: The Life of F. Scott Fitzgerald* (New York: Harcourt Brace Jovanovich, 1981), 183.
5. Andre LeVot, *F. Scott Fitzgerald: A Life* (Garden City, NJ: Doubleday, 1983), 130.
6. Katherine Harper, "W. R. Burnett," in *American Hard-Boiled Crime Writers,* vol. 226 of *Dictionary of Literary Biography,* ed. George Parker Anderson and Julie B. Anderson (Detroit: Gale Group, 2000), 34; hereafter cited in the text as *DLB.*
7. W. R. Burnett, *The Asphalt Jungle* (New York: Knopf, 1949), 16.

F I V E : Deadline at Midnight: Cornell Woolrich's *Night Has a Thousand Eyes*

1. Francis M. Nevins Jr., *Cornell Woolrich: First You Dream, Then You Die* (New York: Mysterious Press, 1988), 4; hereafter cited in the text.
2. Cornell Woolrich, *Blues of a Lifetime: The Autobiography of Cornell Woolrich,* ed. Mark T. Bassett (Bowling Green, IN: Bowling Green State University Popular Press, 1991), 24; hereafter cited in the text.
3. Cornell Woolrich, "Three O'Clock," in *The Cornell Woolrich Omnibus* (New York: Penguin, 1998), 65; hereafter cited in the text.
4. John T. Irwin, *The Mystery to a Solution: Poe, Borges, and the Analytic Detective Story* (Baltimore: Johns Hopkins University Press, 1994), 231–34; hereafter cited in the text.
5. Edgar Allan Poe, *Collected Works of Edgar Allan Poe,* 3 vols., ed. Thomas Ollive Mabbott (Cambridge: Belknap Press of Harvard University Press, 1969–78), 2:398; hereafter cited in the text.
6. Sigmund Freud, *The Standard Edition of the Complete Psychological Works of Sigmund Freud,* 24 vols., trans. James Strachey et al. (London: Hogarth Press, 1955–78),11:99–100.
7. Ovid, *Metamorphoses,* in *Ovid in Six Volumes,* trans. Frank Justus Miller, 3rd ed. (Cambridge: Harvard University Press, 1977), 3:149; hereafter cited in the text.
8. John T. Irwin, *American Hieroglyphics* (Baltimore: Johns Hopkins University Press, 1980), 185–86; hereafter cited in the text.
9. Erich Neumann, *The Origins and History of Consciousness* (Princeton, NJ: Princeton University Press, 1971), 214; hereafter cited in the text.
10. Cornell Woolrich, *Night Has a Thousand Eyes* (New York: Paperback Library, 1967), 10.
11. James M. Cain, *Double Indemnity* (New York: Vintage, 1978), 29.

six: A Puzzle of Character

1. See John T. Irwin, *The Mystery to a Solution: Poe, Borges, and the Analytic Detective Story* (Baltimore: Johns Hopkins University Press, 1994).
2. Willard Huntington Wright, "The Great Detective Stories," in *The Art of the Mystery Story*, ed. Howard Haycraft (New York: Carroll & Graf, 1983), 189, 191; hereafter cited in the text as *TAMS*.
3. R. Austin Freeman, "The Art of the Detective Story," in *TAMS*, 15.
4. E. M. Wrong, "Crime and Detection," in *TAMS*, 24.
5. Dorothy Sayers, introduction to *The Omnibus of Crime*, in *TAMS*, 102.
6. Howard Haycraft, *Murder for Pleasure: The Life and Times of the Detective Story* (New York: Carroll & Graf, 1984), viii; hereafter cited in the text as *MFP*.
7. Jonathan Goodman, *The Slaying of Joseph Bowne Elwell* (London: Harrap, 1987), 73–110.
8. George P. Le Brun, *Call Me If It's Murder!* (New York: Bantam, 1965), 159.
9. Dashiell Hammett, "The Benson Murder Case," in *TAMS*, 382.
10. Raymond Chandler, "The Simple Art of Murder," in *TAMS*, 223.
11. Dashiell Hammett, *The Maltese Falcon* (New York: Vintage, 1972), 15.
12. Raymond Chandler, *The Big Sleep* (New York: Vintage, 1976), 100–101.
13. Edgar Allan Poe, *Collected Works of Edgar Allan Poe*, 3 vols., ed. Thomas Ollive Mabbott (Cambridge: Belknap Press of Harvard University Press, 1969–78), 2:521n.
14. Raymond Chandler, *Farewell, My Lovely* (New York: Vintage, 1976), 138.
15. "William Riley Burnett," in *Twentieth-Century Authors*, ed. Stanley Kunitz and Howard Haycraft (New York: H. W. Wilson, 1942), 225.
16. James M. Cain, *Three by Cain: "Serenade," "Love's Lovely Counterfeit," "The Butterfly"* (New York: Vintage, 1989), 353–54.
17. Ernest Hemingway, *The Green Hills of Africa* (New York: Scribner's, 1935), Foreword.
18. Roy Hoopes, *Cain: The Biography of James M. Cain* (Carbondale: Southern Illinois University Press, 1982), 285.
19. Francis M. Nevins Jr., *Cornell Woolrich: First You Dream, Then You Die* (New York: Mysterious Press, 1988), 20.
20. F. Scott Fitzgerald, *The Great Gatsby*, ed. Matthew J. Bruccoli (New York: Cambridge University Press, 1991), 126.
21. Richard Layman, *Shadow Man: The Life of Dashiell Hammett* (New York: Harcourt Brace Jovanovich, 1981), 141.
22. F. Scott Fitzgerald, *Tender Is the Night* (New York: Scribner's, 1934), 310.
23. F. Scott Fitzgerald, *The Letters of F. Scott Fitzgerald*, ed. Andrew Turnbull (Scribner's: New York, 1963), 540.

seven: Hard-Boiled Fiction and Film Noir

1. James Damico, "Film Noir: A Modest Proposal," in *Perspectives on Film Noir,* ed. R. Barton Palmer (New York: G. K. Hall, 1996), 138; subsequent quotations from Palmer cited in the text.
2. R. Barton Palmer, "*Film Noir* and the Genre Continuum: Process, Product, and *The Big Clock*," in ibid., 141.

3. Charles Gregory, "Living Life Sideways," in ibid., 156.

4. Paul Schrader, "Notes on Film Noir," in ibid., 103.

5. Robert G. Porfirio, "Existential Motifs in the Film Noir," in ibid., 119.

6. Katherine Harper, "W. R. Burnett," in *American Hard-Boiled Crime Writers*, vol. 226 of *Dictionary of Literary Biography*, ed. George Parker Anderson and Julie B. Anderson (Detroit: Gale Group, 2000), 32.

7. Andrew Bergman, *We're in the Money: Depression America and Its Films* (New York: New York University Press, 1971), 7; hereafter cited in the text.

8. John Huston and W. R. Burnett, *High Sierra* (screenplay), ed. Douglas Gomery (Madison: University of Wisconsin Press, 1979), 16; hereafter cited in the text as Gomery.

9. A. M. Sperber and Eric Lax, *Bogart* (London: Weidenfeld & Nicolson, 1997), 117–18; hereafter cited in the text as Sperber.

10. Edward G. Robinson with Leonard Spigelgass, *All My Yesterdays: An Autobiography* (New York: Hawthorn Books, 1973), 181; hereafter cited in the text.

11. W. R. Burnett, *High Sierra* (New York: Bantam, 1950), 177–78.

12. Diane Johnson, *Dashiell Hammett: A Life* (New York: Random House, 1983), 84.

13. John Huston, *The Maltese Falcon* (continuity script), ed. William Luhr (New Brunswick, NJ: Rutgers University Press, 1995), 39–40; hereafter cited in the text as Luhr.

14. Tom Hiney, *Raymond Chandler: A Biography* (New York: Grove Press, 1997), 150.

15. Carlos Clarens, *Crime Movies: From Griffith to "The Godfather" and Beyond* (New York: Norton, 1980), 195.

16. Raymond Chandler, *The Raymond Chandler Papers: Selected Letters and Nonfiction, 1909-1959*, ed. Tom Hiney and Frank MacShane (New York: Atlantic Monthly Press, 2000), 67; hereafter cited in the text as *Papers*.

17. Joseph McBride, *Hawks on Hawks* (Berkeley: University of California Press, 1982), 104; hereafter cited in the text.

18. Peter Bogdanovich, *The Cinema of Howard Hawks* (New York: Museum of Modern Art, 1962), 23–24; hereafter cited in the text.

E I G H T : Hard-Boiled Fiction and Film Noir, Continued

1. Raymond Chandler, *The Raymond Chandler Papers: Selected Letters and Nonfiction, 1909-1959*, ed. Tom Hiney and Frank MacShane (New York: Atlantic Monthly Press, 2000), 117.

2. Roy Hoopes, *Cain: The Biography of James M. Cain* (Carbondale: Southern Illinois University Press, 1982), 268.

3. Maurice Zolotow, *Billy Wilder in Hollywood* (New York: G. P. Putnam's Sons, 1977), 111; hereafter cited in the text.

4. James M. Cain, *Double Indemnity* (New York: Vintage, 1978), 115, 118.

5. Billy Wilder and Raymond Chandler, *Double Indemnity* (screenplay), intro. Jeffrey Meyers (Berkeley: University of California Press, 2000), 70; hereafter cited in the text as Wilder.

6. Edward. G. Robinson, with Leonard Spigelgass, *All My Yesterdays: An Autobiography* (New York: Hawthorn Books, 1973), 236.

7. "Barré Lyndon," in Ephraim Katz, *The Film Encyclopedia* (New York: Thomas Y Crowell, 1979), 745.

8. Bill Brubaker, *Stewards of the House: The Detective Fiction of Jonathan Latimer* (Bowling Green, IN: Bowling Green State University Popular Press, 1993), 1–19.

9. Sigmund Freud, *The Standard Edition of the Complete Psychological Works of Sigmund Freud*, 24 vols., trans. James Strachey et al. (London: Hogarth Press, 1955–78), 17:241.

10. Cornell Woolrich, *Night Has a Thousand Eyes* (New York: Paperback Library, 1967), 274.

Index